Yoga in Jainism

Jaina Studies is a relatively new and rapidly expanding field of inquiry for scholars of Indian religion and philosophy. In Jainism, "yoga" carries many meanings, and this book explores the definitions, nuances, and applications of the term in relation to Jainism from early times to the present.

Yoga in Jainism begins by discussing how the use of the term *yoga* in the earliest Jaina texts described the mechanics of mundane action or karma. From the time of the later Upaniṣads, the word Yoga became associated in all Indian religions with spiritual practices of ethical restraint, prayer, and meditation. In the medieval period, Jaina authors such as Haribhadra, Śubhacandra, and Hemacandra used the term Yoga in reference to Jaina spiritual practice. In the modern period, a Jaina form of Yoga emerged, known as Prekṣā Dhyāna. This practice includes the physical postures and breathing exercises well known through the globalization of Yoga.

By exploring how Yoga is understood and practiced within Jainism, this book makes an important contribution to the fields of Yoga Studies, Religious Studies, Philosophy, and South Asian Studies.

Christopher Key Chapple is the Doshi Professor of Indic and Comparative Theology and Director of the Master of Arts in Yoga Studies at Loyola Marymount University, USA.

Routledge Advances in Jaina Studies
Series Editor: Peter Flügel
School of Oriental and African Studies

Jain Studies have become an accepted part of the study of religion. This series provides a medium for regular scholarly exchange across disciplinary boundaries. It will include edited collections and monographs on Jainism.

1 **Studies in Jaina History and Culture**
Disputes and dialogues
Edited by Peter Flügel

2 **History, Scripture and Controversy in a Medieval Jain Sect**
Paul Dundas

3 **The History of Vegetarianism and Cow-Veneration in India**
Ludwig Alsdorf
Edited by W. Bollée

4 **Jaina Scriptures and Philosophy**
Edited by Peter Flügel and Olle Qvarnström

5 **Yoga in Jainism**
Edited by Christopher Key Chapple

6 **Early Asceticism in India**
Ājīvikism and Jainism
Piotr Balcerowicz

Yoga in Jainism

Edited by
Christopher Key Chapple

Routledge
Taylor & Francis Group
LONDON AND NEW YORK

First published 2016
by Routledge
2 Park Square, Milton Park, Abingdon, Oxon OX14 4RN

and by Routledge
711 Third Avenue, New York, NY 10017

First issued in paperback 2017

Routledge is an imprint of the Taylor & Francis Group, an informa business

British Library Cataloguing in Publication Data
A catalogue record for this book is available from the British Library

Library of Congress Cataloging in Publication Data
Yoga in Jainism / Edited by Christopher Key Chapple.
pages cm. — (Routledge advances in Jaina studies)
Includes bibliographical references and index.
1. Yoga. 2. Jainism. I. Chapple, Christopher Key, 1954- editor.
B132.Y6Y533 2016
294.4′436—dc23
2015017031

ISBN 13: 978-1-138-49344-5 (pbk)
ISBN 13: 978-1-138-82907-7 (hbk)

Typeset in Times New Roman
by Swales & Willis Ltd, Exeter, Devon, UK

Contents

Contributors

Piotr Balcerowicz is a professor of philosophy and Indian studies, currently based in Warsaw, Poland, where he specializes in Indian philosophical tradition. Beside Indian philosophy and the history of Indian religions, he teaches international relations. He has published extensively on Indian philosophy and religion, but also on the Middle East and Central Asia. He has authored a number of books on Indian philosophy, Jainism, and the history of Afghanistan. His books include: *Early Asceticism in India: Ājīvikism and Jainism* (London: Routledge, 2015), and *Encyclopedia of Indian Philosophies*, XIV and XVII: *Jain Philosophy*, Parts II and III (Delhi: Motilal Banarsidass, 2013, 2014) (as co-editor).

Johannes Bronkhorst took up the study of Sanskrit and Pali at the University of Rajasthan (Jaipur, India), then at the University of Pune (India). In Pune he obtained an M.A. in 1976 and a Ph.D. in 1979. He then obtained a second doctorate from the University of Leiden in 1980. In 1987 he was appointed full professor of Sanskrit and Indian Studies at the University of Lausanne (until his retirement in 2011). He has published some 190 research papers and more than 15 books. Some of his recent books are: *Greater Magadha* (Leiden: Brill, 2007), *Buddhist Teaching in India* (Boston: Wisdom Publications, 2009), *Language and Reality* (Leiden: Brill, 2011), *Buddhism in the Shadow of Brahmanism* (Leiden: Brill, 2011), *Karma* (Honolulu: University of Hawai'i Press, 2011), and *Absorption* (Paris: UniversityMedia, 2012).

Christopher Key Chapple is Doshi Professor of Indic and Comparative Theology and Director of the Master of Arts in Yoga Studies at Loyola Marymount University, California, USA. Dr. Chapple received his undergraduate degree from the State University of New York at Stony Brook and his doctorate in Theology at Fordham University. He has published several books on the religions of India, including *Karma and Creativity* (Albany, NY: SUNY Press, 1986), *Nonviolence to Animals, Earth, and Self in Asian Traditions* (Albany, NY: SUNY Press, 1993), *Reconciling Yogas* (Albany, NY: SUNY Press, 2003), and *Yoga and the Luminous* (Albany, NY: SUNY Press, 2008). He has also edited several volumes on religion and ecology, including *Jainism and Ecology* (Cambridge, MA: Center for the Study of World Religions, 2002), and *Yoga and Ecology* (Hampton, VA: A. Deepak Pub., 2009). He serves as editor of the journal *Worldviews: Global Religions, Culture, and Ecology*.

John E. Cort is Professor of Asian and Comparative Religions at Denison University in Granville, Ohio, USA. In addition to being the author of several dozen articles on the Jains, and religion, history, and culture in western India, he has written *Jains in the World: Religious Values and Ideology in India* (New York: Oxford University Press, 2001) and *Framing the Jina: Narratives of Icons and Idols in Jain History* (New York: Oxford University Press, 2010). He co-authored with Lawrence A. Babb and Michael W. Meister *Desert Temples: Sacred Centers of Rajasthan in Historical, Art-Historical and Social Context* (Jaipur: Rawat, 2008).

Andrea R. Jain is Assistant Professor of Religious Studies at Indiana University–Purdue University Indianapolis and author of *Selling Yoga: From Counterculture to Pop Culture* (Oxford: Oxford University Press, 2014). She is a co-author (with Jeffrey J. Kripal) of *Comparing Religions: Coming to Terms* (Malden, MA: Wiley-Blackwell, 2014). Her areas of interest include the history of modern Yoga, especially Yoga's twentieth-century popularization and intersections with consumer culture. She is currently writing on defining Yoga, nationalism and Yoga, Yoga among disenfranchised communities, and the intersections of gender, sexuality, and Yoga. She is a regular contributor to *Religion Dispatches* and co-chair of the Yoga in Theory and Practice Group of the American Academy of Religion.

Sagarmal Jain holds an M.A., and Ph.D in Philosophy. He has authored more than 25 books and 150 research articles. He served for many years as Professor at Parshwanath Vidyapeeth, Varanasi, India and is the Founder and Director of the Prachya Vidyapith Shajapur (M.P.). He is the recipient of numerous awards, including the Gautam Ganadhar Samman (Prakrit Bharti) in 2008, and the Samata Puraskar Gauhati (Assam) in 2012. He is the general editor of the *Encyclopedia of Jaina Studies*.

Smita Kothari received her Ph.D. in Religion, South Asian Studies, and Environment from the University of Toronto in September 2013. Her thesis, *Dāna and Dhyāna in Jaina Yoga: A Case Study of Prekṣādhyāna and the Terāpantha*, is a textual and ethnographic study that explores notions of charity and meditation practices through a case study of a particular sect of Jainism. Smita is a Faculty Associate in the School of History, Philosophy, and Religion at Arizona State University, where her current research focus is on Dalit conversions to Buddhism and Jainism.

Jeffery D. Long is Professor of Religion and Asian Studies at Elizabethtown College in Elizabethtown, Pennsylvania, where he has taught since he received his Ph.D. from the University of Chicago Divinity School in the year 2000. He is the author of *A Vision for Hinduism: Beyond Hindu Nationalism* (London: IB Tauris, 2007), *Jainism: An Introduction* (London: IB Tauris, 2009), the

Historical Dictionary of Hinduism (Lanham, MD: Scarecrow Press, 2011), and the forthcoming *Indian Philosophy: An Introduction*, along with a companion reader of primary sources (*Indian Philosophy: The Essential Sources*). He has also published numerous articles and has served as chair of the Dharma Academy of North America (DANAM).

Olle Qvarnström is Professor of History of Religions at Lund University, Sweden. He has conducted research on Brahmanism, Buddhism, and Jainism, especially philosophical and theological traditions, their doctrinal system and praxis, mutual influence, and conflict. In 2002 he published a translation of *The Yogaśāstra of Hemacandra* (Cambridge, MA: Harvard University Press, 2002), the first translation of its kind to be published in a Western language. In the field of Jaina systematic philosophy, he has studied philosophers such as Siddhasena Divākara, Haribhadrasūri, and Hemacandra. His current research on Jainism involves Jain art and the relationship between Jainism and Islam during the Delhi Sultanate.

Kamal Chand Sogani received his Ph.D. in Philosophy with an emphasis in Ethical Doctrines in Jainism from the University of Rajasthan in 1961. He served in the Department of Philosophy, at M.L. Sukhadiya University in Udaipur for 24 years and established the department of Jainology, Prakrit and Agama-Ahimsa-Samata Sansthan. He is the editor of the *Jainvidya* and *Apabhramsa Bharti* journals. For his contributions in the field of Prakrit, Dr. Sogani has received the Acharya Kundakunda award (1996), the New Delhi, Agama Manisha Puraskara award (2004), and the Jalganva, Shruta Samvardhana Puraskara (2006) merit award.

Jayandra Soni retired in May 2012 from the Department of Indology and Tibetology, Philipps-Universität Marburg, Germany, where he taught Indian languages (Sanskrit, Hindi, Gujarati) and Indian philosophy from October 1991. Born and brought up in South Africa where he did his B.A., he studied further in India (Banaras Hindu University Ph.D. in 1978) and Canada (McMaster University Ph.D. in 1987). He presently lives in Austria and teaches part-time courses on Indian philosophies and religions at the University of Innsbruck. He continues his research in Indian philosophy, including special studies in Jaina philosophy on which he has also written several articles.

Introduction

Christopher Key Chapple

This book will investigate the usage of the term *yoga* within the Jaina religious tradition. Jainism arose prior to Buddhism, taking form in northeastern India perhaps as early as 800 B.C.E. Around 500 years later, Jainism spread south, where the Digambara tradition of naked male ascetics took root and west, developing into the Śvetāmbara tradition, characterized by male and female White-Clad monastics. Today, both forms of Jainism can be found throughout the subcontinent and, starting a century or more ago, lay Jains began to migrate to East Africa, the British Isles, and with the liberalization of immigration policies in the 1960s, to North America. Jainism constitutes the most ancient of the surviving Śramaṇa traditions, which are distinct from the Brahmanical ideas and practices that have come to be associated with the term Hinduism. Śramanical traditions generally eschew elaborate rituals, do not adhere to the *Vedas*, posit neither a creator nor controlling God, were founded by charismatic teachers who serve as objects of veneration, and emphasize the importance of the purification that arises from adherence to strict disciplines of ethics and meditation. Brahmanical traditions promote the performance of rituals based on the instructions contained in the *Yajur Veda*, often worship forms of Viṣṇu or Śiva or other gods and goddesses, proclaim that the *Ṛg Veda*, the source document for their beliefs and practices, had no author, and often declare that correct ritual practice and clear thinking are more important than effortful meditation.

The word *yoga* has a long history of usage within all the religious traditions of India. The mapping of a term or practice such as *yoga* over the course of India's long philosophical and religious history presents a daunting task. The linguistic legacy of any single Sanskrit word can open a Pandora's box of early usages, later usages, literal renderings, *double entendres*, metaphorical meanings, puns, apposite intentions, and so forth. The word *yoga* is no exception. It hails from Indo-European antiquity. *Yoga* in the *Ṛg Veda* refers to the process of yoking horses to a chariot. It has been traced by linguists to the English word yoke. The Monier-Williams and Apte Sanskrit dictionaries give a layered sense of the word *yoga*, with Apte suggesting 42 different numbered meanings[1] and Monier-Williams (1899/1995: 856) listing more than 100 synonyms, citing usage in agriculture (yoking a team of horses), warcraft, magical arts, various schools of philosophy (including Sāṃkhya, Buddhism, and Jainism), grammar, and astronomy. The early Pali usage of the word refers to bonds and attachments, and the early Jaina use of the word refers to the process by which fettering karmas attach to the soul. Not until the later Upaniṣads do we find what seems to be the first "spiritual" reference to Yoga, as part of a list in the *Taittirīya Upaniṣad* (ca. sixth century B.C.E.), along with the terms faith (*śraddhā*), righteous artistry (*ṛta*), the true (*satya*), the self (*ātman*), and the great (*mahas*). Fully developed discussions of Yoga as a spiritual description appear in the *Śvetāśvatara* and *Maitri Upaniṣads* (ca. fourth and third century B.C.E., respectively) and in the *Bhagavad Gītā* (ca. fifth to second century B.C.E.).

The *American Heritage Dictionary* defines *yoga* as follows:

> *yoga*. also Yoga. 1. An ascetic Hindu discipline involving controlled breathing, prescribed body positions, and meditation, with the goal of attaining a state of deep spiritual insight and tranquility.
>
> 2. A system of stretching and positional exercises derived from this discipline to promote good health, fitness, and control of the mind.

The dictionary goes on to provide the following information:

> Word History: The word yoga comes from Sanskrit *yogaḥ*, "yoking, joining together" and by extension "harnessing of one's mental faculties to a purpose" and thus "yoga." The Sanskrit word descends from the Indo-European root *yeug-, "to join, yoke." In the Germanic branch of the Indo-European language family, *yeug- developed into yuk-, represented in Old English by geoc, the ancestor of Modern English yoke. The root *yeug- is continued by words in most of the branches of the Indo-European language family, which indicates that the speakers of Proto-Indo-European used draft animals to pull their plows and draw their wagons.[2]

In its modern American English language usage, the many alternative usages of the term *yoga* have been set aside in favor of the association of the term with the spiritual practices of Yoga as articulated in the Upaniṣads, the *Bhagavad Gītā*, and the *Yoga Sūtra*. In this volume, the usage of the term will be capitalized when referring to Yoga as a spiritual practice following the convention of capitalizing the words Buddhism or Jainism and *yoga* will be kept in lower case and in italics when discussed in the earlier sense of the word, as it appears in the *Ṛg Veda*, the Pali Buddhist canon, and the *Tattvārtha Sūtra*.

In its spiritual sense, Yoga can be seen as a process developing mental and physical focus for the cultivation of a refined and often peaceful state of being. Methods to practice Yoga can include the holding of physical poses, the regulation of breath, and worshipful actions such as gazing upon an image (*dṛṣṭi/darśana*), silent sitting, recitation of *mantra*, and study of sacred texts. Yoga helps a person develop mental and physical acuity through the careful training of emotional states, control of the senses, and discipline of body and breath. Yoga has the capacity to generate states of accomplishment and power as well as inner and outer calm.

Buddhist texts provide some of the earliest meditation instructions. Buddhists specify four positions for meditation: sitting, standing, walking, and lying down. The *Satipaṭṭhāna Sūtra* advises one to observe whether the breath is long or short. Within two centuries following the death of founder Śakyamuni Buddha, statues were installed at Buddhist temples, providing a visual focus for meditation. The extensive corpus of Buddhist literature, like the *Vedas*, was originally transmitted orally and committed to memory. Like with the Brahmanical tradition, short segments of text eventually produced the Buddhist tradition of repeated chants recited to bring about a state of concentration through the practice of *mantra.*

Instructions for Brahmanical or Hindu forms of meditation first appear in the Upaniṣads listed above. These include the sixfold practice of the *Maitri Upaniṣad*: restraint of breath (*prāṇāyāma*), gathering inward of the senses (*pratyāhāra*), meditation (*dhyāna*), concentration (*dhāraṇā*), contemplation (*tarka*), and a state of absorption (*samādhi*) (MU 6:18). Patañjali later revised this list, adding ethical practices (*yama* and *niyama*) as well as reference to bodily movements that bring strength and ease (*āsana*). He dropped contemplation as a separate stage. The *Bhagavad Gītā* describes positive human qualities such as ethical comportment, firm resolve, and equanimity throughout its 700 verses. It also lists three philosophical Yogas: Karma Yoga, performing action without being attached to the results; Jñāna Yoga, discernment of the eternal nature of the soul, in contrast to the constantly changing realm of manifestation as expressed through the three constituents of reality (*tamas* or heaviness, *rajas* or passion, and *sattva*, illumination); and Bhakti Yoga, the cultivation of devotional sentiment. Like the meditation texts of early Buddhism and the Yoga practice instructions found in the *Maitri Upaniṣad*, the sixth chapter of the *Bhagavad Gītā* provides instructions for seated meditation and control of breath.

The shift in meaning of *yoga* from bondage to karma or the yoking of the mind through the senses to the world to its spiritualized sense takes place with the articulation or definition of Yoga as *viyoga*, contrasted with *saṃyoga*. According to Sāṃkhya philosophy, which itself has a long history with many variant interpretations, the root cause of suffering can be found in the attachment (*yoga*) prompted by past actions (*karma/saṃskāra*) which results in a fundamental misperception of identity. In Sāṃkhya, as expressed in the second chapter of the *Bhagavad Gītā*, one's true identity can be found in pure consciousness (*puruṣa*), not in the realm of change and activity (*prakṛti*) that produces ego, thoughts, and sensory attachment to objects (*ahaṃkāra, manas, indriya, mahābhūta*). Through the generation of insightful wisdom (*jñāna*) one comes to extirpate the limited karma-laden sense of identity, pronouncing "I am not, there is no 'I,' I own nothing" (*nāsmi, nāham, na me*). This formulaic expression, found both in Buddhist literature and in the *Sāṃkhya Kārikā*, signals entry into a life of freedom, characterized by the adoption of the Brahma Vihāra in Buddhist, Yoga, and Jaina literature, the ongoing application of friendliness, compassion, joy, and equanimity (*maitrī, karuṇā, muditā, upekṣā*). The term Yoga, qualified as a distancing or separation (*viyoga*) from afflicted karma, transforms from a word indicating linkage with the trouble of karma into a generalized description of the many practices required to attain states of freedom.

This book explores the definitions, nuances, and applications of the term Yoga in Jainism from early times to the present. The term Yoga for Jainism carries multiple levels of meaning. In the early Jaina tradition, the term *yoga* described the process by which karmas bind themselves to the soul (*jīva*). In the medieval period, Yoga came to refer to spiritual practice. This sense of the word remains in general usage today.

It is important to note that a dynamic interaction transpired among the many spiritual traditions throughout Indian history. The *Bhagavad Gītā* describes the culmination of spiritual practice as Brahma-nirvāṇa, hybridizing Upaniṣadic and Buddhist terms (BG II: 72). Key ideas and practices from Jainism can be found in the classical Yoga Darśana, as articulated in Patañjali's *Yoga Sūtra*, particularly in its listing of the observance of ethical vows (YS II: 30–39) and the operations of karma (YS IV: 7–17). The earliest surviving Jaina text, the *Ācārāṅga Sūtra* (ca. 350 B.C.E.), holds non-violence to be the primary religious practice, supported by truthfulness, not stealing, sexual restraint, and non-possession. These identical precepts appear in the *Yoga Sūtra* (ca. 200–400 C.E.) as the first rung of Patañjali's eightfold Yoga practice. The *Yoga Sūtra* also describes the operations of karma in a manner similar to that found in Jaina texts, it refers to the final goal of Yoga, *kaivalyam*, in a manner and terminology akin to that used by Jainas, who refer to the goal of freedom as *kevala*.

Whereas the philosophical system known as Yoga bears similarities to some aspects of Jainism, the actual usage of the term "*yoga*" in early Jaina texts such as Umāsvāti's *Tattvārtha Sūtra* carries a different sensibility than that indicated in Patañjali's definition of Yoga as *citta vṛtti nirodha*, a state of mental control. Umāsvāti proclaimed that *yoga* refers to the process whereby karmas become attached to the soul and hence impede its energy, consciousness, and bliss (*vīrya, caitanya, ānanda*). At first glance, this seems to indicate that Yoga would be the antithesis of the desired outcome of freedom from all bondage. However, Umāsvāti also indicated that connecting or yoking with positive actions can in fact help one advance toward the state of freedom. Nonetheless, the use of the term *yoga* in Jaina texts prior to the middle of the first millennium of the Common Era referred to the mundane action of performing action within the confines of cause and effect.

From the time of the later *Upaniṣads*, as indicated above, Yoga provided a pan-Indian approach to spirituality through its practices of ethical restraint (*yama*), prayer (*japa*), and cultivating states of concentration (*dhāraṇā*) and meditation (*dhyāna*). Patañjali's eightfold Yoga rose to prominence by the year 500 C.E., presenting a universally recognizable string of practices that indicate a commitment to the spiritual path. The Śvetāmbara Jaina author Haribhadra Virahāṅka (550 C.E.) employed the term Yoga to indicate spiritual practice and Haribhadra Yākinī-putra (750 C.E.) newly interpreted Jaina ideas in an eightfold structure similar to that posited by Patañjali. In the twelfth century, the Śvetāmbara Jaina court philosopher Hemacandra wrote extensively of an eightfold practice of Jaina

Yoga. This manual still remains in use as the prime guidebook for Śvetāmbara spiritual practice. This eightfold approach to Yoga was further expanded upon in the work of the seventeenth-century Jaina scholar Yaśovijaya and has become incorporated into the twentieth-century practices of Prekṣā meditation described in this volume.

Among the Digambara Jainas, Kundakunda (ca. 400 C.E.) developed a train of thought similar to parallel developments in Mahāyāna Buddhism and Advaita Vedānta, positing that life must be understood from two perspectives, absolute (*niścaya naya*) and transactional or worldly (*vyavahāra naya*). By fasting and other spiritual disciplines, one can apply techniques to identify with the former rather than the latter, thereby experiencing the self in its true nature. Rāmasena and Śubhacandra (ca. 950 C.E.) continued this emphasis on meditation (*dhyāna*) on the true self (*sva, ātman, jīva*) as a means leading toward liberation, a practice still central to the Digambara tradition. Digambara meditation texts include the *Dhyānastava* of Bhāskaranadi (ca. 1050 C.E.) and the *Paramātmaprakāśa* of Yogīndu (disputed dates range from 550 to 950 C.E.), translated poetically into French by Nalini Balbir, and the *Jñānārṇava* of Śubhacandra, which is discussed in detail in this volume by Professor Sogani (Chapter 8).

Yoga is practiced by yogis, a term used interchangeably with *sādhu* or *muni* in all four traditions (Hindu, Buddhist, Jaina, Sikh) of India. Yogis, including Jaina adepts, are said to develop extraordinary powers (*ṛddhis*) and attainments (*labdhis*), including the ability to cure disease through touch, to take any form at will, and develop penetrating mental abilities. The Dādāgurus provide one example of accomplished Jaina yogis who inspired religious fervor and provided protection to the Jaina community. From the time of Kundakunda to the modern period, yearning for the auspicious presence of a yogi indicates seriousness on the Jaina path whereby one seeks to become free of karma and its entanglements.

In the modern period, Ācārya Mahāprajña (1920–2010) developed a Jaina form of Yoga meditation, known as Prekṣā Dhyāna, that draws from Buddhist and Hindu Yoga meditation techniques. This movement seeks to provide tools for everyday people to participate in a path of Jaina Yoga, including the physical postures and breathing exercises well known due to the globalization of Yoga practice.

Survey of existing literature on Jaina Yoga

Two significant books on Jaina Yoga are thought to have highlighted the Jaina adoption of the term Yoga as a general referent for spiritual practice. The first, Nathmal Tatia's *Studies in Jaina Philosophy* (1951), summarizes the pioneering work of Haribhadra Yākinī-putra, who mixes the stages of Yoga with the worship of the goddess as well as with the shared goal of total freedom. The second, *Jaina Yoga: A Survey of the Mediaeval Śrāvakācāras* (Williams 1963), meticulously examines the system of vows (*vrata*) that distinguish the Jaina faith. Williams provides a remarkable chronology of primary Jaina thinkers, with separate sections on the major figures of the Śvetāmbara and Digambara lineages. He provides a cross-sectarian analysis of each of the major categories of Jaina faith and practice, including analyses of the 12 primary vows, listings of acceptable professions, and lists of prescribed meditations (*dhyāna, bhāvanā*) and activities (*kriyā*). Although making note of the importance of the works of Haribhadra Virahāṅka (sixth century), Haribhadra Yākinī-putra (eighth century), and Hemacandra (1089–1172), he does not provide a summary of their works: at the time of Williams' work, they had not been edited or published. Paul Dundas (2012: 151) notes that this book "its title notwithstanding . . . in fact relates to the monastic literature legislating for lay behavior [and] barely mentions the topic of meditation."

Various translators have helped to remedy what had been a major lacuna in the field. K. K. Dixit, through the L. D. Institute for Indology, published translations of several Jaina Yoga texts, including the *Yogaśataka* and the *Yogabindu* of Haribhadra Virahāṅka (1965, 1967) and the *Yogadṛṣṭisamuccaya* of Haribhadra Yākinī-putra (1970). Chapple completed a fuller study of the latter text in his work *Reconciling Yogas: Haribhadra's Collection of Views on Yoga, with a New Translation of the Yogadṛṣṭisamuccaya* (2003). Chapple offers a new translation of the fivefold Yoga found in Haribhadra Virahāṅka's *Yogabindu* in this volume. Qvarnström's translation of Haribhadra's *Yogaśāstra* (2002) opened a window into greater understanding of the role of Yoga in the Jaina faith. This text even today serves as a primary manual for applied spirituality throughout the Śvetāmbara community and heavily influenced the development of the modern form of meditation known as Prekṣā Dhyāna. The eighth chapter of the *Yogaśāstra* borrowed heavily from Śubhacandra's *Jñānārṇava*, the Digambara meditation manual that in turn adopts practices of mantra and yantra from the tantric tradition. Sogani's chapter in this volume, drawing from his earlier study, *Ethical Doctrines in Jainism* (2001), examines the significance of Śubhacandra's *Jñānārṇava* (Chapter 8).

Anthologies on Jaina, Tantra, and Yoga traditions published in the past several years include important material on Yoga in Jainism. Paul Dundas discusses the role of mantra in his groundbreaking chapter "Becoming Gautama: Mantra and History in Śvetāmbara Jainism" in *Open Boundaries: Jain Communities and Cultures in Indian History,* edited by John E. Cort. Patañjali lists the recitation of a sacred syllable as an important part of the practice of Yoga (YS I: 28, *taj japas tad artha bhāvanam*). Dundas documents how this practice became standard within Jaina ritual, building on the work of M. B. Jhavery's *Comparative and Critical Study of Mantraśāstra.* In addition to discussing the contemporary Jaina recitation of short seed (*bīja*) mantras, Dundas describes in detail the *sūrimantra*, used widely in Śvetāmbara monastic liturgical recitation. In a later work, Dundas translates a tale wherein Jaina monks resist the influence of Nāth yogis, particularly through the efficacious use of mantra by the Jaina monk Jinadatta. Dundas also notes that the most widely used Jaina prayer is the Pañcanamaskāra Mantra, often referred to as the Ṇamōkāra Mantra, which honors the *tīrthaṅkaras*, the *siddhas*, the *ācāryas*, the *upādhyāyas*, and the vowed monastics (Dundas, 2000). Dundas' most recent study of Jaina Yoga centers on the Digambara monk Rāmasena (tenth century), who, like Haribhadra Yākinī-putra, refers to the eightfold Yoga of

Patañjali in his *Tattvānuśāsana*. The following verse, translated by Dundas (2012: 157), demonstrates the rhetorical importance of Yoga in this text: "Deploying the mighty hand gesture, the mighty mantra and the mighty mandala, the yogin, in becoming Lord Pārśva, is in possession of a body made fully integrated."

One feature of Yoga as described in the Yoga Sūtra is the attainment of powers (*vibhūti, siddhi*). Though Patañjali warns that these are merely signs of accomplishment and not to be confused with the true yogic discernment (YS III: 37), in Jaina lore these powers indicate an important sign of an adept's status. Kristi Wiley (2012: 145–194) undertakes an exhaustive study of powers (*labdhi, ṛddhi*) in Jaina literature, including the ability to read minds and to travel through the air in her contribution to the book *Yoga Powers: Extraordinary Capacities Attained through Meditation and Concentration.* This topic is taken up in this volume by Piotr Balcerowicz, who investigates clairvoyance in Jaina narratives (Chapter 4). The negative aspects of the accumulation of yogic powers have been described extensively by David Gordon White in the book *Sinister Yogis* (2009). The Jaina narratives regard yogic powers, tempered by the strict adherence to monastic vows, to be a positive indication of spiritual accomplishment.

Overview of the present work

This book is divided into three parts. The first part examines textual sources for understanding the usage of the term *yoga*/Yoga in the early phase of Jainism. In the first chapter, Sagarmal Jain notes that Jainism, like the other religions of Indian origin, attaches supreme importance to Yoga and meditation (*dhyāna*) as the means to spiritual advancement and emancipation. This chapter gives the reader a grand overview of Jaina Yoga spanning from the pre-canonical age (before the sixth century B.C.E) to the twenty-first century. Sagarmal Jain explores the major movements and thinkers of these periods. He also compares Jaina Yoga with Hindu and Buddhist Yogas, noting influences across traditions.

Jayandra Soni examines the term *yoga* in early Jaina philosophical literature (Chapter 2). Umāsvāti defines yoga in the *Tattvārtha Sūtra* 6, 1 as: *kāyavāṅ-manaḥkarma yogaḥ*, which S. A. Jain (1992) translates as: "The action of the body, the organ of speech and the mind is called yoga (activity)." In his *Studies in Jaina Philosophy*, Nathmal Tatia says: "In Jainism the term cāritra (conduct) is the exact equivalent of the general term yoga."[3] Soni explores these two usages of the term *yoga*/Yoga as given in the fifth century with the two earliest commentaries on the *Tattvārtha Sūtra,* the *Svopajñabhāṣya* and Pūjyapāda's *Sarvārthasiddhi.*

Johannes Bronkhorst (Chapter 3) argues that Kundakunda's ideas of the true nature of the self must be understood as an attempt to introduce or perhaps reintroduce the Sāṃkhya notion of an inactive soul (*puruṣa*). Kundakunda adjusted this concept to accommodate Jaina doctrine. The Sāṃkhya system, like Jainism, believes in rebirth and karmic retribution. It also asserts that knowledge of the true, inactive, nature of the self is an essential step toward the ultimate goal of liberation. Classical Jainism had not conceived of the self in this manner, but this changed with Kundakunda.

The final chapters in this section present arguments and counterarguments on the topic of extrasensory perception (*yogi-pratyakṣa*) in Jainism and its soteriological implications. Piotr Balcerowicz (Chapters 4 and 5) examines the special abilities (*siddhi/ṛddhi*) that arise in practitioners of Yoga. The idea of *yogi-pratyakṣa* was often related to omniscience (*sarva-jñāna*) in Indian philosophical and religious traditions, including Buddhism and the systems of Nyāya-Vaiśeṣika. It was in Jainism, however, that the correlation between extrasensory perception and omniscience became most conspicuous. The Jainas were also probably the first to develop rational arguments such as the "gradual development" argument, already present in Kundakunda's works, which were used to justify the radical claim of the Jaina's omniscience. An indispensable logical step in these arguments relied on the assumption of the existence of extrasensory perception. Further, Jaina philosophers treated the idea of *yogi-pratyakṣa* as an intermediate stage to ultimate perfection of knowledge, i.e., to omniscience, a hallmark quality of the liberated soul. These chapters demonstrate the precise doctrinal and philosophical reasons that made the link between extrasensory perception and omniscience so important.

The second part of the book explores medieval appropriations of the term Yoga as a path of spiritual practice. Chapple (Chapter 6) explores the fivefold Yoga of Haribhadra Virahāṅka (sixth century) as found in the *Yogabindu*. Haribhadra Virahāṅka explains Jaina Yoga as a path of purification. The pathgoer (*cāritrin*) traverses the five steps of introspection (*adhyātma*), cultivation (*bhāvanā*), meditation (*dhyāna*), equanimity (*samatā*), and the quieting of all mental states (*vṛttisamkṣaya*). These stages are examined in light of Umāsvāti's traditional analysis of the 14 stages of spiritual ascents (*guṇasthāna*). Haribhadra Virahāṅka highlights yogic practices such as mantra recitation (*japa*), appropriate behavior (*svaucityālocana*), and ritualized confession (*pratikramaṇa*) as important aspects of spiritual comportment. This chapter also discusses the eightfold Jaina Yoga of Haribhadra Yākinī-putra (eighth century) as an example of Jaina interaction with the Buddhist, Hindu, and Tantric traditions of Yoga.

Olle Qvarnström (Chapter 7) gives a biographical account of Hemacandra, the great eleventh-century Śvetāmbara monk and scholar, as well as a summary of one of his most influential works, the *Yogaśāstra*. Hemacandra's lucid scholarship has made him tremendously influential among Jaina and non-Jainas alike, who have come to regard his exposition as arguably the most systematic and clear work of its kind. His magnum opus is the *Yogaśāstra,* whose influence is still vibrantly present among Jaina communities across the globe.

The next chapter, by Kamal Chand Sogani (Chapter 8), explores the relationship between ethics and mysticism in Jaina spirituality, examining the 12 incentives that inspire an individual to take up the path toward sainthood, the five vows well known within the Yoga and Jaina traditions, and the stages of meditation (*dhyāna*) taught within the *Jñānārṇava* of Śubhacandra. The chapter ends with a study of mysticism as explained through the Jaina levels of spiritual ascent (*guṇasthānas*). The primary textual sources drawn upon include the *Sarvārthasiddhi* of Pūjyapāda, his commentary on the *Tattvārtha Sūtra*, the *Mūlācāra* of Vaṭṭakera, the *Kārttikeyānuprekṣā*, the *Pravacanasāra* of Kundakunda, and especially the *Jñānārṇava* of Śubhacandra.

Jeffery Long's chapter (Chapter 9) investigates Yaśovijaya's view of Yoga. A seventeenth-century Śvetāmbara scholar, Yaśovijaya focused specifically on points of both contrast and commonality between Jaina and non-Jaina thinkers and movements, including the *Bhagavad Gītā*. In terms of Jaina intellectual history, Yaśovijaya's view is of particular interest due to his location at the cusp of what are widely known as the "classical" and "modern" periods. This chapter emphasizes ways in which Yaśovijaya can be seen as a transitional figure between these two periods, with aspects of his thought demonstrating strong continuity with classical Jaina (especially Śvetāmbara) philosophy, and other aspects anticipating modern trends, such as an emphasis on yogic experience (*anubhāva*) as a valid source of authentic knowledge.

The third and final part of the book discusses Yoga and Jainism in modernity, beginning with a chapter by John E. Cort (Chapter 10). Cort notes that a yogī is someone who engages in the performance of the technical embodied spiritual disciplines of Yoga. Yogī also refers more generally in South Asian religious culture to anyone who has in one way or another renounced the world, and thereby engages in conduct that runs counter to the norms of the householder. South Asian literature is replete with descriptions of yogīs in this second sense. These include Jain yogīs. This chapter investigates the literary trope of the ideal yogī (also *muni, sādhu*) in the Digambara tradition. The trope first emerges in the middle of the first millennium C.E. in two texts to be read by mendicants as part of their regular practice, the Prākṛt and Sanskrit *Yogī Bhaktis*. The former is attributed to Kundakunda and the later to Pūjyapāda, but most likely these are simply attributions of important liturgical texts to mendicant authors viewed as authoritative "church fathers" by the later tradition. The trope is found in medieval literature, such as the Apabhraṃśa works of Yogīndu that have been analyzed by Colette Caillat. Finally they are found in a large number of Hindi texts composed in North India in the seventeenth through nineteenth centuries. This chapter argues that the frequent performative articulation of this ideal helped to create situations in which the ideal yogī was alive in the Digambara imagination, even when there had been few, if any, living Digambara *munis* for many centuries, and so helped to create a favorable setting for the revival of the institution of the naked *muni* in the twentieth century.

Smita Kothari (Chapter 11) probes into two aspects of religious practice among Jaina communities: giving (*dāna*) and meditation (*dhyāna*) This chapter examines the practice of *dhyāna* (meditation) as a ritual within Jaina Yoga through a case study of Prekṣā Dhyāna, a late-twentieth-century innovation of the Terapanthi Śvetāmbara Jaina leader Acarya Mahāprajña (1920–2010). It also includes material on the advocacy of giving in order to support community and construction activities, as well as field data on the teaching of Prekṣā Dhyāna at camps in India.

The chapter by Andrea R. Jain (Chapter 12) also takes up the study of Prekṣā Dhyāna, comparing Mahāprajña to other Jain Yoga gurus who participated in the development and popularization of Yoga in the twentieth century. Mahāprajña prescribes Prekṣā Dhyāna as a form of preventative medicine, a health and fitness discipline, and a physiotherapeutic practice for the enhancement of the body and the reduction of stress. He integrates classical Yoga ideas and practices with biomedical discourse about anatomy, physiology, and endocrinology. This chapter also explores the popular dissemination of Prekṣā Dhyāna worldwide by the *samaṇīs*, nuns who have not yet taken their final vows. The *samaṇīs* teach physical techniques, postures and breathing exercises, aiming at physical and spiritual enhancement to students in India, the United States, and Britain, whose interests are primarily in Yoga's perceived physiotherapeutic benefits. This chapter also evaluates the intersection of this practice with classical schools of Yoga.

The final chapter, also by Chapple (Chapter 13), provides a contemporary narrative account of Jaina Yoga as a modern global phenomenon. Based on field experience, Chapple narrates his experiences with Jaina Yoga as taught by Muni Mahendra Kumar and Acarya Shiv Muni from the Śvetāmbara tradition and Pujya Ganini Shri Gyanmati Mataji of the Digambara tradition. Mention is also made of persons of Jaina origin who have been communicators of Yoga in the contemporary world: Chandra Mohan Jain/Rajneesh/Osho and Hansaji Jayadeva Yogendra. The chapter concludes with acknowledgment of the presence of Jaina Yoga on the worldwide web and observations about the flexible approach evident in the synergy between Jainism and Yoga.

In summary, the usage of the term *yoga* during the early years of Jainism explained the process through which the impulses of karma adhered to and hence occluded the luminosity of the soul. Responding to a shift in cultural usage of this term that probably arose during the later Upaniṣads, Jaina thinkers began to describe their religious practices in light of a new definition of Yoga as referring to techniques employed to achieve a state of mental quiescence. The systematization of Yoga by Patañjali in the *Yoga Sūtra* drew the attention of scholars such as Haribhadra Yākinī-putra, Hemacandra, and Yaśovijaya, who mapped the practices of Jaina spiritual discipline in a format similar to Patañjali's threefold and eightfold schematics. In the contemporary period, practices have been formulated that incorporate modern scientific research on Yoga as well as practices from Buddhist traditions. Paul Dundas (2012: 151) has noted, "There exists no systematic discussion of the historical development of meditation and yoga in Jainism in any western language." This book hopefully will spark an interest for further research into this area, including the generation of new critical editions and translations on the topic of Jaina Yoga.

This volume arose from two conferences. The first, The International Seminar on the Yogic Traditions of India with Special Reference to Jaina Yoga, December 7–9, 2006, took place at the India International Centre in New Delhi, sponsored by the Bhogilal Leherchand Institute of Indology and the Sri Jain Shwetambar Nakoda Parshvanath Tirth. Dr. Jitendra B. Shah of the L.D. Institute of Indology in Ahmedabad served as co-director with Christopher Chapple. Participants included A. Ramulu, Ashok Kumar Singh, Atusushi Uno, Bansidhar Bhatt, Christopher Key Chapple, D.C. Jain, D.N. Bhargawa, G.C. Pandey, Ian Whicher, Ishwar Bharadwaj, Jitendra B. Shah, Jai Prasad Balodhi, Kamala Jain, Knut A. Jacobsen, Laura Cornell,

Mukul Raj Mehta, Nalini Balbir, Oliver Lamers, Olle Qvarnström, Peter Flugel, Piotr Balcerowicz, R.C. Jain, R.K. Chhabra, Ramashankar Tripathy, Ratna Purohir, S.R. Vyas, Sagarmal Jain, Samani Malli Prajnaji, Samani Mangal Prajnaji, Shashiprahha Kumar, Shri Shrutiprakash Swami Sadhu, Shubhada Vanjape, Shugan Chand Jain, Vimala Karnataka, Vijay Kumar Jain, and Shri Gani Yashovijayaji. The other major gathering that fostered the publication of this volume was the 12th annual Jaina Studies Workshop hosted by the Centre of Jaina Studies of the School of Oriental and African Studies at the University of London. Welcome blessings were offered by Svastiśrī Cārukīrti Paṇḍitācāryavarya Mahāsvāmījī, Samaṇī Prasannaprajñā, and Samaṇī Rohitaprajñā. Participants in the conference included Peter Flugel, Christopher Chapple, Olle Qvarnström, Sagarmal Jain, Bansidhar Bhatt, Samani Prasannaprajña, Samani Rohitaprajña, John E. Cort, Johannes Bronkorst, Jeffery D. Long, Piotr Balcerowicz, Smita Kothari, and Robert Zydenbos.

Many people helped with the compilation and editing of this book, including Jodi Shaw, Hunter Joslin, and Kija Manharé. Deep gratitude goes to Sulekh Jain and Shugan Jain for their unwavering support for the field of Jaina studies, and to Padmanabh S. Jaini.

Notes

1 joining; union; contact; employment; mode; consequence (mostly at the end of comp. or in abl.); a yoke; a conveyance; an armour; fitness; an occupation; a trick; an expedient; endeavour; remedy; a charm; gain; the equipment of an army; fixing; a side; an occasion; possibility; wealth; a rule; dependence; etymology or derivation of the meaning of a word; the etymological meaning of a word; deep and abstract meditation; the system of philosophy established by Patañjali; a follower of the yoga system of philosophy; (in arith.) addition; (in astr.) conjunction; a combination of stars; 34.name of a particular astronomical division of time (27 such yogas are usually enumerated); the principal star in a lunar mansion; devotion; a spy; a traitor; an attack; steady application; ability; equality. *Digital Dictionaries of South Asia, The Practical Sanskrit –English Dictionary, s.v.* "yoga," accessed December 9, 2014, http://dsal.uchicago.edu/dictionaries/apte/.

2 *American Heritage Dictionary Online,* "yoga," accessed December 8, 2014, https://ahdictionary.com/word/search.html?q=Yoga&submit.x=0&submit.y=0.

3 Tatia, Nathmal. *Studies in Jaina Philosophy.* Banaras: Jain Cultural Resarch Society, 1951, p. 262.

Bibliography

American Heritage Dictionary Online, "yoga," accessed December 8, 2014, https://ahdictionary.com/.

Balbir, Nalini and Collette Caillat. *Lumière de l'Absolu.* Paris: Editions Payt & Rivages, 1999.

Bhāskaranadi. *Dhyānastava.* Edited and translated by Suzuko Ohira. Varanasi: Bharatiya Jnanapitha, 1973.

Bronkhorst, Johannes. *The Two Traditions of Meditation in Ancient India.* Stuttgart: Franz Steiner, 1986.

Chapple, Christopher Key. "Haribhadra's Analysis of Patañjala and Kula Yoga in the *Yogadṛṣṭisamuccaya.*" In *Open Boundaries: Jain Communities and Cultures in Indian History*. Edited by John E. Cort. Albany: State University of New York Press, 1998, pp. 15–30.

Chapple, Christopher Key. "Centrality of the Real in Haribhadra's Yoga Texts." In *Approaches to Jaina Studies: Philosophy, Logic, Rituals and Symbols*. Edited by N.K. Wagle and Olle Qvarnström. Toronto: University of Toronto Centre for South Asian Studies, 1999, pp. 91–100.

Chapple, Christopher Key. "Life Force in Jainism and Yoga." In *The Meaning of Life in the World Religions.* Edited by Joseph Runzo and Nancy M. Martin. Oxford, England: Oneworld Publications, 2000, pp. 137–152.

Chapple, Christopher Key. *Reconciling Yogas: Haribhadra's Collection of Views on Yoga, with a New Translation of Haribhadra's Yogadṛṣṭisamuccaya.* Translation by Chapple and John Thomas Casey. Albany: State University of New York Press, 2003.

Chapple, Christopher Key. "Purity and Diversity in the Yoga Traditions of Patanjali and Haribhadra." In *Jainism and Early Buddhism: Essays in Honor of Padmanabh S. Jaini.* Edited by Olle Qvarnström. Fremont, California: Asian Humanities Press, 2003. Appeared 2004, pp. 415–425.

Chapple, Christopher Key. "Disciplines and Vows (*Yamas* and *Vratas*): How the Mystical Yields to the Ethical in Yoga and Jainism." *Archiv für Religionsgeschichte* 9 (2007), pp. 9–21.

Cort, John E. "Worship of Bell-Ears the Great Hero, A Jain Tantric Deity." In *Tantra in Practice.* Edited by David Gordon White. Princeton: Princeton University Press, 2000, pp. 417–433.

Desai, S. M. *Haribhadra's Yoga Works and Psychosynthesis.* Ahmedabad: L. D. Institute of Indology, 1983.

Digital Dictionaries of South Asia, The Practical Sanskrit –English Dictionary, s.v. "Yoga," accessed December 9, 2014, http://dsal.uchicago.edu/dictionaries/apte/.

Dixit, K. K. tr. *Haribhadrasūri's Yogaśataka with Auto-Commentary along with his Brhmasiddhāntasamuccaya.* Edited by Mumirāja Śri Puṇyavijayajī. Ahmedabad: Lalbahi Dalpatbhai Bharatiya Sanskriti Vidyamandira, 1965.

Dixit, K. K. *The Yogabindu of Ācārya Haribhadrasūri.* Ahmedabad: Lalbhjai Dalpatbhai Bharatiya Sanskriti Vidyamandira, 1967.

Dixit, K. K. *Yogadṛṣṭisamuccaya and Yogaviṃśika of Ācārya Haribhadrasūri.* Ahmedabad: Lalbhai Dalpatbhai Bharatiya Sankriti Vidyamandira, 1970.

Dundas, Paul. "Becoming Gautama: Mantra and History in Śvetāmbara Jainism." In *Open Boundaries: Jain Communities and Cultures in Indian History.* Edited by John E. Cort. Albany: State University of New York Press, 1998, pp. 31–52.

Dundas, Paul. "The Jain Monk Jinapati Sūri Gets the Better of a Nāth Yogī." In *Tantra in Practice.* Edited by David Gordon White. Princeton: Princeton University Press, 2000, pp. 231–338.

Dundas, Paul. "A Digambara Jain Description of the Yogic Path to Deliverance." In *Yoga in Practice.* Edited by David Gordon White. Princeton: Princeton University Press, 2012.

Dundas, Paul. "Losing One's Mind and Becoming Enlightened: Some Remarks on the Concept of Yoga in Śvetāmbara Jainism and its Relations to the Nāth Siddha Tradition." In *Yoga: The Indian Tradition.* Edited by David Carpenter and Ian Whicher. London: Routledge Curzon, 2003, pp. 130–142.

Jain, S. A. *Reality: English Translation of Shri Pujyapada's* Sarvārthasiddhi. Madras: Jwalamalini Trust, 1992.

Jaini, Padmanabh S. *The Jaina Path of Purification.* Berkeley: University of California Press, 1979.

Jhavery, M. B. *Comparative and Critical Study of Mantraśāstra.* Ahmedabad: Sarabhai Manilal, Nawal, 1944.

Kansara, N. M., and G. C. Tripathi, editors. *Studies in Haribhadrasuri: Papers presented at a Seminar in the B. L. Institute of Indology, Delhi.* Delhi: Bhogilal Leherchand Institute of Indology, 2014.

Monier-Williams, Monier, Sir. *A Sanskṛit-English Dictionary.* Oxford: Clarendon Press, 1899/1995.

Muniji, Archarya Sh. Shirish. *The Doctine of Karma & Transmigration in Jainism.* 2nd ed. Chennai: Sanskar Jain Patrika, 2007.

Muniji, Archarya Sh. Shirish. *The Doctrine of the Self in Jainism.* 2nd ed. Punjab: Bhagwan Mahavir Meditation Research Centre Trust, 2007.

Muniji, Archarya Sh. Shirish. *The Fundamental Principles of Jainism.* 2nd ed. Punjab: Bhagwan Mahavir Meditation Research Centre Trust, 2007.

Muniji, Archarya Sh. Shirish. *The Jaina Pathway to Liberation.* 2nd ed. Punjab: Bhagwan Mahavir Meditation Research Centre Trust, 2007.

Muniji, Archarya Sh. Shirish. *The Jaina Tradition.* 2nd ed. Punjab: Bhagwan Mahavir Meditation Research Centre Trust, 2007.

Muniji, Archarya Sh. Shirish. *Self-Meditation: Nature and Practice.* 1st ed. Punjab: Bhagwan Mahavir Meditation Research Centre Trust, 2009.

Qvarnström, Olle. "Jain Tantra: Divinatory and Meditative Practices in the Twelfth Century *Yogaśāstra* of Hemacandra." In *Tantra in Practice.* Edited by David Gordon White. Princeton: Princeton University Press, 2000, pp. 595–604.

Qvarnström, Olle. "Jain Tantra: Divinatory and Meditative Practices in the Twelfth-Century Yogaśāstra of Hemacandra." In *Tantra in Practice,* Vol. 8 of *The Princeton Readings in Religions Series.* Edited by David Gordon White. Princeton: Princeton University Press, 2000, pp. 595–604.

Qvarnström, Olle. tr. *The Yogaśāstra of Hemacandra: A Twelfth Century Handbook on Jainism.* Cambridge, MA: Harvard University Press, 2002.

Qvarnström, Olle. "Jain Yoga of the Terapanthi Tradition." In *Yoga in Practice*, pp. 365–382. Edited by David Gordon White. Princeton: Princeton University Press, 2012.

Qvarnström, Olle and Jason Birch. "Universalist and Missionary Jainism: Jain Yoga of the Terāpanthī Tradition." In *Yoga and Practice.* Edited by David Gordon White. Princeton: Princeton University Press, 2012, pp. 365–382.

Sogani, Kamal Chand. *Ethical Doctrines in Jainism.* Sholapur: Jaina Samskriti Samrakshaka Sangha, 2001.

Tatia, Nathmal. *Studies in Jaina Philosophy.* Banaras: Jain Cultural Resarch Society, 1951.

Uditaprabha, Sadhvi. *Jain Dharm meṃ Dhyān kā Aitihāsik Vikās Kram.* Byavar: Muni Sri Hajarimal Smrti Prakashan, 2007.

White, David Gordon. *Sinister Yogis.* Chicago: University of Chicago Press, 2009.

Wiley, Kristi. "Supernatural Powers and Their Attainment in Jainism." In *Yoga Powers: Extraordinary Capacities Attained through Meditation and Concentration.* Edited by Knut. A. Jacobsen. Leiden: Brill, 2012.

Williams, R. *Jaina Yoga: A Survey of the Medieval Śrāvakācāras.* Delhi: Motilal Banarsidass. 1963.

1 The historical development of the Jaina Yoga system and the impacts of other Yoga systems on Jaina Yoga

A comparative and critical study

Sagarmal Jain

Jainism, like the other religions of Indian origin, attaches supreme importance to *yoga* and *dhyāna* (meditation) as a means to both spiritual advancement and emancipation. According to the *Uttarādhyayanasūtra* (one of the four Mūlasūtras of the Jaina canon), one can know the real nature of self through right knowledge; one can have faith in it through right vision or right attitude. Similarly, one can have control over it through right conduct, but the purification of self can only be achieved through right *tapas.*[1] As per Jainism, *tapas* (penance) has two supreme wings, which are known as Śukla-Dhyāna (meditation, or concentration) and *kāyotsarga,* i.e. non-attachment toward one's own body as well as worldly belongings. The Jaina believes that emancipation, which is the ultimate goal of our life, can only be achieved by Śukla-Dhyāna, which is the state of pure self-awareness, or knowership. Thus, according to Jainism, emancipation can only be achieved by *dhyāna,* which is also the seventh limb of the Yoga-system of Patañjali. Thus we can say that *dhyāna* and Yoga are essential factors in Jaina religious practices.

If we want a brief historical account of the development of Jaina Yoga, its meditation methods, and the impact of other Indian Yoga systems upon it, we should first divide the development of the Jaina Yoga system into the following five stages:

1 pre-canonical age (before sixth century B.C.);
2 canonical age (fifth century B.C. to fifth century A.D.);
3 post-canonical age (sixth century A.D. to twelfth century A.D.);
4 age of tantra and rituals (thirteenth to nineteenth century A.D.);
5 modern age (twentieth century).

Pre-canonical age

The concepts of Yoga and meditation are as old as Indian culture itself. From the earliest period, we find two types of evidences regarding Yoga and meditation. Firstly, there is sculptural evidence, and secondly there is literary evidence. For the first phase of Yoga and meditation, both types of evidence are available, but it is very difficult to say that these evidences support the Jaina method of Yoga and meditation. We can only say that this earliest phase of Yoga and meditation belongs to the Śramanic culture, of which Jainism, Buddhism, Ājīvika, Sāṃkhya Yoga, as well as some other minor Śramanic trends, are the offspring. For this reason every Indian system of Yoga has the right to claim it as its own. This is why there are Jaina scholars who claim that these evidences belong to their own tradition. The earliest sculptural traces regarding Yoga and meditation are found in Mohenjodaro and Harappa. In the excavation of Mohenjodaro and Harappa there were seals found depicting yogis either seated or standing in meditation postures.[2]

This proves that in that period meditative and yogic practices had been prevalent. The culture of Mohenjodaro and Harappa may be called the earliest phase of the Śramanic culture of India. It is clear that, while the Vedic tradition was engaged in performing *yajña* or sacrifices, the Śramanic tradition was taking interest in yogic and meditative practices. I am of the opinion that this early Śramanic tradition has been divided over time into various branches, such as Jainism, Buddhism, Saṃkhya, Yoga, and Ājīvika, as well as other minor sects. Despite the Upaniṣadic trend of that period to try to make a synthesis between the Śramanic and the Vedic it was primarily dominated by Śramanic traditions. The Saṃkhya and Yoga systems may also be the result of this synthesis, yet we must be aware that the Śramanic features are a dominant force for them as well.

Impact of other systems on Jaina Yoga in this period

In the first phase, i.e. in the pre-canonical age, it is very difficult to trace the impact of other systems of Yoga on Jaina Yoga, because in this period we do not find any information about organized schools of yogic and meditational practices, except that of Ramaputta, from whom Lord Buddha had learned some methods of meditation. It is interesting to note that Ramaputta was mentioned in some Jaina canonical texts as well, such as *Sūtrakṛāṅga*, *Antakrta-Dasanga*, and *Ṛṣibhāṣita*.[3] I believe that the original forms of Vipassanā and Prekṣā meditation from that period basically originated with Ramaputta.

Canonical age

Traditionally it is believed that Jaina Yoga and meditative practices originated from Ṛṣabhadeva, the first Tīrthaṅkara, but as far as the historical evidences are concerned, the earliest mention of yogic practices and meditation was found in early Jaina canonical works such as *Ācārāṅga, Sūtrakṛāṅga*, and *Ṛṣibhāṣita*. In "Upadhānaśruta," the ninth chapter of the *Ācārāṅga*, there are records of the yogic and meditative practices which were followed by Lord Mahāvīra himself, in which we find the trāṭaka meditation method.[4] In the *Sūtrakṛāṅga's* sixth chapter, Prekṣā meditation is also mentioned. In it Lord Mahāvīra was presented as the best meditator or seer who knew the real nature of religious practices, like steadiness of mind and Prekṣā (self-awareness).[5] In the eighth chapter of the *Sūtrakṛāṅga* it states that the ultimate means for emancipation are *dhyāna,* yoga, and *titikṣā* (tolerance).[6] At their end yogic and meditation practices can be completed by giving up the attachment towards one's own body (8/26), which is known in Jainism as *kāyotsarga.*

In this second phase, which is known as the canonical age, some common features can be seen between Patañjali's eightfold Yoga system and the Jaina Yoga system. Patañjali's system has the following steps of yogic practices:

1 *yama* (vows)
2 *niyama* (supporting vows)
3 *āsana* (bodily postures)
4 *prāṇāyāma* (controlling of respiration)
5 *pratyāhāra* (controlling of sense organs)
6 *dhāraṇā* (controlling of mental activities)
7 *dhyāna* (concentration of mind)
8 *samādhi* (equanimity of mind, or cessation of mind).

In Jaina canonical works we also find these eight limbs of yogic *sādhanā*, but with different names. Ācārya Atmaramaji of the Sthānakavāsī Jaina sect, in his book entitled *Jaina Agamon Mem Aṣtanga Yoga,* compares the eight limbs of Patañjali's yoga system with a Jaina system of *sādhanā.* According to Ācārya Atmaramaji, what Patañjali calls the five *yamas* correspond to the five mahāvratas of the Jaina system. In fact, the individual names of the *mahāvratas* and the yamas are the same. In the Jaina cannon they are: (1) ahiṃsā (non-violence); (2) satya (truthfulness); (3) asteya (non-stealing); (4) brahmacarya (celibacy); and (5) aparigraha (non-possessions). In the *Yoga Sūtras* Patañjali mentions these five yamas in the name of five mahāvratas.

The second limb of yogic sādhana is niyama. The five *niyamas* in Patañjali's *Yoga Sūtra* are: (1) *śauca* (piousness); (2) *santoṣa* (satisfaction); (3) *tapas* (penance); (4) *svādhyāya* (study of the scriptures) and (5) *īśvara-praṇidhāna* (meditation on the nature of God or the pure self). In Jain scriptures there are correlations with these niyamas, though often with different names. For example, in the *Bhagawati Sūtra,* Lord Mahāvīra explains to Somila that his lifestyle is of six types: (1) *tapas*; (2) *niyama*; (3) *samyama*; (4) *svādhyāya*; (5) *dhyāna*; and (6) *āvaśyaka* (observance of essential duties with self-awareness).[7] Here *samyama* appears where Patañjali had *santoṣa*, and *dhyāna* aligns with Patañjali's *īśvara-praṇidhāna*. *Śauca* appears in the first chapter of the *Isibhāsiyāṃ*, though *śauca* does not mean bodily purity for the Jainas, but rather mental purity, i.e., piousness of the heart. In both Jainism and Patañjali's *Yoga Sūtras,* the *niyamas* support the yamas and the *mahāvratas*. We can also say that the 26 bhāvanās of the five *mahāvratas*, and the 32 Yoga saṃgrahas of Jainism are analogous to the *niyamas* of Patañjali.

Āsana (bodily posture) is the third limb of Patañjali's yogic *sādhana*. Many of these *āsanas* are accepted in Jainism under the auspice of *kayaklestapa*, which is the sixth kind of external *tapas*. We also find the names of various types of *āsanas* in Jaina scriptures, like *bhagawati*, *aupapatike*, and *dasarutaskanda*.[8] It is said that Lord Mahāvīra attained the *kevala jñāna* in *goduhasana*.[9]

The fourth limb of Patañjali's yoga system is *prāṇāyāma* (control of respiration). Even though there is no clear instruction regarding *prāṇāyāma* in the Jaina canonical works, there is a kind of *prāṇāyāma* described in the commentary of the *Āvaśyaka-sūtra*. Here it states that during the yearly penitential retreat (*pratikramana*), one should observe the meditation (*kāyotsarga*) of 1,000 breaths; during the fourth monthly *pratikramana* one should meditate upon 500 breaths; on the fourth nightly *pratikramana* one should meditate upon 200 breaths, during the daily *pratikramana* one should mediate upon 100 breaths, and a meditation on 50 breaths should be observed for the nightly *pratikramana*.[10] In my opinion, this is the same as both the *ānāpānasati* of Vipassanā Buddhist meditation, and the *swasaprekṣā* meditation of the Terapantha sect's Ācārya Mahāprajña. I have not found any references to *prāṇāyāma* practices like *kumbhaka*, *puraka*, or *recaka* in early Jaina canonical texts, though various types of *prāṇāyāma* are mentioned in the later period, for example in the *Jñānārṇava* of Ācārya Śubhacandra and in Hemacandra's *Yogaśāstra*.[11]

The fifth limb of Patañjali's *Yoga Sūtra* is *pratyāhāra*, which means to have control over one's sensory organs. This has been widely discussed in the Jaina canon under the name *pratisamlinta* as the sixth kind of external austerity. It has also been described in various Jaina agamas as *indriya-saṃyama*, and is discussed at some length in the 13th chapter of the *Uttarādhyayanasūtra*.[12] Many equivalents to the fifth limb of yoga can be found referenced throughout the Jaina canonical works.

The sixth, seventh, and eighth limbs of Patañjali's Yoga are respectively *dhāraṇā*, *dhyāna*, and *samādhi*. In the works of Jaina logic, the fourth kind of *matijñana* is known as *dhāraṇā*. The Jaina concept of *dhāraṇā*, or retention, is different than Patañjali's understanding of *dhāraṇā*, which means concentration of the mind, while in Jainism dhāraṇā means retention of the experience. Patañjali's concept of *dhāraṇā* resembles more closely the Jaina concept of *dhyāna*.

In the Jaina tradition *dhyāna* generally means concentrating the mind on some object or mental image. According to them our thoughts, and their instrument, the mind, are restless, and their regulation and concentration is called *dhyāna*. Jainism describes four kinds of *dhyāna*: (1) *ārta-dhyāna* – the concentration of the mind on fulfilling worldly desires; (2) *raudra-dhyāna* – the concentration of thoughts on violent activities; (3) *dharma-dhyāna* – the concentration of the mind on auspicious thoughts, or on the well-being of one's self as well as the well-being of others; (4) *śukla-dhyana* – here the mind gradually shortens its fields of concentration and at last becomes *nirvikalpa*, steady and motionless.[13] According to Patañjali, *samādhi* is the motionless state of mind, body, and speech. In other words, it is the state of trance in which the connection of the self with the outer world is broken.

Patañjali's three internal limbs of Yoga, *dhāraṇā*, *dhyāna*, and *samādhi*, align with the Jaina concept of meditation. *Dhāraṇā* and *dhyāna* may be summed up in various stages of *dharma-dhyāna*, while *samādhi* resembles *śukla-dhyāna*.

Another way we can understand Patañjali's last three limbs in a Jaina context is to think of them in relationship to *kāyotsarga* (non-attachment to one's body and worldly things). It is important to remember that in Patañjali's Yoga, *dhāraṇā*, *dhyāna*, and *samādhi* are not only the internal limbs of yogic *sādhana*, but are also dependent upon one another through a link of process, meaning that without *dhāraṇā*, *dhyāna* is not possible, and without *dhyāna*, *samādhi* is impossible.

From the above it can be inferred that Jaina Yoga held many similarities with Patañjali's eightfold yoga; none the less the Jaina sādhana of the canonical age was centered on a three- or fourfold path of emancipation, i.e., right faith, right knowledge, right conduct, and right austerity. Umāsvāti and some of the other Jaina *ācāryas* prescribed a threefold path because they considered right conduct and right austerity to fall under the same category. There are similar threefold paths in Hinduism as well as in Buddhism. The Hindu path, as set forth in the *Bhagavad Gītā*, is Bhakti Yoga, Jñāna Yoga, and Karma Yoga, while the Buddhist threefold path is *śīla*, *samādhi*, and *prajña*. Jaina right knowledge can be compared to Jñāna Yoga of Hinduism and to *prajña* of Buddhism, right faith is similar to Bhakti Yoga and to *saṃyak samādhi*, while right conduct lines up with Karma Yoga in the *Gītā,* and with *śīla* in Buddhism.[14] It is important to note that there are some Hindu thinkers who hold that the cultivation of any one of these constituents is sufficient in attaining emancipation, which stands in stark contrast to the Jaina thinking which holds that the absence of any one of these makes emancipation impossible. Jainism believes in the synthesis of these three Yogas. These three Yogas of Jainism can be summed up in the practice of *sāmāyika* or Samatva Yoga, which is the excellent blend of right faith, right knowledge, and right conduct. The *Uttarādhyayanasūtra* states: *nadamsanissa nanam, nanena vina na hunti ceranguna. Agunissa natthi mokkho, natthi amokkhassa nivbvanam* (28:30). [Knowledge is impossible without a right view, or faith, and without right knowledge right conduct is impossible; without right conduct liberation remains unattainable.] Thus all three are needed for the attainment of emancipation.

Samatva Yoga: the fundamental Yoga of Jainism

Sāmāyika or Samatva Yoga is the principal concept underlining Jainism. It is the first and foremost of the six essential duties of both monks and householders. In order to explicate the nuanced meaning and use of this word we must first explore how it is translated and defined in various sources. The Prakrit term s*amaiya* can be translated into English in a variety of ways, such as observance of equanimity, viewing all living beings as oneself, conception of equality, harmonious state of one's behavior, integration of personality, as well as righteousness in the activities of mind, body, and speech. Ācārya Kundakunda uses the term samahi (*samādhi*) in the same sense as *sāmāyika,* meaning a tensionless state of consciousness, or state of self-absorption. In a general sense the word *sāmāyika* means a particular religious practice through which one can attain equanimity of mind. It is an end as well as a means in itself. As a means it is a practice for attaining this equanimity, while as an ends it is the state in which the self is completely free from the flickerings of alternative desires and wishes, excitements and emotional disorders. It is the state of self-absorption, or of resting in one's own self. In Ācārya Bhadra's *Avasyakaniryukti,* he writes that *sāmāyika* is nothing but one's own self in its pure form. Thus, from a transcendental point of view, *sāmāyika* means the realization of one's own self in its real nature.[15] It is the state in which one is completely free from attachment and aversion. Within the same work Ācārya Bhadra lists equanimity, equality, righteousness, the state of self-absorption, purity, peace, welfare, and happiness, which are all synonyms for *sāmāyika.*[16]

Sāmāyika is explained in a myriad of ways in the *Anuyogadvarasūtra*, the *Avasyakaniryukti,* and in Kundakunda's *Niyamasāra*. For example, one who has given up the movement of uttering words, who has realized himself with non-attachment, is said to have supreme equanimity (*sāmāyika*). He who is detached from all injurious or impious actions, who observes the threefold control of the body, mind, and speech, and who restrains his senses is said to have attained equanimity. One who behaves equally towards himself and all living beings, both mobile and immobile, is said to have equanimity. Furthermore, one who observes self-control, vows, and austerities, who is neither innervated nor disturbed by attachment or aversion, and who always refrains from indulgence, sorrow, and ennui is said to have attained equanimity or *sāmāyika.*[17]

Ultimately this practice of equanimity is equated with religion itself. In *Ācārāṅga* it is said that all worthy people preach religion as equanimity. Thus, for Jainas the observance of religious life is nothing but the practices of *sāmāyika* for the attainment of equanimity. According to them it is the essence of all types of religious activities which are prescribed only in order to attain it. Equanimity is valued not only in Jainism but in Hindu sources as well. The *Bhagavad Gītā* defines Yoga as equanimity,[18] and in the *Bhāgavat Purāṇa* it is said that the observance of equanimity is the worship of the lord.

The whole framework of Jaina *sādhana* has been built on the foundation of *sāmāyika,* and all the religious tenets are made for it. Ācārya Haribhadra maintains that one who observes the equanimity of *saṃabhava* will surely attain emancipation whether his is Bauddha or the follower of any other religion.[19] Jaina religious texts hold that even those who observe hard penances and austerities, such as eating only once in a one- or two-month period, or those who make donations of crores of golden coins every day cannot attain emancipation or liberation unless equanimity has been attained.[20] Emancipation only comes with the equanimity of the mind. Ācārya Kundakunda writes, "What is the use of residing in the forest, the mortifications of the body, the observance of multiple fasts, the study of scriptures, and the vow of silence etc., to a saint who is devoid of equanimity?"[21]

Now, we arrive at a very salient question. How does one go about attaining this equanimity of the mind? The mere verbal claim to observe this equanimity, and to refrain from committing any type of injurious act is meaningless unless we emphatically practice it in our daily lives. The first step in this process is to discern what causes the disturbances of the mind and then endeavor to eradicate them. To say that one should observe this equanimity is easy, but to practice it is very difficult. Our mental faculty is always in the grips of attachment and aversion, therefore, whatever we think or do is always motivated by either one of these. Because the vectors of attachment and aversion are solely responsible for the disturbances of the mind the attainment of mental equanimity depends on the eradication of them both. As long as we are stuck in the processes of attachment and aversion we will be unable to attain equanimity, or Samatva Yoga.

The impact of other Yoga systems on Jaina Yoga in this period

As previously noted, evaluating any clear differentiation between Yogas of the pre-canonical age is very difficult, not only because of insufficient archeological and literary evidence, but also because the early Śramanic movement was not codified into multiple schools, each with definite philosophical backgrounds. However, during the canonical age different schools of thought formed which had particular names and doctrines, like Jainism, Buddhism, Ājīvika, Saṃkhya, and Yoga etc. We find a great deal of similarities between Jaina Yoga, Buddhism, and Patañjali in this period. In his introduction to the *Tattvārthasūtra,* Pt. Sukhalaji discusses these commonalities in detail. The clear similarities make any concrete proof of one's impact on another tenuous at best, though it is generally accepted that these systems have a common source from which they developed. That common source is the Indian Śramanic tradition. The similarities are quite apparent during the *sūtra* age; in particularly between Patañjali's *Yoga Sūtras* and Umāsvāti's *Tattvārthasūtra*, yet their names and explanations are quite different from one another. Even though Pt. Sukhalaji gives 21 common points of conceptual similarity between *Tattvārthasūtra* and Yoga *darśana*[22] in his introduction to the text, they are similarities in meaning with very different names, and thus we cannot really say that one system borrowed from another. It shows simply that they share a common source. We do know that in the canonical age the Śramanic movement had formed into distinct groups with clear lines of thought, one of which is Jainism.

Jainism had its own method of meditation, and its own understanding of how emancipation could be achieved. In the Jaina canonical works, as well as in Jinabhadra's *Dhyāna-Sataka* (sixth century A.D.), meditation was considered to be of four kinds, i.e., Ārta-Dhyāna, Raudra-Dhyāna, Dharma-Dhyāna, and Śukla-Dhyāna. The first two, Ārta-Dhyāna and, Raudra-Dhyāna, were considered to be the causes of bondage, while the last two, Dharma-Dhyāna and Śukla-Dhyāna, were the causes of emancipation. As far as I know this fourfold classification of meditations is solely the product of Jaina *ācāryas*, and they are not found with either these names or in this type of grouping within any other Indian Yoga system.

Just as common features have been found among the *Yoga Sūtras* and the *Tattvārthasūtra,* there are similarities between the key Jaina concept of Samatva Yoga within Buddhism and Hinduism (and within the *Bhagavad Gītā* in particular). Yet, we cannot say that Jainism borrowed this idea from Hinduism, because the *Ācārāṅga*, which propounds Samatva Yoga, pre-dates the *Bhagavad Gītā*. To claim the opposite, that Hinduism borrowed from Jainism, is beyond the interests of this chapter. In this exploration of the canonical age I wish simply to direct our attentions away from concrete assumptions about one group's influence upon another, and rather see the ambiguity of divergence that arose from a common source.

Post-canonical age

The post-canonical age is very important for our understanding of the development of Jaina Yoga for two reasons: the first is that during this period there were a great deal of Jaina Yoga works composed, while the second is that the impact of other Yoga systems upon the Jaina system can be clearly seen. As stated above, the canonical age gives us some scattered references to Yoga practices in regards to the five yamas (*Mahāvrata*), the five *niyamas*, some of the bodily postures, the control of sense organs, various aspects of meditation, along with some philosophical and religious preaching, but these works cannot solely be considered the works of Jaina Yoga literature. In my opinion the first work on Jaina meditation is Jinbhadra's *Dhyāna-Sataka* (sixth century A.D.).

The *Dhyāna-Sataka* is devoted to Jaina meditation, and is based on Jaina canonical works like *Sthanga*. *Sthanga* deals with four kinds of *dhyānas* and their subclasses: (1) their objects; (2) their signs (*lakṣaṇa*); (3) their condition (*ālambana*); and (4) their reflections (*bhāvanā*). This description of *dhyāna* is on a par with the canonical works except for some of the specific details, such as the appropriate type of place for meditation, right time of meditation, right posture, right qualities of a meditator, and results of meditation.[23] In Jinbhadragani's *Dhyāna-Sataka* he deals minimally with the first two inauspicious *dhyānas* (*ārta* and *raudra dhyāna*), but explores the two auspicious *dhyānas* (*dharma* and *śukla dhyāna*) in detail. According to him, since the first two *dhyānas* are the causes of bondage, the second two, which are the means for emancipation, are the only *dhyānas* which can be considered limbs of Yoga *sādhana*.

The next great contributor in the development of Jaina yoga was Haribhadra. He was a Jaina *ācārya* who not only helped construct, or reconstruct, Jaina Yoga, but he also made extensive comparative studies between Jaina Yoga and a number of other Yoga systems. Haribhadra composed four major books on Jaina Yoga: *Yogaviṃśika, Yogaśataka*, *Yogabindu*, and *Yogadṛṣṭisammucaya.* It was Haribhadra who reformulated the meaning of the word *yoga* within the Jaina context. Initially *yoga* was considered to be the cause of bondage.[24] Haribhadra ostensibly said that that which joins to the emancipation is Yoga, and according to him all spiritual and religious activities that lead to final emancipation are Yoga.[25] It is important to note that within his works he explained Yoga in different ways. In his *Yogaviṃśika* he describes a fivefold Yoga: (1) practice of proper posture (Sthāna Yoga); (2) correct utterance of sound (Urṇa Yoga); (3) proper understanding of the meaning of canonical works (Artha); (4) concentration of the mind on a particular object, such as on a Jina image (Ālambana); and (5) concentration of thoughts on abstract qualities of a Jina or Self (Anālambana). The fifth stage may also be considered as the state without thought (Nirvikalpa-Daśā).[26] In this fivefold Yoga of the *Yogaviṃśika,* the first two constitute the external aspects of

Yoga sādhana, while the last three are the internal aspects. Or, to put it another way, the first two are Karma Yoga, while the last three are Jñāna Yoga.

In the *Yogabindu* Haribhadra introduces another fivefold Yoga: (1) spiritual vision (Adhyātma Yoga); (2) contemplation (Bhāvanā Yoga); (3) meditation (Dhyāna Yoga); (4) mental equanimity (Samatā Yoga); and (5) cessation of all activities of mind, speech, and body (Vṛttisaṃkṣaya).[27] In his *Yogadṛṣṭisammucaya* Haribhadra elucidates on a threefold yoga: (1) willingness for the self-realization or yogic *sādhana* (Icchā Yoga); (2) the follow-up of scriptural orders (Śāstra Yoga); and (3) development of one's spiritual powers and the annihilation of spiritual inertia (Sāmarthya Yoga).[28] The facets of this threefold yoga propounded in Haribhadra's *Yogadṛṣṭisammucaya* may be compared with the three jewels of Jainism. The three jewels, right vision, right knowledge, and right conduct, are a *mokṣa mārga*, a path of emancipation, and thus are Yoga. Even though Haribhadra purports a variety of Yogas in his books, the consistent line of thought regarding Yoga throughout is that Yoga is that which unites one to emancipation. His eightfold Yoga is summarized by Chapple in this volume.

Following Haribhadra there were two *ācāryas* who made remarkable contributions in the field of Jaina Yoga. There was Śubhacandra (eleventh century), a Digambara whose most notable Yoga work was entitled *Jñānārṇava*, and Hemacandra (twelfth century), a Śvetāmbara, who wrote the *Yogaśāstra*. In the Yoga *sādhana* of the *Jñānārṇava*, Śubhacandra prescribes four virtues: (1) friendship with all beings (*maitri*); (2) appreciation of the merits of others (*pramoda*); (3) sympathy towards those in need (*karuṇā*); and 4) equanimity, or indifference regarding the unruly (*madhyastha*). These virtues are to be cultivated as the prerequisite for auspicious meditation.[29] The same four virtues, with some variance on the names, can also be found in Buddhist monastic practices, as well as the *Yoga Sūtras* of Patañjali. In the *Jñānārṇava,* when Śubhacandra discusses the Dharma Dhyāna, he breaks it down further into four types: *piṇḍastha*, *padastha*, *rūpastha*, and *rūpātīta*. This is in conjunction with five types of *dhāraṇās*: *parthivi*, *agneya,* vāyavi *(svasana*), *vārūṇē*, and *tattva-rūpavati*[30] of the Piṇḍastha Dhyāna. It is important to bear in mind that these four types of *dhyānas* and five types of *dhāraṇās* are present in early Buddhist and Hindu tantric texts, but not in that of the early Jainas.

Hemacandra follows Śubhacandra as another important figure of Jaina Yoga. Hemacandra's *Yogaśāstra* is a blend of Jaina ethics, religion, and meditation, mixed with Patañjali's *Yoga Sūtras*. There are also influences from tantric practices, Hindu Haṭha Yoga, as well as Buddhist yogic sādhana. By reviewing each chapter of Hemacandra's *Yogaśāstra* we can try to see the impact of earlier Jaina and non-Jaina *ācāryas* on this text.

The first chapter of the *Yogaśastra* deals with both the importance of yogic *sādhanā*, as well as the five *mahāvratas* (great vows), *pañcasamitis*, and the three *guptis*. These form the basic code of conduct for Jaina monks and nuns. Here Hemacandra follows the Jaina canonical tradition. At the end of this first chapter of the *Yogaśastra* Hemacandra discusses the 35 *mārgānusāri* (qualities of a householder). Though we do not find any reference to these 35 qualities of a householder in Jaina canonical works, they are discussed by Haribhadra in his work. I suspect Hemacandra borrowed this idea from Haribhadra.

The second and third chapters of the *Yogaśāstra* explain the meaning of *samyak-darśana* (right vision) along with detailed descriptions of the 12 vows of a householder, both of which are based not only on Jaina canonical works, but other traditional works as well, such as Umāsvāti's *Tattvārthasūtra*. It is interesting to note when Hemacandra introduces a new element. An example of this can be found in his elucidation on the vow of non-stealing, where he writes "ill luck, slavery, cutting off the organs of any living being, and poverty are also the same as stealing"[31] (2:65).

The fourth chapter of the *Yogaśāstra* is devoted to Jaina spirituality, the science of meditation, along with the practice of equanimity, which, as explained above, is the base of Jaina spiritual *sādhana*. Along with Hemacandra's descriptions of meditation he explains the four basic feelings (*bhāvanās*) necessary for meditation practice along with the appropriate *āsanas* (bodily postures). With the exception of the *āsana* portion, there is nothing presented in this chapter which is outside Jaina canonical and traditional texts.

The *Yogaśāstra's* fifth chapter is devoted to *prāṇāyāma* (breath control). Here we can see the direct impact of Patañjali's *Yoga Sūtras*, the *Haṭhayoga Pradīpikā*, as well as the *Gheraṇḍasaṃhitā*. In the first verse Hemacandra writes, "Having obtained mastery of various postures, Patañjali and others advocated the necessity of *prāṇāyāma*, for securing meditational power, as otherwise there will be no control over the mind" (5:1). In earlier Jaina traditions *prāṇāyāma* was not accepted as an essential limb of yogic *sādhana*, with the exception of Haribhadra, who renamed *prāṇāyāma* as *diprā* in the *Yogadṛṣṭisammucaya* verse 57. In the fifth chapter Hemacandra gives a detailed account of *prāṇāyāma*, but in the sixth chapter he rejects the necessity of *prāṇāyāma* practice:

> tatrāpnoti manaḥ svāsthyaṃ prāṇāyāmaiḥ kadarthitaṃ
> prāṇasyāyamane pīthā tasyāṃ sayāccittaviplavaḥ (4)
> pūraṇe kumbhane caiva recane ca pariśramaḥ
> citta-saṃkleśa-karaṇān makteḥ pratyūhakāraṇaṃ (5)

> The mind does not get stability if it is troubled by exercises of breath-control because, while controlling the breath, the body also undergoes discomfort and distress, and this again becomes the cause of mental imbalance. Inhaling, suspending, and exhaling involve hard labors. This, on its part produces grief; and the aggrieved state of mind thus blocks the way to salvation.[32]

From this we can say that in the fifth chapter of the *Yogaśāstra* Hemacandra clearly borrowed from texts like the *Yoga Sūtra* and the *Haṭhayoga Pradīpikā,* while the sixth chapter reflects the fact that he was a Jaina Ācārya, and thus rejected the necessity of *prāṇāyāma* because it was not considered an essential feature of Jaina Yoga *sādhanā* even by Haribhadra, a founder of the Jaina Yoga system. Along with the discussion of *prāṇāyāma*, the fifth chapter of the *Yogaśāstra* explores various ways to predict the time of death. Hemacandra delves into the ways to forecast death in great detail, from exploring it via the movement of the breath in the *nāḍis*, external signs, dreams, shadows, and other physiological symptoms such as the absence of taste, hearing, and smell; these subsections on death divination take up nearly 200 verses in this chapter. I have tried to uncover the original sources of these verses, but have been unable to find them. Pujya Muni Jambuvijaya has not given us any trace of the origins of theses verses either. All that I have found are some traces in the *Bhaviṣyapurāṇa* and the *Gariṭhapurāṇa*. As mentioned above, the sixth chapter of the *Yogaśāstra* is fully devoted to the negation of the necessity or utility of *prāṇāyāma*. This chapter ends in only eight verses.

The seventh chapter of the *Yogaśāstra* introduces the various levels of meditation. Here he discusses the four types of Dharma-Dhyāna, i.e., the *piṇḍastha*, *padastha*, *rūpastha*, *rūpātīta*, and the five *dhāraṇās*. These thought processes are based on the five elements of earth, fire, wind, water, and the real nature of the self. (7:9)

> pārthivī syād athāgneyī mārutī vāruṇī tathā
> tatra bhūḥ pañcamī ceti piṇḍasathe pāñca dhāraṇāḥ (a)
>
> When it comes to [meditation] on [imagined] objects (*piṇḍa*), there are five [different] acts of concentration: one related to the earth [element], one to the fire [element], one to the wind [element], one to the water [element], and a fifth [related to] the [non-material] Self. (7:9)[33]

We do not find anything in regard to these four types of *dhyānas* and five *dhāraṇās* in either earlier Jaina canonical works, or in the Yoga texts of Ācārya Haribhadra. We should note that these four Dharma-Dhyānas (*piṇḍastha*, *padastha*, *rūpastha*, *rūpātīta*), as well as the five types of *dhāraṇās* (*pārthīvī*, *āgneyī*, *vāyavī*, *vāruṇī*, and *tattvarūpavati*) can be found in Buddhist and Hindu Tantric literature.

Though Hemacandra discusses the three jewels of Jainism – right knowledge, right vision, and right conduct – in his *Yogaśāstra,* he places the greatest stress on right conduct. In his description of meditation methods he goes into an elaborate discussion of the above-mentioned *dhyānas* and *dhāraṇās*. Many scholars are of the opinion that he borrowed these ideas from the *Jñānarṇava* of Śubhacandra,[34] or possibly directly from the *Gheraṇḍasaṃhitā*. Since Śubhacandra borrowed these classifications of *dhyāna* and *dhāraṇās* from the Hindu Tantra, and Hemacandra was then inspired by Śubhacandra's explications of these *dhyānas* and *dhāraṇās*, we can easily say that in this period the impact of the other systems of Yoga *sādhanā* on Jaina Yoga is evident.

The eighth chapter of Hemacandra's *Yogaśāstra* is devoted to Padastha Dhyāna, or Māntrika Sādhanā. Hemacandra may have been influenced by Hindu mantras, but he approached mantra practice in a way that allowed them to function in accordance with Jaina tradition. This is a task he had taken up from earlier Ācāryas like Haribhadra and Śubhacandra, as well as others.

The ninth chapter is on the *rūpastha dhyāna,* which is the focus on the outward form of the Jina. The tenth chapter is devoted to the nature of liberated souls along the four subtypes of Dharma Dhyāna (i.e. *ājñāvicaya, apāyavicaya, vipākavicaya,* and *saṁsthānavicaya*).

> Thus the mind of a mendicant (*muni*) which is immersed in the ambrosia of the four kinds of meditation – [*piṇḍastha, padastha, rūpastha*, and *rūpavarjita*] – [and] which has directly experienced the reality of the world, attains purity of Self. (10:6) Also from another perspective virtuous meditation is fourfold by making a distinction between [the following] objects of meditation: (i) the teaching (*ājñā*) [of the Jina], (ii) the evil (*āpāya*) [consequences of *karma*], (iii) the nature (*vipāka*) [of *karma*], and (iv) the structure [of the universe] (*saṁsthāna*). (10:7) [35]

He gives an introductory explanation to the four subtypes in verse 10:7 (quoted above) and then elaborates on each of these in accordance with Jaina canonical works and dhyāna śataka.

The 11th chapter of the *Yogaśāstra* discusses the Śukla-Dhyāna (pure self-awareness), its four subtypes, and the special qualities of the Arhat or the Tīrthaṅkar. The process of *samuddhata* and achieving liberation (*siddha gatī*) are elaborated on as well. The contents of this chapter are all based on Jaina traditional literature.

The 12th, and final chapter explores the four gradations of mind: *vikṣipta, yātāyāta, śiliṣṭa*, and *sulīna,* and how through disciplined practice the restless mind (*vikṣipta*) can be coalesced into a mind of deep steadiness (*sulīna*). Hemacandra borrowed this kind of division of the mind, along with various terms that Qvarnström translates as "no mind" [36] which are found in chapter 12, from Gorakṣanātha's *Amanaskayoga*.

Muni Shri Jambuvijayaji's contribution in this field is remarkable. He has given both a comparative as well as an exhaustive list of the verses from the *Yogaśāstra* as well as the above-mentioned works, in the third volume of the *Yogaśāstra* within its first appendix. Similarly, from the above-mentioned texts he ascertained the information about seeing the signs of age and death. Thus, we can conclude that, while writing the *Yogaśāstra,* Hemacandra was influenced by other Indian Yoga systems, particularly Patañjali's *Yogasūtra*, the *Haṭhayoga Pradīpikā*, the *Amanaskayoga* of Gorakṣanātha, and the *Gheraṇḍasaṃhitā* of the Hindu tradition, Nāgasena's *Tattvānuśāsana* of the Buddhist tradition, as well as Śubhachadra's *Jñānārṇava* of the Digambara sect. Here it is to be noted that in writing his *Yogaśāstra,* Hemacandra primarily depended on Śubhachadra's *Jñānārṇava* along with some Śvetāmbara texts such as *Dhyānaśataka* and its *Haribhadriyatika*, the *Praśamarati* of Umāsvāti, the *Brahatkalpabhāṣya*, etc.

The impact of other Yoga systems on Jainism in this period

The first Yoga work of the post-canonical age is the *Dhyāna-Sataka.* Since the four types of meditation found within are based on Jaina canonical works, we can conclude that other Yoga systems had no impact on this text. Conversely, the impact of other Yoga systems is evident in other works from this period, such as those written by Haribhadra, Śubhacandra, and Hemacandra.

Since Haribhadra had been born a Brahmin, and later converted to Jainism, it is not surprising to find Brāhmanical influences in his work. Nonetheless, he remained faithful to Jainism while explicating Jaina Yoga in his various works on the subject. Haribhadra offers us different Yoga *sādhana* schemes within his variant Yoga texts. If we peruse some of his Yoga principles we can more easily compare them to analogous systems found in the texts of other traditions.

In Haribhadra's *Yogadṛṣtisamuccaya* he mentions three Yogas: (1) Icchāyoga; (2) Śāstrayoga; and (3) Samārthyayoga. These are based on the three jewels of Jainism. Similarly, in the *Yogavāsiṣṭha,* we find three stages of Yoga *sādhana*: (1) total devotion; (2) mental peace; and (3) total cessation of the activities of the mind and the body. Icchāyoga in the *Yogadṛṣtisamuccaya* is similar to total devotion found in the *Yogavāsistha,* while Samārthyayoga resembles the two other states of mental peace, and the cessation of the activities of the mind and the body.

In the *Yogabindu* Haribhadra describes five types of yoga: (1) Adhyātma Yoga (spiritualization); (2) Bhāvanā Yoga (contemplation); (3) Dhyāna-Yoga (meditation); (4) Samatā Yoga (equanimity of mind); and (5) Vṛttisaṃṣaya Yoga (cessation of all activities of the mind, body, and speech). Adhyātma is what is accepted in other systems as Mahāyoga. Bhāvanā and Dhyāna are also present in Hindu Yoga systems. Samatā Yoga and Vṛttisaṃṣaya Yoga are not only present in the *Yogavasiṣṭha,* but can be found in Laya Yoga as well.

In his *Yogaviṃśika* Haribhadra lists four types of yogas: (1) *āsana* (posture); (2) *urṇa* (recitation of mantras); (3) *ālambana*; and (4) *anālambana*. *Āsana* is found in Patañjali's *Yoga Sūtra*. *Urṇa* is referred to within the Hindu context as *mantra* or *japa*, while *ālambana* is akin to Bhakti Yoga and *anālambana* is similar to Laya Yoga. In like manner, Haribhadra's eight Yoga *dṛṣtis* are arranged along the same lines as the eight limbs of Patañjali. Haribhadra incorporated these various concepts from Buddhist and Hindu Tantric systems, yet fashioned them in a way that is in accordance with the Jain tradition.

When it comes to the categories of *piṇḍastha*, *padastha*, *rūpastha*, and *rūpātīta dhyānas* along with their *pārthiv*, *āgneyī*, *vāyavi*, and *vāruṇī dhāraṇā*, we find them in Jain works like Śubhacandra's *Jñānarṇava* and Hemacandra's *Yogaśāstra,* which were influenced by Hindu tantric texts, as well as Patañjali's *Yoga Sūtra*. The impact of these non-Jaina texts is evident in their work, and we must accept that these Acaryas were influenced by Patañjali and Hindu tantric works.

The age of rituals and the impact of Tantra (thirteenth century–nineteenth century)

The four centuries between Hemacandra and Yaśovijaya spanning from the thirteenth to the sixteenth century can be considered a dark age for Jaina Yoga. The original spiritual nature of Jaina Yoga was shoved into the background during this period, when tantra and its rituals became of prime importance. No longer was emancipation the ultimate goal of Yoga *sādhanā*, but rather worldly achievements held sway. The spiritual goal of Yoga *sādhanā* was completely forgotten and replaced by material welfare. There were still some commentaries composed on the canonical and other Jaina works, but the dominant features of this age were works on tantra, mantra, and rituals. The Jaina Acaryas wrote texts on Jaina rituals, tantra, and mantra sādhanā during this period.

In the seventeenth century Yaśovijaya revived the spiritual nature of Jaina Yoga. He wrote commentaries on Haribhadra's Yoga works along with original Yoga texts such as *Ādhyātmasāra, Jñanasāra*, and *Ādhyatmopanisad*. Along with these works Yaśovijaya also wrote a commentary on the *Yoga Sūtra* of Patañjali.

Along with Yaśovijaya, another important spiritual thinker in this age was Anandaghana who also revived Jaina spirituality and Yoga *sādhanā* through his *padas* and songs written in praise of the 24 Tirthankaras. Both of these thinkers are deeply influenced by Haribhadra, yet some influences from Patañjali, Raja Yoga, and Haṭha Yoga can also be seen. As stated above, the dominant feature of this age was the heavy influence of Hindu tantra and ritual performance on Jaina Yoga.

The modern age

The modern age brings tremendous changes and developments to the practice of Jaina Yoga. During this period the common man became drawn to Yoga, and there was a development of meditation as a means to relieve tension. Today the human race is held in the grip of self-created tensions built and fueled by ambition and greed. Fortunately, Shri S.N. Goyanaka returned to India from Burma in the late 1960s and revived the ancient Buddhist practice of Vipassanā meditation, a practice which was once prevalent in Jainism as well. Ācārya Mahāprajña of the Terapantha Jaina sect studied this technique with Goyanakiji. He recalibrated this meditation method based on his knowledge of the Jaina canon as well as Patañjali's *Yoga Sūtra* to form the Jaina system he called Prekṣā-Dhyāna. Prekṣā meditation is the dominant feature of Jaina Yoga in the modern period. Acaryas of different Jaina sects have attempted to evolve their own methods of meditation and Yoga, but theirs is nothing new and simply a blend of Prekṣā and Vipassanā. Of course, we should note that Prekṣā meditation is a blend of Buddhist Vipassanā, Patañjali's Aṣṭānga Yoga, Haṭha Yoga, and contemporary psychology.

I would like to conclude this chapter with a beautiful verse from the *Samayika Patha* of Acarya Amitagati:

> Sattveṣu maitriṃ guniṣu pramodaṃ
> Kliṣteṣu jiveṣu kṛpaparatvaṃ
> Madhyasthabhavaṃ viparita vṛttau
> Sadā mamātma vidadatudeva
> O Lord! I should be friendly to all creatures of the world,
> and feel delight in meeting virtuous people.
> I should always be helpful to those who are in miserable conditions,
> and tolerant towards my opponents.[37]

Notes

1 *Uttarādhyayanasūtra* 28/35.
2 R. C Majumdar, A. D. Pusalker, and A. K. Majumadra, editors, *The History and Culture of Indian People,* Vol. 1. *The Vedic Age* (London : Allen & Unwin, 1951), plate VII.
3 See *Sūtrakṛāṅga* 3/62, *Sthānāṅga* 10/113, and *Ṛṣibhāṣita* Chapter 23.
4 *Ācārāṅga* 9/5.
5 *Sūtrakṛāṅga* 6/13, 6/17.
6 Ibid. 8/27.
7 *Bhagavatīsūtra* 6/3.
8 *Daśaśrutaskandha* 6/3.
9 *Pajjosavaṇākappo* (Ladnun) 81.
10 *Āvaśyakacūrṇi.*
11 *Jñānārṇava, sarga* 37–40. *Yogaśāstra* 7/8–9.
12 *Uttarādhyayna* 32/21–106.
13 *Yogaśāstra* 12/5.
14 Sagarmal, Jain, *Jaina Buddha, Aura Gītā ke ācāradarśanoṃ adhyayaan,* Vol II, p. 1 (Jaipur, Rajasthan, 1982).
15 *Āvaśyakaniryukti,* 1048.
16 Ibid. 1046.
17 *Niyamasāra,* 122, 155, 133. *Anuyogadvāragāthā,* 127–128. *Āvaśyakaniryukti,* 797–800.
18 *Bhagavadgītā,* 2/48.
19 Haribhadra, *Lokatattvanirṇya,* 1–2.
20 Pt. Sukhalaji's Hindi introduction to the *Tattvārthasūtra,* 55.
21 *Niyamasāra* 124.
22 Pt. Sukhalaji's Hindi introduction to the *Tattvārthasūtra,* 55.
23 *Dhyānaśataka* 1–5, and 100–105.
24 *Tattvārthasūtra,* 6/13.
25 *Yogaśataka* 2. *Yogaviṃśikā* 1.
26 *Yogaviṃśikā* 2.
27 *Yogabindu* 31.
28 *Yogadṛṣṭisamuccaya* 2.
29 *Jñānārṇava* 27/4–15.
30 *Jñānārṇava, sarga* 37–40.
31 Translation mine.
32 Translation mine.
33 Translation: Qvarnström, Olle, trans., *The Yogaśāstra of Hemacandra: A Twelfth Century Handbook on Śvetāmbara Jainism, Harvard Oriental Series,* Edited by Michael Witzel, Vol. 60 (Cambridge: Harvard University Press, 2002), 146.
34 Tatia, Nathmal, *Studies in Jaina Philosophy* (Banaras: Cultural Research Society, 1951), 290.
35 Translation: Qvarnström, Olle, trans., *The Yogaśāstra of Hemacandra: A Twelfth Century Handbook on Śvetāmbara Jainism.* p. 169.
36 Ibid. pp. 191–194.
37 Jinendra Varni. *Jain Dharma Saar* (Varanasi: Sarva Seva Sangha, 1974), Śloka, p. 71.

2 Yoga in the *Tattvārthasūtra*

Jayandra Soni

Umāsvāti defines *yoga* in *Tattvārthasūtra* (TS) 6, 1 as: *kāyavāṅmanaḥkarma yogaḥ*, which S. A. Jain (in *Reality*: see Umāsvāti 1955) translates as: "The action of the body, the organ of speech and the mind is called *yoga* (activity)." It is significant, for the meaning of the term, that Jain retains the original word *yoga* in his translation, rendering it as "activity" only in brackets and indicating, thereby, that it has a special meaning here. In his *Studies in Jaina Philosophy*, Nathmal Tatia (1994: 262) says: "In Jainism the term *cāritra* (conduct) is the exact equivalent of the general term *yoga*." It is well known that Jainism uses several philosophical terms in a specific sense, and this is the case here with the term *yoga* (the term *syāt* would be another example in Jaina *anekāntavāda*). Since Umāsvāti's *c.* fifth-century TS is a basic work for practically every aspect of basic Jaina philosophy, this paper attempts to see what the work says about *yoga*, in consultation with two earliest commentaries (the *Svopajñabhāṣya* (*Svobhā*) and Pūjyapāda's *Sarvārthasiddhi* (SS)).

The seven basic truths which constitute reality (*tattva*) make up the background against which Umāsvāti discusses Jaina *yoga* in Chapter 6, (*ṣaṣtho 'dhyāya*) of his TS. The seven categories (*padārthas*) are given in TS 1, 4 and the first three are *jīva, ajīva,* and *āsrava.* In introducing the contents of Chapter 6, both the earliest commentaries to the TS, the *Svobhā* and Pūjyapāda's SS, refer to the sequence of these three when they say, to the same effect, that now *āsrava* will be described, indicating thereby that the explanation of *jīva* and *ajīva* has now been concluded. The first two sūtras of TS (6:1, 2) introduce Jaina *yoga* in this way:

> *kāyavāṅmanaḥkarma yogaḥ* |
> *sa āsravaḥ* |
>
> (TS 6: 1,2)

This means that, according to the TS, *yoga* (which is defined as a threefold activity or karma of the body, of speech, and of the mind) is *āsrava*, an influx, influence or flowing in (of *pudgala,* which then turns into fine karma particles). In other words, when TS (6, 1) says that *yoga* is the activity of the body, etc., and the next sūtra says that this *yoga* is *āsrava,* then it is clear that this chapter begins with an explanation of the third of the seven basic categories in Jaina philosophy.

It is well known that the TS is the authoritative text for the basics of Jaina philosophy and that both the Digambara and Śvetāmbara versions hardly disagree on the fundamentals of Jaina ontology, metaphysics, and epistemology. This paper attempts to discuss Jaina *yoga* on the bases of selected sections of the two commentaries and to see what, if any, significant differences they entail in their interpretation of the respective basic sūtras, as is the case with some topics.[1]

In its commentary to TS 6, 1 the SS begins by saying that the meanings of the words *kāya*, etc., have been explained (*kāyādayaḥ śabdā vyākhyātārthāḥ*).[2] This hint is useful for the fact that the word *yoga* in the TS 6, 1 has to be seen in the context of Jaina philosophy as a whole, namely, that Jaina *yoga* is concerned with more than the mere statements of the sūtra alone, a point that is probably explicit in the next sūtra, TS 6, 2, where it is said that this *yoga* is *āsrava*, a term that constitutes one of the seven basic Jaina truths (TS 1, 4). The *Svobhā*, on the other hand, begins by briefly saying what these actions are, as will be seen below in detail when both these commentaries will be quoted.

The first time that *āsrava* is mentioned is, as already pointed out, in TS 1, 4 and the *Svobhā* says only that "we shall describe in detail later" (*purastād vistareṇopadekṣyāmaḥ*) their definition and their differences (*tāṃllakṣaṇato vidhānataś ca*). The SS gives the following by way of an initial understanding of the term in TS 1, 4 (the relevant portions are extracted out of the commentary to the whole *sūtra*): *āsrava* is what has a form (of matter or *pudgala*) through the coming in of meritorious and unmeritorious karma (*śubhāśubhakarmāgamadvārarūpa āsravaḥ*). The commentary then goes on to say that the main causes of transmigration are *āsrava* and *bandha* (bondage).[3] With this brief contextual background the commentaries to TS 6, 1–2 can now be explored in more detail. It is useful to keep in mind that in TS 6, 1–2 the words *karma, yoga,* and *āsrava* are used by and large synonymously in the sense of action and/or activity, with *āsrava* also retaining its specific meaning of influx, inflow, or influence.

Svobhā on TS 6, 1:

> *kāyikaṃ karma vācikaṃ karma mānasaṃ karma ity eṣa trividho yogo bhavati* | *sa ekaśo dvividhaḥ* | *śubhaś cāśubhahaś ca* | *tatrāśubho hiṃsāsteyābrahmādīni kāyikaḥ, sāvadyānṛtaparuṣapiśunādīni vācikaḥ, abhidhyāvyāpāderṣyāsūyādīni mānasaḥ* | *ato viparītaḥ śubha iti* |

> Action performed with the body, action consisting in words, action performed in the mind, this is the threefold *yoga*. Each is twofold: meritorious and unmeritorious. Here unmeritorious [actions] performed with the body are violence, stealing, unchaste [conduct], etc.; [unmeritorious action] consisting in words are [what is] objectionable, not true, harsh/severe/unkind, malignant/slanderous/treacherous, etc.; [unmeritorious] actions performed in the mind are desire/wish/longing for [something], ruin/death [of someone], envy [of another's success], displeasure/indignation (*asūyā*) [especially at the merits or the happiness of another, as also in envy and jealousy], etc. The opposite of [each of] this is meritorious [action].

The gist of the *Svobhā* commentary makes it clear that the TS here is basically concerned with ethical behavior because the reference is to meritorious and unmeritorious action, the former leading to good or auspicious results and the latter to bad or inauspicious results (see below).

SS on TS 6, 1:

> *kāyādayaḥ śabdā vyākhyātārthāḥ | karma kriyā ity anarthāntaram | kāyavāṅmanasāṃ karma kāyavāṅmanaḥkarma yoga ity ākhyāyate | ātmapradeśaparispando yogaḥ | sa nimittabhedāt tridhā bhidyate | kāyayogo vāgyogo manoyoga ity |*
>
> The meaning which the words body, etc. have, has been explained.[4] [The word] karma (in the sūtra) has the other meaning *kriyā*, action. The action of the body, speech and the mind is called the *yoga* (activity) of the body, speech and mind. *Yoga* (activity) is the vibration of the soul.[5] On account of the difference of the cause this (*yoga*/activity) is divided into three kinds: body-*yoga*, speech-*yoga* and mind-*yoga* [respectively].

The crux of the SS comment is the interesting point that *yoga* (activity) is a vibration (*parispanda*) on the part of the soul (*ātman*) and that this vibration in fact is of three kinds. The SS commentary on TS 6, 1 then goes on to describe exactly what each of these kinds of vibration is. For the purposes here it is not necessary to quote in detail the rest of the commentary to this *sūtra*, but only to refer to each of the three kinds of vibrations of the soul in the words of the commentary itself: *ātmapradeśaparispandaḥ kāyayogaḥ . . . ātmanaḥ pradeśaparispando vāgyogaḥ . . . ātmapradeśaparispando manoyogaḥ*, namely, the vibration of the soul which is the *yoga* (activity) of the body, of speech, and of the mind.

The *Svobhā* does not introduce the purpose of the next very short sūtra (TS 6, 2), *sa āsravaḥ*, in any particular way. The SS commentary, on the other hand, seems to bear in mind that *yoga* (activity) is connected, or has something important to do, with *āsrava* (influx) and so, after describing the three kinds of vibrations which make up the three kinds of *yoga* (activity), returns to the theme of the chapter and asks: what characteristic does *āsrava* have (*kim lakṣaṇa āsravaḥ*)? And gives the link to the next short sūtra by saying: what was expressed by the word *yoga* (activity) with regard to a person in the world, this (*yoga*) is *āsrava* (TS 6, 2). Thus, according to the SS commentary, a clear sequence seems to emerge: *yoga* is karma, karma means *kriyā*, so *kriyā* is *yoga*, *yoga* is vibration, vibration is in fact three kinds of *yoga* and this *yoga* is *āsrava*.[6]

Śvetāmbara version:

> TS 6, 3: *śubhaḥ puṇyasya |*
> Meritorious [*yoga* (action)] is [the *āsrava (*influx)] of good/auspicious [results of action].
>
> TS 6, 4: *aśubhaḥ pāpasya |* Unmeritorious [*yoga* (action) is [the *āsrava* (influx)] of bad/ inauspicious [results of action].

The Digambara version combines both these statements into one sūtra:

> TS 6, 3: *śubhaḥ puṇyasyāśubhaḥ pāpasya* |

The *Svobhā* commentary on TS 6, 3–4 entails just one short sentence for each sūtra:

> *śubho yogaḥ puṇyasyāsravo bhavati* and *tatra sadvedyādi puṇyaṃ vakṣyate* | *śeṣaṃ pāpam iti* |
>
> Meritorious *yoga* (action) is the inflow of good/auspicious [results of action]. Good/auspicious [results of action] like *sadvedya* will be explained there.[7]

This indicates that the *Svobhā* postpones its comments on auspicious karma, like *sadvedya*, etc., for later.

What has been established thus far is that human beings indulge in activity through the body, speech, and mind and that these activities in the final analysis are conducted by the soul itself.[8] The question about why the soul should be involved in activity at all can be answered by pointing out the fact that one of the three main and inherent qualities of the soul is *vīrya* or energy and that its manifestation or implementation is a natural and inherent function. The soul (*jīva*), as a substance (*dravya*), is eternal and its qualities are therefore likewise eternal, with the proviso that these qualities can manifest themselves ideally and unlimitedly only in the absence of karma which hinders and restricts its natural functions. Karma, as we saw above, is activity (*yoga*), and this activity leads to an influx of *pudgala* or matter which in its subtle karma-form limits the scope of what the soul can do. This implies that, depending on whether the soul is under the influence of passions or not, the effect of the influx is accordingly restrictive or not. If the manifestation or implementation of *vīrya* is a natural and inherent function of the soul, in other words if the activity through the body, speech, and mind—which require the use of this energy—is "natural" human action, then the question is whether human beings are in a position to control the manifestation and implementation of this natural inherent energy. This is where Jainism calls upon human beings to channel this energy in such a way that it leads to meritorious rather than unmeritorious effects.[9] In other words, in dealing with Jaina *yoga* we are concerned with Jaina ethics, a code of conduct which is an exemplification of Jaina virtues and norms of behavior.

The point just made about the influence of passions is mentioned in TS 6, 4/5 (Jain's tr.): "[There are two kinds of influx, namely] that of persons with passions, which extends transmigration (*sāmparāyika*), and that of persons free from passions, which prevents or shortens it."[10] The two types of persons are in fact human beings with passions (*sakaṣāya*) and those without passions (*akaṣāya*) like the Jinas and the Siddhas of the Jaina tradition.[11] Attention will be paid here only to the former.

According to the karma theory in Jainism, every human activity (of the body, speech, and mind), without exception, leads to an influx of karma. The more the "amount" of karma is accumulated by such activity, the more is the soul under its pressure and influence. That is, the inherent *vīrya* or power of the soul (*jīva*) to manifest its natural and inherent functions is restricted to the extent the amount of karma that "covers" and thereby restricts it.[12] The point is that human beings cannot avoid the influx (*āsrava*) of karma but that this influx can be "regulated" in terms of the "intensity" of the action, if one can learn how to control the attitude behind an act.[13] TS 6, 6/7 hints at this point: "Influx is differentiated on the basis of intensity or feebleness of thought-activity, intentional or unintentional nature of action, the substratum and its peculiar potency" (Jain's translation in Pūjyapāda 1992).[14]

In Indian philosophy most schools share the presupposition that the knowledge of reality (in whatever way the school describes it) is the liberating factor from the suffering that underlies human existence. Jainism offers its own view and this is the content of the very first sūtra of the TS 1, 1: "Right faith, right knowledge and right conduct [together] constitute the path to liberation" (*samyagdarśanajñānacāritrāṇi mokṣamārgaḥ*). This fundamental position has significant implications for ethical behavior in the world and Chapter 6 of the TS presupposes this basic philosophical standpoint. The question is how can one know what is "right" faith, knowledge and conduct. Some of the hints in Chapter 6 supply a basic orientation for right conduct and four sūtras may be quoted here, in Jain's translation (Pūjyapāda 1992):

> TS 6, 10/11:
> Spite against knowledge, concealment of knowledge, non-imparting of knowledge out of envy, causing impediment to acquisition of knowledge, disregard of knowledge and disparagement of true knowledge, lead to the influx of karmas which obscure knowledge and perception.
>
> TS 6, 11/12:
> Suffering, sorrow, agony, moaning, injury and lamentation, in oneself, in others or in both, lead to the influx of karmas which cause unpleasant feeling (*asadvedya*).
>
> TS 6, 12/13:
> Compassion towards living beings in general and the devout in particular, charity, asceticism with attachment etc. . . . contemplation, equanimity, freedom from greed—these lead to the influx of karmas that cause pleasant feeling (*sadvedya*).[15]
>
> TS 6, 14/15:
> Intense feelings induced by the rise of the passions cause the influx of the conduct-deluding karmas.

Jaina ethics is first and foremost concerned with rules of behavior for ascetics, with certain relaxations of them for the lay person (TS 7, 20/15: "one who observes the small vows is a householder"). As far as the views quoted above are concerned, these apply for all persons. In other words, a certain ascetic attitude is called for in the case of the laity as well, as may be evident in the statement above about "contemplation, equanimity, freedom from greed," which would apply generally. Chapter 7 of the TS is an extension of Chapter 6 insofar as it goes into more detail regarding the nature of *āsrava* (recall the sequence mentioned above: *yoga* is karma, karma means *kriyā*, so *kriyā* is *yoga*, *yoga* is vibration, vibration is in fact three kinds of *yoga* and this *yoga* is *āsrava*), and lists the vows applicable to ascetics and laity.

Taking a vow is a solemn act in general. It may be said in the case of Jaina ethics that taking vows forms the basis of Jaina religious behavior; it is a commitment to fulfill a promise which is often solemnized by a ritual act, although vows may also be taken individually, making it a private affair. In taking a vow, especially in making it public, there is a qualitatively different aspect to it than merely making a promise to do some thing or the other. The person taking a solemn vow is publicly committed to abide by it and has to constantly remember it. In this way, taking a vow becomes a religious act, with the metaphysical implications being directly or indirectly involved —it is done for the sake of "merit," for the sake of accumulating "pleasant" karma which, in turn indicates that one has a free choice in actively regulating one's life.

A vast amount of material has been composed from early times in the history of Jainism to regulate lay conduct. These texts serve as guidelines for lay conduct (*śrāvakācāra*) and the standard work on this is still Williams' *Jaina Yoga* (1983).

Notes

1 See, for example, TS 2, 8–9 on *upayoga* and the two earliest commentaries on them. Soni (2007), fn. 13, points out a significant difference between the commentaries on this. See the same place for basic information and further references about the TS and its commentaries, including the point that there are Śvetāmbara and Digambara versions of the TS. See also Ohira (1982).

2 The reference is probably to TS 5, 19 which (in taking *śarīra* as a synonym of *kāya*) says: *śarīra-vāṅmanaḥprāṇāpānāḥ pudgalānām,* "(The function) of matter (is to form the basis) of the body and the organs of speech and mind and respiration" (Umāsvāti 1955: 144, tr. Jain). The synonym of the word *kāya* also appears in TS 2, 36, where the five types of bodies (*śarīrāṇi*) are mentioned and then described in the rest of the sūtras, TS 2, 37–53, of the chapter (Jain's index to *Reality* proved quite useful here). The word *vāc* is not given in Jain's index but the word "word" (which is his translation of *vāc* in TS 6, 1) is said to appear on p. 151. In this case *vāc* has to be seen as a synonym of *śabda* or sound, also in the sense of the sounds of a language and, thereby, speech. *Manas* (with *vāc*) is also described in TS 5, 19, as given above here; the SS comments on this sūtra in a bit more detail than the *Svobhā.*

3 *Saṃsārasya pradhānahetur āsravo bandhaś ca.* This part of the commentary indicates once again how the scope of *yoga* is further widened, from being the activities of the body, etc., to being an influx (*āsrava*) of karma, to now being one of the two main causes of rebirth.

4 See fn. 2 above.

5 The word *pradeśa* in *ātmapradeśa* is to be taken here in the sense of "with a part of the body, e.g. *kaṇṭha-hṛdaya-[pradeśa]*", see Monier-Williams under *pradeśa*. The word also has a technical meaning, see Jaini (1979), p. 113: "The precise amount (pradeśa) of karma . . . " See ibid. pp. 112—116 on "vibrations (yoga)." TS 6, 1–2 and this section of the SS is quoted by him on p. 112, fn. 17, but not translated literally. The English translations of the SS are largely based on Jain's (Umāsvāti 1992).

6 Only a few selected sūtras of TS 6 will be dealt with here. Note the minor differences in the enumeration of the two versions of the TS, with hardly any difference in the content.

7 TS 8, 8/9: *sadasadvedye*, "The two karmas which cause [a] pleasant feeling and [an] unpleasant feeling respectively are the two types of feeling-producing karmas", tr. Jain, Pūjyapāda 1992 [*vedya* here stands for *vedanīya-karma*]. 8/9 refers to the sūtra numbers of the Digambara and Śvētāmbara versions of the TS respectively, and this method will be used in the rest of the paper whenever needed. The Hindī tr. and commentary of the *Svobhā* on TS 6, 4 (Umāsvāti 1932) says that *sadvedya* will be explained in TS 8, 36, which I have not been able to find; TS 8 has only 26 sūtras (the SS includes *Svobhā* TS 8, 3 in 8, 2 and has one more sūtra in the chapter). The word *sadvedya* also appears in TS 8, 25/26, which Jain translates as "The good variety of feeling-producing karmas."

8 See Jaini (1979), pp. 102–106 for an excellent description of the soul's qualities, including *caitanya* and *sukha*.

9 It is to be remembered that both meritorious and unmeritorious karma are in fact limiting factors, albeit for human conduct the former is more "pleasing." The aim, of course, is through the support of meritorious actions to lead finally to absolute dispassion (*vairāgya*) by following "the Jaina path of purification" of all karmas.

10 TS 6, 4/5: *sakaṣāyākaṣāyayoḥ sāmparāyikeryāpathayoḥ* | Literally: [activity, *yoga*] with passions are favorable for future existences and those without passions would be proper religious behavior (*īryāpatha*) in terms of Jaina virtues. On *kaṣāya* see, for example, Jaini (1979), at various places, and the article by Wiley (2000).

11 Technically these types of inflow are related to the 14 quality states (*guṇasthāna*) of the soul in which the first type of passion applies to the first ten of the quality states and the second type from states 1–13. On those who act without passion, see again the article by Wiley (2000).

12 The impression should not be given that the *jīva* is in any way "weaker" than *ajīva*. Both *jīva* and *ajīva* are *dravya* (substances) and in terms of Jaina ontology have an equal status. The point about the purification of all karmas is to realize the need to "return" to the "natural" state of the *jīva*, where its existence is naturally without any attachment to *ajīva*. How *ajīva* "originally" got attached to *jīva* is another question, which cannot be dealt with here now.

13 Jaini (1979), p. 113: "The precise amount (*pradeśa*) of karma that engulfs the soul after a given activity is said to depend upon the *degree of volition* with which that activity was carried out" (emphasis in the original). In the fn. to this, Jaini quotes TS 6, 6/7 which is being discussed here.

14 TS 6, 6/7: *tīvramandajñātājñātabhāvādhikaraṇavīryaviśeṣebhyas tadviśeṣaḥ* | The word *vīrya* is omitted in the *Svobhā* version of the sūtra, although it is mentioned in the commentary.

15 What has been omitted here is Jain's explanation in brackets after "asceticism with attachment etc.": " i.e. restraint-cum-non-restraint, involuntary dissociation of karmas without effort, austerities not based on right knowledge".

Bibliography

Jaini, Padmanabh S. (1979) *The Jaina Path of Purification*. Delhi: Motilal Banarsidass.

Ohira, Suzuko. (1982) *A Study of Tattvārthasūtra with Bhāṣya. With Special Reference to Authorship and Date*. L. D. Series 86. Ahmedabad: L. D. Institute of Indology

Soni, Jayandra. (2007) "Upayoga, According to Kundakunda and Umāsvāti." *Journal of Indian Philosophy*, 35: 299–311.

Tatia, Nathmal (1994) *Tattvārtha Sūtra. That Which Is*. Umāsvāti/Umāsvāmī, with the combined commentaries of Umāsvāti/Umāsvāmī, Pūjyapāda and Siddhasenagaṇi, translated with an introduction by Nathmal Tatia. With a foreword by L. M. Singhvi and an introduction to the Jaina faith by Padmabh S. Jaini. San Francisco: Harper Collins.

Umāsvāti (c. fifth century) (1932) *Sabhāṣyatattvārthādhigamasūtra*. Bambaī: Manilāla, Revāśaṃkara Jagajīvana Jhaverī.

Umāsvāti (c. fifth century) (1955) *Sarvārthasiddhi* (a commentary on Umāsvāti's *Tattvārthasūtra*), edited (and translated into Hindī) by Phūlacandra Śāstrī. Kāśī: Bhāratīya Jñānapīṭha.

Umāsvāti (c. fifth century) (1992) *Reality. English Translation of Shri Pujyapadacharya's Sarvarthasiddhi*, 2nd ed. Tr. S. A. Jain. (reprint of the first edition published in Calcutta: Vira Sasana Sangha, 1960). Madras: Jwalamalini Trust.

Wiley, Kristi, L. (2000) "Colors of the Soul: By-products of Activity or Passions." *Philosophy East and West*, 50 (3): 348–366.

Williams, R. (1983) *Jaina Yoga. A Survey of the Mediaeval Śrāvakācāras*. (first ed. Oxford, 1963). Delhi: Motilal Banarsidass.

3 Kundakunda versus Sāṃkhya on the soul

Johannes Bronkhorst

There have been several conceptions of the soul in the history of Jainism. Probably the oldest text of the Śvetāmbara Jaina canon, the *Ācārāṅga Sūtra* / *Āyāraṃga Sutta,* has some passages that reveal an idea about the soul that is very different from what came to be the classical Jaina conception. Dalsukh D. Malvania (1981) and others have drawn attention to *Āyāraṃga* 176, which describes the soul in the following terms:

> It is not long nor small nor round nor triangular nor quadrangular nor circular; it is not black nor blue nor red nor green nor white; neither of good nor bad smell; not bitter nor pungent nor astringent nor sweet; neither rough nor soft; neither heavy nor light; neither cold nor hot; neither harsh nor smooth. It does not have a body, is not born again, has no attachment and is without sexual gender. While having knowledge and sentience, there is nonetheless nothing with which it can be compared. Its being is without form, there is no condition of the unconditioned. It is not sound nor form nor smell nor flavour nor touch or anything like that.
>
> (tr. Jacobi, 1884: 52, emended as in Dundas, 2002: 43)

Āyāraṃga 171, moreover, states: "That which is the soul is that which knows, that which is the knower is the soul, that by which one knows is the soul" (tr. Dundas, 2002: 44). The classical Jaina concept of the soul finds expression in other texts of the Śvetāmbara canon. A verse of *Uttarajjhayaṇa* Chapter 36 states: "The dimension of perfected [souls] is two-thirds of the height which the individual had in his last existence" (tr. Jacobi, 1895: 212, modified). The *Viyāhapannatti* (7.8) compares the soul, which may cover the volume of an elephant or of a louse, with a lamp that lights up the space in which it is placed, sometimes a hut, sometimes the space determined by a cover (Deleu, 1970: 139). A short reference to the body-like size of the soul is also found in one of the concluding stanzas of the *Uvavāiya* (171). This classical concept – as I have been able to show in another publication (Bronkhorst, 2000) – appears to have been formed under the influence of Abhidharma Buddhism.

It seems likely that the classical Jaina concept of the soul, whether under the influence of Buddhism or otherwise, was developed along with the special ideas of karma that came to occupy Jaina thinkers. But whatever its historical justification, it represents a somewhat idiosyncratic development which remained, as far as we can see, the exclusive property of Jainism. And even here it appears to have little to connect it with the origins of this religion. One reason for thinking so is constituted by the early canonical passages which I mentioned. Another one is that this classical concept barely fits in the surroundings from which Jainism arose, and to which it originally belonged. Let us have a closer look at these surroundings.

I have studied and analyzed the cultural background of Jainism, Buddhism, and other movements that were originally situated in the region east of the confluence of the two rivers Gaṅgā and Yamunā in a book called *Greater Magadha* (Bronkhorst, 2007). Jainism shared with some of the other religious movements a preoccupation with karmic retribution, which in their case meant the belief that all acts inevitably will have an effect, often in a future life. Many of these religious movements were concerned to avoid the new lives that would come about as a result of acts carried out in present and preceding lives. Early Jainism emphasized the need to abstain from all physical and mental activity. In other words, the advanced practitioner should abstain from all acts, with the result that he would not create new bases for karmic retribution. Acts that had been carried out before, whether in this or a preceding life, could be immunized, i.e., forced to bear fruit in this life, through the pain produced by ascetic practices. Since the ascetic practices that were believed to bring this about consisted themselves largely in the abstention from all activity, the physical and mental immobilization pursued by the advanced Jaina ascetic served a double purpose: no new bases were laid for further karmic retribution, and the traces of acts carried out earlier were destroyed.

This specific method of attaining liberation from rebirth and karmic retribution did not crucially depend on any specific vision as to the true nature of the soul. Such a specific vision may have accompanied early Jainism, but we have already seen that the oldest canonical texts provide us with preciously little information to go by. There were however other religious movements at the same time and in the same region of northern India in which the concept of the soul did play a crucial role. These were the movements that believed that the soul, i.e., the real self of the human being (and of all other living beings for that matter), does not and cannot act by its very nature. Activity belongs to the body and the mind, both of which are essentially different from the inactive self. Karmic retribution, too, belongs for this reason to the realm of body and mind, without affecting the real self of a person. Knowledge of one's real self frees one from rebirth and karmic retribution, because knowledge of the self amounts to the realization that in deepest reality one does not act and has never acted.

This notion of a real self that never acts lies at the heart of most philosophical thought that came to be associated with Brahmanism. It is very visible in Sāṃkhya, which divides all that exists in two totally distinct categories: on the one hand the selves, essentially and fundamentally inactive, and on the other hand all that which is active, whether physical or mental. The fundamental idea finds expression in a verse of the *Bhagavadgītā,* which states[1]: "Actions are, all of them, undertaken by the guṇas of Prakṛti. He who is deluded by egoism thinks 'I am the doer'." The *guṇas* of Prakṛti are, in Sāṃkhya and therefore in texts like the *Bhagavadgītā* which accept the fundamental ideas of Sāṃkhya, that which makes up all that is active, i.e., all that is different from the inactive self. The self, for its part, is not involved in any acts, and indeed, if a person thinks that she is thus involved, she is deluded by egoism. It is Prakṛti that acts, and the self remains inactive throughout. The *Bhagavadgītā* adds some practical teachings of its own. It does not teach that one should abstain from all activity. No, one should rather act in accordance with one's own nature. The terms used to designate the nature of a person are *prakṛti* and *svabhāva*; these coincide, according to the *Gītā,* with a person's own duty (*svadharma*), i.e., the duties associated with one's position in life. The warrior Arjuna, for example, is told to carry out his duties as a warrior in a war that opposes him to members of his own family. The way to carry out such a task is by not being attached to the fruits, i.e., the results, of one's acts.

This short excursion into the teaching of the *Bhagavadgītā* is useful as an introduction to the thought of Kundakunda as it expresses itself primarily in his *Samayasāra*, a work which "has greatly influenced Digambara thinking for centuries, and has been acclaimed by them as the most profound exposition of the Jaina doctrine" (Jaini, 1976: 30/92).[2] Before turning to him, let me summarize what has been said so far. We are very poorly informed about the ideas on the self that were current in early Jainism. We do know that Jainism abandoned these early ideas, whatever they were, and turned to the idiosyncratic concept of the soul that accompanied it henceforth. We do not know for sure why the idea of an essentially inactive soul, which became so fertile in other currents of thought, was not incorporated in the classical beliefs of Jainism; I have already made the suggestion that the way in which Jainas elaborated their ideas about karma had a role to play in this.

These ideas about an inactive soul were not completely abandoned, however. Kundakunda's ideas of the true nature of the self, I propose, have to be understood as attempts to introduce, perhaps reintroduce, them into Jainism, not, of course, in their original and primitive form, but adjusted to Jaina doctrine as it had taken shape in the meantime.

Recall, at this point, that the notion of a totally inactive soul or self, where it is accepted, is inseparable from the belief in rebirth and karmic retribution. More precisely, knowledge of the true, inactive, nature of the self is always presented as an essential step toward the ultimate goal of liberation. The implication of this fact is that the way in which karmic retribution is conceived is closely connected with the way the self is thought of. Briefly put, the self is free from all those features that are responsible for rebirth and karmic retribution. For most currents of thought in ancient India, these features cover all acts carried out by a person. It goes without saying that, if others were to believe that only certain acts, not all of them, lead to karmic retribution, they are free to postulate the existence of a self that is only free from those specific acts, not necessarily free from all of them.

In other words, they may believe in a self whose activity is limited to such acts as do not bring about karmic retribution.

This, I submit, is the position of Kundakunda in his *Samayasāra*. His main point is similar to the one that finds clearest expression in Sāṃkhya and related texts, viz., that an essential step on the road to liberation is the realization that one's self is different from activity that leads to karmic retribution. The ripening of the fruit arising from karma does not belong to the self, we read in verse 208, for the self is different from it. The Jinas, verse 210 adds, have pointed out that there are many such ripenings, but these are not my own natures: I am only a knower by nature. However, he who still has even ever so little attachment or other faults left does not know his self, however learned he may be (211).

The similarity between Sāṃkhya and the thought propounded by Kundakunda is undeniable. The similarity is however only superficial, and there are important differences. As a matter of fact, Sāṃkhya is mentioned and criticized in the *Samayasāra*. What is more, the teaching of the *Bhagavadgītā* is criticized, too, be it implicitly. Let us begin with the latter.

Verse 335 states that one becomes liberated when one gives up the fruit of one's deeds. This is close to the main teaching of the *Bhagavadgītā*. However, the verse 336 following adds an important specification. The ignorant person, it states, since he resides in the own nature (*svabhāva*) of Prakṛti, experiences the fruit of his deeds; he who possesses knowledge, on the other hand, knows the fruit of his deeds but does not experience it as arisen.[3] The use of the words *svabhāva* and *prakṛti*, so typical for the *Bhagavadgītā*, confirms our suspicion that Kundakunda here criticizes this text in particular. Unlike the *Bhagavadgītā*, he is of the opinion that only an ignorant person will follow his own prakṛtic nature. Only the person incapable of liberation (*abhavya*)[4] will not give up Prakṛti, verse 338 adds. The knowing person neither carries out nor experiences the various kinds of acts; however, he knows their result, as he knows bondage, merit and demerit (340).

However, Kundakunda does not only voice criticism of the practical path taught by the *Bhagavadgītā*. He is of the opinion that the underlying Sāṃkhya philosophy is not up to the mark, either. Indeed, if all that is active is, for that reason, part of Prakṛti, the conclusion must be that Prakṛti is the only agent around. Prakṛti, however, is unconscious. Unconscious Prakṛti would in this way turn the self into one that has a correct or incorrect understanding of the world (vv. 353, 354). And all selves would be inactive (366). Kundakunda does not accept this. For him the soul is subject to change. Indeed, he points out in an earlier verse (127; cf. 124) that if the soul did not undergo modifications, there would be no cycle of rebirths (*saṃsāra*) and the Sāṃkhya philosophy would be correct.[5]

According to Kundakunda, then, the soul *is* active, at least to some extent. Verse 127, just considered, states that the soul is modified by *bhāva*s such as anger (*krodha*). Kundakunda makes a point of regularly using the verb "to do, to make" (Skt. *kṛ*) in connection with words denoting the soul. What, then, is it that the soul makes or does? The word often used as object in such situations is *bhāva*.[6] Recall that anger was called a *bhāva* in the verse just considered. We may assume that *bhāva*s are states of the soul, which the latter "makes" or "produces," presumably by a process of modification. The soul, we learn in another verse (28), can be connected with many *bhāva*s.[7]

An important verse states that the self makes a *bhāva* and is its agent from the highest point of view, while from a practical, and therefore lower, point of view, it is the agent of material karma.[8] This is to be understood in the light of the fact that karma in Jainism is thought of as a material substance which clings to the soul and is responsible for the cycle of rebirths it undergoes. Freedom from this substance signifies freedom from rebirth. Total inactivity on the part of the soul is not required. The soul, in Kundakunda's opinion, *is* active: some of this activity has as consequence that material karma attaches itself to the soul, with the results we know. Activities of the soul that do not cause material karma to cling to it do not have this effect; they do not involve the soul in the endless cycle of rebirths. It follows that the soul must act in the right manner in order to be freed from *saṃsāra*. In Sāṃkhya the soul could not do a thing to bring about its liberation; it depended on the activity of Prakṛti. Kundakunda's soul *can* do something, and is indeed ultimately responsible for its own liberation.

The self, verse 88 points out, is an agent by its own *bhāva*, but it is not the agent of all the *bhāva*s produced by material karma.[9] The following verse explains this further: From the highest standpoint the self makes nothing but itself and experiences itself.[10] How does the self produce and experience itself, or rather its own *bhāva*? Verse 93 appears to present the answer: "Just as the self makes its own *bhāva* because of material karma, so it experiences its own *bhāva* because of material karma."[11]

It is clear from what precedes that Kundakunda distinguishes between *bhāva*s that belong to the soul and are in a certain way identical with it, and such that are not. This is confirmed by verse 94, which states that error and *bhāva*s such as anger are of two kinds: they are either the soul (*jīva*) or not the soul (*ajīva*).[12] It follows from verse 95 that the difference lies in what is called *upayoga*, which is often translated *application of consciousness*.[13] Ignorance, intemperance, and error are *jīva*, on condition that they are *upayoga*.[14] Indeed, they are modifications of *upayoga* connected with confusion; these modifications fall into three main categories: error, ignorance, and intemperance.[15] *Upayoga* is in this way of three kinds, and itself a *bhāva* that is pure and unsullied; whatever further *bhāva* it creates, it is its agent.[16]

So far the discussion deals with activities that take place within the self and which for this reason have themselves no karmic consequences. However, material substance modifies itself in accordance with what happens in the self: "Whatever *bhāva* the self produces, it is its agent; [however,] material substance modifies itself in relationship to that, and turns itself into karma."[17] At this point confusion is likely to enter: "The soul consisting of ignorance makes something else into itself, and itself into something else. It becomes in this way the agent of the karmas."[18] The soul thinks it becomes the agent of the karmas, but this is due to ignorance. In reality it is not. The soul possessed of correct knowledge knows better: "The soul consisting of correct knowledge does not make something else into itself, and itself into something else. It is not the agent of the karmas."[19] "He who knows that the self does not make the modifications of material substance [such as] the obstructions of knowledge, he possesses correct knowledge."[20]

The picture which develops out of these and other verses is the following. There are two fundamentally different realms: that of karma, which is a material substance, and that of the soul. The soul, though not without activity, is not the agent of anything that takes place in the karma which belongs to the material realm. However, it can have a causal effect on karma, through its activity within its own realm. One can therefore say that the soul produces karma, but only metaphorically: "Having seen the modification of bondage, the soul being its cause, it is said that karma has been produced by the soul, but only metaphorically."[21] "Even though a battle is carried out by soldiers, people say that it is carried out by the king. In the same way, the obstruction of knowledge and other such things are produced by the soul [only] from a practical point of view."[22]

The distinction, in this discussion, between a higher point of view and a practical point of view is unavoidable.[23] Indeed, it is the confusion between these two which is responsible for the fact that most people do not see the road to liberation. This is not only true of Kundakunda's thought. It applies with equal force to the Sāṃkhya system of thought which Kundakunda criticizes. There, too, the failure to see the distinction between the realm of the soul and the realm of Prakṛti keeps people tied up in the world of eternal transmigration. This is not to say that Kundakunda's thought is identical with Sāṃkhya. Unlike Sāṃkhya, the soul as conceived of by Kundakunda *is* capable of certain activities, which are however limited to its own domain. All this we have seen.

The verses of the *Samayasāra* present, sometimes in quick succession, the two different points of view just mentioned. This can easily lead to confusion. Since all verses do not explicitly state whether they present the highest or the practical point of view, the impression is often created that they contradict each other. The contradictions, it seems to me, can almost always be resolved by keeping the two points of view in mind, and assigning, of two contradictory verses, one to the highest point of view, the other to the practical point of view. Kundakunda's main point, unsurprisingly, is to emphasize that the soul is not, and cannot be, the agent of what happens in the material world of karma. This is essential, because it is this knowledge that allows of a dissociation of the self from all that which leads to karmic retribution. Kundakunda's ideas about the realm of the self in which the self *can* be an agent constitute a theoretical elaboration meant to distinguish his thought from Sāṃkhya – which he obviously looks upon as a close competitor – and no doubt to allow place for certain traditional Jaina notions as to the possibility of the soul to be an agent after all. Indeed, verse 127 points out that if the soul did not transform itself into states such as anger, this would signify the end of the cycle of rebirths, *or the acceptance of Sāṃkhya*.[24]

The preceding analysis of the thought of the *Samayasāra* reveals a vision of the place of the soul in the world and of its place on the path to liberation that is coherent and credible. This depiction of the self does *not* "very much resemble that of the Upaniṣadic and Advaitic Brahman or Ātman", as it has been claimed.[25] It resembles the self of Sāṃkhya in some respects, but differs from it in certain others, voluntarily so, as we have seen. Nor do I see any reason to look upon the *Samayasāra* as a "heterogeneous repository of accumulated Digambara teaching, [. . .] rather than the imperfectly preserved work of an individual heterodox philosopher".[26] This is not to deny that its author used traditional material, nor do I wish to claim that he was necessarily a complete innovator. But in reading the *Samayasāra*, I do have the impression of being confronted with the work of someone who wished to incorporate into Jainism a notion that had become very fruitful and useful in other currents, primarily Sāṃkhya, but also elsewhere. The author of the *Samayasāra* is explicit about his concern to take over the central idea of Sāṃkhya, at the same time improving upon it. In order to do so, he had to think out a competing system, an attempt in which he succeeded to at least some extent. The fact that the *Samayasāra* can, by and large, be read as a text expressive of a coherent thesis is the best argument there could be to maintain that it had one single author, whether he was called Kundakunda or otherwise.[27]

Some other works ascribed to Kundakunda represent by and large the same thesis as the one propounded in the *Samayasāra*. The *Pravacanasāra*, in particular, has some verses that state in so many words that the soul *can* be active, but only in its own domain. According to *Pravacanasāra* II.92, "The self, making its own nature, becomes the agent of its own *bhāva*, but not the agent of all the *bhāva*s that consist of material substance."[28] Two verses further, the same text states: "The [self], now being the agent of its own modification born from its [own] substance, is sometimes taken [and sometimes] freed by the dust of karma."[29] *Pravacanasāra* I.9 attributes to the soul (*jīva*) itself three states: "While the soul, whose nature is modification, modifies into something auspicious by means of an auspicious [state], into something inauspicious by means of an inauspicious [state], it becomes pure by means of a pure [state]."[30] "If the self itself is not auspicious or inauspicious by nature, there will be no cycle of rebirths for embodied beings."[31] The *Pañcāstikāyasāra* contains similar statements, among them the following: "Since it makes its own *bhāva*, the self is the agent of its own *bhāva*, not of the material karmas; this is how the words of the Jina must be understood."[32] It is on account of a modification in the soul that karma attaches itself to it (v. 128).

We can contrast this with the *Paramātmaprakāśa* of Yogīndu, which is sometimes claimed to continue the thought of Kundakunda; this text does not contain any statement supportive of Kundakunda's vision of the soul's nature. Quite on the contrary, it states in no uncertain terms that the highest point of view is that the self does nothing whatsoever.[33]

Notes

1 *Bhagavadgītā* 3.27: *prakṛteḥ kriyamāṇāni guṇaiḥ karmāṇi sarvaśaḥ / ahaṅkāravimūḍhātmā kartāham iti manyate //.*

2 I have not had access to the "bewildering number of editions, reprints and commentaries" that exist of Kundakunda's main works. They have been conveniently enumerated and presented by Royce Wiles (2001). The editions used by me in this study are specified in the "References" at the end of this article.

3 *Samayasāra* 336: *aṇṇāṇī kammaphalaṃ payaḍisahāvaṭṭhido du vededi / ṇāṇī puṇa kammaphalaṃ jāṇādi udidaṃ ṇa vededi //* (Sanskrit: *ajñānī karmaphalaṃ prakṛtisvabhāvasthitas tu vedayate / jñānī punaḥ karmaphalaṃ jānāti uditaṃ na vedayate //*).

4 Cf. Jaini, 1977.

5 *Samayasāra* 127/3.54: *apariṇamaṃte hi sayaṃ jīve kohādiehi bhāvehiṃ / saṃsārassa abhāvo pasajjade saṃkhasamao vā //* (Sanskrit: *apariṇamamāne hi svayaṃ jīve krodhādibhiḥ bhāvaiḥ / saṃsārasyābhāvaḥ prasajyate sāṃkhyasamayo vā //*).

6 e.g. *Samayasāra* 190.

7 *bahubhāvasamjutto*; Skt. *-saṃyuktaḥ*.

8 *Samayasāra* 24: *jaṃ kuṇadi bhāvam ādā kattā so hodi tassa bhāvassa / ṇicchayado vavahārā poggalakammāṇa kattāraṃ //* (Sanskrit: *yaṃ karoti bhāvam ātmā kartā sa bhavati tasya bhāvasya / niścayataḥ vyavahārāt pudgalakarmaṇāṃ kartā //*).

9 *Samayasāra* 88/3.14: . . . *kattā ādā saeṇa bhāveṇa / puggalakammakadāṇaṃ ṇa du kattā savvabhāvāṇaṃ //* (Sanskrit: . . . *kartā ātmā svakena bhāvena / pudgalakarmakṛtānāṃ na tu sarvabhāvānām //*).

10 *Samayasāra* 89/3.15: *ṇicchayaṇayassa evaṃ ādā appāṇam eva hi karedi / vedayadi puṇo taṃ ceva jāṇa attā du attāṇaṃ //* (Sanskrit: *niścayanayasyaivam ātmātmānam eva hi karoti / vedayate punas taṃ caiva jānīhi ātmā tv ātmānam //*).

11 *Samayasāra* 93: *poggalakammaṇimittaṃ jaha ādā kuṇadi appaṇo bhāvaṃ / poggalakammaṇimittaṃ taha vedadi appaṇo bhāvaṃ //* (Sanskrit: *pudgalakarmanimittaṃ yathātmā karoti ātmanaḥ bhāvam / pudgalakarmanimittaṃ tathā vedayati ātmano bhāvam //*).

12 *Samayasāra* 94/3.19: *micchattaṃ puṇa duvihaṃ jīvam ajīvaṃ taheva aṇṇāṇaṃ / avi radi yogo moho kodhādīyā ime bhāvā //* (Sanskrit: *mithyātvaṃ punar dvividhaṃ jīvo 'jīvas tathaivājñānam / aviratir yogo mohaḥ krodhādyā ime bhāvāḥ //*).

13 On this term, see Johnson (1995: 97 ff.); Soni (2007).

14 *Samayasāra* 95/3.20: *poggalakammaṃ micchaṃ jogo aviradi aṇṇāṇam ajjīvaṃ / uvaogo aṇṇāṇaṃ aviradi micchatta jīvo du //* (Sanskrit: *pudgalakarma mithyātvaṃ yogo 'viratir ajñānam ajīvaḥ / upayogo 'jñānam aviratir mithyātvaṃ ca jīvas tu //*).

15 *Samayasāra* 96/3.21: *uvaogassa aṇāī pariṇāmā tiṇṇi mohajuttassa / micchattaṃ aṇṇāṇaṃ aviradibhāvo ya ṇādavvo //* (Sanskrit: *upayogasyānādayaḥ pariṇāmās trayo mohayuktasya / mithyātvam ajñānam aviratibhāvaś ceti jñātavyaḥ //*).

16 *Samayasāra* 97/3.22: *edesu ya uvaogo tiviho suddho ṇiraṃjaṇo bhāvo / jaṃ so karedi bhāvaṃ uvaogo tassa so kattā //* (Sanskrit: *eteṣu copayogas trividhaḥ śuddho niraṃjano bhāvaḥ / yaṃ sa karoti bhāvam upayogas tasya sa kartā //*).

17 *Samayasāra* 98/3.23: *jaṃ kuṇadi bhāvam ādā kattā so hodi tassa bhāvassa / kammattaṃ pariṇamade tamhi sayaṃ poggalaṃ davvaṃ //* (Sanskrit: *yaṃ karoti bhāvam ātmā kartā sa bhavati tasya bhāvasya / karmatvaṃ pariṇamate tasmin svayaṃ pudgaladravyam //*).

18 *Samayasāra* 99/3.24: *param appāṇaṃ kuvvadi appāṇaṃ pi ya paraṃ karaṃto so / aṇṇāṇamao jīvo kammāṇaṃ kārago hodi //* (Sanskrit: *param ātmānaṃ karoti ātmānam api ca paraṃ kurvan saḥ / ajñānamayo jīvaḥ karmaṇāṃ kārako bhavati //*).

19 *Samayasāra* 100/3.25: *param appāṇam akuvvī appāṇaṃ pi ya paraṃ akuvvaṃto / so ṇāṇamayo jīvo kammāṇam akārago hodi //* (Sanskrit: *param ātmānaṃ akurvann ātmānam api ca param akurvan / sa jñānamayo jīvaḥ karmaṇām akārako bhavati //*).

20 *Samayasāra* 108/3.33: *je puggaladavvāṇaṃ pariṇāmā hoṃti ṇāṇa āvaraṇā / ṇa karedi tāṇi ādā jo jāṇādi so havadi ṇāṇī //* (Sanskrit: *ye pudgaladravyāṇāṃ pariṇāmā bhavanti jñānāvaraṇāni / na karoti tāny ātmā yo jānāti sa bhavati jñānī //*).

21 *Samayasāra* 112/3.37: *jīvamhi hedubhūde baṃdhassa ya passidūṇa pariṇāmaṃ / jīveṇa kadaṃ kammaṃ bhaṇṇadi uvayāramatteṇa //* (Sanskrit: *jīve hetubhūte baṃdhasya ca dṛṣṭvā pariṇāmam / jīvena kṛtaṃ karma bhaṇyate upacāramātreṇa //*).

22 *Samayasāra* 113/3.38: *yodhehiṃ kade juddhe rāeṇa kadaṃ ti jaṃpade logo / taha vavahāreṇa kadaṃ ṇāṇāvaraṇādi jīveṇa //* (Sanskrit: *yodhaiḥ kṛte yuddhe rājñā kṛtam iti jalpate lokaḥ / tathā vyavahāreṇa kṛtaṃ jñānāvaraṇādi jīvena //*).
23 See on this distinction Bhatt (1974).
24 See above, note 3.
25 Singh (1974: 85), as cited by Johnson (1995: 238). Nor do Kundakunda's teachings resemble early Advaita Vedānta, as claimed by Dhaky (1991), referred to in Dundas (2002: 291 n. 52).
26 Johnson (1995: 265).
27 Johnson (1995: 111) does not seem to think otherwise: "as far as I know, the *upayoga* doctrine does not appear in this form in any recorded source prior to Kundakunda. Indeed, commentators frequently remark upon the peculiarity, or uniqueness of Kundakunda in this respect. For all hermeneutic purposes, therefore, he must be taken as the originator of this particular form of the *upayoga* doctrine."
28 *Pravacanasāra* II.92: *kuvvaṃ sabhāvam ādā havadi hi kattā sagassa bhāvassa / poggaladavvamayāṇaṃ ṇa du kattā savvabhāvāṇaṃ //* (Sanskrit: *kurvan svabhāvam ātmā bhavati hi kartā svakasya bhāvasya / pudgaladravyamayānāṃ na tu kartā sarvabhāvānām //*).
29 *Pravacanasāra* II.94: *sa idāṇiṃ kattā saṃ sagapariṇāmassa davvajādassa / ādīyade kadāī vimuccade kammadhūlīhiṃ //* (Sanskrit: *sa idānīṃ kartā san svakapariṇāmasya dravyajātasya / ādīyate kadācid vimucyate karmadhūlibhiḥ //*).
30 *Pravacanasāra* I.9: *jīvo pariṇamadi jadā suheṇa asuheṇa vā suho asuho / suddhena tadā suddho havadi hi pariṇāmasabbhāvo //* (Sanskrit: *jīvaḥ pariṇamati yadā śubhenāśubhena vā śubho 'śubhaḥ / śuddhena tadā śuddho bhavati hi pariṇāmasvabhāvaḥ //*). On the difference between *śuddha* "pure" and *śubha* "auspicious", see *Pravacanasāra* III.45: "Śramaṇas have pure consciousness and auspicious consciousness . . . ; among them those who have pure consciousness are without *āsrava*s and the others are with *āsrava*s" (*samaṇā suddhuvajuttā suhovajuttā ya hoṃti samayamhi / tesu vi suddhuvajuttā aṇāsavā sāsavā sesā //*; Sanskrit: *śramaṇāḥ śuddhopayuktāḥ śubhopayuktāś ca bhavanti samaye / teṣv api śuddhopayuktā anāsravāḥ sāsravāḥ śeṣāḥ //*); see further Johnson (1995: 112 f).
31 *Pravacanasāra* I.46: *jadi so suho va asuho ṇa havadi ādā sayaṃ sahāveṇa / saṃsāro vi ṇa vijjadi savvesiṃ jīvakāyāṇaṃ //* (Sanskrit: *yadi sa śubho vā aśubho na bhavati ātmā svayaṃ svabhāvena / saṃsāro 'pi na vidyate sarveṣāṃ jīvakāyānām //*).
32 *Pañcāstikāyasāra* 61: *kuvvaṃ sagaṃ sahāvaṃ attā kattā sagassa bhāvassa / ṇa hi poggalakammāṇaṃ idi jiṇavayaṇaṃ muṇeyavvaṃ //* (Sanskrit: *kurvan svakaṃ svabhāvam ātmā kartā svakasya bhāvasya / na hi pudgalakarmaṇām iti jinavacanaṃ jñātavyam //*).
33 *Paramātmaprakāśa* I.65cd: *appā kiṃpi vi kuṇai ṇavi ṇicchau euṃ bhaṇei* (Sanskrit: *ātmā kimapi karoti naiva niścaya evaṃ bhaṇati*). Cf. Balbir (1998: 300); Balbir and Caillat (1999: 113).

Bibliography

Balbir, Nalini (1998): "Glossaire du Paramātmaprakāśa et du Yogasāra." *Bulletin d'Études Indiennes,* 16, 249–318.

Balbir, Nalini, and Caillat, Colette (1999): *Lumière de l'Absolu.* Paris: Payot & Rivages.

Bhatt, Bansidhar (1974): "Vyavahāra-naya and Niścaya-naya in Kundakunda's Works." *Zeitschrift der deutschen Morgenländischen Gesellschaft,* (Suppl. 2), 279–291.

Bronkhorst, Johannes (2000): "Abhidharma and Jainism." In *Abhidharma and Indian Thought. Essays in Honor of Professor Doctor Junsho Kato on his Sixtieth Birthday.* Committee for the Felicitation of Professor Doctor Junsho Kato's Sixtieth Birthday, Nagoya. Tokyo: Shuju-sha, pp. 578–581 ([13]–[30]).

Bronkhorst, Johannes (2007): *Greater Magadha. Studies in the Culture of Early India.* Handbook of Oriental Studies, Section 2 South Asia, 19. Leiden: Brill.

Deleu, Jozef (1970): *Viyāhapannatti (Bhagavaī): The Fifth Anga of the Jaina Canon.* Introduction, critical analysis, commentary and indexes. Lala Sundar Lal Jain Research Series, 10. Reprinted: Delhi: Motilal Banarsidass, 1996.

Dhaky, M. A. (1991): "The Date of Kundakundācārya." = Dhaky and Jain (1991), pp. 187–206.

Dhaky, M. A., and Jain, S. (eds.) (1991): *Aspects of Jainology,* Vol. III. *Pt. Dalsukhbhai Malvania Felicitation Volume I.* Varanasi. (not seen).

Dundas, Paul (2002): *The Jains*, 2nd ed. London: Routledge.

Jacobi, Hermann (1884): *Jaina Sūtras, translated from the Prākrit.* Part I: *Ācārāṅga Sūtra, Kalpa Sūtra.* Sacred Books of the East, 22. Oxford University Press. Reprinted: Delhi: Motilal Banarsidass, 1980.

Jacobi, Hermann (1895): *Jaina Sūtras, translated from Prākrit.* Part II: Uttarādhyayana Sūtra, Sūtrakritāṅga Sūtra. Sacred Books of the East, 45. Reprinted: Delhi: Motilal Banarsidass, 1968.

Jaini, Padmanabh S. (1976): "The Jainas and the Western Scholar." In: *Sambodhi.* L. D. Institute of Indology, Ahmedabad, pp. 121–131. Reprinted: Jaini (2000), pp. 23–36; Soni (2001), pp. 85–98 (references to the reprints).

Jaini, Padmanabh S. (1977): "Bhavyatva and Abhavyatva: A Jain Doctrine of 'Predestination'." In *Mahāvīra and His Teachings.* Edited by A. N. Upadhye et al. Bombay: Bhagavān Mahāvīra 2500th Nirvāṇa Mahotsava Samiti, pp. 95–111.

Jaini, Padmanabh S. (2000): *Collected Papers on Jaina Studies.* Delhi: Motilal Banarsidass.

Johnson, W. J. (1995): *Harmless Souls. Karmic Bondage and Religious Change in Early Jainism with Special Reference to Umāsvāti and Kundakunda.* Delhi: Motilal Banarsidass.

Kundakunda: *Samayasāra.* (1) The original text in Prakrit, with its Samskrit renderings, and a translation, exhaustive commentaries, and an introduction, by Rai Bahadur J. L. Jaini, published by Pandit Ajit Prasada at The Central Jaina Publishing House, Ajitashram, Lucknow, 1930. (Sacred Books of the Jainas, 8.) (2) Original text, romanization, English translation and annotations (with scientific interpretation) by Jethalal S. Zaveri, assisted by Muni Mahendra Kumar, Jain Vishva Bharati University, Ladnun, 2009. References are to, and citations from, edition (1).

Kundakunda: *Pravacanasāra.* Edited and translated by A. N. Upadhye. Agas: Shrimad Rajachandra Ashrama, 1964.

Kundakunda: *Pañcāstikāyasāra.* Edited and translated by A. Chakravartinayanar and A. N. Upadhye. New Delhi: Bharatiya Jnanpith, 1975.

Malvania, Dalsukh D. (1981): "Beginnings of Jaina Philosophy in the Ācārāṅga." In *Studien zum Jainismus und Buddhismus. Gedenkschrift für Ludwig Alsdorf.* Edited by Klaus Bruhn and Albrecht Wezler. ANISt, 23. Wiesbaden: Franz Steiner, pp. 151–153.

Singh, Ram Jee (1974): *The Jaina Concept of Omniscience.* L. D. Series, 43. Ahmedabad: L. D. Institute of Indology. (not seen).

Soni, Jayandra (ed.) (2001): *Vasantagauravam: Essays in Jainism Felicitating Professor M. D. Vasantha Raj of Mysore on the Occasion of his Seventy-Fifth Birthday.* Mumbai: Vakils, Feffer and Simons.

Soni, Jayandra (2007): "Upayoga, According to Kundakunda and Umāsvāti." *Journal of Indian Philosophy,* 35(4), 299–311.

Wiles, Royce (2001): "The Works of Kundakunda: An Annotated Listing of Editions, Translations and Studies." = Soni (2001), pp. 183–224.

Yogīndu: *Paramātmaprakāśa (Paramappapayāsu).* Edited by A. N. Upadhye. Agas: Shrimad Rajachandra Ashram, 1937.

4 Extrasensory perception (*yogi-pratyakṣa*) in Jainism, proofs of its existence and its soteriological implications*

Piotr Balcerowicz

0.1. Most classical Indian philosophical schools accepted the idea of suprasensory, supernatural, or mystic perception, usually known as *yogi-pratyakṣa*, i.e., the perception of a yogin, or sometimes *ārṣa-pratyakṣa*, i.e., the perception of seers (*ṛṣi*), or *yogi-jñāna*, cognition of a yogin. The idea of *yogi-pratyakṣa* was occasionally related to omniscience (*sarva-jñāna*) in Indian philosophical and religious traditions, such as Buddhism or the systems of Sāṃkhya-Yoga or the post-fifth-century Nyāya-Vaiśeṣika. It was in Jainism, however, that the correlation between supernatural perception and omniscience became most conspicuous and pronounced.

The Jainas were also probably the first to develop rational arguments – such as argument from progression, already present in Kundakunda's works, etc. – which were supposed to substantiate their radical claim of the Jina's omniscience. An indispensable logical step in these arguments relied on the assumption of the existence of some kind of supernatural perception unmediated by senses. Further, Jaina philosophers treated the idea of *yogi-pratyakṣa* as an intermediate stage to ultimate perfection of knowledge, i.e., to omniscience.

This chapter analyzes (1) what doctrinal and philosophical reasons made the link between supernatural perception and omniscience so important in Jaina tradition; (2) what were the implications for the Jaina doctrine of liberation; and (3) which particular doctrinal tenets of Jainism made such arguments possible. The focus of the chapter is to collect a range of rational arguments in which the idea of supernatural perception plays a crucial role. Further, (4) I will try to identify possibly the earliest formulations of some such arguments, both within Jaina tradition and outside of it, as well as refer to their epistemologically most developed forms, up to the time of Hemacandra-sūri.

In my analysis I will frequently refer to Hemacandra-sūri's *Pramāṇa-mīmāṃsā*, where a number of earlier arguments for supernatural perception and omniscience were gathered, but I will also try to show earlier formulations of such arguments.

As against a common stereotype that Indian traditions were unanimous in their acceptance of supernatural perception, there were at least three notable exceptions to be mentioned, namely the followers of the schools of the early Nyāya-Vaiśeṣika until the beginning of the fifth century,[1] Mīmāṃsā and the materialists, or Cārvāka / Lokāyata. In their realistic approach, these philosophical schools rejected the suprasensory sphere, albeit for different reasons. The criticism of extrasensory perception meted out by the two latter schools will be the subject of Chapter 5, "Extrasensory perception, (*yogi-pratyakṣa*) in Jainism and its refutations" (references to this chapter below are as "see counter-arguments").

Against the criticism of these three main antagonists, the Jainas, later Naiyāyika-Vaiśeṣikas and Buddhists strove to validate their admission of supernatural perception and its corollary, omniscience.

0.2. To understand the nature of supernatural perception, the way it constituted an object of doctrinal belief in some philosophical systems, we should first summarize the main features of ordinary, sensory perception (*pratyakṣa, loka-pratyakṣa*), against the backdrop of which the former was posited.

Sensory perception of ordinary people was variously defined in different philosophical schools and by different philosophers, but it was generally understood to be characterized by a range of features: innately possessed by all people, being mediated by a particular sense organ, being of five kinds depending on the mediating sense organ, being based on either a direct contact with or a specific relation to the object, grasping spatially and temporarily present objects alone, being characterized by some kind of immediacy (*sākṣāttva, sākṣāt-saṃprayoga-jatva*) and distinctness (*viśadatva*), typically non-erroneousness, leading to a judgment or producing a cognitive decision, primarily non-conceptual character, although its conceptual variety was generally also recognized (with some notable exceptions, e.g., that of Diṅnāga). Its scope was proximate, gross (*sthūra*), or macroscopic material objects.[2]

Various aspects or dimensions of ordinary perception were emphasized in a range of definitions produced in various philosophical systems. For instance, the Nyāya defined perception as "cognition [which is] produced by a [direct] contact of an object with a sense organ, [which is] non-verbal, [which is] unerring, the nature [of which] is decision,"[3] one of the implications being that even visual perception necessitated such direct sense–object contact, which ultimately prompted a theory of eye rays (*cakṣū-raśmi*) emitted by the eye to directly "touch" the object.

The early Mīmāṃsā emphasized the fact that the mere presence of a perceptible object suffices to produce perception, provided sense organs are unimpaired: "Perception is the production of cognition when a contact of a person's senses with a [really] existing [thing takes place]."[4] As Pārthasārathi, a later proponent of the system, explains in the *Śāstra-Dīpikā* (ŚDī), its scope is limited to macroscopic objects, but also includes introspection, albeit it cannot provide any information about moral law (*dharma*) etc.: "Perception, to begin with, occurs as being produced by a contact of a sense organ and an object, inasmuch as it apprehends present [objects]; it is not a ground [for our knowledge] of moral law."[5] Its status is rooted in the character of respective sense organs which produce perception as cognition which is distinct (*viśada*):

> What is the defining feature of a sense organ and how does it relate to eye etc. and to the mind? It is explained: That which produces cognition as a distinct representation of an [object] in contact is called "sense organ." Further, it is

twofold: external and internal. The external sense organ is five-fold: consisting in smell, taste, eye, skin and ear. The internal [sense organ] is one: the mind.[6]

In addition to the property of distinctness qualifying sensory cognition, Pārthasārathi names immediacy (*sākṣāttva*), i.e., being produced through an unmediated, direct contact with the object of cognition (*sākṣāt-saṃprayoga-jatva*), as another constitutive feature.[7]

In contrast, older Sāṃkhya tradition presented perception merely as "the operation of the senses,"[8] for which it was vehemently criticized by most other schools as reducing its functioning to material elements that constitute sense organs and leaving out its cognitive / epistemic aspect.

Buddhist philosophers of the so-called *pramāṇa* tradition, such as Diṅnāga and Dharmakīrti, emphasized the purely non-conceptual and veridical character of perception, which was said to be "free from conceptual construction and non-erroneous,"[9] whereas if any cognitive error, illusion creeps in the moment, the content of the original non-erroneous act of perception subsequently becomes an object of interpretation, categorization, and conceptualization.

As divergent and complex as were interpretations of what constitutes a genuine perception and its definitions among Indian philosophers in general, so was the Jaina approach.[10] An interpretation of perception, which concludes a century-long classical tradition of Jaina epistemology but which also shows dependence on other systems, especially on Mīmāṃsā and Buddhist Yogācāra-Sautrāntika, is provided by Hemacandra: "Perception is clear [cognition]. Clearness is either independence of other cognitive criteria or a distinct representation [of the object] of the form: 'this'."[11] The first feature, i.e., independence of other cognitive criteria (Mīmāṃsā influence), means that perception is a unique means of cognition, the scope and procedure of which do not overlap with those of other kinds of cognition, and it is undeniable and obvious in its self-explanatory character, in not requiring any additional justification for its revealed epistemic contents to be accepted as true. In contradistinction to verbal knowledge and inference, perception does not depend on any other cognitive criteria in the form of cognition of a word or inferential sign as far as its rise is concerned.[12] The other feature, i.e., a distinct representation of an object of the form "this," is ostention, or an unmediated presenting of a thing in its uninterpreted character, especially in a non-conceptual way, to the perceiver (Buddhist influence). Worth mentioning in passing in Hemacandra's definition of perception is the similarity to the Cartesian idea of "clear and distinct perception."

Three separate but related problems related to perception in Jainism were: what actually constituted a genuine perception (whether it was essentially sensory or extrasensory), what was the actual instrument of perception (whether a sense organ or the ultimate perceiver, i.e., the soul), and which term, i.e., whether *pratyakṣa* or *mati-jñāna* / *ābhinibodhika-jñāna*, could correctly apply to what one understood as perception or to one of its subvarieties. Since these issues are generally not directly relevant to the idea supernatural perception, I will not delve into them.

This short overview of how (ordinary) perception was understood in classical India, very sketchy and incomprehensive, is meant to merely present a backdrop to the other variety of perception, which was believed not to be related to or based on sense organs, which is in the actual purview of this chapter.

0.3. A proper understanding of what constituted supernatural perception in Jainism would not be possible without a more general context set for it by a similar idea in other philosophical systems in India, one of the most eminent and well-elaborated expositions found in the system of Nyāya-Vaiśeṣika after the fifth century.

In general, what was known as *yogi-pratyakṣa* or *yogi-jñāna* was claimed to be possessed only by adepts of Yoga, mystics, or ascetics by virtue of some accomplishment (usually believed to be accompanied by some kind of moral superiority) gained through spiritual practice, either meditation / contemplation (*bhāvanā, dhyāna*) or asceticism (*tapas*). Its scope was agreed by a range of thinkers to encompass past (*atīta*) and future (*anāgata*) objects, as well as things (especially those present) which are subtle (*sūkṣma*), concealed from sight (*vyavahita, dūra*) and distant (*viprakṛṣṭa*). Even the wording in such classifications of the scope of *yogi-pratyakṣa* in various schools was usually identical (Table 4.1), which may attest to mutual borrowings and an intersystemic development of the idea.[13]

Also critics of the supernatural, including extrasensory perception, took notice of such views, as is attested by Kumārila, who recapitulates this idea in his *Mīmāṃsā-śloka-vārttika:*

> Some profess that the perception of yogins as well as of the liberated beings (i.e. Arhants in Buddhism and Siddhas in Jainism) [grasps] past and future objects, as well as subtle and concealed (from sight).[14]

It seems that a belief in some kind of extraordinary perception was there in Indian religious and philosophical traditions from quite an early phase, perhaps as an extension of a belief in supernatural phenomena, but the term *yogi-pratyakṣa* (or similar) is certainly of rather late origin and found its way into philosophical treatises at a rather late date. A correlated concept is *ārṣa-pratyakṣa*, which is a particular variety of supernatural perception of the seers (*ṛṣi*), who possess it "genetically": they are born with it by virtue of their past good deeds. This seems to be a slightly more specialized concept than *yogi-pratyakṣa*.

Some systems, such as the Nyāya or Vaiśeṣika, gradually changed their attitude to the idea of extrasensory perception. For instance, the concept of *yogi pratyakṣa* is entirely absent from the early *Vaiśeṣika-Sūtra*, and it is introduced into the system much later, around the fourth/fifth century, or even slightly later. The idea of *yogi-pratyakṣa* developed later within a section of the system of Nyāya-Vaiśeṣika, and is entirely absent from Candramati's *Daśa-Padartha-Śāstra* (DPŚ), which could be an indication that another section of the system did not endorse the new developments. As we shall also see, the concept of supernatural, extrasensory perception of any form (*yogi-* or *ārṣa-pratyakṣa*) is related to the idea of omniscience, or absolute knowledge (*sarva-jñāna / kevala*), and

Table 4.1 Comparative descriptions of extrasensory perception

	Subtle	*Past and future*	*Concealed*	*Distant*
*Yoga-Sū*tra (YS)[1]	*sūkṣma*	–	*vyavahita*	*viprakṛṣṭa*
Yoga-Bhāṣya (YBh)[2]	*sūkṣma*	*atīta-anāgata*	*vyavahita*	*viprakṛṣṭa*
*Vaiśeṣika-Sū*tra (VS(C)) *and Praśastapāda-Bhāṣya* (PBh)[3]	*sūkṣma*	–	*vyavahita*	*viprakṛṣṭa*
Śābara-*Bhāṣya* (ŚBh)[4]	*sūkṣma*	*bhūta-bhaviṣyat*	*vyavahita*	*viprakṛṣṭa*
*Mīmāṃsā-*Ś*loka-vārttika* (MŚV)[5]	*sūkṣma*	*atīta-anāgata*	*vyavahita*	*dūra*
Āpta-*M*īmāṃsā (ĀMī)[6]	*sūkṣma*	–	*antarita*	*dūra*
Nyāya-Bindu (NB)[7]	*svabhāva-viprakṛṣṭa*	*kāla-viprakṛṣṭa*	*deśa-viprakṛṣṭa*$_1$	*deśa-viprakṛṣṭa*$_2$
Vākya-padīya (VP)[8]	*avasthā-bheda*	*kāla-bheda*	*deśa-bheda*$_1$	*deśa-bheda*$_2$

Notes

1 YS 3.25: *pravṛtty-āloka-nyāsāt sūkṣma-vyavahita-viprakṛṣṭa-jñānam.*

2 YBh 1.49: n*a câsya sūkṣma-vyavahita-viprakṛṣṭasya vastuno loka-pratyakṣeṇa grahaṇam asti.*

3 PBh1 8.12.2.1, p. 187 = PBh2 22.12.2.a [242]: v*iyuktânāṃ punaś catuṣṭaya-sannikarṣād yoga-ja-dharmânugraha-sāmarthyāt sūkṣma-vyavahita-viprakṛṣṭeṣu pratyakṣam utpadyate; comp. PBh1* 11, p. 321 = PBh2, p. 8*5 [370]: yathâsmad-ādīnāṃ gav-ādiṣv aśvâdibhyas tulyâkṛti-guṇa-kriyâvayava-saṃyoga-nimittā pratyaya-vyāvṛttir dṛṣṭā gauḥ ś*uklaḥ śīghra-gati*ḥ pīna-kakudmān mahā-ghaṇṭa iti. tathâsmad-viśiṣṭānāṃ yogīnāṃ nityeṣu tulyâkṛti-guṇa-kriyeṣu paramâṇuṣu muktâtma-manaḥsu cânya-nimittâsambhavād yebhyo nimittebhyaḥ pratyādhāraṃ vilakṣaṇo 'yaṃ vilakṣaṇo 'yam iti pratyaya-vyāvṛttiḥ, deśa-kāla-viprakarṣe ca paramâṇau sa evâyam iti pratyabhijñānaṃ ca bhavati te 'ntyā viśeṣāḥ. See also VSV(C): sūkṣma-vyavahita-viprakṛṣṭeṣv artheṣu teṣāṃ catuṣṭaya-saṃnikarṣād api pratyakṣaṃ jāyate, tathā asmad-ādi pratyakṣeṣu.*

4 ŚBh 1.2.2, p. 4.7–9: codanā *hi bhūtaṃ bhavantaṃ bhaviṣyantaṃ sūkṣmaṃ vyavahitaṃ viprakṛṣṭam ity evaṃ-jātīyakam arthaṃ śaknoty avagamayitum, nânyat kiñcanêndriyam.*

5 M*ŚV 2.141cd (Codanā-sūtra): sūkṣmâtītâdi-viṣayaṃ jīvasya parikalpitam // See* also MŚV 114cd: dūra-sūkṣmâ*di-dṛṣṭau . . . , MŚV 4.26ab (Pratyakṣa-sūtra): atītânāgate 'py arthe sūkṣme vyavahite 'pi ca / pratyakṣaṃ yogināṃ iṣṭaṃ kaiścin muktâtmanām api //* ; MŚV 6.119cd-120ab (Śabda-nityatâdhikaraṇa): yeṣ*āṃ tv aprāpta evâyaṃ ś*abdaḥ śrotreṇa *gṛhyate // teṣām aprāpti-tulyatvaṃ dūra-vyavahitâdiṣu /*

6 ĀMī 5: sūkṣ*mântarita-dūrârthāḥ pratyakṣāḥ kasyacid yathā / anumeyatvato 'gny-ādir iti sarva-jña-saṃsthitiḥ // See also P*MīV 1.16 § 55, p. 14: *sūkṣmântarita-dūrârthāḥ kasyacit pratyakṣāḥ prameyatvāt, ghaṭavad iti.*

7 NB 2.27: anyathā cânupalabd*hi-lakṣaṇa-prāpteṣu deśa-kāla-svabhāva-viprakṛṣṭeṣv artheṣv ātma-pratyakṣa-nivṛtter abhāva-niścayâbhāvāt.*

8 VP 1.32:
avasthā-deś*a-kālānāṃ bhedād bhinnāsu śaktiṣu /*
bhā*vānām anumānena prasiddhir atidurlabhā //*

plays a crucial role in establishing the latter's existence. Unsurprisingly, proofs of the existence or possibility of supernatural perception are likewise of generally late date.

A classical exposition of the nature of supernatural perception is provided by the Vaiśeṣika in a passage which is a later addition to the *Vaiśeṣika-Sūtra* and probably slightly antedates or is contemporaneous with Praśastapāda, a passage which distinguishes two kinds of adepts possessed of it:[15]

[A: The state of a yogin who is *yukta* = *yuñjāna* (lit. "concentrated"), i.e. temporarily engrossed in meditation:]
[13] Due to particular connection of the self and the mind in the self [there arises] perception of the self.[16]
[14] [This perception] also [grasps] other substances, [i.e. atoms[17] of five elements, time, space, mind].

[B: The state of a yogin who is *viyukta* (lit. "no longer concentrated"), i.e. no longer engrossed in meditation:]
[15, interpolation:[18]] And [also] due to the contact of the self, sense-organ, mind and object [there arises supernatural perception].
(≈ VS(Ś): And [also] those whose internal organ (mind) is no [longer] concentrated, whose concentration has been interrupted, [acquire perception] of these [other substances].)
[16] And [there is also supernatural perception] of actions and qualities, since they inhere in [the other substances].
[17] And [also there is supernatural perception] of qualities of the self, since they inhere in the self.[19]

Two levels of a practitioner endowed with such suprasensory vision can clearly be distinguished in the passage. The first is called in the text *yukta*, which might theoretically cover a range of meanings. One which may immediately be recalled would be related to the discipline of Yoga, an interpretation seemingly most natural in this context. Hence *yukta* would mean "engrossed in the practice of Yoga" or "disciplined." Consistently, its correlate *viyukta* in the passage would mean "not engrossed in the practice of Yoga" or "not disciplined," something which was hardly the intention of the authors, because this kind of extrasensory perception is available to a very elite group of practitioners who are disciplined by Yoga, and not to everybody. Alternatively, *yukta* could rather be taken, more specifically, to derive from the verbal root √*yuj* of the fourth class (A, Dhātu-pāṭha 4.68): *yujA* samādhau ("The verbal root *yuj* of the fourth class is used in the sense of concentration"), hence *yukta* = "concentrated," or engrossed in deep meditation (*samādhi*). Its correlate *viyukta* would accordingly denote a practitioner who has ended his deep state of meditation, i.e., an adept who is temporarily "not concentrated," which would make good sense in this particular context. The third option would be to derive *yukta* from the verbal root √*yuj* of the seventh class (A, Dhātu-pāṭha 7.7): *yujIR yoge* ("The verbal root *yuj* of the seventh class is used in the sense of connection") and to take it to mean "connected," and *mutatis mutandis viyukta* as "disconnected." That would, however, not seem appropriate in view of the ambiguity of what connection would here be implied: certainly it could not be a connection (or lack of connection: *vi*) of the self with the mind or with the sense organs, inasmuch as in the case of *yukta*, the contact is between the self and the mind, whereas in the case of *viyukta*, the contact relates the self, sense organ, mind, and object, viz. the actual picture is just the opposite to what the third interpretation would suggest. Further, the term *yukta* means the same as the term *yuñjāna* (the present middle participle: "being himself temporarily engrossed [in meditation]") found in the Nyāya-bhāṣya, which speaks of a perception "of a [yogin] temporarily engrossed [in meditation], which is born in the state of concentration in Yoga" (NBh 1.1.3: *yuñjānasya yoga-samādhi-jam; vide supra*, n. 16).

Some conclusions about the nature of extrasensory perception can be drawn from the above *Vaiśeṣika-Sūtra* passage:

1 It is a result of the connection of the self with other components or factors.
2 It is not a direct, innate function of the self, inasmuch as it requires additional factors (beside the self) to occur.
3 It has two subdivisions: one occurring in a state of deep meditation, when the self is in contact with the mind only, the other taking place outside of meditation, when the self is in contact with the mind, sense organ, and object.
4 This twofold subdivision reveals a hierarchy of supernatural perception:
(a) the **yukta-pratyakṣa* (i.e., the perception of a yogin temporarily engrossed in meditation) is subtler, its object being either primarily immaterial and non-physical (the self) or material, physical but immanently not amenable to ordinary perception (such as atoms, time, space, and mind), and it being based on a contact between the self and the mind, whereas:
(b) the **viyukta-pratyakṣa* (i.e., the perception of a yogin who is no longer engrossed in meditation) seems to be lower and more mundane, it being based on a contact of the self, sense organ, mind, and object, and its object being material and physical, including also objects which are potentially perceptible by everyone, but not sensorily accessible at the moment of perception (e.g., due to distance in time or space or due to some physical barrier);[20] both of these kinds being supernatural, the former would be extrasensory, i.e., fully dissociated from the operation of sense organs, whereas the latter, strictly speaking, would also be supernatural, but not fully extrasensory, because a sense organ is somehow engaged in the process of supernatural perception of the *viyukta* practitioner.
5 It is partly related to the idea of liberation, which is implied by the fact that the one possessed of it can enter a meditative trance of *samādhi*, which should ultimately lead to liberation.[21]

Supernatural perception occupies a prominent place in Praśastapāda's commentary; he distinguishes the same two kinds of extrasensory perception, but seems to have slighly modified the scope of both kinds of supernatural perception, retaining the hierarchical order with the **yukta-praktaykṣa* (possessed by *yukta*-yogins, i.e., those engrossed in meditation and superior to ordinary humans beings) being superior, above the **viyukta-pratyakṣa* of those not engrossed in meditation who perceive merely material, physical objects distant in time or space or separated from ordinary sight by some kind of barrier:

> [240] The grasping of the highest universal (*mahā-sāmānya*) and of [intermediate universals such as] substantiality, qualitativeness, and mobility etc.,

> inherent in a perceptible substratum, through sense-organs which grasp [their] substratum is the [ordinary] perception of people like us. [241] However, in yogins who are temporarily engrossed in meditation (*yukta*) [and] who are superior to us, through the mind influenced by moral excellence (*dharma*) produced by [the practice of] Yoga, there arises an unerring perception of the intrinsic nature with respect to [such invisible substances as] their own self, the self of others, ether, space, time, air, atoms, mind as well as qualities, actions, universals, individuators which are inherent in these [substances]. [242] On the other hand, in [yogins who are] no longer engrossed in meditation (*viyukta*) due to the contact of the four [viz. the self, sense-organ, mind and object and] thanks to the efficacy of the influence of moral law produced by [the practice of] Yoga, there arises perception with respect to objects which are subtle, concealed [from sight] and distant.[22]

Praśastapāda's elaboration of the *Vaiśeṣika-Sūtra* classification, being itself a later interpolation, introduces some new insights as to the nature of supernatural perception:

6 The precondition for supernatural perception, especially the superior kind, or **yukta-pratyakṣa*, is the practice of Yoga and moral law (*dharma*), whereas it is not clear whether one requires any moral standard to possess **viyukta-pratyakṣa*.

7 Praśastapāda extends the scope of the **yukta-pratyakṣa* to embrace one's own and other people's selves, ether, space, time, air, atoms and the mind as well as qualities, actions, universals, individuators which are inherent in these substances, whereas the **viyukta-pratyakṣa* is limited to objects which are subtle, concealed from sight and distant.

He further describes how and on what basis adepts of Yoga distinguish between objects perceived supernaturally:

> [370] Similarly to people like us who experience the differentiation in cognition occasioned by equal shapes, qualities, actions, parts or relations, with reference to cows, etc. [as different] from horses, etc. – [e.g. in the form] "[this] cow is white, of swift pace, with a fat neck hump, with a large bell" – in a similar manner yogins, who are superior to us, [experience] the differentiation in cognition with reference to permanent [entities like] atoms as well as minds and souls of liberated people that [all] have identical shapes, qualities and actions. Since there is no other factor [that would make such a differentiation between seemingly identical things possible], the factors thanks to which [the yogins are able to distinguish] each and every substratum [of qualities and actions in the form]: "this is different, that is different", and [thanks to which in those yogins] a recognition arises: "this is that [atom]" with regard to an atom in distant place and time, are ultimate individuators. [371] Suppose, on the other hand, without [postulating the existence

> of] ultimate individuators, that the yogins possessed such a discrimination through cognition as well as recognition [of individual atoms, which they could acquire] through moral law (*dharma*) produced by [the practice of] Yoga, what would happen then? It would not be possible [for them to distinguish between atoms etc.] in this way, [i.e. merely through such a supernatural perception]. Just like the cognition of white in something which is not white or a recognition of something completely invisible does not arise through moral law produced by [the practice of] Yoga, and if it could [arise] it would be false, in the same manner the yogins can possess neither discrimination through cognition nor a recognition through moral law born of [the practice of] Yoga without [the existence of] ultimate individuators.[23–24]

The actual position of the fifth-century authors responsible for the above interpolation in the *Vaiśeṣika-Sūtra* being unknown, it seems that, for Praśastapāda, it was the **yukta-pratyakṣa* which necessitated some kind of moral statute (*dharma*) for it to be acquired, whereas it was not necessarily the case with the inferior kind of **viyukta-pratyakṣa*. To distinguish between atoms by means of a supernatural perception of the ultimate individuators (*antya-viśeṣa*) was the domain of the **yukta-pratyakṣa*: the "recognition of individual atoms" could be acquired "through moral law (*dharma*) produced by the practice of Yoga."

This Vaiśeṣika concept of supernatural perception also found its way into the system of Nyāya and was elaborated by representatives of the twin school. Of particular note is the exposition of Bhāsarvajña, who does not really distinguish between **yukta-pratyakṣa* and **viyukta-pratyakṣa* on the basis of their different scopes but according to the kind of connection between the self and other relata. The former presupposes only a connection between the self and the mind, whereas the latter requires the co-operation of the four elements (the self, the mind, a sense organ, and the object):

> [NSā:] Supernatural perception is the grasping of an object distant in place, time and its own (subtle) nature. [NBhū:] Distant in place [means] places far away like existent worlds etc.; concealed from sight means] hellish abodes etc.; distant in time [means] past etc.; distant in terms of one's own nature [means] atoms, ether etc. This takes place in both states: in the state of the "concentrated" (*yukta*) and in the state of the "not concentrated" (*viyukta*). Among these two, in the state of the "concentrated" only due to the connection of the self and the mind there arises the grasping of the complete object, and this is said with respect to the highest yogins. However, an ordinary yogin does not have the grasp of the complete object.[25]

Further, the **yukta-pratyakṣa* is said to cognize a complete object (whatever that exactly means), not just its spatial slice (e.g., the surface of the object) or its temporal snapshot (e.g., its present condition), which alone remain perceptible to the **viyukta-pratyakṣa*. Also this account of Bhāsarvajña preserves a noticeable hierarchy: the former, more comprehensive, is possessed by highest yogins (*parama-yogin*) alone, whereas the latter is the domain of ordinary yogins (*yogi-mātra*).

A very special kind of supernatural perception, particularly distinguished in the Nyāya-Vaiśeṣika system, was the seers' perception (*ārṣa-pratyakṣa*), also called intuition (*pratibha* or *pratibhā*). We find this idea in the *Vaiśeṣika-Sūtra*: "And the seers' perception is the perfect seeing of the *dharma* [and other things]."[26] However, this *sūtra* must again be a later interpolation, for we find it in Candrānanda's recension (VS(C)), but it is absent, e.g., in Śaṅkaramiśra's *Upaskāra* (VS(Ś)).

The passage was appended at the very end of the chapter, with no direct connection to the preceding portion. It was apparently a reaction to the claims of the Mīmāṃsā school that the Vedic revelation, the way it was interpreted and ritually practiced by that school, was the only means to know the *dharma*. Here, with a new kind of supernatural perception, the Nyāya-Vaiśeṣika could reject the Mīmāṃsā ritualistic claim and substantiate its independent access to moral law.

0.4. Jaina epistemology relied heavily on the general epistemological paradigm developed by other schools, especially that of early Nyāya-Vaiśeṣika.

Despite Jaina epistemological classification's original terminological incompatibility with the rest of epistemological traditions in classical India – the term *pratyakṣa* (universally: "perception"; in Jainism: "direct cognition") was reserved for a range of supernatural cognitions, whereas the actual sensory perception was known as *abhinibodha* or *mati-jñāna* – both kinds of perception were clearly distinguished in the quintuplet of cognitions: sensuous cognition (*abhinibodha*, mati; lit. "apprehension," "mental process"), testimonial cognition (*śruta*; lit. "the heard"), clairvoyance (*avadhi*; lit. "mental infiltration"), telepathy, or mind-reading (*manaḥ-paryāya* or *manaḥ-paryaya*; lit. "penetration of the mind") and perfect knowledge, or omniscience (*kevala*; lit. "the singular one"), all being later grouped under two headings of indirect cognition (*parokṣa*) and direct cognition (*pratyakṣa*), respectively.[27]

What would correspond to ordinary, sensory perception was known as sensuous cognition (*abhinibodha, mati*), a natural cognitive endowment of all living beings. The Jainas tried to clearly distinguish it from other kinds of cognition, partly under the influence of the Nyāya-Vaiśeṣika epistemology, and came to define it as cognition that originates in the contact of a sense organ, the mind, and an object. It was not purely non-conceptual or exclusively derived from sensory data. In fact, it also comprised inner apprehension of mental images and memories, or mental insight. Its understanding was rather unspecific: within it sensations, perceptions, and mental processes overlapped and it covered a range of epistemic events and cognitive processes. It not only covered sensations derived from particular sense organs and their awareness but also mental processes triggered by such sensations, including processes of simple reasoning, sensation of doubt, acts of deliberation and cogitation, and recognition. Alongside testimonial cognition (*śruta*; lit. "the heard"), which covered all cognition that was not based on direct experience of the cognizing subject but on verbal communication of another person, particularly scriptural testimony, sensuous cognition consituted twofold indirect cognition (*parokṣa*), i.e., mediated by either a sense organ or mind, or both.

The heading of direct cognition proper (*pratyakṣa*) comprised three varieties of what one could call supernatural perception, with no intermediary of sense organs or mind, conceived of as a quasi-sense organ. Clairvoyance (*avadhi*) traditionally comes first. It was believed to grasp material macroscopic objects that were considered physically beyond the reach of ordinary, sensuous perception or testimonial cognition. Further, this kind of extrasensory perception was not accessible to everyone: one had to either be born with it or to acquire it through special ascetic practices. In terms of cognitive faculties (*upayoga*) we can speak of two kinds of clairvoyance (*avadhi*): clairvoyant perception and clairvoyant knowledge (*avadhi-darśana* and *avadhi-jñāna*). However, it is also twofold in terms of its origin[28]: conditioned by birth, i.e., possessed by denizens of hell and divine beings, as well as occasioned by destruction-cum-subsidence of karman, possessed by denizens of hell, divine beings, animals, and people. The Jainas would further distinguish six varieties of it: "not-accompanying" (*anānugāmika*), viz. present only in a given place; "accompanying" (*ānugāmika*), viz. it accompanies the person after he or she has left the place where he or she obtained it; regressive (*hīyamānaka*); progressive (*vardhamānaka*); oscillating (*anavasthita*); and stable (*avasthita*), that will accompany the person until the moment of death or attainment of omniscience.[29]

Much subtler was telepathy, or mind-reading (*manaḥ-paryāya / manaḥ-paryaya*), which was supposed to directly grasp others' thoughts, i.e., all contents of other minds. Inasmuch as one could achieve it only through a process of spiritual development and as a result of the uplifting of best virtues, it was available only to those morally most advanced humans. This concept presupposed an idea, which is a pan-Indian belief, that mental phenomena, including all states of mind of other people, are somatic,[30] i.e., they extend in space and are spatially located. For this very reason telepathy, the way it was conceived of in Jainism, was a subtle, sophisticated kind of perception which grasped extremely fine percepts located in the mind. The difference between clairvoyance and telepathy concerned clarity (*viśuddhi*), place (*kṣetra*), possessor (*svāmin*), and domain (*viṣaya*).[31] Thus, only telepathy was believed to be restricted to the restrained, or spiritually advanced human beings (*manuṣya-saṃyata*), viz. it was conditioned by high moral standards. This precondition resembles the requirement, postulated by the Vaiśeṣika and other systems, of "the moral law produced by the practice of Yoga" (*yogaja-dharma*).

We may speculate on what were the reasons that prompted the Jainas to accept the existence of clairvoyance or telepathy. Surely, their presence in the structure of Jaina epistemology was not dictated by a reasoned argument, at least not at the initial stage. Probably, these two kinds of direct cognition were accepted as a result of a widespread religious belief in the existence of supernatural cognitive faculties and of supernatural phenomena. But, as we will see, these two kinds of cognition came to fulfill another role, too, being crucial elements in an argumentative structure and rhetorics within Jainism.

A culmination of the hierarchy of the latter of subtler and subtler kinds of supernatural perceptions and the apex of all spiritual and cognitive development as well as the fulfillment of the dream of the imperfect suffering living being was absolute, perfect knowledge, or omniscience (*kevala*). From the Jaina standpoint, the omniscient perfected being's (*kevalin*) perception faced no spatial, temporal, or structural limitations and literally everything was revealed through it all at once – all things past, present, and future, distant and sublime, material and mental. Unlike in Buddhism, for instance, omniscience in Jainism was conceived of not as some kind of potentiality available to the perfected being but a cognitive actuality. The attainment of absolute knowledge is a consummation of mundane existence of a soul transmigrating from times immemorial, being tantamount to liberation and to a complete destruction of all karmic matter.

0.5. A problem which both the Jainas as well as other schools, such as Nyāya-Vaiśeṣika, which advocated the existence of supernatural cognitive faculties, had to face once they entered the public sphere of debate was to counter criticism meted out by the staunch opponents of omniscience, and to do it primarily on rational grounds. It was one thing to believe in supernatural phenomena and extrasensory cognitive faculties, which necessitated no reasoned justification; it was another to defend one's position, which required reasoned argumentation. This had to lead to a development of rational arguments to prove the existence and feasibility of such cognitive faculties. At this stage of research it seems quite difficult to determine which rational arguments for the existence of supernatural cognitive faculties came first. Therefore, I will confine myself to merely collecting them, not necessarily in a chronological order.

1 An argument which is most frequently resorted to by thinkers is the argument from progression. One of its full expositions, outside Jaina literature, can be found in the *Nyāya-mañjarī*. It is recapitulated there by Jayanta Bhaṭṭa, and this attests to its much earlier origin. Jayanta advances it in order to counter the Mīmāṃsakas' counter-argument from the lack of evidence (see counter-arguments, § 8) to the effect that it is not possible to formulate any rational proof of suprasensory perception. In his reply to the question posited by the Mīmāṃsakas, "What would be the proof of supernatural perception that could also cognise *dharma* ?" Jayanta Bhaṭṭa replies:

> The proof [of supernatural perception] is the culmination (gradual perfection) of perception. For it is as follows: a person like us whose sight is limited notices a number of things placed in proximity. Cats [lit. "enemies of mice"], on the other hand, can recognise even a thing that has fallen into a place covered with a layer of mud in the thickest possible darkness. Furthermore, one learns from the Rāmāyaṇa epic that the king of vultures named Sampāti could even see Sītā [lit. the spouse of Daśaratha's son] in the distance of a hundred miles. This precisely is the culmination (gradual perfection) of perception like the culmination (perfection) of such qualities as white etc. which is based on gradation.

> Hence it is understood that there is the highest culmination (perfection) without any further gradation (perfection). And therefore those in whom there is the highest intensity (consummation) of this [perception] are praised as yogins. And the highest culmination (intensity) means that [yogins'] perception has as its domain [things] that are subtle, concealed (from sight), distant, past, future etc.[32]

Of special importance in the argument is the actual meaning of the central term *atiśaya*, which normally means "excellence," "superiority," "eminence," "pre-eminence," or "ascendancy," which I render here as "progression," "gradual perfection" ("gradual development"), "culmination," or "gradation," depending on context. What it means in this particular context is, as Jayanta Bhaṭṭa aptly clarifies, a gradual ascending process of perfection from a rather feeble competence / faculty, or unpronounced feature, through intermediate stages / gradation, up to absolute consummation or ultimate perfection of the faculty, the gradation or improvement of which is no longer possible.

This argument from progression was used by other schools, e.g., by the Buddhists and the Jainas, as well. A good classical exposition of it is found in Hemacandra's *Pramāṇa-mīmāṃsā:*

> The proof of this [supernatural perception (sc. omniscience) follows] from the argument that there is completion of the culmination (gradation) of understanding, and from other [proofs].[33]

Hemacandra himself supplies a few instantiations of this argument:

> [Let's first take] the culmination of understanding. Progression [must have] its completion somewhere, because of culmination, just like the culmination of magnitude. Because of this argument, since it is proved that there is understanding with no higher limit, [we have] the proof of this absolute knowledge, because the proof of [the existence of] absolute knowledge depends on the same structure (*rūpa*) as the proof of such [understanding with no higher limit].[34]

What the example "like the culmination of magnitude" (*parimāṇatiśayavat*) means is that things progress from smallest atoms (*paramaṇu*) as the lowest limit to the whole space of the universe (*loka*) as the highest limit. Similarly, we can observe, Hemacandra argues, such a progress of cognition / understanding from a very limited one to the cognition of maximum magnitude, i.e., omniscience. We find similar progression, or gradual perfection of the scope of our knowledge, in the case of astronomy, too.[35]

What is important, as Hemacandra emphasizes, is that clairvoyance and telepathy constitute two consecutive stages of clarity or purity that eventually lead to omniscience:

> Clairvoyance and telepathy follow gradual progression of this [destruction of karman].[36]

The structure of the argument provides a proper allocation of clairvoyance (*avadhi*) and telepathy (*manaḥ-paryāya / manaḥ-paryaya*) within a structured typology of the five kinds of cognition traditionally accepted by the Jainas. Being intermediary stages from limited cognitive faculties, these two served earlier religious and folk beliefs in the supernatural and rare human faculties to grasp it apart, to prove the strong Jaina claim of omniscience. In other words, for the Jainas, *yogi-pratyakṣa* was treated just as an intermediate stage to perfection of knowledge, a "visible" corroboration that progression toward perfection is possible.

This approach can be identified already with Kundakunda, who in his *Samaya-sāra* emphasizes that the five kinds of cognition ultimately share the same nature. However they can be arranged hierarchically from sensuous cognition as the lowest to the absolute knowledge as the highest, with no further progress:

> Sensuous cognition, testimonial cognition, clairvoyance, telepathy and absolute knowledge are one and the same state. When that which is the ultimate is attained, there arises liberation.[37]

Putting aside the question of whether the author(s) of the *Pavayaṇa-sāra* is (are) the same person(s) as the author(s) of the *Samaya-sāra*, both texts – composed not earlier than 300 C.E. – have much affinity in terms of ideas and approach, which find expression in the Jaina tradition, which assumes that the author of both is one and the same person. The same idea of hierarchically structured cognitions is found also in the *Pavayaṇa-sāra*:

> [34] Monks have scripture for eyes, all beings have their sense organs for eyes, whereas the divine beings have clairvoyance for eyes. However the liberated beings have eyes that see everything.[38]

The cognition of monks is scriptural, i.e., testimonial cognition (*śruta*), not based on perception. Every living being is endowed with sensory perception, which is the lowest kind, lower than monks' scriptural cognition. A more supreme kind is clairvoyance (*avadhi*), and presumably also telepathy (*manaḥ-paryāya*). The highest of all is the omniscience of liberated beings.

Another passage from the same *Pavayaṇa-sāra* sheds additional light on what links the five kinds of cognition:

> [45] Perfected souls (saints) [achieve their condition] as a result of merit (or: auspicious karman). Their activity is, however, a natural development, which is free from [inauspicious karman such as] confusion etc., and therefore it is known as "resulting from the destruction [of karman]" (*kṣāyika*)."[39] [46] If the soul itself could not become either good or bad by virtue of its own essential nature alone, there would be no mundane world (transmigration) for all the bodies endowed with a soul.[40]

The saints (*arhant*) who have reached the level of perfection are endowed with absolute knowledge (*kevala*), which is the apex of the ascending development of cognitive faculties. As Kundakunda explains, this highest cognitive status is a result of the destruction of karmic impurities, which keep the souls in the world of death and rebirth. What is significant is the argument that the souls become good and perfect (but also bad and imperfect) by virtue of their own essential natures alone, without any involvement of some external factor. That coincides with the idea that all the five cognitions, from the least pure to the most pure absolute knowledge, are in a line of spiritual development which is based on a gradual process of perfection and purification of the souls. And the process of purification (but also of pollution) is effectuated by the soul itself, an important observation which emphasizes the soul's role as the only and ultimate ethical agent. By implication, the innermost nature of all souls is pure, all impurities being external to them. Indirectly, the passage provides a method of how to achieve perfection and absolute knowledge: one should first identify the causes of limited perception and then remove them through practice. This motif will recur in the argument from purification (§ 5).

The implication of the above passage, compounded with the conviction that cognitive faculties are organized hierarchically in a progressive sequence with omniscience at the apex, is a basis for future argument from progression. As a rule, Kundakunda does not openly argue with opponents, does not rationally justify his position, and does not engage in a rational dispute where religious dogmas are supported and consolidated with reasoned arguments. That is why we would not find a well-structured argument from progression to prove omniscience in Kundakunda's works. But what is already present there are the building blocks for such an argument to be explicitly formulated in the future.

This task is undertaken by Samantabhadra,[41] who uses these threads to weave an argumentative fabric in his *Āpta-mīmāṃsā*:

> [4] A complete destruction of defects and karmic veils is possible, because a complete consummation [of the gradual purification process] is [possible], just like a [complete] annihilation of both external and internal blemishes in particular cases with the help of respective causes.[42] [5] Objects that are subtle, concealed [from sight] and distant remain [always] directly perceptible to someone, because they are inferable, just as fire etc. [is inferable from visible smoke] – such is a proof of the omniscient [Jina].[43]

The argument, introduced in verse 4, can be formally arranged as follows[44]:

> Thesis (*pratijñā*): There exists complete destruction of defects and karmic veils (*doṣavaraṇayor hānir niḥśeṣasti*),
>
> Logical reason (*hetu*): Because there is a completion of progression, i.e. the consummation of gradual purification process (*atiśāyanāt*),
>
> Example (*dṛṣṭānta*): Like a complete annihilation of both external and internal blemishes in particular cases with the help of respective causes (*kvacid yathā sva-hetubhyo bahir antar mala-kṣayaḥ*).

The thesis amounts to the claim that "there exists omniscience," inasmuch as "complete destruction of defects and karmic veils" is identical with attaining omniscience, and provisionally liberation. The actual structure of the argument is the following:

> An invisible perfect condition *x* of a particular faculty *F* (e.g. liberation, omniscience, extrasensory perception) is possible, because there can be a gradation of the respective faculty.

And indeed, as Jayanta Bhaṭṭa notices, the crux of the argument from progression is that "there is the highest culmination without any further culmination" (*param api niratiśayam atiśayam*).

In fact, the way in which this specific argument is found with Samantabhadra can be understood to work two ways. First, there is a gradation of purification (a hierarchy of purer and purer cognitions, which terminates with absolutely pure omniscience). Alternatively, there is a gradation of destruction of pollution (a hierarchy of states in which karmic veils and defects are more and more destroyed, till a state is reached when all karmic veils and defects are fully destroyed). Whichever way we take it, both formulations ultimately amount to one and the same result: pure cognition in a state of complete destruction of karmic veils and defects.

Further, verse 5,[45] which supplements the argument of verse 4, establishes a connection between the scope of *yogi-pratyakṣa* (supernatural perception) and *kevala* (omniscience), which serves as a support for the argument. In fact, it also constitutes an argument in its own right as the argument from potentiality (*vide infra*, § 6).

The argument from progression, explicated in verse 4, bases its elaboration in a commentary *Aṣṭa-śatī* by Akalaṅka (eighth century):

> And in this way the complete (consummate) destruction of defects etc. is somehow capable of annihilating all [karmic] blemishes. Thus, why should a proof of a blemish-free condition not be possible? The expunction of dirt etc. [in the case of a gem] does not entail the destruction of the gem [and similarly the annihilation of karman does not destroy the soul], because it does not stand to reason that something really existent [such as a soul] could be totally annihilated.[46]

What Akalaṅka emphasizes in addition is that the process of purification, through the annihilation of impurities, does not necessarily lead to a destruction of the object to be purified. That is particularly important in Jaina context, which understands the soul as the only and ultimate ethical agent which is both the object which undergoes a purification process and the agent which effectively carries it out.

Akalaṅka refers to the argument in his other work, the *Laghīyas-traya*, too:

> If excellence (gradation in skills) of man is possible, why should there be no person who could see objects in an extra-sensory manner?[47]

As we can see, the argument from progression was applied by various Śvetāmbara and Digambara authors, from Kundakunda to Hemacandra-sūri, but its use was not restricted to Jaina authors. Jayanta Bhaṭṭa, a representative of Nyāya-Vaiśeṣika who used this argument, has already been mentioned, but we find it also with other systems.

An early example is Bhartṛhari, whose argument evinces some similarity with the statements found in the *Praśastapādabhāṣya* (*vide supra*, n. 22):

> However, one knows of cognition, encompassing all sense organs, [of imperceptible universals] on the part of [the omniscient] who are superior to us that it [comes about] from a continued practice, similarly to [professional knowledge] of particular things such as gems, silver etc. on the part of specialists in these [things].[48]

Further, he lays down the principle of progression which enables one to compare between two similar qualities, or substances possessed of similar qualities, and establish a hierarchy based on the respective intensity of a given quality.

> A quality is explained to be independently a ground for superiority [of one quality over another quality]. It is solely due to such quality on which another quality is depended that one recognises its superiority over the other quality.[49]

Another instance, albeit in a slightly modified form, is found also in Buddhist literature, e.g., in Dharmakīrti's oeuvre (*vide infra*, n. 56).

The argument from progression was employed also by other schools of Indian thought where it served to prove the superiority of other qualities, not only omniscience. It is found, for instance, in the tradition of the Pātañjala Yoga to demonstrate the pre-eminence of god (*īśvara*), which attests to a wide popularity of this kind of argumentative structure:

> Further, his (god's) supremacy is without any equal excellence [that could compare with it]. To begin with, [his] excellence is not exceeded by any other excellence, [because] that very thing which would be excelling over [it] would necessarily be this very excellence [of god]. Therefore, where the excellence reaches its upper limit that is god. Moreover, there is no excellence that is equal to his [excellence]. Why? [Because] when out of two [seemingly] equal things one thing is desired at the same time [and] the thing is selected (lit. established) as follows: "This one must be new; that one must be old," then it automatically follows that the other is inferior because it falls short of [satisfying] the desired expectation. And it is not the case that for two [seemingly] equal things they are achieved as the desired object simultaneously, because the object would stand in contradiction. Therefore the one whose supremacy is without any [seemingly equal] excellences is god.[50]

All these instances, and certainly there will be a lot of more to be traced in various works, attest to a wide popularity of this argument, despite its fundamental logical flaws. One of these could be briefly mentioned here. Let the symbol $\rightarrow$ stand for any kind of precedence, whether hierarchical, temporal, causal etc.; "" means "x is superior in degree to y." The main premise of the argument is:

> 'For any thing y there exists some other thing x such that x is superior in degree to y (or "y is subordinate to x"),' i.e. $\forall yx\ (x \rightarrow y)$.

From this, one tends to draw a conclusion:

> "There exists one thing x which is superior in degree to all ys," i.e. $\exists x \forall y\ (x \rightarrow y)$.

Clearly, such a move, i.e. $\forall y \exists x\ (x \rightarrow y) \Rightarrow \exists xy\ (x \rightarrow y)$, constitutes a logical fallacy, for it is logically not permissible to interchange the places of the qualifiers.[51]

If, in addition, we know x as well as $x + 1$, we can know $(x + 1) + 1$, so we can know $(x + 1) + 1 + \ldots + n$, etc. There is nothing logically binding that means that this sequence has to terminate at any point. At the same time, the infinite continuity of the series, i.e., continuous expansion of our knowledge by accumulation, cannot lead to omniscience because the process takes place within a limited time in which only a limited section of the series can unfold (and provision has to be made for no loss of the already accumulated knowledge, i.e., loss of memory).

The structure of the proof resembles a proof of god's existence, which we find in Thomas Aquinas' *Summa Theologiae* as "the fourth way," or the argument "from the degrees of perfection." Just as an argument from hierarchy of beings attempts to prove that a sequence of ever better entities must end with a fully perfect being, so functions the argument from progression to prove omniscience. The logical flaw of these arguments is similar to two other arguments of god's existence ("from the prime mover" and "from the first cause," or cosmological argument), formulated for the first time by Aristotle at the beginning of his *Metaphysics*.

2 A variant of argument from progression is what could be called reverse argument from progression. It is found in an embryonic form, for instance with Kundakunda:

> [236 / 222] When the same conch-shell, having abandoned its white nature, would become of black nature, then it would abandon its whiteness. [237 / 223] Just like a conch-shell, when it has lost its white nature due to [another] substance, it would become of black nature, then it would give up its whiteness. [238 / 223] In the same manner, also the same cogniser, when he – having lost his cognitive nature – would be modified through nescience, he would become of nescient nature.[52]

In fact, this is a reverse argument from progression by analogy. Just as a conch-shell may gradually lose its whiteness and turn black, in the same way a knowing soul may gradually become bereft of any capacity to cognize. Why Kundakunda uses this argument is another question: it serves probably both to demonstrate that progression works in two ways (towards perfection and towards imperfection) and to warn religious followers not to be negligent in their religious practice. For just as there is a progression from whiteness down to blackness and, by analogy, from a state of ordinary, mundane consciousness down to a state of complete cognitive defunctness, there must also be a progression from ordinary, mundane consciousness up to omniscience.

As long as one wishes that the argument could serve to prove a hierarchy of ever-diminishing cognitions, down to inanimate senseless objects (*jaḍa*), the problem would be that the argument, at least as far as Jaina ontology goes, is not a good analogy. Omniscience amounts to perfection, with suprasensory perception as an intermediate stage: in this case there is no continuum with ever higher degrees of a quality (here: cognition), but we can rather speak of termination of a sequence which has its apex with omniscience. With a downward progression with ever-diminishing cognition, one would *mutatis mutandis* expect some kind of a termination of the sequence, i.e., absolute lack of consciousness. But that is clearly not the case in Jainism: even the lowest possible living beings in the state of nigoda, with just one sense active, possess some residual consciousness and cognition related to that singular sense organ. In other words, in Jainism one never finds a living being downgraded to a state of a complete absence of cognition and consciousness.

3 Another variant of the argument from progression is what could be called an argument from progression by necessity. It emphasizes that the gradual process towards absolute perfection through various stages is in a way necessarily determined. Its late version is found in Hemacandra-sūri's *Pramāṇa-mīmāṃsā*:

> When there is the accomplishment (intensity) of the three jewels[53] practised assiduously for a long time, without interruption and with utmost care by force of reflection, analysis and meditation over one [and the same thing and] when there is complete annihilation of obstructing karmans that veil cognition and [perception], [there is a manifestation] of the soul whose own nature is consciousness (sc. it knows itself) and whose own nature is illumination (sc. it knows external objects).[54]

The general structure of the argument from progression ("a progression of a gradable quality / faculty *F* may lead to a perfect condition *x* of that quality / faculty") is extended to embrace one more element: once one discovers the method to upgrade the faculty or quality and fully and properly implements it, one necessarily achieves the final state of perfection of that faculty or quality. Interestingly, in its second assumption, also this argument confuses two (or three) modalities: (1) possibility, potentiality or probability, on the one hand, and, on the other, (2) necessity, or determination, or (3) actuality. Clearly, from the premise "one can achieve a condition *x*," it does not follow that "one will achieve a condition *x*."

Interestingly, Hemacandra seems to directly rely on Dharmakīrti's and Dharmottara's formulations found in the *Nyāya-bindu* (NB 1.11), except for some necessary doctrinal adjustments.[55]

Dharmakīrti defines supernatural perception as follows:

> Yogin's cognition is produced by the accomplishment (intensity) of contemplation of existing objects.[56]

Dharmakīrti's commentator, Dharmottara, explains that "contemplation of (meditation on) an entity is the perpetual (lit. again and again) keeping in mind of [that entity]."[57] He also emphasizes the gradual process of perfection that finally leads to supernatural perception and emphatically divides the process into three stages[58]: the consummation (intensity) of contemplation (*bhāvanā-prakarṣa*),[59] the ultimate state of the intensity (*prakarṣa-paryantavasthā*),[60] and yogin's perception, *yogi-pratyakṣa*, as the final stage.[61,62]

As in the later argument formulated by Hemacandra, also here in Dharmakīrti's argument two elements are conspicuous: (1) supernatural perception is a culmination of a longer process (argument from progression); and (2) it is achieved through meditation (the method). Hemacandra's is however a stronger claim. Whereas for Dharmakīrti, this version of the argument from progression brings us to a supernatural perception, which does not have to imply an attainment of full omniscience, such a fully omniscient condition is implied in Hemacandra's formulation. Nevertheless, it is Dharmakīrti's definition of supernatural perception (*yogi-pratyakṣa*) above which at the same time provides a nucleus of a proof of *yogi-pratyakṣa*, which in its crudest form would assume the form: "supernatural perception is possible, because it can be achieved by consummation (perfection) of some practice (meditation)." In other words, uninterrupted spiritual practice and meditation, carried out properly, have to necessarily lead to their culmination in the form of supernatural perception.

4 An interesting argument for the existence of omniscience, in which it provides guarantee for a possibility of any cognition, is found in Kundakunda's *Pavayaṇa-sāra*. I would call it argument from the collapse of all knowledge:

> [48] For the one who does not know simultaneously the objects that exist in [all] the three time periods and are situated in [all] three worlds it is not possible to know even a single substance with its [infinite] modes. [49] A single substance is possessed of infinite modes. Infinite are aggregates of substances. If one does not know them simultaneously, how can he know them all. [50] If knowledge arises for the knower gradually, dependent on an object, that [knowledge] is not permanent, does not result from the destruction [of *karman*] and is not all-pervasive. [51] The [knowledge] of the Jinas knows simultaneously all variegated occurrences, diversified

> into both [those that exist] in the three time periods and those that are permanent, in every respect. Indeed great is [their] knowledge.[63]

This argument contends that omniscience (*kevala*) is a guarantee, or a logical prerequisite, that we can know anything: If one does not know everything, how can one know even a single thing with all its features? Without admitting omniscience, or rather that there is an omniscient being, one runs a risk that one might not know anything. To know even a single thing one would have to know it in its all facets, and if knowledge of all its facets is possible, why should knowledge of all things not be possible? Clearly, the argument conflates two kinds of infinities: the infinity of all entities as such and the infinity of aspects of one entity. According to the argument, both are two sides of one and the same equation.

The argument is patently counterfactual: we do happen to know quite a number of things, albeit our cognitions may not encompass all aspects of individual things. That does not prevent us from acquiring some cognition, even in imperfect dimensions. Cognition, albeit partial, is not only possible, it is a fact and something on which we can usually rely on in our lives.

Further, the argument confuses two (or even three) modalities: possibility with actuality (and even with necessity), because it rests on a premise that "if it is possible to know *P*, then one knows *P*" (or even, "if it is possible to know *P*, then one necessarily knows *P*"), where *P* is any aspect, condition, or facet of a thing *x*. This premise is also a precondition for the reasoning: "if one knows *x* in one aspect, one knows (or: necessarily knows) *x* in all its aspects." This premise is likewise erroneous. However, as we shall see, the confusion of modalities will resurface in another argument too (*vide infra*, § 6).

5 This argument, in a significantly modified form, reoccurs in a Jaina text *Nyāyavatāra-vivṛti* by Siddharṣigaṇi, where it is mentioned alongside yet another argument for omniscience. We can call the latter the argument from purification. In its elaborate form it runs in two stages. The first stage has the form:

> [1. The thesis:] The cognitive subject is such whose complete purification is possible,
>
> [2. the logical reason:] because the means for [his] purification exists;
>
> [3. the invariable concomitance accompanied by the example:] in this world, whatever is such the means for the purification [of which] exists is [also] such the complete purification of which is possibly existent,[64] like a particular gem for the purification of which the means exists, [namely] prolonged calcination in a clay furnace[65] with the alkali, etc.;
>
> [4. the application:] and indeed the cognitive subject is such for whose purification the means exists, [namely] repeated practice of cognition, etc.;
>
> [5. the conclusion:] hence [the cognitive subject is] such whose complete purification is possibly existent.[66]

The argument starts with two premises: (1) if we have a method to purify an object, that object is "purifiable"; (2) we do have means to purify the soul, which is the ultimate cognitive subject. These lead to a conclusion that the soul, being the cognitive subject, can be purified. The aspect of cognitive faculties is crucial here because it is supposed to imply potential omniscience of the soul. However, this argument, the way it is formulated, only proves, formally speaking, that purification of the soul is possible, but it does not prove that supernatural perception or omniscience is possible. In other words, from the fact alone that a state of completely pure soul exists does not follow that omniscience, understood as completely purified cognition, is possible.

Therefore, the whole argument requires a second stage. And, indeed, Siddharṣigaṇi explicitly supplements it with the following equation: "cogniser = cognition":

> And the cognitive subject, [when] completely purified, is called the absolute, because there is no difference at all between cognition and cogniser.[67]

This is a recurrent theme in Jaina literature to equate the soul with cognition and to treat it as the ultimate perceiving organ, or "the eye" (*akṣa*) per se, as attested, e.g., in the works of Kundakunda or Siddharṣigaṇi:

> Therefore the living element (soul) is cognition. The cognoscible is the substance, which is proclaimed to be threefold. Substance is further the soul and the other [five inanimate substances], which are connected with transformation.[68]

> Concerning that, the linguistic unit "perceiving organ" – with regard to ultimately real perception well-known from the Canon – is well-known as a synonym of the living element (soul).[69]

Only equipped with the second stage, the whole argument from purification may aspire to prove that, since there is a method to purify the soul, and since the soul, being the cognizer, is ultimately also cognition, therefore a complete purification of the soul is tantamount to a completely purified cognition, i.e., omniscience. This inference would still require one more element to be proved, namely that completely purified cognition amounts to omniscience. A hidden premise in the whole argument is that such cognition in the completely purified condition faces no more impairment, understood as a cognitive limit. Therefore, such cognition, being freed from impurities, becomes at the same time freed from all limitations, in temporal, substantial, qualitative, or quantitative terms: it is cognition in all times, of all substances, of all their qualities, and in all possible numbers.

This was a decisive step to identify the soul, or the cognizing subject, with cognition / knowledge, not only with the locus of cognition / knowledge, as was the case in the Nyāya-Vaiśeṣika or Mīmāṃsā, which had a much weaker claim of the *ātman*, i.e., the cognitive subject, being the receptacle and site of knowledge, namely that:

> Knowledge is located only in the self. It is [therefore] understood that this [self] is the cogniser of this [knowledge]. And this [self] also has efficacy to remember and associate [things].[70]

The idea of immanent purity of the soul, which has to purify itself to regain its omniscience, was a recurrent motif in Jaina argumentation for omniscience, and we find it as early as with Kundakunda's *Samaya-sāra*:

> [278] Just as a gem made of [transparent] rock quartz crystal, being pure, does not modify itself because of red (*rāga*) and other colours, but only it is illuminated by other substances which are red etc., [279] similarly the cogniser, being pure, does not modify itself because of desire (*rāga*) and other [emotions], but only it is illuminated by other defects which are red etc.[71]

These two verses express a well-grounded conviction in Jainism that the soul's nature is cognition, and forms a nucleus of a future argument based on analogy. The identity of the soul and cognition is also expressed by Kundakunda in the *Pavayaṇa-sāra*:

> The cogniser is of the nature of cognition. Objects are the cognisable expanse for the cogniser, just like colours are [the cognisable expanse] for the eyes. They do not occur for each other, [i.e. they function for the congiser].[72]

On numerous occasions it is stated by Kundakunda and other Jaina writers that the soul is indestructible in its nature, also as a cognitive subject, and therefore it can endure both the negative implications of karmic matter that adheres to it as well as a burning-like purification process that expunges the karmic dirt from it:

> Just as gold, however much it is heated, never loses its nature of gold, similarly the cognitive subject, however much he is burnt by the rise of karman, never loses his nature of the cognitive subject.[73]

The belief in the indestructible and cognitive nature of the soul was crucial for the argument to prove omniscience for two reasons. It served as the second indispensable step in the argument from purification, and it provided assurance that the soul or its faculties would not be destroyed in the process. An important idea was that the substance, the way the Jainas understood it, retained its character throughout all processes and transformations it was undergoing. The idea was frequently expressed, e.g., by Kundakunda in the *Samaya-sāra*:

> [130] Such [golden] occurrences (sc. entities) as earrings etc. originate from a [substance] made of gold by nature, just as [iron] chains etc. originate from a [substance] made of iron by nature. [131] Also [all] such numerous occurrences (sc. states) of an ignorant person originate from a [substance] made of

> ignorance (sc. karman). On the other hand, all occurrences (sc. states) of the cognising subject originate from a [substance] made of cognition.[74]

The argument from purification in Jainism did not always have recourse to the idea of a gem enwrapped in impurities. In his proof, Hemacandra avails himself of a different example, not of a precious stone, but of clouds veiling the sun and the moon:

> The veiling of [the self] of knowing essence is possible through cognition-veiling and other types of karman just like the moon and the sun [can be covered] by dust, fog, cloud, veil etc.; and like a blow of wind strong enough can remove [the veils obscuring] the moon and the sun, so can meditation and contemplation [remove veils obscuring the knowing self].[75]

The opponent is quick enough to point out that the veiling of the moon and the sun can have its end because it has a beginning,[76] in accordance with the widespread conviction in India that "whatever has a beginning can have its end" (but the reverse implication does not hold, viz. "whatever can have its end must have a beginning"). But the analogy is not adequate, inasmuch as the veiling of the soul's cognitive faculties does not have its beginning, hence it does not follow that it can terminate. Hemacandra then reverts to the well-known analogy of the precious stone and similar objects, which seem to provide a much better illustration:

> Even though the dross [covering] an ore of gold has no beginning, one can see that the [dross] can be removed by [the process of] calcination in a clay furnace with the alkali, etc. Precisely in the same way even though cognition-veiling and other types of karman have no beginning, it is possible to remove them through repeated practice of the three jewels (see n. 53) which are [the proper] counteractive measures.[77]

To recapitulate, the complete argument from purification amounts to the following: "One can purify oneself completely, because there is a method. Since one's nature is consciousness, then once one is absolutely pure, one is endowed with absolute knowledge." This kind of proof was possible only within the framework of Jaina ontology and required three ontological presuppositions on which to rest: (1) a peculiar understanding of the soul's nature as intrinsically pure and omniscient; (2) the equation of cognition and the cognizer; and (3) the idea of karman as subtle matter that obstructs innate capacities of the soul, but does not transform its inner nature, for it was only in Jainism that the soul was considered the cognitive subject (i.e., the subject that experiences / processes knowledge), cognitive agent (*jñātṛ* = *jñāna-kartṛ*) and cognitive instrument (*akṣa*).

It is impossible to say who formulated the argument from purification for the first time and in what period, but it seems that Kundakunda's oeuvre might belong to the earliest corpus of works to which the argument may be traced back with certainty, at least in a condensed formulation, if not in a full-fledged proof formula (*prayoga*) of five or ten members (*pañcavayava, daśavayava*). And that should be probably located within the period of the fourth to fifth centuries. However, the building blocks for this argument are traceable much earlier, even if they are not given a form of proof. The earliest historical source, perhaps going back to the first two centuries B.C.E., could be the non-canonical *Isi-bhāsiyāiṃ*, which contains some doctrinal building blocks for a future argument:

> [21] All the time, moment after moment, the prudent and wise should eradicate blemishes of his own soul just like one removes [the dross covering an ore] of gold. [22] After one has seen [how consistently / how slowly] the destruction of the black tincture [of the golden ore], or the erection of an ant-hill, or the collection of honey [proceeds], [one understands that] the exertion in ascetic restraint is superior.[78]

These two verses already contain a conviction that the soul bears likeness to a precious mineral, in this case gold, not a gem, which can be purified through a gradual process of purification, or repeated practice, as well as that such a process takes place by gradually going through various stages.

6 An argument which briefly surfaced in the preceding (*vide infra*, § 1) is argument from potentiality, drafted by Samantabhadra in his *Āpta-mīmāṃsā* (ĀMī 5)[79]:

> [5] Objects that are subtle, concealed [from sight] and distant remain [always] directly perceptible to someone, because they are inferable, just as fire etc. [is inferable from visible smoke] – such is a proof of the omniscient [Jina].

The verse speaks of "objects that are subtle, concealed from sight and distant," which are generally known in India to naturally fall under the scope of supernatural perception (*yogi-pratyakṣa*), but here we deal with an apparently much stronger claim. The argumentative structure is as follows:

> Thesis (*pratijñā*): Objects that are subtle, concealed from sight and distant necessarily remain always directly perceptible to someone (*sūkṣmantarita-dūrarthāḥ pratyakṣāḥ kasyacid*),
>
> Logical reason (*hetu*): because they are inferable (*anumeyatvataḥ*),
>
> Example (*dṛṣṭānta*): just as fire etc. is inferable from visible smoke (*yathā 'gny-ādiḥ*).

What is not explicitly stated in the argument, but is taken for granted, is at least one premise: everything which is inferable (*anumeya*) is potentially perceptible (*pratyakṣa*) to someone, which makes the argument enthymematic. Being rather poor logic, the argument as such could only attempt to prove the existence of supernatural perception, which was believed to grasp the range of normally imperceptible objects. However, the argument is brought forth with the purpose of proving omniscience. That being the case, it presupposes another premise based on the argument from progression, in this case a progression not of subtlety or purity but of scope or magnitude: it is attested (or rather assumed) that some inferable objects can be perceived through supernatural perception, the scope of which is limited; therefore there must be a supernatural cognition that cognizes all inferable objects.

Samantabhadra was not the only one to deploy this argument. Centuries later Hemacandra takes recourse to the same argument, in fact quoting Samantabhadra (*sūkṣmantarita-dūrarthāḥ pratyakṣāḥ kasyacid*), with a significant modification, though:

> Objects that are subtle, concealed [from sight] and distant remain [always] directly perceptible to someone, because they are cognisable in a valid way (*prameya*), like a pot.[80]

He replaces "inferable" (*anumeya*) with "cognisable" (*prameya*) of much wider scope, which comprises proving properties, or probantia, i.e., "perceptible" and "inferable." Why he does so may be slightly puzzling, but one possible reason may have been the enthymematic premise, or invariable concomitance, that everything which is inferable (*anumeya*) is potentially perceptible (*pratyakṣa*), which does not really have to be the case. Another possible reason may have been an influence of the Vaiśeṣika claim, which I call the knowability thesis, viz. "whatever is existent is also nameable and knowable,"[81] which also served the Nayāyika-Vaiśeṣika to prove god's omniscience.[82,83] The argumentative structure, therefore, is therefore almost identical, with the logical reason of more comprehensive scope:

> Thesis (*pratijñā*): Objects that are subtle, concealed from sight and distant necessarily remain always directly perceptible to someone (*sūkṣmantarita-dūrarthāḥ kasyacit pratyakṣāḥ*),
>
> Logical reason (*hetu*): because they are cognisable (*prameyatvāt*),
>
> Example (*dṛṣṭānta*): like a pot (*ghaṭavad*).

The argument from potentiality – but it is also a defect from which two other arguments suffer, namely argument from the collapse of all knowledge and argument from progression by necessity – confuses two (or three) modalities: (1) possibility, potentiality or probability, on the one hand, and, on the other, (2) necessity, or determination, or (3) actuality.

Both the predicate of Samantabhadra's and Hemacandra's thesis (*pratyakṣa*, or "perceptible") and the logical reasons (*anumeya*, or "inferable" for Samantabhadra, and prameya, or "cognizable" for Hemacandra) are gerundives, which cover a range of meanings, including obligation, prescription, necessity, fitness, expectation, likelihood, possibility, etc., as described by Pāṇini (A 3.3.164; A 3.3.164;

A 3.3.164; A 3.3.169; A 3.1.125; A 3.3.170–171; A 3.3.170–171; A 3.3.171–172 and Kāś ad loc.). Being optatives (potentials) by default, they function as passive-like alternatives to the imperative and subjunctive modes, to the construction of the verb root arh with infinitive and to the future, and the optative mood (liṅ-suffixed of the sarvadhātuka type).[84]

It comes as no surprise that when one and the same grammatical device can express both possibility and necessity, ambiguity may easily follow. That explains the crucial step in the argument, i.e., the equation "*x* can be perceived," to "*x* must be perceived." It is quite obvious that what follows from "*x* can be perceived" is certainly not necessity ("*x* is necessarily perceived") or actuality ("*x* is actually perceived"), but merely possibility or absence of necessity ("it is not necessarily the case that *x* cannot be perceived").

But this (perhaps unintended, perhaps deliberate) confusion of modalities plays a crucial role in the argument, for it is one thing to claim that "subtle and other objects are perceptible" in the sense of possibility or potentiality (it is not impossible that an ordinary person may perceive them), which does not entail any omniscience claim, and quite another that "subtle and other objects are perceptible" in the sense of necessity (they have to be perceived by someone, viz. their being perceptible requires someone to perceive them), which is about the omniscience claim.

Such ambiguity plays a crucial role in the argument on potentiality, whose consecutive stages can be disambiguated as follows:

> Premise: Objects which are subtle, concealed from sight and distant are inferable (*anumeya*; possibility: "can be inferred"; *Samantabhadra*), or cognizable (*prameya*; possibility: "can be cognised"; *Hemacandra*).
>
> Step 2. Everything which is inferable (*anumeya*; possibility: "can be inferred") or cognizable (*prameya*; possibility: "can be cognized") is perceptible (*pratyakṣa*; possibility: "can be perceived").
>
> Step 3. These objects are perceived by someone (*pratyakṣa*; necessity: "must be perceived," or actuality: "are perceived").
>
> Conclusion: There is / must be (actuality: "is," or necessity: "must be") someone who perceives them, and that person is omniscient, the Jina.

This argument is found with other authors, too, and perhaps the most elaborate expression is given by Siddharṣigaṇi, who still uses Samantabhadra's logical reason that "all things are inferable" (*anumeya*):

> [1. The thesis:] The clear perception (sc. omniscience), whose domain is the range of all real things (sc. omniscience), is possible,
>
> [2. the logical reason:] inasmuch as the inference whose domain are [all] these [things] can be drawn;

[3. the invariable concomitance accompanied by the example:] in this world, for any *x*, if inference, whose domain is *x*, is drawn, perception grasping *x* reaches somehow the path of rising (sc. occurs), like [the inference as well as the perception] of fire, [viz. fire can be inferred as well as perceived];

[4. the application:] and inference is [indeed] drawn, whose province are all objects;

[5. the conclusion:] hence, there must be also a clear perception, that recognises these [all objects].[85]

The argument from potentiality is a clear case of equivocation, which uses one and the same term *pratyakṣa* ("perceivable") in two different meanings related to two different modalities: one conveys possibility ("can be perceived") and the other necessity ("must be perceived") or actuality ("is actually perceived"). Being based on such equivocation, the argument is a case of a logical fallacy. There are other logical fallacies this argument involves, one of them being circularity.[86]

7 A variety of this argument is what I would call the reductio argument from impossibility, and it is found in Akalaṅka Bhaṭṭa's *Siddhi-viniścaya*, and later quoted by Hemacandra[87]:

> If the cognition of a thing which is absolutely imperceptible is not possible, how is it possible that there is unanimity among people about, say, astronomy? If it is said: because of testimony, that furnishes another proof [of the existence of an omniscient being].[88]

Its structure can be analyzed as follows[89]:

Premise 1. Things which are absolutely imperceptible (e.g., subtle or distant) cannot be cognized.

Premise 2. People (e.g., astronomers) know of some things (e.g., celestial bodies, etc.) which are absolutely imperceptible to humans.

Premise 3. They have this knowledge supplied by someone or derive it from the scripture.

Conclusion 1. Premise 1 has to be abandoned.

Conclusion 2. That "someone" who provides the knowledge of imperceptible things must be omniscient.

The argument proceeds from the predicate "absolutely imperceptible" (*atyanta-parokṣe*) to the assumption that people do happen to have knowledge about such seemingly imperceptible things (*jñānavisaṃvāda*). That means that they either have to infer the existence of such absolutely imperceptible things or obtain it through testimony. In both cases, they have to derive their knowledge via another cognitive criterion (*pramāṇa*), which presupposes the existence of someone who must have a direct knowledge (*pratyakṣa*) of the imperceptibles, for both inference and testimony are claimed to be ultimately based on perception. That leads to a conclusion that things which are absolutely imperceptible to ordinary people turn out to be perceptible to those who are capable of perceiving them, i.e., to the omniscient. And this is where the argument from potentiality is hidden.

In addition to the modality equivocation, this argument involves circularity. For how can one obtain a knowledge that there exist objects which are so subtle that an ordinary person cannot perceive them, such as atoms or karmic matter, or objects which are permanently and inherently concealed from an ordinary person's sensory reach (sight etc.) or are so distant that one's senses can never reach them, and one will never be able to know these objects directly, i.e. one will never have any direct cognitive access to them? If such objects are there, they should be permanently barred from our knowledge and they would never be capable of entering our minds. The answer is, Akalaṅka argues, rather straightforward: because one can know of these objects via the scriptural testimony (*śruta*), i.e., via the statements of the omniscient. But then, how do the omniscient know these objects? Because they perceive them directly. And how can we know that the omniscient perceive these things directly, if we cannot verify this perceptually? Because this is what they tell us.

8 A peculiar argument of omniscience – which I would call the argument from the overlapping extensions – is found, again, with Kundakunda, who formulates it in his *Pavayaṇa-sāra*:

> [23] The soul is of the expanse[90] of cognition. Cognition is explained to be of the expanse of cognisible objects. The cognoscible is the world (*loka*) and non-world (*aloka*). Therefore, cognition is present everywhere.
>
> [24] For someone who [says that] the soul is not of the expanse of cognition, one thing is certain: the soul has to be either smaller or larger than the soul.
>
> [25] If [the soul were] smaller, then such cognition [larger from the soul] would be unconscious and would not cognise [anything].
>
> If [the soul were] larger than cognition, how could the soul cognise [anything] without cognition?[91]

This argument, if I understand Kundakunda's intention correctly, apparently rests on the idea of the somatic nature of mental phenomena, including cognitions, to demonstrate that the soul is omniscient by nature and its knowledge can embrace everything. It establishes the following extensions of entities:

> Premise 1: The soul is co-extensive with cognition, because its nature is cognition.

If it is not co-extensive with cognition, then:

(a) either it is smaller, but then the cognition of larger extension has to be partly uncognized by the soul;

(b) or it is larger, then some parts of the soul have to be unconscious, bereft of cognitive faculty.

Premise 2: Cognition as such is co-extensive with cognizable things, including the whole world inhabited by various substances (both animate and inanimate) and the infinite expanse beyond the world (*aloka*), because if things are cognizible, then they have to be reached by cognition, which in turn has to be of their extension.

Conclusion: The soul's cognition is co-extensive with cognizible things also in numerical terms: being co-extensive with all things, the soul can cognize them all.

This argument presents a number of difficulties, including the major premise that the soul and its cognition are one and the same. Putting it aside, first, it would run counter to the Jaina claim that souls are spatially limited under ordinary circumstances. As long as the soul remains in the cycle of rebirth (*saṃsāra*), its outer limits are restricted to the space within the body it inhabits.[92] When it becomes liberated, its size is diminished by one-third of the size of its last inhabited mundane body. The only moment in its career when its size equals that of the world (*loka*), but never goes beyond it into the expanse of the non-world (*aloka*) (due to the absence of the medium of motion, or *dharma*, in the non-world), is during the process of samudghāta, when the soul expands until it reaches the boundary of the world and thereby permeates the whole world for a single time unit, and the purpose of it is to shed off the remainders of karmic matter before the final liberation.[93] It is certainly not the moment when the soul cognizes anything in particular, and it could not be what Kundakunda would have intended. Second, equally problematic is the claim that the extension of cognition has to equal the extension, either spatially or numerically, of the objects it can cognize. Third, the argument also seems to present a case of equivocation in which the spatial extension is confused with numerical extension.

9 In addition to the above arguments, the Jainas have developed some more arguments to prove omniscience from the very nature of inference. One of them is the argument from an addressee of the omniscient lore, phrased by Hemacandra as a reply to a *Śābara-Bhāṣya* passage (ŚBh 1.2.2, see n.):

> [The Mīmāṃsaka say] "The injunction enables [people] to know anything of the following sort: past, present, future, subtle, concealed [from sight] and distant; there is no other instrument [to know these]" (ŚBh 1.2.2).[94] – Anyone who says so indeed intends that the knowledge of things that are past etc., [as explained in the Vedas, is meant] for some

> person (an addressee). Otherwise, for whom would the Veda communicate its contents about things that belong to the three time periods? Thus, the [Veda] communicating [the knowledge of all things to an addressee] gains (sc. presupposes) the entitled [addressee] who indeed knows the truth of things in the three time periods (sc. he becomes omniscient). This has been expressed [by Akalaṅka in his *Siddhi-viniścaya*]: "For whom would the Veda communicate the truth the objects (referents) of which belong to the three time periods, if the human, because of having indestructible veils, would not comprehend [the truth] in such a [all-comprehensive] manner?" In this way, because the communication of real things in the three time periods would be otherwise inexplicable, [we have] the proof of the supernatural absolute knowledge (omniscience).[95]

The argument used by Hemacandra was not his own, as he himself indicated, but phrased, probably for the first time, by Akalaṅka in the *Siddhi-Viniścaya*. The argument, as the context itself reveals, is directed against the Mīmāṃsaka, i.e., the followers of the Vedic tradition who at the same time reject the idea of omniscience; the opponents could not be the Naiyāyika-Vaiśeṣika, likewise the followers of the Vedic tradition, who however accepted the idea of an omniscient being, or god.

The structure of the argument from an addressee of the omniscient lore is as follow:

1 The scripture contains all knowledge, i.e. the knowledge of all things, including imperceptible things.
2 We know this because the scripture speaks of the imperceptible things.
3 For the scripture to be meaningful and purposeful, its content has to be known and communicable to at least certain people, i.e., to its addressees.
4 To be an addressee of the scripture means to be a competent receptacle of its knowledge that is fully transferable from the scripture to the addressee.
5 As a consequence, the contents of the scripture equals the knowledge of the addressee.

To conclude, to say that Vedas have an addressee is tantamount to saying that "there are people who know extrasensory things," which for Hemacandra implies nothing but omniscience.

Needless to say, there is a number of logical flaws in this argument, just to mention four. One is the validity of the first premise, i.e., that a scripture presents all knowledge of all things in all their aspects and at all times, i.e., all "atomic facts" which stand for any event, occurrence, thing in its momentary occurrence, an aspect of a thing, etc. Such atomic facts are necessarily endless in number, because things and their aspects and occurrences are infinite. Suppose one sentence reflects one piece of knowledge, which is a piece of knowledge related to one particular atomic fact. That being the case, to have a scripture which would contain all knowledge reflecting all atomic facts – and only such a scripture could meaningfully present knowledge which, while acquired by somebody, would amount to omniscience – it would have to consist of an infinite number of sentences, a sheer impossibility.

The second problem is, even granting a possibility of a scripture which potentially presents complete knowledge of everything, to have such a scripture is not identical to having a person who has actively acquired its full contents. In the case of a far less comprehensive compendium of knowledge, let's say *Encyclopaedia Brittanica*, once having read its full contents is not identical with active acquisition of all its contents, i.e., knowledge of everything it has to communicate.

Third, the impermissible stratagem Hemacandra employs is to equate knowing something from the scripture with having a direct knowledge of it, i.e., perceiving it directly: **āgama-balaja-jñāna* = *yogi-pratyakṣa*, inasmuch as the knowledge supposedly successfully derived from the scripture, when it concerns all atomic facts, is identified by Hemacandra with omniscience, which is a kind of supernatural perception (*pratyakṣa*) for the Jainas by default.

Fourth, like in most Jaina arguments to prove omniscience, they implicitly argue for the identity of supernatural perception, which clearly does not have to be perception of all things but merely of some, with omniscience.

10 A rather unsophisticated argument is the argument from the scripture, which in Hemacandra's formulation runs as follows:

> Only the [true] scripture which is in conformity with perception and inference is a proof for the existence of someone who perceives suprasensory things. And there is the following conformity: everything which is the scope of the [true] scripture [and is subject to] modal description is also the scope of perception etc. (sc. and of inference).[96]

Like in many other arguments, also in this case someone who is possessed of supernatural perception, i.e., "someone who perceives suprasensory things" (*atīndriyartha-darśin*), is equated with an omniscient person.

The argument can be systematically reconstructed as follows:

1 The scripture teaches that there are omniscient beings.
2 The content of the scripture is in agreement with perception and inference in the sense that:
   (a) It is contradicted neither by perception nor by inference.
   (b) Its scope is the same as the scope of perception and inference.
3 Hence there are omniscient beings whose existence can be perceived and inferred.

The argument is, of course, circular and rests on an unproven (and unprovable) premise that the scopes of perception, inference and scriptures fully overlap. From a Jaina perspective, however, this counterfactual assumption is doctrinally justifiable, because they claim that their scriptures, being an (ultimately indirect) emanation of the wisdom of the omniscient, describe the whole world, which is at the same time the scope of the omniscient's knowledge, or perception. But this presupposition is also circular in character.

11 Of more interest is the argument from ordinary perception:

> Even though [ordinary] sensory perception does not have as its domain the cognition of extrasensory [things], nevertheless the supernatural perception as such, produced by force of meditative concentration makes one know both external things as well as itself, hence this [ordinary] perception provides a proof of this [omniscience].[97]

At first this argument is rather unclear, but it boils down to the fact that we can directly perceive yogins of whom we know that they are engaged in certain practices which yield supernatural perception as a result, or in more detail:

1 With the help of ordinary sensory perception, we see yogins.
2 Yogins are engaged in meditative concentration.
3 The result of meditative concentration is supernatural perception.
4 Hence, the yogins enjoy supernatural perception, or omniscient knowledge.

The argument in this shape would lead Hemacandra to accept that any yogin, also outside of the religious confines of Jainism, whom he sees and who practices meditative concentration, is also endowed with supernatural perception and is at the same time omniscient. And this is certainly something he would not like to accede to. Therefore, the more accurate reconstruction of this argument would probably be as follows:

1 With the help of ordinary sensory perception, we see yogins.
2 Yogins are engaged in meditative concentration.
3 The result of meditative concentration is supernatural perception.
4 The yogins enjoy lower forms of supernatural perception.
5 Since supernatural perception can be graded, there are higher forms of it.
6 Hence, there must be a yogin who enjoys a perfect form of supernatural perception, which is omniscience.

The argument phrased in the above form would allow us to exclude "ordinary" yogins from the class of omniscient beings and reserve the special omniscient status for the selected ones of the Jaina creed. The argument in this shape would run in two stages: the first would be the argument from ordinary perception, and the second stage would be the argument from progression.

One of the problems with the argument from ordinary perception is that a mere observation (ordinary sensory perception) has a behavioristic character: we can observe the outward behavior of the person, but on the mere basis of such observation we can never tell whether the person outwardly appearing to be engaged in Yoga practice is really engaged in meditative concentration or has merely fallen asleep. Granted that it were possible to distinguish between different mental states of such a person by mere observation, it does not suffice to claim that the person is capable of perceiving extrasensory things, because we have no epistemic access to that person's actual cognitive states. All we can do is to rely on that person's own testimony.

12 Another strategy to prove omniscience is by way of demonstrating that is it not possible to disprove it; and if omniscience cannot be disproved, it has to be accepted. One version of it is the argument from the empty subject, which Hemacandra phrases as the following reductio-type paradox:

> Inference cannot disprove this [omniscience] either. Because no inference can be formulated without the grasp (i.e. acceptance) of the subject of inference (property-possessor). And if [we can] grasp the subject of inference (property-possessor), such an inference [against omniscience] can in no way be produced because it is subverted by the valid cognitive procedure that grasps this subject of inference (property-possessor)].[98]

The idea behind this argument is that any valid statement, including logical proofs, must have an existent subject, viz. the subject of a proposition to be meaningful requires denotation. A thesis (*pratijñā*) of a proof formula (*prayoga*) has to likewise be a meaningful sentence, ergo it requires a subject which has a denotation, i.e., which directly refers to an existing thing. That is stipulated by a principle actively promoted by the Nyāya school of logic: any meaningful subject of a sentence has to correspond to a real thing, because otherwise it would not be possible to ascribe any truth value to a sentence with a vacuous subject. For instance, it is not possible to determine whether the following sentences are true or false: "a square circle is a square" and "a square circle is not a square," or "a square circle is a circle" and "a square circle is not a circle." For an assertoric (i.e., non-modal) sentence to be meaningful it is required to be either true of false. Such entities as "square circle" or Pegasus are empty subjects, and not only Alfred North Whitehead and Bertrand Russell were well aware of the problem, but also Indian logicians.

This is precisely the principle which Hemacandra attempts to employ in his peculiar way: when we formulate a negative inference about *x* to deny its existence, and if *x* does not exist, then the inference with such an empty subject "*x*" in the thesis cannot be valid. If such a statement as "omniscience does not exist" is invalid, with omniscience regarded as non-existent and therefore vacuous, then the contrary statement has to be true: "omniscience exists." Further, if we are able to rationally speak of *x*, then any inference denying the existence of *x* is also invalid.

However, if that argument were logically valid, we would never be able to deny the existence of non-existent things; for instance, a sentence "solid liquid does not exist" would force us to accept the opposite "solid liquid exists" by reductio.

To accept the requirement at its face value that the subject must denote, i.e., refer to something existent, for the sentence to be meaningful and truth-value-decidable, what we would really mean by "*x*" as a subject of a proposition would actually be "the existing *x*." Consequently, "The existing x does not exist" would plainly be self-contradictory, and we would therefore have to reject it and deny the proposition: "The existing *x* does not exist"; that is, we would be obliged to affirm: "The existing *x* exists." The argument as such has to be fallacious, for otherwise it would be all too easy to prove the existence of anything one cares to imagine. For instance, one could not meaningfully assert that "The unicorn does not exist," because of the requirement that, for the sentence to be meaningful, "unicorn" has to denote, i.e., refer to a real object. But why are such arguments fallacious?

First, there is obviously no necessary connection between the existing and the description implicit in subject terms "omniscience," "solid liquid," or "unicorn." But how does this conform to the condition that the subject term should have a denotation?

This is quite easy to demonstrate by appealing to the theory of denotation and contextual analysis, for instance, and by analyzing such sentences as "omniscience does not exist" to atomic propositions:

> For some *x*, (i) *x* is omniscience and, (ii) for all *y*, if *y* is omniscience then $y = x$, and, (iii) there is no such *x*.

Thanks to this analytical application of the method of the elimination of the denotations of denoting phrases that actually express vacuous or non-denoting concepts, we can see that the above is a molecular formula of a more complex structure. In fact, this reveals that the actual subject term which Hemacandra wants to see in the proposition is not "omniscience" but it consists of two ideas: *x* and $\exists x$ (where *x* stands for omniscience). This analysis reveals also circularity of the argument: existence is necessarily attached to the subject term in the premise of an argument whose conclusion is to confirm this existence.

With this defective logic, Hemacandra finds himself in quite good company. What he actually did in his proof was very similar to Anselm's and Descartes' methods applied in their respective ontological arguments for the existence of god: they linked existence in a necessary way to god, which consequently was expected to make it impossible to deny his existence in the proposition "god does not exist," where "god" in fact means "existing god."

13 Hemacandra adds one more argument to show that it is a logical impossibility to deny omniscience of any given person because there is no way to falsify omniscience of someone who is omniscient. It is only possible to confirm that someone is not omniscient. Let us call this proof the argument from partial description:

> When you formulate the proof to deny this [omniscience in the following manner]: "The particular person under discussion is not omniscient,

> because he is a speaker . . . , like a man in street", this is not correct, because [the logical reason "speaker" is not a complete statement:] if [the logical reason "speaker" means] that there is a speaker of [true] things comprehended through valid cognitive procedures, then [your proof] is self-contradictory, because any speaker of this sort [who always tells the truth] is no one else but an omniscient person! If [the logical reason "speaker" means] that there is a speaker of false things then this is a case of [an argument] in which what you want to prove is [already] proved (viz. a particular kind of fallacy), because it is generally accepted that people who speak things contradicted by valid cognitive procedures are not omniscient.[99]

The above argument rests on a semantic theory, of crucial importance for the Jainas, that every sentence is necessarily incomplete and its intent should be delimited by or derived from a particular context to which it applies. According to this theory, we always use incomplete descriptions or statements and to properly comprehend them we have to first disambiguate them, viz. to specify precisely their context and meaning. This idea – occasionally expressed by the Jainas with a maxim (*nyāya*): "Every sentence functions with a restriction" – lies also at the core of their syād-vāda and naya-vāda, called respectively a "complete account" (*sakaladeśa*) and "incomplete account" (*vikaladeśa*).[100]

Certainly, we can imagine a situation, as a theoretical experiment, when all a person has said so far has always proved true. However, this does not guarantee that all the person will say will necessarily be true in the future. The reasoning Hemacandra has in mind is that of sampling (§§ 14, 17) when we carry out a limited number of tests verifying a certain hypothesis "all x are P" and on the basis of these tests we conclude that, since "a number n of our observations verified that the n cases of x are P," therefore "all x are P." The generalization clearly does not logically follow from the limited number of observations, and this is a well-known case of induction. And to verify the truth value of all the propositions the speaker has to say about all the existent things in all their past, present and future aspects is impossibility, also because it is impossible for such a speaker to express all such statements in a limited time, e.g., one's lifetime.

14 The argument from no counter-proof, which Kumārila Bhaṭṭa recounts succinctly himself, must have also been used by the Jainas, although I have been unable to trace its formulation in any Jaina work which would with certainty predate Kumārila:

> If there is an omniscient person [who knows everything] through all six cognitive criteria, who can deny this?[101]

This argument shifts the weight of proof on to the other side: now it is the opponent's task to disprove the existence of an omniscient being, if such is his claim. The implication of the argument is that it is not possible to disprove the idea of omniscience from the level, or perspective, of a non-omniscient person, whereas it is only on the level of omniscience ("meta-level") that one may evaluate the truth of statements uttered on the lower level of non-omniscience ("first level).

This argument was known to Samantabhadra, who however is most probably later than or a younger contemporary of Dharmakīrti and hence Kumārila (*vide supra*, n. 41):

> Only you, being faultless, are such [an omniscient person], whose statements are contradicted neither by reasoning nor by scriptural testimony (sc. you are the pramāṇa). There is no contradiction, [because] what is accepted by you [as a tenet of your teaching] is not sublated by what is well proven.[102]

We find this argument also with Hemacandra:

> [Omniscience exists] because there is no counter-proof. – [In this sūtra] the syntactical relation is: it is proved "both because it is firmly determined and because a cognitive criterion (sc. cognitive procedure) that would disprove it is impossible, [and omniscience can be experienced] like pleasure etc." (LT 1.4). For it is as follows: is perception the counter-proof disproving omniscience or is another cognitive criterion [the counter-proof]?[103]

The argument is extensive and covers a few sections (§§ 59–62), in the course of which he essays to demonstrate that any kind of cognition, whether of (sensory or extrasensory) perceptual, inferential or scriptural character, which should serve to disprove omniscience, would ultimately have to be such as to comprise all objects in all places and in all the three times (*sakala-deśa-kāla-viṣaya*), but that would necessarily amount to omniscience. No cognition whose scope in place and time (*niyata-deśa-kāla-viṣaya*) is limited could adjudicate whether a particular person's cognition can indeed grasp all objects everywhere and at all times.

First Hemacandra mentions a counter-argument against supernatural perception, namely: 'This [supernatural perception] is subverted not by operative perception but by inoperative [perception],'[104] which means that we can prove that there is no supernatural perception not because we see a positive fact of the absence of supernatural perception, but precisely because we do not see any positive instance of supernatural perception. In his reply, Hemacandra shows that such an argument is inconclusive: we can predicate of instances we have examined directly, but there a wide range of cases we will never be able to examine:

> If this [falsifying perception] operates by having as its object something in a particular place and time, we agree. But if it operates by having as its object everything in all places and times, then it is not possible without direct perception of an assembly of people present in all places and times! Hence your thesis is not proved.[105]

We can only know particular instances and we cannot make any generalization on their basis. Therefore, even if we can verify that in a number of places there is no observable case of supernatural perception, it proves only what it says: that there are no cases of supernatural perception in situations investigated by us. But this is not a solid basis for any generalized, universal judgment. Interestingly enough, the Jainas avail themselves of the same method against the Mīmāṃsaka as the Mīmāṃsaka (e.g., Kumārila) applied in order to show that it will never be possible to fully know invariable concomitance (*vyāpti*) as the basis for our inferences and reasonings, for our knowledge of it will always have to be partial and inconclusive. All we are capable of doing is to determine that a postulated vyāpti relation does not hold, i.e., we can falsify it. This issue of generalization from individual instances is very much akin to Karl Raimund Popper's criticism of the nature of induction, and the solution he proposed. Only falsification has a definitive character, whereas any number of instances of verification are never sufficient. Hemacandra's argument goes on, however, where Karl Popper left off. Hemacandra adds that if Jaimini or anyone else had the capacity to know that there is no supernatural perception in the whole world, that would precisely amount to omniscience, or supernatural cognition, for someone who is capable of formulating such a conclusion is by definition omniscient.

The above argument was in fact borrowed by Hemacandra from Siddharṣigaṇi:

> [Can you deny the possibility of omniscience] [1] by the invariable concomitance [limited to] a specific place and time or [2] by ascending to all places and times? [Ad 1] If the first alternative [is assumed], then just the way the quintuplet of cognitive criteria – negating the domain which is that [particular pot] – proves the absence of the pot, etc., in a certain place, in the same way that [quintuplet of cognitive criteria] – negating also the domain which is the sensation of all real things – could prove the absence [of the sensation of all real things] delimited by a specific location and [specific] circumstances, but not everywhere. And consequently, that [sensation of all objects] would be difficult to negate, like the pot, etc. [Ad 2] If the second alternative [is maintained], it is not possible at all, for [only a person] perceiving directly sensations of the lot of people occurring in all places and times is entitled to express himself in that manner, namely "There is no sensation of all objects anywhere," [but] not you because [you] do not accept the possibility [of existence] of such a person. In the opposite case, precisely such a [person] who – having determined [the facts himself] – stated [explicitly the denial of the possibility of an omniscient person] in this manner, indeed such a [person] would be someone who has insight into the cognition pervading the range of all real things.[106]

In the remaining portions of the argument Hemacandra borrows from a longer passage of Akalaṅka Bhaṭṭa's *Laghīyas-traya*:

> This [extra-sensory perception (*atīndriya-jñāna*), i.e. omniscience,] exists, both because it is firmly determined and because a cognitive criterion (sc. cognitive procedure) that would disprove it is impossible, [and the extra-sensory perception can be experienced] like pleasure etc. [A cognitive

> criterion (sc. cognitive procedure) that would disprove it is impossible,] because a complete knowledge of a whole assembly of people, each of whom is devoid of cognition that pervades all existent cognoscible things, would be inexplicable without this [extra-sensory perception]. There is no one who would know the truth that this [extra-sensory perception] does not exist, because no one like that is apprehended – [such a person would be non-existent] like a sky flower.[107]

The difficulty with the argument is more of rhetorical or metalogical character than merely logical. Anyone proposing a thesis is also obliged to provide a rational justification for it: a hypothesis requires some kind of validation. The Jainas do have their thesis of omniscience, which obviously stands in need of proof. Even though their opponents may seem to likewise forward their own thesis contradicting it ("omniscience does not exist"; see counter-arguments, § 10), these two are not on a par with each other, and the difference lies not merely in the fact that one is an assertion and the other negation. It is not justified on the part of the Jainas to shift the burden of proof on to those who deny their thesis, because it is they who postulate some positive entity whose existence is under ordinary circumstances imperceptible.

15 There is still one curious case – the argument on sacrilege – which hardly fulfills any rigid criteria of a rational proof, inasmuch as it appeals to the emotional side and religious fury inflamed by irreverence. Nevertheless, it does occasionally feature in a list of proofs of omniscience. Again, we find it in Hemacandra, who having first provided a number of rational arguments is still confronted with the following argument:

> Fine, let us admit that there is omniscience in case of a divine being (e.g. *Viṣṇu* or *Śiva*), but it is not possible in case of any man, even though he is endowed with knowledge and [good] conduct,[108]

Hemacandra simply explodes in fury, and going out of any limits merely throws invectives for several lines, without producing any reasonable rejoinder. It all begins with:

> O! You sinner guilty of [the sin of] disavowing the omniscient being! You lie-teller![109]

His reply clearly does not appeal to the rational side: How can one be in a position to deny the existence of the omniscient being who has done so much for humankind and has suffered so much for the sake of humankind? Whether or how such an attitude is commensurable with the Jaina precept of ahiṃsā, which also involves the avoidance of verbal offense, is a separate question.

This kind of emotional interlude in argumentation is certainly not a solitary case. We find it also with other authors of other philosophical schools in very similar contexts, for instance in Bhāsarvajña's *Nyāya-bhūṣaṇa*: this does not try to prove the existence of supernatural perception but takes recourse to a moral-soteriological argument of psychological nature: "if you deny it, you'll go to hell, because it's a sin":

> The existence of yogins [possessed of supernatural perception'][110] is well known (sc. needs no proof) from texts of revelation, texts of authoritative tradition, from mythical texts, stories and from a few treatises on Yoga. Any denial of those [yogins endowed with supernatural perception] generates outspokenly the highest sin, which is the cause of rebirth in hell and other [lower regions] as well as [the cause] of infinite torments.[111]

16 Perhaps unsurprisingly, Indian authors hardly ever deploy an argument in which the knowledge of the existence of an omniscient person is authoritatively derived from the scripture the validity of which is based on its all-knowing author, because the circularity it involves is too conspicuous. An unusual exception is Haribhadra-Sūri:

> [594] The proof of [the existence / authority of] an [omniscient being] is through the scripture, because [the idea of] such [a person] is a result of scriptural injunction. Further, the scripture[112] is both intrinsically valid and eternal like [Vedic] revelation. [626] To conclude, it is logically correct to establish as distinct righteousness and unrighteousness in this way on the basis of the scripture, the contents of which is everything, which has been revealed by the omniscient, not in any other way whatsoever.[113]

We can call it an argument from the scripture.

17 We also come across a variant of the above argument, the argument from verifiability of the speaker's statements, which is not overtly circular but suffers from other logical deficiencies. It is found in Jinabhadra-gaṇin's *Viśeṣavaśyaka-bhāṣya*:

> There [may be] some suspicion as to why [I am] omniscient. It is because I remove all doubts. Or, you may ask about anything which you do not know [and I will reply] so that you would have confidence.[114]

In it the alleged omniscient person asks us to verify all his statements. A process of verification has to necessarily be restricted in time: it is not possible to ask all questions about everything in real time, so the only available method is by sampling.

It is logically flawed on at least two counts. First, even if we have positively verified the truth of a person x's reply r as well as his next reply $r + 1$, and his subsequent replies $(r + 1) + 1$ up to $(r + 1) + \ldots + n$, it does not follow that his reply $(r + 1) + \ldots + n + (n + 1)$ is equally accurate. Even if 999,999 replies prove accurate, a millionth reply may still be false or he may not know the answer to the millionth question. This is the same problem as in the case of induction. Second, the replies may concern a range of things which cannot be known, are imperceptible or practically unverifiable. And this is where the circularity creeps in: to be able to accept the veracity of the person *x*'s reply about such a practically unverifiable issue, we have to rely on the person's authority alone, and the person's authority rests on our acceptance of the person's replies.

18 There is an argument to prove extrasensory perception, but not omniscience, found in the Vaiśeṣika literature whose Jaina counterpart I have failed to find, probably because it could by definition not be used to prove omniscience. I would call it the argument from an analogy of a newly married girl, and it is found at the very end of the following passage from the *Praśastapādabhāṣya*:

> The seer's perception is described as such cognition which makes things known as they are (sc. in correspondence to truth) and which arises, by virtue of the contact of the soul and the mind and due to special moral endowment (*dharma*), in the seers, who are revealers of the Vedic lore, as the insight into past, future and present, and into extrasensory things such as moral law etc., which are expounded in the scriptures and which are not expounded [at all]. This [supernatural perception] is possessed by gods and seers in an extensive form, [but] also sometimes by ordinary people, for instance when a newly married girl says: "my heart tells [me] that tomorrow my brother will come".[115]

The Vaiśeṣika distinguish this kind of intuition (*pratibhā*) from *yogi-pratyakṣa*, even though the critics of the idea, the Mīmāṃsakas and the Cārvākas, take these two (*yogi-pratyakṣa* and *ārṣa-pratyakṣa*) jointly. Such an intuition is used by Praśastapāda to provide an empirical example that extrasensory perception does exist.[116] For the Jainas, this argument would not serve the purpose because, obviously, such a bride's extrasensory perception, even though it would be demonstrated via such an instantiation, could not be immediately equated with Jina's omniscience.

19 We can summarize the arguments for supernatural perception (*yogi-pratyakṣa*), equated with omniscience (*sarva-jñāna, kevala*), so far collected in the following list:

argument from progression (§ 1)
reverse argument from progression (§ 2)
argument from progression by necessity (§ 3)
argument from the collapse of all knowledge (§ 4)
argument from purification (§ 5)
argument from potentiality (§ 6)
reductio argument from impossibility (§ 7)

argument from the overlapping extensions (§ 8)
argument from an addressee of the omniscient lore (§ 9)
argument from the scripture (§ 10)
argument from ordinary perception (§ 11)
argument from the empty subject (§ 12)
argument from partial description (§ 13)
argument from no counter-proof (§ 14)
argument from sacrilege (§ 15)
argument from the scripture (§ 16)
argument from verifiability of the speaker's statements (§ 17)
argument from an analogy of a newly married girl (§ 18).

The list is certainly not exhaustive and more argumentative devices will certainly be found in future research.

20 As we have seen, classical Indian thinkers, especially representatives of Jainism, Buddhism, the systems of Sāṃkhya-Yoga and the post-fifth-century Nyāya-Vaiśeṣika, formulated a whole range of arguments to prove the existence of omniscience and an omniscient being, either a human or suprahuman, i.e., god (*īśvara*). Even though none of these arguments was logically tight and refutation-proof, they were all in use, some of them winning a particular popularity which was not at all associated with their more sound logical structure than others'. Whether a particular proof was opted for depended, it seems, more likely on individual liking and "dogmatic" preference rather than on strictly logical grounds. Some of these arguments were used by non-Jaina thinkers "merely" to prove the existence of extrasensory perception, not necessarily omniscience.

However, two arguments stand out as uniquely Jainistic. These are the argument from progression with its versions (§§ 1–3) and the argument from purification (§ 2.5).

The first of these, the argument from progression, was also used by representatives of other philosophical schools. The Jaina peculiarity, however, was that the argument was advanced not to prove an "ordinary" extrasensory perception (*yogi-pratyakṣa*), grasping normally imperceptible objects but with a limited compass. In fact, as indicated before, the argument was produced in order to prove omniscience, which was implicitly, in the argumentative structure, identified with omniscience.

It should be remembered that for the Jainas the idea of extrasensory perception connoted two different things. First, it was a generic description for the three types of direct perception which was neither mediated by sense organs nor by a quasi-sense, or the mind: clairvoyance (*avadhi*), telepathy or mind-reading (*manaḥ-paryāya* / *manaḥ-paryaya*), and perfect knowledge or omniscience (kevala), and with its first two varieties (*avadhi* and *manaḥ-paryaya*) it was comparable to what was almost universally called *yogi-pratyakṣa* in other schools. And indeed, extrasensory perception in Jainism was sometimes likewise called *yogi-pratyakṣa*, even though the term itself never occurred in taxonomic descriptions of cognitive faculties in Jainism. Instead, the Jainas used different terms – *avadhi, manaḥ-paryāya / manaḥ-paryaya*, and *kevala* – treated as more or less synonymous with *yogi-pratyakṣa* in certain contexts, albeit in no way co-extensive with each other.

In its second meaning, extrasensory perception is equated with omniscience, especially in such proofs as those described above. In most of them, the distinction between these two meanings of extrasensory perception was intentionally blurred and was often an integral part of the argumentative structure: all these arguments could prove was, at most, existence of some kind of suprasensory faculty, not of cognition grasping all that exists, existed and will exist.

As a matter of fact, for the Jainas the idea of supernatural perception indicates the existence of intermediate stages leading towards the apex, perfect cognition (*kevala*). The precondition for *yogi-pratyakṣa* was the practice of Yoga and moral law (*dharma*), for instance in Vaiśeṣika. In Jainism it was not, at least not in the case of the lowest type of extrasensory perception, clairvoyance (*avadhi*) which, as it was believed, could also be obtained by denizens of hell. So clairvoyance exceeded ordinary perception, but was still limited in scope, in subtlety and in moral predispositions. Higher than that was mind-reading (*manaḥ-paryaya*), which required high moral standing and provided most subtle vision. This progression would culminate in the cognition that was highest and most subtle of all, namely omniscience. As we can see, the typological hierarchy of types of direct, extrasensory cognition (*pratyakṣa*) reproduced the same pattern on which the argument from progression was based: the types of supernatural perception replicate the upward ladder of epistemic faculties.

The progression of ever subtler, more extensive, and perfect cognitive faculties fits well into an ontological presupposition of the Jaina system, namely the idea that our cognitive faculties are limited by ordinary matter, in the form of sense organs and the mind, as well as by subtle matter in the form of karman, conceived of as a subtle veil enveloping and restricting our cognitive instruments. The lowest forms of cognitive faculties were various stages of ordinary sensory perception, and then the subvarieties of the two main types of extrasensory perception, viz. *avadhi* and *manaḥ-paryaya*, believed to be obscured by corresponding subvarieties of the so-called veiling karmans (*āvaraṇīya-karman*). A gradual removal of such veils would, it was claimed, automatically result in a gradual rise in cognitive faculties and progressive growth of the scope of extrasensory perception. An effect of a complete removal of such karmic veils would be absolute knowledge, or omniscience.

In this manner, both clairvoyance (*avadhi*) and telepathy (*manaḥ-paryāya / manaḥ-paryaya*) were not merely corollaries of a range of religious or magical beliefs, prevalent among various groups in South Asia, in diverse supernatural phenomena and extraordinary cognitive faculties that some advanced spiritual practitioners were postulated to possess, which had to somehow be accommodated within established tenets. At the same time these two kinds of extrasensory perception were given their adequate space within the typology of cognitive faculties not only as some kind of usual faculties people believed existed, but also as necessary transitional phases on the progressive path to perfection, in the form of omniscience as its logical concomitants.

In this sense, even though they probably entered Jainism at the very outset as a piece and parcel of early beliefs in supernatural faculties, gradually they came to be logical requirements not only of the spiritual path to perfection but also, and perhaps primarily for Jaina thinkers at a later historical stage, of argumentative and rhetorical exigency.

In this sense, the argument from progression was embedded in Jaina epistemology in quite a unique fashion.

Even more unique was the argument from purification, which could not be formulated within the ontological and epistemological framework of any other school of Indian thought, including Nyāya and Vaiśeṣika.

An integral part of the argument was the conviction that the purification process of the self (*ātman*), or soul (*jīva*), i.e., the ultimate cognitive subject, had a direct impact on the purity of its cognitive faculties, and vice versa, because both were ultimately one and the same substance. The prime source of impurity of the self was believed to be subtle karmic matter of various types and material limitations. Since an impurity-free condition of the self was conceived of as real possibility, it had to correspond to a similar limit-free condition of cognitive faculties. Anything that affected, positively or negatively, the nature of the self had to also affect the quality of the cognitive apparatus and faculties to the same measure.

Nyāya and Vaiśeṣika could not devise a similar argument from purification because the idea that knowledge is the nature of the soul did not exist.

The equation of the self with its cognition was an indispensable element of the argument from purification. The identity of both was usually taken for granted and treated as an established, definite tenet, as something not in need of any additional proof. However, sometimes a need was felt to provide some kind of rational justification for it. Several attempts have been made among Jaina philosophers to prove the intrinsically conscious or knowing nature of the soul (*jīva, ātman*), conscious or knowing in both aspects: conscious of its own self (*sva-nirbhāsin, cetanā-svabhāva*) and conscious of objects external to it (*anya-nirbhāsin, prakāśa-svabhāva*). One such proof, highly interesting from the perspective of comparative history of philosophical ideas, was employed as a second stage of the argument from purification, meant to prove the identity of the self and its cognition, by Hemacandra in *Pramāṇa-mīmāṃsā* in order to establish that conscious character of the cognitive subject, or soul:

> The self has a knowing essence, because he/she cannot doubt his own essence. If *x* does not have a knowing essence, *x* is not someone who cannot doubt his/her essence, like a pot. And the self is not of this sort, for as everyone knows nobody [can entertain] the doubt "Do I exist or not?".[117]

The argument addresses the question of doubt as an essential element to establish one's own existence, and its underlying elements seem to be some sort of a forerunner of the Cartesian argument, although the structure appears a little different from the Cartesian cogito ergo sum argument. Hemacandra formulates two other arguments of similar structure, with different logical reasons (hetu):

> The self has a knowing essence, because he is a conscious agent,[118]

i.e. he able to represent objects in his/her consciousness; and

> The self has a knowing essence, [because he/she is the agent of the act of knowing (*jñapti-kriyā-kartṛtvāt*)[119]].[120]

Since in Jainism the true nature of the soul was knowledge, then naturally a complete self-realization, or perfection understood as a full accomplishment of one's own nature, in its case had to necessarily amount to omniscience.

In the light of the above, the admission of extrasensory perception (*yogi-pratyakṣa*) in Jainism – in the form of two lower forms (clairvoyance and telepathy) and the "cognitive vertex" in the form of perfect omniscience – came to be also a logical requirement in the arguments which ultimately were to prove a possibility of liberation, as a necessary corollary of omniscience.

Notes

* Some ideas of the present chapter were communicated during a lecture '*Yogi-pratyakṣa* in Jainism and its background' on June 5, 2002 at Abteilung für Indologie, Universität Zürich. Some ideas of this chapter were presented at the International Seminar on Yogic Traditions of India with special reference to the Jaina Yoga, December 7–9, 2006, Delhi, organized by Bhogilal Leherchand Institute of Indology. A preliminary version of the chapter was delivered at the conference on Jainism and Yoga, organized by the Centre of Jaina Studies of the School for Oriental and African Studies at the University of London on March 18–19, 2010. A significant part of the present research has been generously supported by the National Science Centre of Poland (Research Project: History of Classical Indian Philosophy: non-Brahmanic Schools, National Science Centre, 2011/01/B/HS1/04014).

1 Supernatural perception was absent in the original *Vaiśeṣika-Sūtra*, as it existed prior to Praśastapāda; see: Wezler (1982), Honda (1988), Isaacson (1993), and Balcerowicz (2010: 308 ff.).

2 Secondary literature on the subject is extremely ample; a good introduction to the topic is Sinha (1934) and Matilal (1986). An excellent critique on the subject by a classical Indian philosopher is Jayarāśi Bhaṭṭa's *Tattvôpaplava-siṃha* (TUS), especially its first chapter on perception.

3 NS 1.1.4 *indriyartha-sannikarṣôtpannaṃ jñānam avyapadeśyam avyabhicāri vyavasāyatmakaṃ pratyakṣam.*

4 MS 1.1.4: *sat-samprayoge puruṣasyêndriyāṇāṃ buddhi-janma tat pratyakṣam.*

5 ŚDī$_2$ ad MS 1.1.4, p. 35.20: *pratyakṣaṃ tāvad indriyartha-saṃprayoga-janyatvena vidyamānôpalambhanatvād bhaviṣyati dharme na nimittam.*

6 ŚDī$_2$ ad MS 1.1.4, p. 36.13–14: *kiṃ punar indriya-lakṣaṇaṃ cakṣur-ādiṣu manasi canusyūtam. ucyate: yat saṃprayukte viśadavabhāsaṃ vijñānaṃ janayati tad indriyam ity ucyate, tac ca dvi-vidham, bāhyam ābhyantaraṃ ca, bāhyaṃ pañca-vidhaṃ ghrāṇa-rasana-cakṣus-tvak-śrotratmakam. āntaraṃ tv ekaṃ manaḥ.*

7 ŚDī$_2$ ad MS 1.1.5, p. 49.10–12: *tasmād avaśyaṃ sākṣāt-saṃprayoga-jatvaṃ lakṣaṇam ity aṅgī-kartavyam, ataḥ śukti-rajata-vedane 'pi vyabhicarābhavād anarthakas tat sator vyatyayaḥ. satyam—sākṣāt-saṃprayoga-jatvaṃ lakṣaṇam.*

8 YDī ad SKā 5, p. 76: *"śrotr-ādi-vṛttiḥ" iti vārṣagaṇaḥ,* as well as YDī ad SKā 1ab, p. 5.11: *śrotr-ādi-vṛ ttiḥ pratyakṣam.*

9 NB 1.4: *tatra pratyakṣaṃ kalpanapoḍham abhrāntam.*

10 For various models in the period to the eighth century C.E., we can distinguish at least 14 models of cognitive faculties which assign various roles to perception, which is one of these faculties: see Balcerowicz (forthcoming/a).

11 PMī 1.13–14: *viśadaṃ pratyakṣam. pramāṇantaranapekṣêdantayā pratibhāso vā vaiśadyam.*

12 PMīV 1.13 § 46, p. 11: *na hi śābdanumānadivad pratyakṣaṃ svôtpattau śabda-liṅgadi-jñānaṃ pramāṇantaram apekṣate.*

13 For details, see Balcerowicz (2005).

14 MŚV 4.26:

> *atītanāgate 'py arthe sūkṣme vyavahite 'pi ca /*
> *pratyakṣaṃ yogināṃ iṣṭaṃ kaiścin muktatmanām api //*

15 See Wezler (1982), Honda (1988) and Isaacson (1993) and Balcerowicz (2010: 308 ff.)

16 See NBh 1.1.3, p. 9.8–9: *pratyakṣaṃ yuñjānasya yoga-samādhi-jam "ātmany ātma-manasoḥ saṃyoga-viśeṣād ātmā pratyakṣaḥ" iti.* – "[Another proof of the existence of soul, beside verbal testimony of an authority or inference, is] perception of a [yogin] presently engrossed [in meditation], which is born in the state of concentration in yoga [in accordance with] the following [sūtra of VS(C) 9.13]: 'Due to particular connection of the self and the mind in the self [there arises] perception of the self'." The fact that VS(C) 9.13 is cited in NBh attests to the temporal priority of Vaiśeṣka into which the idea of extrasensory perception was first introduced.

17 Thus according to Candrānanda, VSV(C): . . . *vyāpaka-dravyeṣv ātmanasaṃyukteṣv apratiṣiddhatma-saṃyogeṣu ca paramaṇv-ādiṣûbhābyāṃ saṃyukteṣu* . . .

18 See Isaacson (1993) and Honda (1988).

19 VS(C) 9.13–17, VS(Ś) 9.1.11–15, VS(D) 9.11–13:

> 13: *ātmany ātma-manasoḥ saṃyoga-viśeṣād ātma-pratyakṣam.*
> [VS(D) : absent]
> 14: *tathā dravyantareṣu.*
> [VS(Ś) 12: *tathā dravyantareṣu pratyakṣam.*]
> [VS(D) : absent]
> 15: *ātmêndriya-mano-'rtha-sannikarṣāc ca.* [= VS(D)]
> [VS(Ś) 13: *asamāhitantaḥ-karaṇā upasaṃhṛta-samādhayas teṣāṃ ca.*]
> 16: *tat-samavāyāt karma-guṇeṣu.* [= VS(D)]
> 17: *ātma-samavāyād ātma-guṇeṣu.* [= VS(D)]

20 See Candrānanda's gloss: ad VS 1.16 (*viyukta-pratyakṣa*): "In these ['disconnected/undisciplined' yogins] there arises perception of objects which are subtle, concealed (from sight) and distant due to the contact of the quadruple (the self, sense-organ, mind and

object). And also of things perceptible to people like us." – VSV(C) ad VS 1.16 (*viyukta-pratyakṣa*): *sūkṣma-vyavahita-viprakṛṣṭeṣu artheṣu teṣāṃ catuṣṭaya-sannikarṣād api pratyakṣam jāyate. tathasmad-ādi-pratyakṣeṣu.* On the quadruple (*catuṣṭaya*) of the self, sense organ, mind, and object, see DPŚ$_2$ 146, pp. 191–192: . . . *yad jñānaṃ tasyatmêndriya-mano-'rtha-catuṣṭaya-sannikarṣaḥ karaṇam.* Cf. also the sequence of connection in NBhū, p. 170 *(apropos of NSā: viprayuktavasthāyāṃ catuṣṭaya-traya-dvaya-sannikarṣād grahaṇaṃ yathā-saṃbavena yojanīyam): [catuṣṭaya:] tatra rasana-cakṣus-tvācām . . . ātmā manasā saṃyujyate, mana indriyeṇa, indriyam arthenêti. [traya:] śrotreṇartha-grahaṇe trayāṇām ātma-manaḥ-śrotrāṇāṃ sannikarṣaḥ. [dvaya:] manasartha-grahaṇe dvayor ātma-manaso sannikarṣa iti.*

21 Cf. NS 1.1.9: *tad-atyanta-vimokṣo 'pavargaḥ* (*tad* = *duḥkha*).

22 PBh$_1$ 8.12, p. 187 = PBh$_2$ 240–242: [240] *bhāva-dravyatva-guṇatva-karmatva-dīnām upalabhyadhāra-samavetānām āśraya-grāhakair indriyair grahaṇam ity etad asmad-ādīnāṃ pratyakṣam. [241] asmad-viśiṣṭānāṃ tu yogināṃ yuktānāṃ yoga-ja-dharmanugṛ hītena manasā svatmantarakāśa-dik-kāla-paramaṇu-vāyu-manaḥsu tat-samaveta-guṇa-karma-sāmānya-viśeṣeṣu samavāye cavitathaṃ svarūpa-darśanam utpadyate. [242] viyuktānāṃ punaś catuṣṭaya-sannikarṣād yoga-ja-dharmanugr aha-sāmarthyāt sūkṣma-vyavahita-viprakṛ ṣṭeṣu pratyakṣam utpadyate.*

23 The idea of the individuators that make it possible for the yogins to distinguish between various atoms is recapitulated in YBh 3.53, p. 313.7.

24 PBh$_1$ 11, p. 321–322 = PBh$_2$ 370–371: [370] *yathasmad-ādīnāṃ gav-ādiṣv aśvadibhyas tulyakṛti-guṇa-kriyavayava-saṃyoga-nimittā pratyaya-vyāvṛttir dṛṣṭā gauḥ śuklaḥ śīghra-gatiḥ pīna-kakudmān mahā-ghaṇṭa iti, tathasmad-viśiṣṭānāṃ yogināṃ nityeṣu tulyakṛti-guṇa-kriyeṣu paramaṇuṣu muktatma-manaḥsu canya-nimittasambhavād yebhyo nimittebhyaḥ pratyādhāraṃ vilakṣaṇo 'yaṃ vilakṣaṇo 'yam iti pratyaya-vyāvṛttiḥ, deśa-kāla-viprakarṣe ca paramaṇau sa evayam iti pratyabhijñānaṃ ca bhavati te 'ntyā viśeṣāḥ.* [371] *yadi punar antya-viśeṣam antareṇa yogināṃ yoga-jād dharmāt pratyaya-vyāvṛttiḥ pratyabhijñānaṃ ca syāt tataḥ kiṃ syāt? naîvaṃ bhavati. yathā na yoga-jād dharmād aśukle śukla-pratyayaḥ saṃjāyate atyantadṛṣṭe ca pratyabhijñānam, yadi syān mithyā bhavet, tathêhapy antya-viśeṣam antareṇa yogināṃ na yoga-jād dharmāt pratyaya-vyāvṛttiḥ pratyabhijñānaṃ vā bhavitum arhati.*

25 NSā, p. 170: *yogi-pratyakṣam tu deśa-kāla-svabhāva-viprakṛṣṭartha-grāhakam, and NBhū,* p. 170: *deśa-viprakṛṣṭāḥ satya-lokadayo 'tidūrasthā vyavahitāś ca nāga-bhuvanadayaḥ, kāla-viprakṛṣṭās tv atītanāgatāḥ, svabhāva-viprakṛṣṭāḥ paramāṇv-ākāśadaya iti, teṣāṃ tri-prakārāṇāṃ viprakṛṣṭānāṃ vyavasthānāṃ va grāhakaṃ pratryakṣaṃ yogi-pratyakṣam ity ucyate. tac cavasthā-dvaye bhavati: yuktavasthāyām ayuktavasthāyāṃ ca. tatra* yuktavasthāyām ātma-manaḥ-saṃyogād eva dharmādi-sahitād aśeṣartha-grahaṇaṃ bhavati. etac ca parama-yogi-vivakṣayôktam, na tu yogi-mātrasyaśeṣarthasya grahaṇaṃ bhavati.

26 VS 9.28 (C): *ārṣaṃ siddha-darśanaṃ ca dharmebhyaḥ.* Candrānanda in his exposition (p. 71) recapitulates PBh$_2$ 2.12.2.d.1 [288].

27 For details and a development of the classifications of cognitive faculties and cognitions in Jainism, see Balcerowicz (forthcoming/a).

28 TS 1.21: *dvividho 'vadhiḥ.* TBh 1.21: *bhava-pratyayaḥ kṣayôpaśama-nimittaś ca.*

29 Cf. TS and TBh 1.22–23.

30 On the concept of somatism in traditional Indian philosophy and psychology see Schayer (1936), Dandekar (1941), and Kunst (1968).

31 TS 1.26 and PMī 1.19.

32 NMa$_2$ 2, vol. I, p. 157.1–7: *darśanatiśaya eva pramāṇam. tathā hy asmad-ādir apekṣitaloko 'valokayati nikaṭa-sthitam artha-vṛndam, undura-vairiṇas tu sāndra-tama-tamaḥ-paṅka-paṭala-vilipta-deśa-patitam api saṃpaśyanti. sampāti-nāmā ca gṛdhra-rājo yojana-śata-vyavahitām api daśaratha-nandana-sundarīṃ dadarśêti rāmayaṇe śrūyate, so 'yaṃ darśanatiśayaḥ śukladi-guṇatiśaya iva tāra-tamya-samanvita iti gamayati param api niratiśayam atiśayam. ataś ca yatrasya paraḥ prakarṣas te yogino gīyante. darśanasya ca paro 'tiśayaḥ sūkṣma-vyavahita-viprakṛṣṭa-bhūta-bhaviṣyad-ādi-viṣayatvam.*

33 PMĪ 1.16: *prajñatiśaya-viśrānty-ādi-siddhes tat-siddhiḥ.*

34 PMĪV 1.16 § 55, p. 13: *prajñāyā atiśayaḥ. tāratamyaṃ kvacid viśrantam, atiśayatvāt, parimāṇatiśayavad ity anumānena niratiśaya-prajñā-siddhyā tasya kevala-jñānasya siddhiḥ, tat-siddhi-rūpatvāt kevala-jñāna-siddheḥ.*

35 PMĪV 1.16 § 55, p. 14: *jyotir-jñānavisaṃvādanyathānupapatteś ca tat-siddhiḥ.*

36 PMĪ 1.18: *tat-tāratamye 'vadhi-manaḥ-paryāyau ca.*

37 SSā$_1$ 219 = SSā$_{2,3}$ 204:

> *abhiṇi-sudôhi-maṇa-kevalaṃ ca taṃ hodi ekkam eva padaṃ /*
> *so eso paramaṭṭho jaṃ lahiduṃ ṇivvudiṃ jādi //*

38 PSā 3.34:

> *āgama-cakkhū sāhū iṃdiya-cakkhūṇi savva-bhūdāṇi /*
> *devā ya ohi-cakkhū siddhā puṇa savvado-cakkhū // 34 //*

39 Cf. TS 10.1: *moha-kṣayāj jñāna-darśanavaraṇantarāya-kṣayāc ca kevalam.*

40 PSā 1.45–46:

> *puṇṇa-phalā arahaṃtā tesiṃ kiriyā puṇo hi odaiyā /*
> mohadīhiṃ virahiyā tamhā sā khāiga tti madā // 45 //
> jadi so suho va asuho ṇa havadi ādā sayaṃ sahāveṇa /
> saṃsāro vi ṇa vijjadi savvesiṃ jīva-kāyāṇaṃ // 46 //
> Vgl. auch SSā$_1$ 219 = SSā$_{2,3}$ 204.

41 Traditionally held to have lived around 550; however, there are valid reasons to maintain that he must have been acquainted with some of Dharmakīrti's works (e.g., certain passages of ĀMĪ seem to betray Dharmakīrti's stamp), *ergo* has to also be considered either later than or younger contemporary of Kumārila. See Balcerowicz (2008: ii) and (2011: 19–20).

42 For analysis of the verse, being a formulation of a proof of liberation, and its soteriological implications, see Balcerowicz (2005).

43 ĀMĪ 4–5:

> *doṣavaraṇayor hānir niḥśeṣasty atiśāyanāt /*
> *kvacid yathā sva-hetubhyo bahir antar mala-kṣayaḥ //*
> *sūkṣmantarita-dūrarthāḥ pratyakṣāḥ kasyacid yathā /*
> *anumeyatvato 'gny-ādir iti sarva-jña-saṃsthitiḥ //*

44 See Balcerowicz (2013: § 4).

45 For the argument exposed in verse 5, see Balcerowicz (2013: § 9).

46 AṣŚ$_1$ 53.9–16 = AṣŚ$_2$ 4.7–9 (ad ĀMĪ 4): *tathā ca doṣader hānir atiśayavatī kutaścit nivartayitum arhati sakalaṃ kalaṅkaṃ iti katham akalaṅka-siddhir na bhavet? na*[†] *maṇer malader vyāvṛttiḥ kṣayaḥ, sato 'tyanta-vināśanupapatteḥ.*

[†] Both editions [Nagin Shah follows AṣŚ$_1$] *have no na [na bhavet? maṇeḥ . . .], although the commentary makes it clear that one should have here a negated sentence:*

AṣS 53.15 ff.: *pradhvaṃsabhāvo hi kṣayo hānir ihabhipretā. sā ca vyāvṛttir eva maṇer kanaka-pāṣāṇād vā (recte: pāṣāṇāder vā) malasya kiṭṭader vā. na punar atyanta-vināśaḥ. sa hi dravyasya vā syāt paryāyasya vā? na tāvad dravyasya nityatvāt . . .*

47 LT (Pramāṇa-praveśa-vivṛti) 1.4: *puruṣatiśaya-sambhave 'tīndriyartha-darśī kiṃ na syāt.*

48 VP 3.1.46:

jñānaṃ tv asmad-viśiṣṭānāṃ† *tāsu sarvêndriyaṃ*‡ *viduḥ /*
abhyāsān maṇi-rūpyadi-viśeṣeṣv iva tad-vidām //

† Cf. VS(C) 2.1.18 [p. 13]: *saṃjñā-karma tv asmad-viśiṣṭānāṃ liṅgam*, and PBh_1 8.12.2.1, p. 187 = PBh_2 22.12.2.a [241]: *asmad-viśiṣṭānāṃ tu yogināṃ yuktānāṃ yoga-ja-dharmanugṛhītena manasā svatmantarakāśa-dik-kāla-paramaṇu-vāyu-manaḥsu tat-samaveta-guṇa-karma-sāmānya-viśeṣeṣu samavāye cavitathaṃ svarūpa-darśanam utpadyate* (for the translation of the passage, see p. XX).
‡ The attribute *sarvêndriyaṃ* ("encompassing all sense organs") of jñānaṃ ("a cognition") unambiguously implies omniscience which transcends limitations of sensory cognition (ordinary perception), which is always restricted to its kind; whereas this particular cognition encompasses all kinds of sensory data (see VP 1.155).

49 VP 1.65:

guṇaḥ prakarṣa-hetur yaḥ svātantryeṇôpadiśyate /
tasyaśritād guṇād eva prakṛṣṭatvaṃ pratīyate //

50 YBh 2.24, p. 56.2–57.4: *tac ca tasyaîśvaryaṃ sāmyatiśaya-vinirmuktam. na tāvad aiśvaryantareṇa tad atiśayyate, yād evatiśāyi syāt tad eva tat syāt. tasmād yatra kāṣṭhā-prāptir aiśvaryasya sa iśvara iti. na ca tat-samānam aiśvaryam asti. kasmat? dvayos tulyayor ekasmin yugapat kāmite 'rthe navam idam astu purāṇam idam astu ity ekasya siddhau itarasya prākāmya-vighātād ūnatvaṃ prasaktam. dvayoś ca tulyayor yugapat kāmitartha-prāptir nasti, arthasya viruddhatvāt. tasmād yasya sāmyatiśayair vinirmuktam aiśvaryaṃ sa evêśvaram.*

51 For details, see Balcerowicz (2013: § 7).

52 $SS\bar{a}_1$ 236–238 = $SS\bar{a}_{2,3}$ 222–223:

jaiyā sa eva saṃkho seda-sahāvaṃ tayaṃ pajahiḍūṇa /
gacchejja kiṇha-bhāvaṃ taiyā sukkattaṇaṃ pajahe // 236 / 222 //
jaha saṃkho poggalado jaiyā sukkattaṇaṃ pajahidūṇa / †
gacchejja kiṇha-bhāvaṃ taiyyā sukkataṇaṃ pajahe // 237 // †
taha ṇāṇī vi hu jaiyā ṇāṇa-sahāvaṃ tayaṃ pajahiūṇa /
aṇṇāṇeṇa pariṇado taiyā aṇṇāṇadaṃ gacche // 238 / 223 //

† $SS\bar{a}_2$ omits this verse. It seems that this verse is a later interpolation, and does not belong to the original structure; neither Amṛtacandra comments on it nor is the term poggalado mentioned or alluded to in his commentary. Further, in $SS\bar{a}_2$ and $SS\bar{a}_3$, poggalado is Sanskritized as paudgalikaḥ, which is simply not posssible. I take it as an ablative.

53 Viz. the correct cognition, correct conation, and correct conduct (samyag-darśana-jñāna-cāritra), see e.g. TS 1.1.

54 PMīV 1.15, § 48, pp. 12.4–12.6: *dīrgha-kāla-nirantara-satkārasevita-ratna-traya-prakarṣa-paryante ekatva-vitarka-vicārav-dhyāna-balena niḥśeṣatayā jñānavaraṇadīnāṃ ghāti-karmaṇāṃ prakṣaye sati cetanā-svabhāvasyatmanaḥ prakāśa-svabhāvasyêti.*

Compare: dīrgha-kāla-nirantara-satkārasevita-ratna-traya-prakarṣa-paryante and NB 1.11: bhūtartha-bhāvanā-prakarṣa-paryantajam

55 Contemplation is here replaced by Hemacandra with the three jewels (instead of *bhūtartha-bhāvanā-prakarṣa-paryantajaṃ* we have *dīrgha-kāla-nirantara-satkārase vita-ratna-traya-prakarṣa-paryante*).

56 NB 1.11: *bhūtartha-bhāvanā-prakarṣa-paryantajaṃ yogi-jñānaṃ cêti*. For Diṅnāga's definition of supernatural perception, which was the basis for Dharmakīrti, see Hattori (1968: 27, 94) and Nagasaki (1988: 348).

57 NBṬ 1.11, p. 67.5: *bhūtasya bhāvanā punaḥ punaś cetasi viniveśanam.*

58 Cf. Nagasaki (1988: 349–350).

59 NBṬ 1.11, p. 67.5–6: *bhāvanāyāḥ prakarṣo bhāvyamānarthabhāsasya jñānasya sphuṭabhatvarambhaḥ.*—"The consummation (intensity) of contemplation is the beginning of [the process in which] cognition [the contents of which is] the image of the object being contemplated represents [this object] in a clear way."

60 NBṬ 1.11, p. 67.6–68.2: *prakarṣasya paryanto yadā sphuṭabhatvam īṣad asaṃpūrṇaṃ bhavati. yāvad dhi sphuṭabhatvam aparipūrṇaṃ tāvat tasya prakarṣa-gamanam. saṃpūrṇaṃ tu yadā tadā nasti prakarṣa-gatiḥ. tataḥ saṃpūrṇavasthāyāḥ prāktany avasthā sphuṭabhatva-prakarṣa-paryanta ucyate.* – "When the representation of [the object] in a clear way by the ultimate intensity is not quite complete. For as long as the representation of [the object] in a clear way is not absolutely complete, this is the progress of the consummation (intensity) of this [contemplation]. But when [it is] complete, then there is no progress [any more]. Therefore, the state prior to the state of complete [representation] is called the ultimate state of the intensity of the representation of [the object] in a clear way."

61 NBṬ 1.11, p. 68.2–3: *tasmāt paryantād yaj jātaṃ bhāvamānasyarthasya sannihitasyêva sphuṭatarakāra-grāhi jñānam yoginaḥ pratyakṣam.* – "Such a cognition which is produced by this ultimate [consummation (intensity) and] which grasps more clear form of the object which is being contemplated as if it were present [in front of the contemplator] is yogin's perception."

62 For further description of the three stages, see NBṬ 1.11 (pp. 68.4–69.2). However, Vinītadeva in his Ṭīkā distinguishes four stages: see Stcherbatsky (1930: II: 31, n. 2) and Nagasaki (1988: 350–354).

63 PSā 1.48–50:

> *jo ṇa vijāṇadi jugavaṃ atthe ti-kkālige ti-huvaṇa-tthe /*
> *ṇāduṃ tassa ṇa sakkaṃ sapajjayaṃ davvam egaṃ vā // 48 //*
> *davvaṃ aṇaṃta-pajjayam egam aṇaṃtāṇi davva-jādāṇi /*
> *ṇa vijāṇadi jadi jugavaṃ kidha so savvāṇi jāṇādi // 49 //*
> *uppajjadi jadi ṇāṇaṃ kamaso aṭṭhe paḍucca ṇāṇissa /*
> *taṃ ṇeva havadi ṇiccaṃ ṇa khāigaṃ ṇeva savva-gadaṃ // 50 //*
> *ti-kkāla-ṇicca-visamaṃ sayalaṃ savvattha saṃbhavaṃ cittaṃ /*
> *jugavaṃ jāṇadi joṇhaṃ aho hi ṇāṇassa māhappaṃ // 51 //*

64 In other words: if there is a means to purify an object, that very object can be, or will be, purified.

65 The puṭa-pāka process is described in Bose–Sen–Subbarayappa (1971: 325): "The substance is subjected to a prolonged heating which is technically called puṭa . . . The source of heat is the fire of cow-dung, and depending on the quantity of the cow-dung cakes used as also the way they are heaped, different degrees are sought to be

given to the substance. The substance itself is placed in an earthen flat container and enclosed by another, and sealed with a mud plaster." For the process of puṭa-pāka and its varieties, cf. D. Joshi (1986: 287 ff.). The process of calcination, or roasting a mineral (e.g., a metal or jewel) in a furnace, technically called puṭa-pāka, forms a part of a pulverization process that aims at converting a particular substance into powder (Rṇv 6.83: bhasmatāṃ gatam), which in its turn is further used to prepare a medicine. Very often the substance to be calcinated is diamond; its pulverization processes are described, e.g., in the vajra-vidhi section of Rṇv (6.65–122), and are referred to as "killing of a diamond" (vajra-māraṇa, Rṇv 6.84); cf. similar expressions: vajraṃ tu mriyate kṣaṇāt (Rṇv 6.88). For the māraṇa-process, see D. Joshi (1986: 10 ff.). Diamond is, in its turn, divided into three varieties depending on their "sex," among which "male" diamonds are regarded as superior (Rṇv 6.68: *puruṣāś ca striyaś caîva napuṃsakam anukramāt*, cf. RRS 4.27: *vajraś ca trividhaṃ proktaṃ naro narī napuṃsakam / pūrvaṃ pūrvam iha śreṣṭham*), as well as into four subtypes according to colour-classes of each of the three gender-subdivisions (Rṇv 6.66*: brāhmaṇāḥ kṣatriyā vaiśyāḥ śūdrāś caîvam anekadhā;* cf. RRS 4.31: *śvetadi-varṇa-bhedena tad ekaîkam catur-vidham / brahma-kṣatriya-viṭ-śudram sva-sva-varṇa-phala-pradam*). The colours – viz., white, red, yellow and dark-bluish – are enumerated in corresponding section of RRSṬ: *catur-vidha-jāti-bhedam āha: "śvetadîti." ādi-śabdena rakta-pīta-kṛṣṇa-varṇa-parigrahaḥ.* The purification (*śodhana*) process of substances other than diamond is further described in the tenth chapter of Rṇv, wherein it is mostly referred to as jāraṇa, and other derivatives of √jæ (e.g. Rṇv 11.35,96: jārayet) are generally used in the context, although the derivatives of √mṛt (Rṇv 11.94: mārayet) do occur, less frequently though, as synonymous with more frequent derivatives of √jæ. Varieties of furnaces and other alchemic equipment are discussed at length by D. Joshi (1986: fifth chapter). See Balcerowicz (2008: n. 551).

Wilhelm Rau (1983: 13–19) cites a passage from the Agastya-saṃhitā[a] (AgS) describing a method of polishing a jewel to obtain a burning lens. The described procedure is, apparently, different from the process of calcination.

There are some striking points to be noted here that may justify the analogy between the soul and a gem as well as the juxtaposition of the process of inner purification of the soul and the process of purification of a gem.

1 The four colours (*varṇa*) of diamond (RRSṬ 4.31) resemble the coloration (*leśyā*) of the soul: *śveta / śukla, rakta / tejas, pīta / padma, kṛṣṇa*. A full list of the traditional six colorings, that correspond to the grade of inner development of an individual comprises black (*kṛṣṇa*; Pkt., *kaṇha*), blue (*nīla*), gray (*kāpota*; Pkt., *kāü*), red (*tejas*; Pkt., *teü*), pinkish yellow (*padma*; Pkt., *paṃha*), white (*śukla*; Pkt., *sukka*); see, e.g. SSi 2.6: *sā ṣad-vidhā: kṛṣṇa-leśyā nīla-leśyā kāpota-leśyā tejo-leśyā padma-leśyā śukla-leśyā cêti,* and TBh 2.6; cf. Glasenapp (1942: 47).
2 The use of derivatives of √jæ, viz., of the term *jāraṇa* with regard to the purifying pulverization processes of a diamond and nirjarā for the purification of the soul, i.e. the removal of karmic matter by ascetic practices.
3 The purification of diamond by its pulverization / calcination does not destroy diamond itself; the process removes only its material impurities.

A comparison of a pious mendicant to a jewel is a well-known motif from Jaina works, e.g. ĀA 176:

śāstragnau maṇivad bhavyo viśuddho bhāti nirvṛtaḥ /
aṅgāravat khalo dīpto malī vā bhasma vā bhavet //

"A [person] competent for liberation, purified [and] restrained, gleams like a jewel in the fire of authoritative treatises; a base man, as one should realise, who burns like charcoal, turns either into filth or into ashes"; cf. ĀA 263cd:

udāsīnas tasya pragalita-purāṇaṃ na hi navaṃ
samāskandaty eṣa spurati suvidagdho maṇir iva //

I do not, by any means, intend to maintain that Jaina salvific doctrine of purification of the soul and its terminology might have influenced in any way the terminology of alchemy, or vice versa. Moreover, personally I am convinced that not only such a relation would be extremely difficult to establish beyond doubt, but also that there was any such direct relation whatsoever. The point I have been trying to make is that certain parallelism concerning both the terminology and processes was responsible for the deliberate choice of particular similes.

[a] Before 1334/5 AD; cf. Rau (1983: 12, n. 30): "*Agastya-proktā agastya-saṃhitā. Buddhabhaṭṭa-racitā ratna-parīkṣā ca. etat pustaka-dvayaṃ paṃ. Buddhi-sāgara-śramaṇaḥ adhyakṣatāyāṃ sarva-darśanacārya paṃ. Kṛṣṇaprasāda Bhaṭṭa Rā'ī ity etaiḥ sampāditam. vīra-pustakalaya-dvārā prakāśitam = purā-tattva-prakāśana-mālā* 15. [Kathmandu / Nepal] vi. saṃ. 2020 [1962/3], pp. 32,22–33.24/."

66 NAV 27.4: *sambhavat-samasta-śuddhika ātmā, vidyamāna-śuddhy-upāyatvād; iha yo yo vidyamāna-śuddhy-upāyaḥ sa sa sambhavat-samasta-śuddhiko; yathā vidyamāna-kṣāra-mṛt-puṭa-pākadi-śuddhy-upāyo ratna-viśeṣas, tathā ca vidyamāna-jñānady-abhyāsa-śuddhy-upāya ātmataḥ sambhavat-samasta-śuddhika iti.*

67 NAV 27.4: *sāmastya-śuddhaś catmā jñāna-jñāninoḥ kathañcid abhedāt kevalam abhidhīyata iti.*

68 PSā 1.36, p. 83.1–2:

tamhā ṇāṇaṃ jīvo ṇeyaṃ davvaṃ tihā samakkhādaṃ /
davvaṃ ti puṇo ādā paraṃ ca pariṇāma-saṃbaddhaṃ //

69 NAV 1.7: *tatra siddhanta-prasiddha-pāramārthika-pratyakṣapekṣayakṣa-śabdo jīva-paryāyatayā prasiddhaḥ.*

70 MŚV 4.122:

ātmany eva sthitaṃ jñānam sa hi boddhatra gamyate /
smaraṇe casya sāmarthyaṃ sandhānadau ca vidyate //

71 SSā_1 300–301 = $\text{SSā}_{2,3}$ 278–279:

jaha phaliha-maṇī suddho[†] *ṇa sayaṃ pariṇamai rāyamāīhiṃ /*
raṃgijjadi aṇṇehiṃ du so rattadīhim davvehiṃ // 278 //
evaṃ ṇāṇī suddho ṇa sayaṃ pariṇamai rayamāīhim /
rāijjadi aṇṇohiṃ du so rāgadīhiṃ dosehiṃ // 279 //

[†] SSā_1: visuddho.
Note the play on the word rāga used in two meanings: "red colour" and "desire."

72 PSā 1.28:

ṇāṇī ṇāṇa-sahāvo aṭṭho ṇeya-ppagā hi ṇāṇissa /
rūvāṇi va cakkhūṇaṃ ṇêva'ṇṇmṇṇesu vaṭṭanti //

73 SSā$_{2,3}$ 6.184:

jaha kaṇayam aggitaviyaṃ pi kaṇaya-bhāvaṃ ṇa taṃ pariccayadi /
taha kammôdaya-tavido ṇa jahadi ṇāṇī du ṇāṇittaṃ //

74 SSā$_{2,3}$ 3.130–131:

kaṇa-mayā bhāvādo jāyaṃte kuṃḍalādayo bhāvā /
aya-mayayā bhāvādo jaha jāyaṃte du kaḍayādi // 130 //
aṇṇāṇa-mayā bhāvā aṇāṇiṇo bahuvihā vi jāyaṃte /
ṇāṇissa du ṇāṇa-mayā savve bhāvā tahā hoṃti // 131 //

75 PMīV 1.15 § 50, p. 12.20–22: *prakāśa-svabhāvasyapi candrarkader iva rajo-nīhāhārabhra-paṭaladibhir iva jñānavaraṇīyadi-karmabhir āvaraṇasya sambhavāt, candrarkader iva prabala-pavamāna-prāyair dhyāna-bhāvanadibhir vilayasyêti.*

76 PMīV 1.15 § 51, p. 12.23.

77 PMīV 1.15 § 51, p. 12.23–25: *anāder api suvarṇa-malasya kṣāra-mṛd-puṭa-pākadinā vilayôpalambhāt, tadvad evanāder api jñānavaraṇīyadi-karmaṇaḥ pratipakṣa-bhūta-ratna-trayabhyāsena vilayôpapatteḥ.*

78 Isibh 28.21–22:

kāle kāle ya mehāvī paṇḍie ya khaṇe khaṇe /
kālāto kancaṇassevêva uddhare malam appaṇo // 21 //
anjaṇassa khayaṃ dissa vammīyassa ya saṃcayaṃ /
madhussa ya samāhāraṃ ujjamo saṃjame varo // 22 //

79 For the argument exposed in verse 5, see Balcerowicz (2013: § 9).

80 PMīV 1.16 § 55, p. 14: *sūkṣmantarita-dūrarthāḥ kasyacit pratyakṣāḥ prameyatvāt ghaṭavad iti.*

81 I.e. Praśastapāda's equation astitva = abhidheyatva = jñeyatva) Uddyotakara's sattva = abhidheyatva = prameyatva. For its discussion see Balcerowicz (2010).

82 See Balcerowicz (2010: § 4.3).

83 Less probable is any Buddhist influence in this case, e.g., from the side of the Sarvāstivādin-Vaibhāṣikas, such as Saṅghabhadra, who in his Nyāyanusāra also expresses a similar idea in a definition of all that exists, to the same effect, viz. everything that exists is cognizable: "To be an object-field that produces cognition (buddhi) is the true characteristic of existence" (see Cox 1995: pp. 138, 375; n. 168).

84 For grammatical details, see Balcerowicz (2013: § 9).

85 NAV 27.3: *samasti samasta-vastu-vistāra-gocaraṃ viśada-darśanaṃ, tad-gocaranumāna-pravṛtteḥ; iha yad-yad-gocaram anumānaṃ pravartate, tasya tasya grāhakaṃ kiñcit pratyakṣam udaya-padavīṃ samāsādayati, yathā citra-bhānoḥ; pravartate ca sakalartha-viṣayam anumānam; atas tad-avalokinā viśada-darśanenapi bhāvyam iti.*

86 For details, see Balcerowicz (2013: § 9).

87 PMīV 1.16 § 55, p. 14.

88 SVi 8.2, p. 526:

dhīr atyanta-parokṣe 'rthe na cet puṃsāṃ kutaḥ punaḥ /
jyotir-jñānavisaṃvādaḥ śrutāc cet sādhanantaram //

89 Cf. Balcerowicz (2013: § 9).

90 It is unlikely that the term *pramāṇa* (*ṇāṇa-pamāṇaṃ*) is used here in its epistemological sense of "cognitive criterion."

91 PSā 1.23–25:

> *ādā ṇāṇa-pamāṇaṃ ṇāṇaṃ ṇeya-ppamāṇam uddiṭṭhaṃ /*
> *ṇeyaṃ loyaloyaṃ tamhā ṇāṇaṃ tu savva-gayaṃ // 23 //*
> *ṇāṇa-ppamāṇam ādā ṇa havadi jassêha tassa so ādā /*
> *hīṇo vā ahio vā ṇāṇādo havadi dhuvam eva // 24 //*
> *hīṇo jadi so ādā taṇ ṇāṇam acedaṇaṃ ṇa jāṇādi /*
> *ahio vā ṇāṇādo ṇāṇeṇa viṇā kahaṃ ṇādi // 25 //*

92 The idea that the soul is spatially co-extensive with its physical body is refuted by Jayarāśi Bhaṭṭa in TUS_1, pp. 76.24–78.5 = TUS_3, pp. 153–155.

93 See Balcerowicz (2011). See also TBh 5.15.

94 The passage is quoted with a slight change: *arthaṃ avagamayati* instead of *arthaṃ śaknoty avagamayitum* in ŚBh 1.2.2.

95 PMīV 1.16 § 56, p. 15: *codanā hi bhūtaṃ bhavantaṃ bhaviṣyantaṃ sūkṣmaṃ vyavahitaṃ viprakṛṣṭam ity evaṃ-jātīyakam arthaṃ avagamayati, nanyat kiñcanên-driyam iti vadatā bhūtady-artha-parijñānaṃ kasyacit puṃso 'bhimatam eva, anyathā kasmai vedas tri-kāla-viṣayam artham nivedayet? sa hi nivedayāṃs tri-kāla-viṣaya-tattva-jñam evadhikāriṇam upādatte. yad āha:*

> *tri-kāla-viṣayaṃ tattvaṃ kasmai vedo nivedayet /*
> *akṣayyavaraṇaîkāntān na ced veda*† *tathā naraḥ // [SVi 8.3]*

iti tri-kāla-viṣaya-vastu-nivedananyathanupapatter atīntriya-kevala-jñāna-siddhiḥ.
† SVi 8.3, p. 527 has: *vetti*, which is the correct reading.

96 PMīV 1.16 § 57: *pratyakṣanumāna-saṃvādaṃ śāstram evatīndriyartha-darśi-sadb hāve pramāṇaṃ. ya eva hi śāstrasya viṣayaḥ syād-vādaḥ sa eva pratyakṣader apîti saṃvādaḥ . . .*

97 PMīV 1.16 § 57: *pratyakṣaṃ tu yady apy aindriyikaṃ natīndriya-jñāna-viṣayaṃ tathapi samādhi-bala-labdha-janmakaṃ yogi-pratyakṣam eva bāhyarthasyêva svasy-api vedakam iti pratyakṣato 'pi tat-siddhiḥ.*

98 PMīV 1.17 § 61, p. 16: *na canumānaṃ tad-bādhakaṃ sambhavati. dharmi-grahaṇam antereṇanumānapravṛtteḥ, dharmi-grahaṇe vā tad-grāhaka-prāmāṇya-bādhitatvād anutthānam evanumānasya.*

99 PMīV 1.17 § 61, p. 16: *atha vivādadhyāsitaḥ puruṣaḥ sarva-jño na bhavati, vaktṛtvāt, puruṣatvād vā rathyā-puruṣavad ity anumānaṃ tad-bādhakam brūṣe, tad asat. yato yadi pramāṇa-paridṛṣṭartha-vaktṛtvaṃ hetuḥ tadā viruddhaḥ, tādṛśasya vaktṛtvasya sarva-jña eva bhāvāt. athasad-bhūtartha-vaktṛtvam tadā siddha-sādhyatā, pramāṇa-viruddhartha-vādinām asarva-jñatvenêṣṭatvāt.*

100 See Balcerowicz (2015: § 3.4, 3.8).

101 MŚV 2.111cd: *yadi ṣadbhiḥ pramāṇaiḥ syāt sarva-jñaḥ kena vāryate //*

102 ĀMī 6:

> *sa tvam evasi nirdoṣo yukti-śāstravirodhi-vāk /*
> *avirodho yad iṣṭaṃ te prasiddhena na bādhyate // 6 //*

103 PMī 17 and PMīV 1.17 § 59 ff.: *bādhakabhavāc ca. "suniścitasambhavad-bādhaka-prāmaṇatvāt sukhadivat"* (LT 1.4) *tat-siddhiḥ iti sambadhyate. tathā hi kevala-jñāna-bādhakaṃ bhavat pratyakṣaṃ vā bhavet pramāṇantaraṃ vā? . . .*

104 PMīV 1.17 § 60: *na pravartamānaṃ pratyakṣaṃ tad-bādhakaṃ kintu nivartamā naṃ tat.*

105 PMīV 1.17 § 60, p. 16: *yadi niyata-deśa-kāla-viṣayatvena bādhakaṃ tarhi sampratipadyāmahe. atha sakala-deśa-kāla-viṣayatvena, tarhi na tat sakala-deśa-kāla-puruṣa-pariṣat-sākṣāt-kāram antareṇa sambhavatîti siddhaṃ na samīhitam.*

106 See NAV 27.4: *pramāṇa-pañcakaṃ tad-gocaraṃ na pravartata iti kathaṃ bhavato nirṇayaḥ? kiṃ niyata-deśa-kāla-vyāptyā yad vā samasta-deśa-kālaskandanenêti? yady ādyaḥ pakṣas, tato yathā ghaṭadeḥ kvacit pramāṇa-pañcakaṃ tad-gocaraṃ nirvartamānam abhāvaṃ sādhayaty, evaṃ samasta-vastu-saṃvedana-gocaram api tan nivartamānaṃ niyata-deśa-daśavacchinnam abhāvaṃ sādhayen, na sarvatra; tataś ca ghaṭadivat tad durnivāraṃ syāt. atha dvitīyaḥ pakṣo, 'sāv asambhavy eva; samasta-deśa-kāla-varti-puruṣa-pariṣat-saṃvedana-sākṣāt-kāriṇo hy evaṃ vaktuṃ yuktaṃ, yad uta na kvacit samastartha-saṃvedanaṃ astîti – na bhavatas, tathā-vidha-puruṣa-sambhavanabhyupagamāt. itarathā ya eva kaścin niścityaîvam abhidadhyāt, sa eva samasta-vastu-vistāra-vyāpi-jñānaloka iti.*

107 LT (Pramāṇa-praveśa-vivṛti) 1.4: *tad (= atīndriya-jñānam) asti suniścitasambhavad-bādhaka-prāmaṇatvāt sukhadivat. yāvaj jñeya-vyāpi-jñāna-rahita-sakala-puruṣa-pariṣat-parijñānasya tad-antareṇanupapatteḥ. tad-abhāva-tattvajño na kaścid anupalabdheḥ kha-puṣpavat.*

108 PMīV 1.16 § 58, p. 15.4–5: *sarva-jñatvam īśvaradīnām astu, mānuṣyasya tu kasyacid vidyā-caraṇavatôpi tad asaṃbhavanīyam.*

109 PMīV 1.16 § 58, p. 15–16: *ā! sarva-jñapalāpa-pātakin! durvada-vādin!...*

110 What is meant by *yogi-sadbhāva* is not simply "the existence of yogins," because they could easily be located anywhere, by "the existence of the yogins" in the true sense, viz. those who possess such a supernatural perception.

111 NBhū, p. 171: *yogi-sadbhāvas tu śruti-smṛti-purāṇêtihāsaneka-yoga-śāstreṣu pra-siddha iti. tad-apalāpaḥ pāpatiśayam eva narakady-ananta-yātanadi-nimittaṃ janayati.*

112 Or: the omniscient; SVK, vol 7, p. 44.7 takes *tasya* to be *sarva-jñasya.*

113 ŚVS 594, 626:

āgamād api tat-siddhir yad asau codanā-phalam /
prāmāṇyaṃ ca svatas tasya nityatvam ca śruter iva // 594 //
sarva-jñena hy abhivyaktāt sarvarthād āgamāt parā /
dharmadharma-vyavasthêyaṃ yujyate nanyataḥ kvacit // 626 //

114 VĀBh 2034:

kidha savaṇṇu tti matī jeṇahaṃ sarrva-saṃsaya-chettā /
pucchasu va jaṃ ṇa yāṇasi jeṇa va te paccayo hojjā //

115 PBh_1, p. 258 = PBh_2 288: *āmnāya-vidhātṛṇām ṛṣīṇām atītanāgata-vartamāneṣv atīndriyeṣv artheṣu dharmadiṣu granthôpanibaddheṣv anupanibaddheṣu catma-manasoḥ saṃyogād dharma-viśeṣāc ca yat pratibhaṃ yathartha-nivedanaṃ jñānam utpadyate tad ārṣam ity ācakṣate. tat tu prastāreṇa deva-ṛṣīṇāṃ, kadācid eva laukikānāṃ, yathā kanyakā bravīti śvo me bhrātagantêti hṛdayaṃ me kathayatîti.*

116 This is refuted by Kumārila (see counter-arguments, n. 9) and Pārthasārathi Miśra (NRĀ ad MŚV 4.32. p. 103: NRĀ ad MŚV 4.32, p. 103: *asmad-ādi-pratibhā tāval liṅgady-ābhāsa-janyā pratyakṣadikam anapekṣya svātantryeṇartham aniścāyayantī naîva pramāṇam, atas tadvad eva yogināṃ apîti.)*: "The intuition of ordinary people like us, to begin with, arises by virtue of fallacies of the inferential sign etc., it does not determine its object autonomously, independent of perception and other cognitive

criteria, [hence it] is not by any means a cognitive criterion; for the very same reason also yogins' [intuition is not a cognitive criterion]." Kumārila demonstrates that any instance of intuition, either mystic or ordinary (such as the case of the girl predicting her brother's visit), is based on unconscious and erroneous reasoning, viz. it is derived from wrong presupposition and erroneous association of facts: the essential elements of the girl's cognition are realistic, but the way they are associated and conclusions drawn is fallacious. Hence such an intuition has no cognitive validity and does not contribute to our knowledge (*niścāya*).

Kumārila rejects the supernatural character of yogins' perception and maintains that there is no qualitative difference between the ordinary perception of common people and the supernatural perception of yogins, insofar as the very definition accepted by all is that perception applies to present things and it depends on some kind of direct relation with the object (not necessarily the contact). The gist of his argument is that the idea of supernatural perception does not fulfill the requirements set by the definition of perception.

117 PMīV 1.15 § 48, p. 12.11–14: *ātmā prakāśa-svabhāvaḥ, asandigdha-svabhāvatvāt, yaḥ prakāśa-svabhāvo na bhavati nasāv asandigdha-svabhāvo yathā ghaṭaḥ, na ca tathatmā, na khalu kaścit aham asmi na vêti sandigdho iti.*

118 PMīV 1.15 § 48, p. 12.14–16: *ātmā prakāśa-svabhāvaḥ, boddhṛtvāt . . .*

119 Viz. *jñapti-kriyā-kartṛtvāt.* This logical reason is not stated explicity, but it is clear from the formulation of the invariable concomitance (*vyāpti*).

120 PMīV 1.15 § 48, p. 12.16–18: *tathā [*ātmā prakāśa-svabhāvaḥ, jñapti-kriyā-kartṛtvāt], yo yasāḥ kriyāyāḥ kartā na sa tad-viṣayo, yathā gati-kriyāyāḥ kartā caitro na tad-viṣayaḥ, jñapti-kriyāyāḥ kartā catmêti.* – "The self has a knowing essence, [because it the agent of the act of knowing]; if x is an agent of the act y, x cannot be the object of y, for instance Caitra is the agent of the act of walking and he is not the object of walking, hence the self is the agent of the act of knowing."

Bibliography

A = Pāṇini: *Aṣṭādhyāyī.* (1) Sumitra Mangesh Katre: *Aṣṭādhyāyī of Pāṇini in Roman Transliteration.* Austin: University of Texas Press, 1987 (reprinted: Motilal Banarsidass, Delhi 1989). (2) Śrisa Chandra Vasu: *The Aṣṭādhyāyī of Pāṇini, edited and translated into English.* 2 Vols., The Pāṇini Office, Al 1891 (reprinted: Delhi: Motilal Banarsidass, 1962, 1977, 1980, 1988). (3) Sharma, Rama Nath: *The Aṣṭādhyāyī of Pāṇini.* Vols. 1–6 (Vol. 1: *Introduction ot the Aṣṭādhyāyī as a Grammatical Device*, Vols. 2–6: *English Translation of Adhāyāyas with Sanskrit Text, Transliteration, Word-Boundary, Anuvṛtti, Vṛtti, Explanatory Note, Derivational History of Examples, and Indices*). Delhi New Delhi: Munshiram Manoharlal Publishers, 2003.

ĀMī = Samantabhadra: *Āpta-mīmāṃsā.* (1) Vaṃśīdhar (ed.): *Aṣṭasahasrī tarkikacakracūḍāmaṇisyādvādavidyāpatinā śrīvidyānandasvāminā nirākṛta.* Bombay: Nirṇaya-sāgara Press, 1915. (2) Nagin Shah (ed., transl.): *Samantabhadra's Āptamīmāṃsā. Critique of an Authority* (along with English Translation, Introduction, Notes and Akalaṅka's Sanskrit Commentary Aṣṭaśatī). Ahmedabad: Sanskritsanskriti Granthamālā 7, 1999. (3) Pannālāl Jain (ed.): *Āpta-mīmāṃsā* of Samantabhadra Svāmi, with two commentaries: *Aṣṭa-śatī* of Bhaṭṭākalaṅka and *Devāgama-vṛtti* of Vasunandi. Kāśī (Benares): Sanātana Jaina Granthamālā 10(7), 1914.

AṣS = Vidyānanda Pātrakesarisvāmin: *Aṣṭa-sahasrī.* See: $ĀMī_1$.

AṣŚ = Akalaṅka: *Aṣṭa-śatī*. See: $ĀMĪ_1$, $ĀMĪ_2$, $ĀMĪ_3$.

Balcerowicz (forthcoming) = Balcerowicz, Piotr: 'Siddhasena Mahāmati and Akalaṅka Bhaṭṭa: A revolution in Jaina epistemology', in: Matthew Kapstein (ed.) *Companion to Classical Indian Philosophy*. Cambridge: Cambridge University Press, forthcoming.

Balcerowicz 2005 = Balcerowicz, Piotr: 'Akalaṅka und die buddhistische Tradition: Von der Nichtwahrnehmung von Unsichtbarem (*adṛśyānupalabdhi*) zu Allwissenheit'. *Wiener Zeitschrift für die Kunde Südasiens* 49, 151–226, 2005.

Balcerowicz 2008 = Balcerowicz, Piotr: *Jaina Epistemology in Historical and Comparative Perspective – A Critical Edition and an Annotated Translation of Siddhasena Mahāmati's Nyāyâvatāra, Siddharṣigaṇin's Nyāyâvatāra-vivṛti And Devabhadrasūri's Nyāyâvatāra-ṭippana*, vols I and II, 2nd ed. Delhi: Motilal Banarsidass, 2008 (1st ed.: *Jaina Epistemology in Historical and Comparative Perspective – A Critical Edition and an Annotated Translation of Siddhasena Divākara's Nyāyâvatāra, Siddharṣigaṇin's Nyāyâvatāra-vivṛti And Devabhadrasūri's Nyāyâvatāra-ṭippana*, vols I and II. Alt- und Neu-Indische Studien 53,1 and 53,2. Stuttgart: Franz Steiner Verlag, 2001).

Balcerowicz 2010 = Balcerowicz, Piotr: 'What Exists for the Vaiśeṣika?' In: Piotr Balcerowicz (ed.) *Logic and Belief in Indian Philosophy*. Delhi: Motilal Banarsidass, 2010: pp. 241–348.

Balcerowicz 2011 = Balceowicz, Piotr: 'The Body and the Cosmos in Jaina Mythology and Art'. In: Piotr Balcerowicz (ed.) *Art, Myths and Visual Culture of South Asia*. Edited in collaboration with Jerzy Malinowski. Delhi: Manohar, 2011, pp. 95–151.

Balcerowicz 2013 = Balcerowicz, Piotr: 'The Authority of the Buddha, the Omniscience of the Jina and the Truth of Jainism'. In: Vincent Eltschinger and Helmut Krasser (eds.) *Scriptural Authority, Reason and Action. Proceedings of a Panel at the 14th World Sanskrit Conference, Kyoto, September 1st–5th 2009*. Vienna: Verlag der Österreichischen Akademie der Wissenschaften, 2013, pp. 319–374.

Balcerowicz 1015 = Balcerowicz, Piotr: 'Do Attempts to Formalise the *Syâd-vâda* Make Sense?' In: Peter Flügel and Olle Qvarnström (eds.) *Jaina Scriptures and Philosophy*. London: Routledge, 2015, pp. 181–248.

Bose–Sen–Subbarayappa 1971 = Bose, D. M., Sen, S.N., and Subbarayappa, B. V. (eds.) *A Concise History of Science in India*. New Delhi: Indian National Science Academy, 1971.

Cox 1995 = Cox, Collett. *Disputed Dharmas. Early Buddhist Theories on Existence. An Annotated Translation of the Section on Factors Dissociated from Thought from Saṅghabhadra's Nyāyānusāra*. Tokyo: The International Institute for Buddhist Studies, 1995.

Dandekar 1941 = Dandekar, R.N. 'Somatism of Vedic Psychology'. *Indian Historical Quarterly* 17, 70–76, 1941.

DhPr = Durveka Miśra: *Dharmottara-pradīpa*. Dalsukhbhai Malvania (ed.) *Paṇḍita Durveka Miśra*'s *Dharmottara-pradīpa* [*Being a Subcommentary on Dharmottara's Nyāya-bindu-ṭīkā, a Commentary on Dharmakīrti's Nyāya-bindu*]. Patna: Kashi Prasad Jayaswal, Research Institute, 1971.

DPŚ = Candramati (Maticandra): *Daśa-padârtha-śāstra* (*Daśa-padārthī*). (1) Hakuju Ui: *The Vaiśeṣika Philosophy According to the Daśapadārtha-śāstra: Chinese Text with Introduction, Translation, and Notes*. London: The Royal Asiatic Society, 1917. (2) Keiichi Miyamoto: *The Metaphysics and Epistemology of the Early Vaiśeṣikas. With an Appendix: Daśapadārthī of Candramati (A Translation with a Reconstructed Sanskrit Text, Notes and a Critical Edition of the Chinese Version)*. Bhandarkar Oriental Series 28. Pune: Bhandarkar Oriental Research Institute, 1996.

Glasenapp 1942 = Glasenapp, Helmuth von. *The Doctrine of Karman in Jain Philosophy*. Translated from the Original German by G. Barry Gifford, Edited by Prof. Hirlal R. Kapadia. Bombay: The Trustees Bai Vijibai Jivanlal Panalal Charity Fund, 1942.

Hattori 1968 = Hattori, Masaaki: *Dignāga, On Perception, being the Pratyakṣa-pariccheda of Dignāga's Pramāṇa-samuccaya, Edition of Tibetan translations and the Sanskrit text as well as the English translation of the Chapter I*. Harvard University Press, Cambridge (Massachusetts) 1968.

Honda 1988 = Honda, Megumu: 'Vaishêshika Sūtora oboegaki II. [Notes on the Vaiśeṣikasūtra II]'. *Indogaku Bukky÷gaku Kenkyū* (*Journal of Indian and Buddhist Studies*) 37,1 (1988) 472–467 (cited after Isaacson (1993)).

Isaacson 1993 = Isaacson, Harunaga: 'Yogic perception (yogipratyakṣa) in early Vaieṣika'. *Studien zur Indologie und Iranistik* 18 (1993) 139–160.

Isibh = *Isi-bhāsiyāiṃ* [*ṛṣi-bhāṣitāni*]. (1) Walther Schubring: *Isibhāsiyāiṃ. Ein jaina Text der Frühzeit*. Nachrichten von der Akad. Wiss. in Göttingen, Philologisch-Historische Klasse, Göttingen 1942: Nr.1, S.481–576, 1952: Nr. 2 S.21–52. (2) Schubring, Walther (ed., transl.): *Isibhāsiyāiṃ. Aussprüche der Weisen aus dem Prakrit der Jainas. Übersetzt nebst dem revidierten Text*. Alt- und Neu-Indische Studien 14. Hamburg: Franz Steiner Verlag, 1969.

Joshi 1986 = Joshi, Damodar: *Rasa-śāstra*. Trivandrum: Ayurveda College, 1986.

Kāś = Vāmana and Jayāditya: *Kāśikā*. (1) Gaṅgadhāra Śāstrī (ed.): *Kāśikā nāma śrī-pāṇini-muni-viracita-vyākaraṇa-sūtrāṇāṃ vṛttiḥ*. Banāras: Vidyāvilāsa Pres, 1908. (2) Aryendra Sharma; Khanderao Despande; D. G. Padhye (eds.) *Kāśikā, A Commentary on Pāṇini's Grammar by Vāmana and Jayāditya*. 2 vols., Sanskrit Academy Series 17, 20. Hyderabad: Osmania University, 1969, 1970.

Kunst 1968 = Kunst, Arnold. 'Somatism: A Basic Concept in India's Philosophical Speculations'. *Philosophy East and West* 18 (1968) 261–275.

LT = Akalaṅka: *Laghīyas-traya*. (1) Kallāpā Bharamāppā Niṭve (ed.): *Laghīyas-trayâdi-saṅgrahaḥ. 1. bhaṭṭâkalaṅka-deva-kṛtaṃ Laghīyas-trayaṃ, Ānantakīrti-racita-tātpārya-vṛtti-sahitaṃ, 2. bhaṭṭâkalaṅka-deva-kṛtaṃ Svarūpa-sambodhanam, 3–4. Anantakīrti-kṛta-Laghu-Bṛhat-Sarvajñasiddhī ca*. Māṇikacandra-Digambara-Jaina-Grantha-mālā 1, Nāthūrām Premī Maṃtrī / Māṇikacandra-Digambara-Jaina-Grantha-mālā-samiti, Bombay 1915. (2) Mahendra Kumār Nyāya Śāstri (ed.): *Nyāya-kumuda-candra of Śrīmat Prabhācandrācārya. A Commentary on Bhaṭṭākalaṅkadeva's Laghīyastraya*. With an introduction (*Prastāvanā*) by Kailāścandra Śāstri. 2 Vols., Sri Garib Dass Oriental Series 121, Delhi: Sri Satguru Publications, 1991. (1st ed.: Bombay 1938–1942). (3) Nyāyâcārya Mahendra Paṇḍita Kumār Śāstri (ed.): *Śrīmad-Bhaṭṭâkalaṅka-deva-viracitam Akalaṅka-grantha-trayam* (*Svôpajña-vivṛti-sahitam Laghīyas-trayam, Nyāya-viniścayaḥ, Pramāṇa-saṅgrahaś ca*). Ahmadābād (Ahmedabad): Sarasvatī Pustak Bhaṇḍār, 1996 (1st ed: Ahmedabad–Calcutta 1939).

Matilal 1986 = Matilal, Bimal Krishna: *Perception. An Essay on Classical Indian Theories of Knowledge*. Oxford: Oxford University Press, 1986 (reprinted: New Delhi 2002).

MS = Jaimini: *Mīmāṃsā-sūtra*. See: ŚBh.

MŚV = Kumārila Bhaṭṭa: *Mīmāṃsā-śloka-vārttika*. Dvārikādāsa Śāstrī (ed.): *Ślokavārttika of Śrī Kumārila Bhaṭṭa with the Commentary Nyāya-ratnâkara of Śrī Pārthasārathi Miśra*. Ratnabharati Series 3. Varanasi: Tārā Publications, 1978.

Nagasaki 1988 = Nagasaki, Hojun. *A Study of Jaina Epistemology*. (With appendixes: 1. 'Transcendent Perception in Jaina Logic with Special Reference to Buddhist Logic.' 2. 'Perception in Yogācāra-bhūmi.' 3. 'A Study of the Pramāṇa-mīmaṃsā: An Incomplete work on Jaina Logic'.) Kyoto: Heirakuji–Shoten, 1988.

NAV = Siddharṣi-gaṇin: *Nyāyâvatāra-vivṛti*. See: Balcerowicz (2008).

NB = Dharmakīrti: *Nyāya-bindu*. See: DhPr.

NBhū = Bhāsarvajña: *Nyāya-bhūṣaṇa*. Svāmī Yogīndrānanda (ed.): *Śrīmad-ācārya-Bhāsarvajña-praṇītasya Nyāya-sārasya svôpajñaṃ vhyākhyānaṃ Nyāya-bhūṣaṇam*. Ṣaḍ-darśana-grantha-mālā 1. Vārāṇasī: Ṣad-darśana Prakāśana Pratiṣṭhānam, 1968.

NBṬ = Dharmottara: *Nyāya-bindu-ṭīkā*. See: DhPr.

NMa = Jayanta Bhaṭṭa: *Nyāya-mañjarī*. (1) K.S. Varadacharya (ed.): *Nyāyamañjarī of Jayantabhaṭṭa with Ṭippaṇi-nyāya-saurabha by the editor*. vols 1 and 2, *Oriental Research Institute Series* 116, 139. Mysore: University of Mysore, 1969, 1983. (2) Gaurinath Sastri (ed.): *Nyāyamañjarī of Jayanta Bhaṭṭa with the Commentary of Granthi-bhaṅga by Cakradhara*. Part 1–3, M. M. Śivakumāraśāstri-Granthamālā 5. Vārāṇasī: Sampūrṇānand Saṃskṛta Viśvavidyālaya, 1982, 1983, 1984.

NRĀ = Pārthasārathi Miśra: *Nyāya-ratnâkara*. See: MŚV.

NSā = Bhāsarvajña: *Nyāya-sāra*. See: NBhū.

PBh = Praśastapāda: *Praśastapādabhāṣya* (*Padārthadharmasaṅgraha*). (1) Vindhyeśvarī Prasāda Dvivedin (ed.): *The Praśastapāda Bhāṣya with Commentary Nyāyakandalī of Śrīdhara*. Vārāṇasī 1895 (2nd ed. Delhi: Sri Satguru Publications, 1984). (2) Johannes Bronkhorst, Yves Ramseier (eds.) *Word Index to the Praśastapādabhāṣya: a complete word index to the printed editions of the Praśastapādabhāṣya*. Delhi: Motilal Banarsidass, 1994.

PMī = Hemacandra-sūri: *Pramāṇa-mīmāṃsā*. (1) Satkari Mookerjee; Nathmal Tatia: *Hemacandra's Pramāṇa-mīmāṃsā. Text and Translation with Critical Notes*. Varanasi: Tara Publications, 1970. (2) *Kavikālasarvajña-Śrī-Hemacandrâcārya-viracitā svopajña-vṛtti-sahitā Pramāṇa Mīmāṃsā*. Ed. by Sukhlāljī Saṅghavī, Mahendra Kumār and Dalsukh Mālvaṇiyā. Ahmedabad: Sarasvatī Pustak Bhaṇḍār, 1998.

PMīV = Hemacandra-sūri: *Pramāṇa-mīmāṃsā-svopajña-vṛtti*. See: PMī.

PSā = Kundakunda: *Pavayaṇa-sāra* [*Pravacana-sāra*]. A.N. Upadhye (ed.) *Śrī Kunda-kundācārya's Pravacanasāra (Pavayaṇasāra), a Pro-Canonical Text of the Jainas, the Prakṛit Text critically edited with the Sanskrit Commentaries of Amṛtacandra and Jayasena*. Śrī Paramaśruta-Prabhāvaka-Maṇḍala. Agās (Gujarat): Śrīmad Rājacandra Āśrama, 1984. (1st ed. Bombay 1935).

Rau 1983 = Rau, Wilhelm: *Zur vedischen Altertumskunde*. Akademie der Wissenschaften zu Mainz, Abhandlungen der Geistes- u. sozialwissenschaftlichen Klasse 1983, No. 1. Wiesbaden: Franz Steiner Verlag, 1983.

Rṇv = *Rasârṇava*. Praphulla Cadra Rāy; Hariś Candra Kaviratna (eds.): *Rasârṇava*. Bibliotheca Indica 175. Calcutta: The Asiatic Society, 1985 (reprinted) (1st ed. 1910).

RRS = *Rasa-ratna-samuccaya*. Vināyaka Ganeśa Āpaṭe (ed.): *Rasa-ratna-samuccaya-ṭīkā*. Ānandāśrama-saṁskṛta-granthāvali 115. Pune: Ānandāśrama-mudranālaya, 1941.

RRSṬ = Maṇiśātri: *Rasa-ratna-samuccaya-ṭīkā*. Ed. by Vināyaka Ganeśa Āpaṭe, Ānan dāśrama-saṃskṛta-granthāvali 115, 1941.

Schayer 1936 = Schayer, Stanisław: 'Über den Somatismus der indischen Psychologie.' *Bulletin International de l'Academie Polonaise des Sciences et des Lettres, Classe de Philologie* (Cracow) 7–10 (1936) 159–168. (Reprinted in: Stanisław Schayer: *O filozofowaniu Hindusów. Artyku³y wybrane*. Ed. by Marek Mejor. Polska Akademia Nauk, Komitet Nauk Orientalistycznych. Warsaw: PWN, 1988, pp. 495–504).

Sinha 1934 = Sinha, Jadunath: *Indian Psychology Perception*. London: Kegan Paul, Trench, Trubner, 1934.

SSā = Kundakunda: *Samaya-sāra*. (1) Rai Bahadur J.L. Jaini (ed., transl.) *The Sacred Books of the Jainas*. Vol. VIII: *Samayasara (The Soul-Essence) by Shri Kunda Kunda*

Acharya. Aitashram, Lucknow: The Central Jaina Publishing House, 1930. (2) Pannālāl Jain (ed.): *Śrīmad-bhagavat-Kundakundâcārya-viracitaḥ Samaya-sāraḥ Ātma-khyāti-Tātpārya-vṛtti-Ātma-khyāti-bhāṣā-vacanikā iti Ṭīkā-trayôpetaḥ*. Śrī Paramaśruta Prabhāvaka Maṇḍala. Agās: Śrīmad Rājacandra Āśrama, 1997. (3) Khemacandra Jaina Sarārph (ed.) *Parama-pūjya Śrīmat-Kundakundâcārya-deva praṇīta Samaya-sāra evaṃ us para parama-pūjya Śrīmad-Amṛtacandra-sūri-viracita saṃskṛta ṭīkā Ātma-khyāti tathā donoṛ para Ādhyātma-yogī Nyāya-tīrtha guruvarya sahajānanda Mahārāja dvārā viracita Sapta-daśâṅgī-ṭīkā*. Meraṭh san: Mantrī Sahajānanda Śāstramālā, 1977.

SSi = Pūjyapāda Devanandin: *Sarvârtha-siddhi*. (1) Phoolchandra Shastri (ed.): *Ācārya Pūjyapāda's Sarvārthasiddhi [The commentary on Ācārya Griddhapiccha's Tattvārtha-sūtra]*. Edited and translated (into Hindi). Varanasi 1934 (reprinted: Jñānapīṭha Mūrtidevī Jaina Grantha-mālā13. Delhi: Bhāratīya Jñānapīṭha Prakāśana, 2000). (2) Jinadasa Śastri (ed.) *Tattvārtha-vṛttiḥ Sarvārtha-siddhiḥ—Pūjyapāda Devanandin*. Śrīsekhārāma Nemicandra Granthāmālā 128. Ṣodaśapur: Devajī Sakhārām Diśī & Māṇikacandra-digambara-jaina-parīkṣālaya-mantri, 1939.

Stcherbatsky 1930 = Stcherbatsky, Th.: *Buddhist Logic*, vols I and II. Leningrad: Izdatel'stvo Akademii Nauk SSSR, 1930 (reprinted: Delhi: Motilal Banarsidass, 1993).

SVi = Akalaṅka Bhaṭṭa: *Siddhi-viniścaya*. Mahendrakumār Jain (ed.) *Siddhi-viniścaya of Akalaṅka edited with the commentary Siddhi-viniścaya-ṭīkā of Anantavīrya*, 2 vols. Vārāṇasī: Bhāratīya Jñānapīṭha Prakāśana, 1959.

SVK = Yaśovijaya: *Syād-vāda-kalpalatā* [*Śāstra-vārtā-samuccaya-vyākhyā*]. Badarī-nath Śukla; Vijaya Prem Sūri; Vijaya Suvanabh (eds.): *Śrīmad Haribhadra-sūri-racita Śāstra-vārtā-samuccaya tathā . . . Śri Yaśovijaya-kṛta Syād-vāda-kalpalatā* [*Vyākhyā*] *kā Hindi-vivecana. Hindi-vivecana-kāra Badarī-nath Śukla, Hindi-vivecana-abhivīkṣaka Vijaya Pre-sūri*, vols. 1–7. Gulālvāḍī, Muṃbaī: Chaukhambhā Oriyanṭāliyā, Vārāṇasī / Divya-darśan Ṭrasṭ, 1977–1089.

ŚBh = Śabarasvāmin: *Mīmāṃsā-śābara-bhāṣya*. *Mīmāṃsā-śābara-bhāṣya*, ed. Yudhiṣṭhira Mīmāṃsaka, vols. 1–6. Śrī Śāntisvarūp Kapūr, Rāmalāl Kapūr Trust Press, Bahālgaḍh Sonīpat – Haryāṇā I: 1987, II: 1990, III: 1980, IV: 1985,V: 1986, VI: 1990.

ŚDī = Pārthasārathi Mīśra: *Śāstra-dīpikā*. (1) L. S. Dravid (ed.): *Tarka-pāda Section edited with Ramakṛṣṇa's Yukti-sneha-prapūraṇī*. Chowkhambā Sanskrit Series 43, Chowkhambā, Vārāṇasī (Benares) 1916. (2) Dharmadatta Jha (ed.): *Shāstradīpikā of Parthasarathi Mishra, With the Commentary Mayukhamalika (From Second Pada of First Chapter to the End) by Somanātha and With the Commentary Yuktisnehaprapurani (For the First Tarkapada) by Rāmakrishna*. Varanasi: Krishnadas Academy, 1988.

ŚVS = Haribhadra-sūri: *Śāstra-vārtā-samuccaya*. K.K. Dixit (ed., Hindi transl.): *The Śāstravārtāsamuccaya of Ācārya Haribhadrasūri with Hindi Translation, Notes and Introduction*. L.D. Series 22. Ahmedabad: Lalbhai Dalpatbhai Bharatiya Sanskriti Vidyamandira, 1969.

TBh = Umāsvāti: *Tattvârthâdhigama-bhāṣya*. See: TS_1, TS_2.

TS = Umāsvāmin: *Tattvârtha-sūtra*. (1) M.K. Mody (ed.): *Tattvarthadhigama by Umāsvāti being in the Original Sanskrit with the Bhāṣya by the author himself*. BINS 1044, 1079, 1118, Calcutta 1903, 1904, 1905. [= Śvetāmbara Recension]. (2) See: SSi. [= Digāmbara Recension].

TUS = Jayarāśi Bhaṭṭa: *Tattvôpaplava-siṃha*. (1) Sukhlalji Sanghavi and Rasiklal C. Parikh (ed.): *Tattvopaplavasimha of Shri Jayarasi Bhatta*. Gaekwad's Oriental Series 87, Baroda: Oriental Institute, 1940. (2) Eli Franco. *Perception, Knowledge and Disbelief: A study of Jayarāśi's scepticism*. Stuttgart: AuNIS 35, 1987. (reprinted: Delhi: Motilal Banarsidas, 1994). (3) Esther Solomon: *Tattvopaplavasiṃha (An Introduction, Sanskrit*

Text, English Translation & Notes). Parimal Sanskrit Series 111. Delhi: Parimal Publications, 2010.

VĀBh = Jinabhadra-gaṇin: *Visesâvassaya-bhāsa* (*Viśeṣâvaśyaka-bhāṣya*). Haragovinda Dās (ed.): *Viśeṣâvaśyaka-bhāṣyaṃ. Maladhāri-śrī-hemacandra-sūri-viracitayā śiṣya-hitânamnayā bṛhad-vṛttyā vibhūṣitam*. Śrī-Yaśovijaya-jaina-grantha-mālā 25, 27, 28, 31, 33, 35, 37, 39. Vārāṇasī: Shah Harakhchand Bhurabhai, 1915.

VP = Bhartṛhari: *Vākya-padīya*. Wilhelm Rau: *Bhartṛharis Vākyapadīya. Die Mūlakārikās nach den Handschriften herausgegeben und mit einem Pāda-Index versehen*. Abhandlungen für die Kunde des Morgenlandes XLII, 4. Wiesbaden: Franz Steiner Verlag, 1977.

VS(C) = Kaṇāda: *Vaiśeṣikasūtra* (Candrānanda's recension). Muni Jambuvijaya (ed.): *Vaiśeṣikasūtra of Kaṇāda with the Commentary of Candrānanda*. Introduction by Anantalal Thakur. Gaekwad's Oriental Series. Baroda: Oriental Institute 136, 1961.

VS(D) = Kaṇāda: *Vaiśeṣika-sūtra*. Anantalal Thakur (ed.): *Kaṇāda-kṛtaṃ vaiśeṣika-darśanam avijñāta-kṛta-pracīna-vyākhyayā samalaṅkṛtam—Vaiśeṣikadarśana of Kaṇāda with an Anonymous Commentary*. Darbhanga: Mithila Institute of Post-Graduate Studies and Research in Sanskrit Learning, 1957.

VS(Ś) = Kaṇāda: *Vaiśeṣika-sūtra* (Śaṅkaramiśra's recension, *Upaskāra*). (1) Jayanārāyaṇa Tarkapañcānana (ed.): *Vaiśeṣika-darśana of Kaṇāda with the Commentaries Vaiśeṣika-sūtrôpaskāra of Śaṅkara Miśra and Kaṇāda-sūtra-vivṛti of Jayanārāyaṇa Tarkapañcānana*. Calcutta: Bibliotheca Indica I 34, 1861.

VSV(C) = Candrānanda: *Vaiśeṣikasūtravṛtti*. Siehe: VS(C).

Wezler 1982 = Wezler, Albrecht: 'Remarks on the definition of "yoga" in the Vaiśeṣikasūtra', in: L. A. Hercus et al. (eds.) *Indological and Buddhist Studies. Volume in Honour of Professor J.W. de Jong on His Sixtieth Birthday*. Canberra: Australian National University, Faculty of Asian Studies, 1982, pp. 643–686.

YBh = *Yoga-bhāṣya*. See: YS.

YDī = *Yukti-dīpikā*. Albrecht Wezler and Shujun Motegi: *Yuktidīpikā. The Most Significant Commentary on the Sāṃkhyakārikā*. Critically edited by Albrecht Wezler and Shujun Motegi. Vol. I. *Alt- und Neu-Indische Studien* 44, Stuttgart 1998.

YS = Patañjali: *Yoga-sūtra*. *Pātāñjala-yogasūtra-bhāṣya Vivaraṇam of Śaṅkara-bhaga vatpāda*, ed. Polakam Sri Rama Sastri and S.R. Krishnamurthi Sastri. Madras: Government Oriental Manuscripts Library, 1952.

5 Extrasensory perception (*yogi-pratyakṣa*) in Jainism and its refutations*

Piotr Balcerowicz

As we can see from Chapter 4, "Extrasensory perception (*yogi-pratyakṣa*) in Jainism, proofs of its existence and its soteriological implications" (references to this chapter below are as "see arguments"), extrasensory perception (*yogi-pratyakṣa*) in Jainism not only was, in the form of its three subdivisions, a part of the taxonomy of epistemic faculties, but also fulfilled a rhetorical and argumentative role to prove a possibility of omniscience and perfection of the human being, in addition to its soteriological role.

The previous chapter presented a compilation of arguments for the existence of extrasensory perception and perfect knowledge (*kevala*), i.e., omniscience, and of an omniscient being advanced by the Jainas. A number of such arguments, as we could see, overlap or are perhaps even borrowed from other schools, primarily from the Nyāya-Vaiśeṣika and Buddhists. Some of them are, however, characteristically Jaina and were only possible granted Jaina specific ontological or epistemological presuppositions.

Such arguments gave rise to a range of counter-arguments, or arguments against the possibility of omniscience or of an omniscient being, formulated by the Mīmāṃsakas and materialists, which often preserved a preliminary objection (*pūrvapakṣa*) in mostly Jaina and Nyāya texts. Usually the counter-arguments are on the whole directed against the Naiyāyika-Vaiśeṣikas, not particularly against the Jainas. In this chapter, I will try to collect such arguments formulated in various schools of thought in ancient India. Since I will frequently refer to the proof of extrasensory perception and omniscience, an adequate appraisal of the counter-arguments outlined in this chapter may require a parallel reading of the arguments described in Chapter 4. As against a common stereotype that Indian traditions were unanimous in their acceptance of supernatural perception, there were at least three notable exceptions to be mentioned, namely the followers of the schools of the early Nyāya-Vaiśeṣika until the beginning of the fifth century,[1] Mīmāṃsā and the materialists, or Cārvāka / Lokāyata. In their realistic approach, these philosophical schools rejected the supra-sensory sphere, albeit for different reasons.

The materialist Cārvāka accepted the world as it was presented to us through our senses, and to illustrate their thesis they would cite the following dictum (*nyāya*): "empirical facts and everyday practice are explicable by this much only" (*iyataiva dṛṣṭa –vyavahāropapatti*).[2] In other words, if an event or phenomenon, e.g., the occurrence of consciousness in a physical body, can be successfully explained without the assumption of some additional hypothetical or disputable entities, by taking recourse to a lesser number of assumptions and in the most economic way, there is no ground for assuming such hypothetical entities. This approach is very much akin to Occam's razor, *entia non sunt multiplicanda praeter necessitatem* ("entities are not to be multiplied without necessity"), a maxim ascribed to William of Ockham.[3]

Similarly, the Mīmāṃsaka did not admit the existence of supernatural perception (*yogi-pratyakṣa*) for the simple reason that it would undermine the authoritative status of the Vedas as the only source of information on moral law (*dharma*), the fundament of all dealings and social interactions in the world. In the system, *dharma* was defined as follows: "Moral law is the desired goal an indication of which is injunction."[4] In his commentary, Śabarasvāmin emphasises not only the moral and eschatological relevance of the Vedic injunction (*codanā*), but also its cognitive scope: "The injunction enables [people] to know anything of the following sort: past, present, future, subtle, concealed [from sight] and distant; there is no other instrument [to know these]"[5]; and precisely these were the things that were believed by, e.g., later Naiyāyikas and Vaiśeṣikas, to be amenable to supernatural perception and were described by them in exactly the same terms.[6] The Vedas are therefore the only means to know the moral law (*dharma*), which regulates all spheres of human life in this world and hereafter.[7] The fear of the Mīmāṃsaka clearly was that the admission of any possibility of supernatural perception would render the Vedas unnecessary as the source of knowledge on extrasensory objects, including the post-mortem human fate, as well as morality and *dharma*. The consequences the admission of extrasensory perception would have for society and the world would be destructive, insofar as the fundament of morality and social and ritual order, i.e., the Vedas, would no longer be held relevant or valid. Kumārila, apparently referring to Praśastapāda's claim that there is something like intuition (*pratibha* or *pratibhā*) called the seers' perception (*ārṣa-pratyakṣa*),[8] explains: 'Just like ordinary intuition, which does not depend on perception or other cognitive criteria, would not be adequate to [provide any reliable] judgement, so is [the intuition] of yogins.'[9]

1 A refutation of the argument from progression in its various forms (see arguments, §§ 1–3), directed rather against Dharmakīrti's version of it (see arguments, § 3) than against the Jainas', is found for instance in the commentaries to the *Mīmāôsā-śloka-vārttika*, i.e. Pārthasārathi Miśra's *Nyāya-Ratnakara*[10] and in Sucaritamiśra's *Kāśikā*:

> "And indeed it is an empirical fact that perfection (intensity, accomplishment) of cause (S = *sādhya*) is pervaded by the perfection (intensity, accomplishment) of the result (H = *hetu*), for instance perfection of craftsmanship of a painter etc. [is pervaded by] perfection of a painting etc. And the cause of [supernatural] perception of any particular yogin who is engrossed in contemplation is undergoing a process of gradual

> perfection." – thus runs [the invariable concomitance (*vyāpti*) of] the logical reason as essential nature [accepted by the Buddhists]. But if this were really so, on what account could the perfection of the cause be known?[11]

In other words, if we accepted the internal logic of the argument from progression, as Sucaritamiśra demonstrates, from perfection of craftsmanship of a painter (H) one can validly infer perfection of a painting (S), etc.: H → S. But the problem the Buddhist or Jaina opponent has to face is the following: on the basis of what can we decide that a painter is indeed accomplished? Generally it is from an excellent painting that one infers that the one who has committed it is an accomplished artist: S → H, not the other way round. Consequently, the argument from progression either reverses the established logic, whereby instead of judging the skill of an artist on the basis of his works it would have us evaluate the quality of an artefact on the basis of the talent of the artist, or is circular, in which: H → S and S → H.

Precisely the same problem is observed in the case of the Buddhist and Jaina argument in which, too, from the intensity of contemplation (H) one infers perfection of supernatural perception (S): H → S, instead of the other way round. Accordingly, the argument that contemplation itself is the cause of perfection which brings about *yogi-pratyakṣa* is circular: we confuse cause and effect, the instrument and action. We can call this counter-argument circularity of the argument from progression.

2 A typical counter-argument is from the non-production of the future and the past, based on the presumption that all kinds of perception, to remain perception, grasp only present objects. Future and past objects are therefore, by definition, inaccessible to any kind of perception. A version of it is found, e.g., in Jayarāśi Bhaṭṭa's *Tattvôpaplava-siṃha*:

> Similarly, the perception of the yogins cannot be produced by the perceived object, because past or future [objects] cannot produce [anything]. Or, if they could produce, they would lose their status of past and future things.[12]

Jayarāśi points out that an admission of supernatural perception, which is directly caused by the object being perceived in the very same moment, involves contradiction: cause and effect cannot be absolutely separated in time and space.

3 Jayarāśi Bhaṭṭa extends this counter-argument to emphasise the inaccessibility of the future and the past:

> Similarly, the perception of the yogins, which [is believed to] arise with regard to past and future objects, cannot make [the yogin] reach the object.[13]

He is clearly alluding to the Nyāya-Vaiśeṣika concept of perception which is maintained to be non-belying, reliable, trustworthy (*avisaṃvādin*), and thus to provide a kind of dependable promise: if one acts in accordance with what a particular act of perception presents to consciousness, one will surely achieve this object. For instance, if perception presents a jug of water, we are justified in acting towards it and grasping it in order to quench our thirst. That principle of "non-belying, reliability, trustworthiness" (*avisaṃvāda*) can certainly not be met in the case of supernatural perception of past or future objects: no matter how much one could try to quench one's thirst with past or future water, the efforts will be futile. In other words, such perception "belies its promise," viz. it does not pass the test of practical verification. Jayarāśi's argument is therefore pragmatic.

In a discussion on whether we should accept testimony (*āgama, śabda*) as another cognitive criterion in the *Nyāya-bhūṣaṇa*, Bhāsarvajña recapitulates a similar proof, albeit more extended, that supernatural perception cannot grasp past and future objects, which is an indirect proof that *yogi-pratyakṣa* cannot exist:

> Furthermore, what would be the connection between supernatural cognition (perception) and past and future objects? It has already been made clear that such objects cannot produce cognition. If you say that the origination of [supernatural cognition] takes place in an uninterrupted series, this is not correct because past and future things cannot produce [any cognition] even in an uninterrupted series. For no cognition can be produced directly by these [objects], in consequence of which one should admit that this [cognition] is produced in an uninterrupted series of other cognitions as a sequence of reproductions of past impressions of these [objects]. [Let us then assume] that a cognition that belongs to the series [of the yogin's cognition] generates it. But this is not the case, because [the cognition of the series] which generates [the final cognition of the yogin] already belongs to the past. But even if [one admits as the cause] a cognition that belongs to the series [of the yogin's cognition], one knowledge produced by something cannot determine another [knowledge], because that would have too far-reaching consequences: [for instance] that would lead to the undesired consequence that one knowledge produced by one object such as a woman, piece of gold etc., would determine [the knowledge] of all women, pieces of gold etc.[14]

4 Still another argument to counter the proof, primarily of Buddhist provenance, from progression by necessity is by pointing out that the actual object-field for a meditative contemplation, or supernatural perception, is merely a series of recollective mental images projected in a present moment (counter-argument from past images). This counter-argument is voiced by Pārthasārathi Miśra in the *Nyāya-Ratnakara*:

> For what you call [supernatural] perception produced by the power of contemplation is not possible, because contemplation consists in a series of memory-images of similar contents and is uninterrupted by [a thought

> of] another [object].[15] And memory has as its contents something which has already been experienced, [hence] it does not refer to something not yet cognised [which is a characteristic of any cognitive criterion (*pramāṇa*); therefore the knowledge we acquire through memory is not valid]. Thus, if dharma could be cognised without any cognitive criterion, what would be the use of contemplation?![16]

The main points in the counter-argument are as follows:

1. Supernatural perception is said to be produced by meditative contemplation, but in fact it presents past images, therefore it is merely a kind of memory (*smṛti*); being such, the knowledge it brings about is not valid, inasmuch as memory (*smṛti*) does not count as a cognitive criterion (*pramāṇa*).
2. If the cognitive procedure of supernatural perception were accepted as valid (*pramāṇa*), that would amount to saying that we could grasp through it objects which are also past, future, distant, etc., but in fact these could be cognized through memory only; therefore meditative contemplation and yoga would become redundant.
3. That would also mean that we could grasp moral law (*dharma*) through memory and no cognitive criteria (valid cognitive procedures) would be necessary.
4. Consequently, that would amount to the collapse of all philosophic inquiry (no validity of acts of cognition), the collapse of morality (*dharma* could be known through methods that are not valid), and collapse of the authority of Vedas.

5 Its variant, the counter-argument from the lack of cause, is briefly presented in Sucaritamiśra's *Kāśikā*:

> By the very [statement that supra-sensory perception grasps] "past and future objects as well" [you] express the idea that there is no cause [of such a perception].[17]

Such supernatural perception would therefore have to be admitted to be fictitious, because it would have no objective basis (*ālambana*), being uncaused.

6 An important and powerful line of reasoning – let's call it the counter-argument from the limited domain – is presented by Kumārila to refute the argument from progression:

> [Even then], in so far as there cannot be any going beyond the own domain [of sense organs], the culmination experienced with regard to some [domain, e.g. vision,] would concern only [e.g.] visual perception of things which are distant, subtle etc.; but this could not be the operation of the sense of hearing with regard to visual aspects.[18]

Again, Kumārila directs his repudiation primarily against the Naiyāyikas, not the Jainas, as confirmed by a subsequent reaction of Jayanta Bhaṭṭa, who quotes Kumārila's verse:

> Let us assume [for a while] that there be culmination [of perception] as long as it does not go beyond its own domain. But [even then] the moral law cannot become the domain for e.g. the eye. As it has been said by Kumārila . . .[19]

Even if we accept that a progression in the case of one sense faculty, say, sight, culminates with a state in which that faculty exceeds its ordinary limits and grasps things normally invisible, being subtle, concealed from sight and distant, nevertheless such a progression in one sense organ could in no way affect a similar development in the remaining sense faculties, and such extrasensory perception would have to be restricted only to the visual aspect of such things, certainly not to all. By implication, that would exclude a possibility of omniscience.

7 Using a similar idea, Kumārila produces another counter-argument, from the overlapping of sensory data:

> If the omniscient person can conceive [of everything] by virtue of any cognitive criterion (cognitively valid procedure), then this [cognitive criterion] could cognise all tastes etc. through the eye.[20]

The commentator Pārthasārathi Miśra adds the following remark:

> Otherwise how could someone who knows the limitation of [sense organs'] own nature, [i.e. the restriction of each of the sense organs to their own respective data only], experience the operation of perception or any other [cognitive criterion] with respect to all things which are not the respective domain?[21]

Supernatural perception, including omniscience, would require that the typical ordering of particular perceptual data as related to particular perceptual cognitions would no longer be there.

This counter-argument could only be formulated and be meaningful given the ontology of systems such as Mīmāṃsā, Nyāya, or Vaiśeṣika, which assume that the self, or soul (*ātman*), normally cognizes only through some medium, e.g., through the mind or sense organs. This argument would formally be a little less effective in the view of the Jaina ontology according to which the ultimate cognizer is the soul and does not necessitate any particular sense organ or other instrument. Jaina classifications generally distinguish five kinds of sensory perception (*indriya-pratyakṣa*), or conventional perception (*sāṃvyavahārika-pratyakṣa*), but do not explicitly draw such distinction in the case of extrasensory perception or omniscience. However, even without formally distinguishing varieties of extrasensory perception related to the five object-fields, the Jainas would find it difficult to meaningfully speak of extrasensory perception in which all kinds of data – auditory, ocular, olfactory, gustatory, and tactile as well as mental (introspective, reflexive) – would mingle: such perception could not serve to make any basic distinctions that normally perception does.

The above verse is quoted by Jayanta Bhaṭṭa, who tries to dispel Kumārila's criticism:

> Also yogins have senses which grasp taste and other sensory data, and like [their] eyes, these [other sense organs] are indeed perfected. Therefore one does not have to assume any operation of [yogins'] eye with respect to taste etc.[22]

What is important, even though Kumārila (MŚV 2.112) speaks of the omniscient person (*sarva-jña*), is that in his rejoinder Jayanta Bhaṭṭa speaks of the perception of the yogins, which only confirms that the difference between *sarva-jñāna* and *yogi-pratyakṣa* was only quantitative and in degree, but not qualitative or in essence.

8 A straightforwardly commonsensical counter-argument is from the lack of evidence, advanced, e.g., by Kumārila:

> [117] Well, we and other people do not see any omniscient person nowadays and a line of reasoning [to prove that such an omniscient person ever] existed is impossible in the same way as one can negate [the existence of such people]. [118] Nor [the existence of] an omniscient person [can be proved] by scripture, because that would be a case of mutual dependence (vicious circle). [Besides], how is the [full] validity of [a text] communicated conceivable?'[23]

The idea is not simply that omniscient persons are never seen. What the argument purports to demonstrate is that their existence cannot be proved through mere observation, i.e., perception as one of the cognitive criteria, but there are no other cognitive criteria, such as inference or scripture, which could provide some kind of evidence for their existence. Reliance on scripture to prove its author's omniscience would involve circularity. That being the case, one can still provide rational arguments against their existence.

This counter-argument from the lack of evidence is recapitulated in a fuller form by Hemacandra:

> There is no cognitively valid procedure at all to prove the omniscient cognition or any other [supernatural perception]. [First,] the functioning of perception is limited to respective domains of colour etc. [for respective sense and] it cannot operate with regard to an extrasensory object. [Second,] neither can inference [grasp the extrasensory object], because it has as its basis that it is produced by force of relation between the inferential sign and the possessor of the inferential sign, both of which are grasped by perception. [Third, it is not

> possible through testimony because] if testimony is [believed to be] related to this [supernatural perception because it is] preceded by extrasensory cognition, then [we have a case of] mutual dependence.[24]

In a separate section of his *Pramāṇa-Mīmāṃsā* alongside the commentary (PMĪ 1.17, and PMĪV 1.17 §§ 59–70, pp. 16–18) devoted to this counter-argument, Hemacandra presents a few more interesting variants of it.

9 Kumārila provides also a counter-argument from misapplied definition:

> The perception of yogins is not at all different from [the perception] of ordinary [people]. Insofar as also this [supernatural perception] is a perception, it should grasp present [objects] as well as it should be produced through the contact with a [really] existing [thing]. The concept which arises in these [yogins] with regard to an absent (sc. either future or past) object is, therefore, not perception, in the same way as desire (about the future object) or remembrance (about the past object) [is not perception].[25]

10 In an ingenious way Kumārila reverses the argument from no counter-proof (see arguments, § 14) into an effective counter-argument against omniscience:

> [134] For how can it be ascertained that "he is omniscient" at the time of his existence by those who wish to know this but are devoid of the awareness of his knowledge (sc. his ability) and of what he knows (the contents of his knowledge), [i.e. are not omniscient themselves]? [135] You would have to assume numerous omniscient men [living contemporaneously], because someone who is not omniscient cannot know that the other person is omniscient. [136] And for someone who cannot [directly] see that a particular person is omniscient the own words of such [a person] have no cognitive validity if he does not know [any scriptural] basis (sc. unless he accepts the testimony of scriptures), just like statements of any other [ordinary person].[26]

In his argument Kumārila points out that the ordinary Buddhists, Jainas, Naiyāyikas or Vaiśeṣikas who admit omniscience of the Buddha, the Jina or Īśvara should be omniscient themselves in order to substantiate the omniscience claim. Besides, that would also entail the necessary plurality of omniscient beings, which would go against the assumption of early Buddhists and Jainas, who believed that the birth of an omniscient Buddha or Jina is a unique event and two Buddhas or Jinas cannot co-exist in the same region side by side. This attitude changed with Mahāyāna Buddhism and in mediaeval Jainism, which admitted of such a simultaneous plurality of omniscient Buddhas or Jinas, respectively, in various worlds (or parts of the universe). But even then they never admitted that two Buddhas or

Jinas could co-exist within the same part of the world and have direct personal contact with each other.

Without being omniscient themselves, the believers in an omniscient being are left to rely solely on the testimonial evidence of those claiming to be omniscient, which would involve a fallacy of a vicious circle (*vide infra*, § 11). Thus to ascribe omniscience to anyone one should be at the level of omniscience ("meta-level") in order to verify it directly in another person: the required level (omniscience) is not accessible from the level of ordinary experience ("first-level").

Comparing two lines of reasoning – see arguments, § 14 (the argument from no counter-proof) and § 10 below (counter-argument from no counter-proof) – we encounter a collision of two conflicting approaches based on the same principle: to judge the other person's omniscience one has to be omniscient. One is a negative reasoning, to deny (falsify) the other person's omniscience, the other is positive, to prove (verify) the other person's omniscience. As indicated above (see arguments, § 14) both these arguments juxtaposed, as Kumārila presents them, are neither a mere play on words and arguments nor an irreconcilable confrontation of arguments and counter-arguments, in analogy to the seemingly irresolvable conflict between theistic and atheistic world views. Kumārila attempts to demonstrate that any claim in philosophical discourse should first be proved and corroborated in order to enter the realm of discourse, otherwise it remains a matter of mere belief; and the weight of proof is always on the side of the propounder of a particular theory. Otherwise, anyone could postulate the existence of any imaginable entity. Not to postulate entities which one cannot prove is some sort of extension of the principle of economy in rational thinking and discourse. This principle of parsimony (*lāghava, kalpanā-gaurava-prasaṅga*) was widely accepted in India, including the Mīmāṃsaka and Cārvāka, who are reported to follow the dictum (*nyāya*): "empirical facts and everyday practice are explicable by this much only" (*vide supra*, n. 2). In other words, if any event – e.g., the occurrence of consciousness in a physical body – can be explained without assuming additional hypothetical or disputable entities, by taking recourse to a lesser number of assumptions and in the most economic way, there is no ground for assuming such hypothetical entities. This approach is very much akin to Occam's razor.

11 In the last line of the above quotation in § 10 (MŚV 2.136cd: *tad-vākyānāṃ pramāṇatvaṃ mūlajñāne*), Kumārila speaks of another requirement, apart from being omniscient, that could enable one to admit another person's omniscience: that person's own testimony. That is precisely the same counter-argument from circularity evoked also on another occasion, where Kumārila turns directly against the Jainas:

> In the same way [as the Buddhists, also the Jainas] admit that a living being (soul) who no longer depends on sense-organs etc.[27] possesses absolute cognition the contents of which are [things that are] subtle, past etc. But this cannot be proved without his own testimony (scriptures), and the [authority of] testimony (scriptures) [cannot be proved] without him.[28]

Kumārila points to the a major logical flaw in such a reasoning, called 'the mutual dependence' (*itaretaraśraya*[29], also known as *anyonyaśraya*), viz. *circulus vitiosus*: to accept omniscience we have to rely on the authority of the scriptures, which are the testimony imparted by the omniscient; and to rely on the authority of the scriptures we have to accept the omniscience of their author. Both ends of the vicious circle are equally imperceptible and cannot be verified solely by reference to our perception of quotidian experience. This paradox, referred to by Kumārila, is a general problem of authoritative character of all revealed monotheistic religions, but not only,[30] and is logically embedded in their doctrinal structure.

12 As was the case in an earlier argument (§ 10), Kumārila reverses the line of reasoning (the scripture and the omniscient author reciprocally validating each other) which was the basis of the previous argument and which suffers from the flaw of mutual dependence, or circularity, and makes out of it a counter-argument against omniscience in a rather surprising manner:

> [130] My statement "The Buddha and others are not omniscient" is true because I am saying this, like in the case [of such statements]: "fire is hot and radiant." [131] And what I am saying is directly verifiable, whereas you should first prove what you are saying. Therefore, my [statement] is a proof (logical reason), whereas your [statement] is either doubtful or unproved [i.e. your proof suffers from the fallacy of the doubtful logical reason or from the unproved logical reason]. [132] How can anyone postulate something (e.g. omniscience) in the case of which [a reason] such as being a cognoscible thing etc. which does not contradict perception etc. can disprove its existence?[31]

In fact, this is quite an ingenious reversal of the argument from verifiability of the speaker's statements (see arguments, § 16). What could be named the counter-argument from one's own verifiable statements rests on one's authority derived by analogy from the speaker's other statements that can easily be verified empirically. Nevertheless, it is clearly logically flawed: even if we have positively verified the truth of a person x's statement p as well as his subsequent statements $p + 1$, and $(p + 1) + 1$ up to $(p + 1) + \ldots + n$, it does not follow that a future statement $(p + 1) + \ldots + n + (n + 1)$ is equally true (the problem of induction). Nevertheless, the reversal does not suffer from the fallacy of mutual dependence (circularity), as does the circular proof of omniscience from the scripture.

13 There is still one more counter-argument which Hemacandra targets with his argument from partial description (see arguments, § 13, n. 107), and which is referred to, e.g., by Dharmakīrti in the *Nyāya-Bindu*, Siddharṣi-gaṇin in the *Nyāyavatāra-vivṛti,* and Bhāsarvajña in the *Nyāya-bhūṣaṇa*:

> This [particular person] is not omniscient, because he is endowed with passion (or: because he is a speaker), like a person in the street.[32]

This counter-argument from passions, indeed rather unconvincing, purports to demonstrate that it is not possible to determine on strictly behavioral grounds whether a particular person, who appears on all counts to be like any other member of society, is omniscient. It is classified by Buddhists, Jainas, and the Naiyāyikas as a fallacy of the example (*dṛṣṭāntabhāsa, udāharaṇabhāsa*) type in which the property of the probandum and the probans is doubtful (*sandigdha-sādhya-sādhana-dharma*; NB, NAV) or in which the probans is doubtful (*sandigdha-sādhana*; NBhū). I have not come across its genuine instantiation in the Mīmāṃsā or Cārvāka literature, and it seems to be known to us only from its references in Jaina and Buddhist literature.

14 As in the case of the arguments for supernatural perception (*yogi-pratyakṣa*) and omniscience (*sarva-jñāna, kevala*), we can also summarise the counter-arguments, in the following list, knowing that it is not exhaustive and more proofs will surface in subsequent research:

counter-argument circularity of the argument from progression (§ 1)
counter-argument from the non-production of the future and the past (§ 2)
counter-argument from the inaccessibility of the future and the past (§ 3)
counter-argument from past images (§ 4)
counter-argument from the lack of cause (§ 5)
counter-argument from the limited domain (§ 6)
counter-argument from the overlapping of sensory data (§ 7)
counter-argument from the lack of evidence (§ 8)
counter-argument from misapplied definition (§ 9)
counter-argument from no counter-proof (§ 10)
counter-argument from circularity (§ 11)
counter-argument from one's own verifiable statements (§ 12)
counter-argument from passions (§ 13).

15 Since no works of Indian materialists (*cārvāka, lokāyata*) survived except for the *Tattvopaplavasiṃha* of Jayarāśi Bhaṭṭa, "a sceptic loosely affiliated to the materialist Cārvāka / Lokāyata school of thought,"[33] we cannot hope to find a plethora of counter-arguments retained first-hand in their works except for some stray excerpts, quotations and reports preserved in works of other schools, such as, e.g., Prabhācandra-sūri's *Prameya-kamala-mārtaṇḍa* (PKM, pp. 247–254). These may yield more interesting counter-arguments.

However, from the extant sources it transpires that the main opponents of the idea of omniscience, i.e., Mīmāṃsakas and materialists, directed their arguments primarily against the schools of Nyāya-Vaiśeṣika and the Buddhists. The Jaina concept of omniscience and proofs thereof produced by them hardly ever became the butt of such criticism, which would attest to a rather secondary role played by Jaina thinkers in the actual development of Indian philosophy, at least the way it was perceived by Indian thinkers who were less interested in discussing the Jaina concept of omniscience as a viable alternative.

Notes

* A significant part of the present research has been generously supported by the National Science Centre of Poland (Research Project: History of Classical Indian Philosophy: non-Brahmanic Schools, National Science Centre, 2011/01/B/HS1/04014).

1 Supernatural perception was absent in the original Vaiśeṣika-sūtra, as it existed prior to Praśastapāda; see: Wezler (1982), Honda (1988), Isaacson (1993) and Balcerowicz (2010: 308 ff.).

2 Cf. e.g. the recapitulation of the Cārvāka's argument in NAV 31.10: *nanu ca kāyakāra-pariṇatāni bhūtāny evatma-vyatirekiṇī? cetanām utkālayanti; sā ca tathā-vidha-pariṇāma-pariṇateṣu teṣu santiṣṭhate, tad-abhāve punas teṃv eva nilīyata iti; tad-vyatirekanubhave 'pi na para-loka-yāyi-jīva-siddhir, iyataiva dṛṣṭa-vyavahārôpapatteḥ.* – "Nothing but gross elements, transformed into the corporeal form, bring consciousness, [that is] different from them, into being. And this [consciousness] persists invariably in (sc. has as its substratum) these [gross elements,] that have been transformed into a transformation of such a kind (sc. transformed into consciousness). When, however, this [transformation of gross elements into consciousness] does not [continue any longer], it disintegrates into these [gross elements] alone. Consequently, it is not established that the living element departs to the next world, even though [he is] experienced as different from these [gross elements], because empirical facts (sc. what is experienced) and everyday practice are explicable by this much only."

3 As a matter of fact, an *expressis verbis* formulation of the maxim is absent from his extant works altogether. The idea, however, was already present in Duns Scotus' writings.

4 MS 1.2: *codanā-lakṣaṇo 'rtho dharmaḥ.*

5 ŚBh 1.2.2, p. 4.7–9: *codanā hi bhūtaṃ bhavantaṃ bhaviṣyantaṃ sūkṣmaṃ vyavahitaṃ viprakṛṣṭam ity evaṃ-jātīyakam arthaṃ śaknoty avagamayitum, nanyat kiñcanęndriyam.*

6 See, e.g., NMa_1, Vol. 1, p. 268.10–11 = NMa_2, Vol. 1, p. 157.6–7: *ataś ca yatrasya paraḥ prakarṣas te yogino gīyante. darśanasya ca paro 'tiśayaḥ sūkṣma-vyavahita-viprakṛṣṭa-bhūta-bhaviṣyad-ādi-viṣayatvam.*

7 MŚV 2.115:

> *bhaviṣyati na dṛṣṭaṃ ca pratyakṣasya manāg api /*
> *sāmarthyaṃ nanumānader liṅgadi-rahite kvacit /*

- "The empirical fact is that with regard to future [events and *dharma*] perception has absolutely no efficacy, even slightest; neither has [the efficacy] inference and other [cognitive criteria] with regard to something that is devoid of any inferential mark."

8 Kumārila does not mention Praśastapāda in accord with his general procedure not to mention his opponents by name. However, his commentator Pārthasārathi Miśra refers to Praśastapāda directly; see NRĀ ad MŚV 4.32: *yathā śvo me bhrātaganęti . . .*

9 MŚV 4.32:

> *laukikī pratibhā yadvad pratyakṣady-anapekṣiṇī /*
> *na niścayāya paryāptā tathā syād yogināṃ api /*

10 NRĀ ad MŚV 4.26, p. 102.15 ff.

11 MŚVK ad MŚV 4.27, p. 215.15 ff.: bhavati *catra kāraṇa-prakarṣo hi kārya-prakarṣeṇa vyāpto dṛṣṭaḥ citra-kāradi-śilpa-prakarṣa iva citradi-karma-prakarṣeṇa. prakṛṣyate ca kasyacid yogino bhāvanā-bala-bhuvaḥ pratyakṣasya kāraṇam iti svabhāva-hetuḥ. athapi syāt kutaḥ kāraṇa-prakarṣo 'vagamyata iti.*

12 TUS_1, p. 168.1–3: *tathā yogi-pratyakṣasya pratīyamānartha-janyatā na sambavati vyatītanāgatayor ajanakatvāt. janakatve vatītanāgatā hīyate.*

13 TUS_1, p. 170.1–3 = TUS_3, p. 64: *tathā yogi-jñānasyatitanāgatarthe samutpannasyartha-prāpakatvaṃ na vidyate.*

14 NBhū, p. 384.3 ff.: *kiṃ cātītanāgatarthaḥ saha yogi-jñānānām api kaḥ sambandhaḥ? na hi tad-arthānām janakatvam astîty uktam prāk. pāramparyeṇa tat utpattir iti cet, na, anāgatarthānāṃ pāramparyeṇapy ajanakatvāt. na hi taiḥ kiṃcij jñānaṃ sākṣād utpāditaṃ yena tad-vāsanôtpatti-krameṇa jñānantarāṇām pāramparyeṇa tad-utpattiḥ kalpyeta. taj-jātīyasyasti janakatvam iti cet, na, janakasyatītatvāt. na ca taj-jātīyatve 'py anyata utpannaṃ jñānam anyat paricchinnatti, atiprasaṅgāt. ekasmāt strī-suvarṇady-arthād utpannasya jñānasya sarva-strī-suvarṇady-artha-paricchedakatva-prasaṅgāt.*

15 This directly refers to NBṬ 1.11, p. 67.5*: bhūtasya bhāvanā punaḥ punaś cetasi viniveśanam* (*vide supra*, see Chapter 4 'Extrasensory Perception (*yogi-pratyakṣa*) in Jainism, Proofs of its Existence and its Soteriological Implications', n. 65).

16 NRĀ ad MŚV 4.29, p. 103.3–4: *na hi bhāvanā-bala-jaṃ pratyakṣaṃ nāma sambhavati, bhāvanā hi samāna-viṣayā vijātīyavyavahitā smṛti-santatiḥ, smṛtiś ca pūrvanubhūta-viṣayiṇī nananubhūtaṃ gocarayati. tad yadi dharmaḥ pramāṇantareṇanubhūtaḥ kiṃ bhāvanayā?*

17 MŚVK ad MŚV 4.26, p. 214.23–24: *ata eva "atītanāgate 'py arthe" ity-ādinā hetv-asiddhi-bījam upadarśitam.*

18 MŚV 2.114:

yatrapy atiśayo dṛṣṭaḥ svarthanatilaṅghanāt /
dūra-sūkṣmadi-dṛṣṭau syān na rūpe śrotra-vṛttitā //

19 NMa_2 2 (I, p. 157.8–9): *nanu sva-viṣayanatikrameṇa bhavatu tad-atiśaya-kalpanā. dharmas tu cakṣuṣo na viṣaya eva. yad uktam:*

yatrapy atiśayo dṛṣṭaḥ svarthanatilaṅghanāt /
dūra-sūkṣmadi-dṛṣṭau syān na rūpe śrotra-vṛttitā // [MŚV 2.114]

20 MŚV 2.112:

ekena tu pramāṇena sarva-jño yena kalpyate /
nūnam sa cakṣuṣā sarvān rasadīn pratipadyate /

21 NRĀ ad MŚV 2.112. *itarathā kathaṃ svabhāva-niyamaṃ jānann aviṣaye sarvarthe pratyakṣasyanyasya vā pravṛttim adhyavasayed iti?*

22 NMa_2 2 (I, p. 158.1–2): *rasadi-grāhīṇy api yoginām indriyāṇi cakṣurvad atiśayavanty evęti na rasadiṣu cakṣu-vyāpāraḥ parikapyante.*

23 MŚV 2.117–18:

sarva-jño dṛśyate tāvan nẹdānīm asmad-ādibhiḥ /
nirākaraṇavac chakyā na casīd iti kalpanā // 117 //
na cagamena sarva-jñaḥ tadīye 'nyonya-saṃśrayāt /
narantara-praṇītasya prāmāṇyaṃ gamyate katham // 118 //

24 PMīV 1.15 § 54, p. 13: *na ca mukhya-pratyakṣasya tadvato vā siddhau kiñcit pramāṇam asti. pratyakṣam hi rūpadi-viṣaya-viniyamita-vyāpāraṃ natīndriye 'rthe pravartitum utsahate. napy anumānam pratyakṣa-dṛṣṭa-liṅga-liṅgi-sambandha-balôpajanana-dharmakatvāt tasya. āgamas tu yady atīndriya-jñāna-pūrvakas tat-sambandhaḥ, tadętarętaraśrayaḥ.* He returns to the issue of the 'no proof' argument again in PMī 1.17, and PMīV 1.17 §§ 59–70, p. 16–18.

25 MŚV 4.28cd–30:

> *na loka-vyatiriktaṃ hi pratyakṣaṃ yogināṃ api //*
> *pratyakṣatvena tasyapi vidyamānôpalambhanam /*
> *sat-samprayogajatvaṃ vapy asmat-pratyakṣavad bhavet //*
> *teṣām avartamāne 'rthe yā* nāmôtpadyate matiḥ /*
> *pratyakṣaṃ sā tatas tv eva nabhilāṣa-smṛtadivat //*

* Dvārikādāsa Śāstrī's edition read vā, whereas the Mīmāṃsā-śloka-vārttika edited with Sucaritamiśra's *Kāśikā* reads yā, which is the reading adopted by me for two reasons. First, it is a natural correlate to sā in the pāda 4.30c: *yā . . . matiḥ . . . sā pratyakṣam*; secondly, also NRĀ ad loc. correlates two clauses in the same way: *yad avidyamāna-viṣayaṃ . . . tat pratyakṣaṃ na bhavatîti.*

26 MŚV 2.134–136:

> *sarva-jño 'sāv iti hy eva tat-kāle tu bubhutsubhiḥ /*
> *taj-jñāna-jñeya-vijñāna-rahitair gamyate katham // 134 //*
> *kalpanīyāś ca sarva-jñā bhaveyur bahavas tava /*
> *ya eva syād asarva-jñaḥ sa sarva-jñam na budhyate // 135 //*
> *sarva-jño 'navabuddhaś ca yenaîva syān na taṃ prati /*
> *tad-vākyānāṃ pramāṇatvaṃ mūlajñāne 'nya-vākyavat // 136 //*

27 Cf. PSā 1.19: he becomes suprasensuous and has full powers being the one who has destroyed *karmans (anindriya = indriya-viṣaya-vyāpāra-rahita).*

28 MŚV 2.141–142ab:

> *evaṃ yaiḥ kevalaṃ jñānam indriyady-anapekṣiṇaḥ /*
> *sūkṣmatītadi-viṣayaṃ jīvasya parikalpitam //*
> *na rte tad-āgamāt siddhyen na ca tenagamo vinā /*

29 NRĀ ad MŚV 2.141, p. 65.25.

30 On the paradox and Mīmāṃsā approach to it, see Biderman (1994). This paradox of monotheistic religions (God is justified by scriptures, scriptures are justified by God) is also found in the Indian tradition, e.g., in the *Yoga-sūtra* 1.24, pp. 54.6–55.1: *yo 'sau prakṛṣṭa-sattvôpādānāt īśvarasya śāśvatika utkṛṣṭaḥ, sa kiṃ sanimittaḥ āhosvit nirnimittaḥ? iti tasya śāstraṃ nimittam. śāstram punaḥ kim-nimittaṃ? prakṛṣṭa-sattva-nimittam. etayoḥ śāstrôtkarṣayor īśvara-sattve vartamānayor anādiḥ sambandhaḥ.* – "This eternal superiority of God results from his appropriation of a superior [kind of the quality of] subtlety. Does it have any justification or is without any justification? Its justification is the scripture. What is the justification of the scripture? Its justification is a superior [kind of the quality of] subtlety. The relation of these two, i.e. the scripture and superiority, both residing in God, is beginningless."

31 MŚV 2.130–131:

> *buddhadīnām asarva-jñam iti satyaṃ vaco mama /*
> mad-uktatvād yathaivagnir uṣṇo bhāsvara ity api // 130 //

pratyakṣam ca mad-uktamtvaṃ tvayā sādhyā tad-uktatā /
tena hetur madīyaḥ syāt sandigdhasiddhatā tava // 131 //
pratyakṣady-avisaṃvādi prameyatvadi yasya ca /
sadbhāva-vāraṇe śaktaṃ ko nu taṃ kalpayiṣyati // 132 //

32 NB 3.125: *asarva-jño 'yaṃ rāgadimattvād, rathyā-puruṣavat* = NAV 24.2; NBhū, p. 324: *nayaṃ sarva-jño rāgadimattvāt, rathyā-puruṣavat.*
33 See Balcerowicz (2011).

Bibliography

Balcerowicz 2008 = Balcerowicz, Piotr: *Jaina Epistemology in Historical and Comparative Perspective – A Critical Edition and an Annotated Translation of Siddhasena Mahāmati's Nyāyâvatāra, Siddharṣigaṇin's Nyāyâvatāra-vivṛti And Devabhadrasūri's Nyāyâvatāra-ṭippana*, vols I and II, 2nd ed. Delhi: Motilal Banarsidass, 2008 (1st ed.: *Jaina Epistemology in Historical and Comparative Perspective – A Critical Edition and an Annotated Translation of Siddhasena Divākara's Nyāyâvatāra, Siddharṣigaṇin's Nyāyâvatāra-vivṛti And Devabhadrasūri's Nyāyâvatāra-ṭippana*, vols I and II. Alt- und Neu-Indische Studien 53,1 and 53,2. Stuttgart: Franz Steiner Verlag, 2001).

Balcerowicz 2010 = Balcerowicz, Piotr: 'What Exists for the Vaiśeṣika?' In: Piotr Balcerowicz (ed.) *Logic and Belief in Indian Philosophy*. Delhi: Motilal Banarsidass, 2010: pp. 241–348.

Balcerowicz 2011 = Balcerowicz, Piotr: 'Jayarāśi [Bhaṭṭa]', in: Edward N. Zalta (ed.): *The Stanford Encyclopedia of Philosophy*, Spring 2011 edition http://plato.stanford.edu/entries/jayaraasi.

Biderman 1994 = Biderman, Shlomo: 'Escaping the Paradox of Scripture: The Mīmāṃsā Solution', in R.C. Dwivedi (ed.) *Studies in Mīmāṃsā. Dr. Mandan Mishra Felicitation Volume*. Delhi: Motilal Banarsidass, 1994, pp. 87–103.

DhPr = Durveka Miśra: *Dharmottara-pradīpa*. Dalsukhbhai Malvania (ed.) *Paṇḍita Durveka Miśra*'s *Dharmottara-pradīpa* [*Being a Subcommentary on Dharmottara's Nyāya-bindu-ṭīkā, a Commentary on Dharmakīrti's Nyāya-bindu*]. Patna: Kashi Prasad Jayaswal, Research Institute, 1971.

Franco 1987 = Franco, Eli: *Perception, Knowledge and Disbelief: A Study of Jayarāśi's scepticism*. Alt- und Neu-Indische Studien 35. Stuttgart: Franz Steiner Verlag, 1987. (reprinted: Delhi: Motilal Banarsidas, 1994).

Honda 1988 = Honda, Megumu: 'Vaishêshika Sūtora oboegaki II. [Notes on the Vaiśeṣikasūtra II]'. *Indogaku Bukky÷gaku Kenkyū* (*Journal of Indian and Buddhist Studies*) 37,1 (1988) 472–467 (cited after Isaacson (1993)).

Isaacson 1993 = Isaacson, Harunaga: 'Yogic perception (yogipratyakṣa) in early Vaieṣika'. *Studien zur Indologie und Iranistik* 18 (1993) 139–160.

MS = Jaimini: *Mīmāṃsā-sūtra*. See: ŚBh.

MŚV = Kumārila Bhaṭṭa: *Mīmāṃsā-śloka-vārttika*. Dvārikādāsa Śāstrī (ed.): *Ślokavārttika of Śrī Kumārila Bhaṭṭa with the Commentary Nyāya-ratnâkara of Śrī Pārthasārathi Miśra*. Ratnabharati Series 3. Varanasi: Tārā Publications, 1978.

MŚVK = Sucaritamiśra: [*Mīmāṃsā-śloka-vārttika-*]*Kāśikā*. K. Sāmbaśiva Sāstrī (ed.): *Mīmāmsā Slokavārtika with the Commentary Kasika of Sucaritamiśra*. Parts I and II, *Trivandrum Sanskrit Series* 23, 29 and 31. Trivandrum: CBH Publications, 1990 (first edition: 1913).

NAV = Siddharṣi-gaṇin: *Nyāyâvatāra-vivṛti*. See: Balcerowicz (2008).

NB = Dharmakīrti: *Nyāya-bindu*. See: DhPr.

NBhū = Bhāsarvajña: *Nyāya-bhūṣaṇa*. Svāmī Yogīndrānanda (ed.): *Śrīmad-ācārya-Bhāsarvajña-praṇītasya Nyāya-sārasya svôpajñaṃ vhyākhyānaṃ Nyāya-bhūṣaṇam*. Ṣaḍ-darśana-grantha-mālā 1. Vārāṇasī: Ṣad-darśana Prakāśana Pratiṣṭhānam, 1968.

NBṬ = Dharmottara: *Nyāya-bindu-ṭīkā*. See: DhPr.

NMa = Jayanta Bhaṭṭa: *Nyāya-mañjarī*. (1) K.S. Varadacharya (ed.): *Nyāyamañjarī of Jayantabhaṭṭa with Ṭippaṇi-nyāya-saurabha by the editor*. vols 1 and 2, *Oriental Research Institute Series* 116, 139. Mysore: University of Mysore, 1969, 1983. (2) Gaurinath Sastri (ed.): *Nyāyamañjarī of Jayanta Bhaṭṭa with the Commentary of Granthi-bhaṅga by Cakradhara*. Part 1–3, M. M. Śivakumāraśāstri-Granthamālā 5. Vārāṇasī: Sampūrṇānand Saṃskṛta Viśvavidyālaya, 1982, 1983, 1984.

NRĀ = Pārthasārathi Miśra: *Nyāya-ratnâkara*. See: MŚV.

PKM = Prabhācandra-sūri: *Prameya-kamala-mārtaṇḍa*. Mahendra Kumar Shastri (ed.): *Prameyakamala-mārtaṇḍa by Shri Prabha Chandra (A Commentary on Shri Manik Nandi's Pareeksha Mukh Sutra)*. Bombay (Muṃbaī): Nirṇaya Sagar Press (Nirṇaya-sāgara Pres), 1941 (first edition: Bombay 1912; reprinted: Delhi: Sri Garib Dass Oriental Series, Sri Satguru Publications, 1990).

PMī = Hemacandra-sūri: *Pramāṇa-mīmāṃsā*. (1) Satkari Mookerjee; Nathmal Tatia: *Hemacandra's Pramāṇa-mīmāṃsā. Text and Translation with Critical Notes*. Varanasi: Tara Publications, 1970. (2) *Kavikālasarvajña-Śrī-Hemacandrâcārya-viracitā svopajña-vṛtti-sahitā Pramāṇa Mīmāṃsā*. Ed. by Sukhlāljī Saṅghavī, Mahendra Kumār and Dalsukh Mālvaṇiyā. Ahmedabad: Sarasvatī Pustak Bhaṇḍār, 1998.

PMīV = Hemacandra-sūri: *Pramāṇa-Mīmāṃsā-svopajña-vṛtti*. See: PMī.

PSā = Kundakunda: *Pavayaṇa-sāra* [*Pravacana-sāra*]. A.N. Upadhye (ed.) *Śrī Kundakundācārya's Pravacanasāra (Pavayaṇasāra), a Pro-Canonical Text of the Jainas, the Prakṛit Text critically edited with the Sanskrit Commentaries of Amṛta-candra and Jayasena*. Śrī Paramaśruta-Prabhāvaka-Maṇḍala. Agās (Gujarat): Śrīmad Rājacandra Āśrama, 1984. (1st ed. Bombay 1935).

Solomon 2010 = Solomon, Esther: *Tattvopaplavasiṃha (An Introduction, Sanskrit Text, English Translation and Notes)*. Parimal Sanskrit Series 111. Delhi : Parimal Publications, 2010.

ŚBh = Śabarasvāmin: *Mīmāṃsā-śābara-bhāṣya*. *Mīmāṃsā-śābara-bhāṣya*, ed. Yudhiṣṭhira Mīmāṃsaka, vols. 1–6. Śrī Śāntisvarūp Kapūr, Rāmalāl Kapūr Trust Press, Bahālgaḍh Sonīpat – Haryāṇā I: 1987, II: 1990, III: 1980, IV: 1985,V: 1986, VI: 1990.

TUS = Jayarāśi Bhaṭṭa: *Tattvôpaplava-siṃha*. (1) Sukhlalji Sanghavi and Rasiklal C. Parikh (ed.): *Tattvopaplavasimha of Shri Jayarasi Bhatta*. GOS 87: 1940. (2) Franco (1987). (3) Solomon (2010).

Wezler 1982 = Wezler, Albrecht: 'Remarks on the definition of "yoga" in the Vaiśeṣikasūtra', in: L. A. Hercus et al. (eds.) *Indological and Buddhist Studies. Volume in Honour of Professor J.W. de Jong on His Sixtieth Birthday*. Canberra: Australian National University, Faculty of Asian Studies, 1982, pp. 643–686.

6 The Jaina Yogas of Haribhadra Virahāṅka's *Yogabindu*

Christopher Key Chapple

Haribhadra Virahāṅka (sixth century) describes a fivefold Yoga system in his 527-verse Sanskrit text, the *Yogabindu.* Whereas the later *Yogadṛṣṭisamuccaya,* written by Haribhadra Yākinī Putra, minimizes the technical presentation of Jaina karma theory and sparingly engages vocabulary from the *Karmagrantha* literature, the *Yogabindu* includes multiple references to these ideas and practices. Furthermore, rather than seeking to legitimize and perhaps harmonize Jaina ideas with Buddhism and Vedānta, the *Yogabindu* makes a case for Jainism to stand forth as a system of religious practice not in need of external confirmation or agreement. The author attempts to explain Jaina Yoga in a systematic fashion, most notably as a path of purification through the stages of the pathgoer (*cāritrin*), who traverses the five steps of self-reflection (*adhyātma*), cultivation (*bhāvanā*), meditation (*dhyāna*), equanimity (*samatā*), and the quieting of fluctuations (*vṛttisaṃkṣaya*). This chapter will examine this system in light of Umāsvāti's traditional analysis of the 14 *guṇasthānas* and also highlight Haribhadra Virahāṅka's discussion of yogic practices such as mantra recitation (*japa*), appropriate behavior (*svaucityālocana*), and ritualized confession (*pratikramaṇa*).

Jainism and Yoga

According to Patañjali, the author of the *Yoga Sūtra* (*ca.* 200 C.E.), karmas are suffused with the five afflictions of ignorance, egoism, attraction, repulsion, and clinging to life which taint each individual's perception of the world. However, although one may be caught within the morass of these karmic influences, Patañjali also states that one can master and control the process of worldly engagement, transforming it into creative endeavor through the application of yogic principles and practices. The purpose of Yoga is to avoid repeating the mistakes of the past: *heyaṃ duḥkhaṃ anāgatam* (YS II:16). The ethical disciplines and observances (*yama* and *niyama*) hold the key to self-purification, allowing one to countermand the habits generated by the afflictions. The greatest accomplishment of Yoga is to move beyond the fetters of past afflicted karma and dwell in a place free of afflicted action: *tataḥ kleśa karma nivṛttiḥ* (YS IV:30).

For this process of purification to take place, the Yoga aspirant must gain control and exert power over the tendency to slip back into afflicted behaviors.

Various practices give rise to this control: developing a regular practice (*abhyāsa*) coupled with non-attachment (*vairāgya*), mastering the breath, applying various forms of mental discipline (*samāpatti, savitarkā, nirvitarkā, savicārā, nirvicārā, sabīja, nirbīja samādhi*), behaving correctly in accord with friendliness, compassion, joy, and equanimity, and so forth. One could list over four dozen ways in which Patañjali encourages the practice of Yoga. Each of these techniques brings forth a sense of mastery, a power that enables one to lessen attachment and move closer to freedom.

Jainism stands in a unique relationship with the broader tradition of Yoga in India as described above. The *Ācārāṅga Sūtra* sets forth the core practices of non-violence, truthfulness, not stealing, sexual restraint, and non-possession that anchor a major portion of Patañjali's eightfold path (II:29–39). The *Tattvārthasūtra* specifies colorations linked with various gradations of karma, a clearly Jaina theme also taken up by Patañjali (IV:7). Perhaps due to Patañjali's apparent widespread usage and popularity, both Haribhadra Yākinī Putra and Hemacandra use Patañjali's eightfold path as a schematic for their own Jaina articulations of Yoga. In the *Yogabindu*, however, this is not the case. The author presumes familiarity with the 14-fold ladder of ascent (*guṇasthānas*). Although clearly familiar with Patañjali and particularly Vyāsa (evident in his usage of the terms burned seeds [423], *saṃprajñāta* [421], cloud of dharma [422]), the author of the *Yogabindu* does not defer to Patañjali or attempt to fit the paths of Yoga into an eightfold or even threefold system. Instead, he sets forth a clear fivefold path that assumes familiarity with Umāsvāti's 14-fold path and makes reference to subtle nuances within the *guṇasthānas* that are not known widely outside Jainism, particularly the reference to the ladder (*śreni*) of ascent.[1]

Yoga stages: six, three, eight, five, seven

Perhaps the earliest articulation of a Yoga system dates back to the *Maitri Upaniṣad* (*ca.* 300 B.C.E.), which outlines a sixfold system. The *Bhagavad Gītā* (*ca.* 200 B.C.E.) specifies three distinct Yogas (*jñāna, karma, bhakti*), though these are not laid in a progressive fashion. The *Yoga Sūtra* (*ca.* 200 C.E.) describes a threefold Yoga plus an eightfold Yoga. The *Yogabindu* (*ca.* 550 C.E.), a Jaina text and the primary focus of this chapter, explains a progressive fivefold Yoga. The *Yogadṛṣṭisamuccaya* (*ca.* 750), another Jaina text, develops a threefold and an eightfold Yoga, refers to Patañjali's systems, and describes two additional eightfold Yogas. The *Yogavāsiṣṭha* (*ca.* 1050 C.E.), a Kashmiri text influenced by Yogācāra Buddhism, describes a sevenfold Yoga. Hemacandra's *Yogaśāstra* (1150 C.E.), another Jaina text on Yoga, aligns the states of Jaina spiritual practice with Patañjali's eightfold system.

The *Maitri Upaniṣad* (6.18) outlines a sixfold Yoga beginning with control of breath and culminating in *samādhi*: (1) control of breath (*prāṇāyāma*); (2) inwardness (*pratyāhāra*); (3) meditation (*dhyāna*); (4) concentration (*dhāraṇā*); (5) contemplation (*tarka*); and (6) absorption (*samādhi*). Patañjali, a few hundred years later, adds ethical precepts first articulated by the Jainas in the *Ācārāṅga Sūtra* (*yama*) as well as observances (*niyama*), and physical postures (*āsana*). He places meditation after concentration, and subsumes contemplation (*tarka*) within his descriptions of *samādhi*, but in variant linguistic forms (*vitarka, savitarka, nirvitarka*). Hence, Patañjali's eightfold Yoga includes the following: (1) ethics (*yama*); (2) observances (*niyama*); (3) postures (*āsana*); (4) control of breath (*prāṇāyāma*); (5) inwardness (*pratyāhāra*); (6) concentration (*dhāraṇā*); (7) meditation (*dhyāna*); and (8) absorption (*samādhi*).

As we will see in greater detail below, Haribhadra Virahāṅka posits five steps to Yoga: (1) self-reflection (*adhyātma*); (2) cultivation (*bhāvanā*); (3) meditation (*dhyāna*); (4) equanimity (*samatā*); and (5) the quieting of fluctuations (*vṛttisaṃkṣaya*).

Haribhadra Yākinī Putra (*ca.* 700–770 C.E.) aligns Patañjali's eight stages of Yoga with his own imaginative rendering of goddess-like stages: (1) friendly (*mitrā*); (2) protector (*tārā*); (3) powerful (*balā*); (4) shining (*dīprā*); (5) firm (*sthirā*); (6) pleasing (*kāntā*); (7) radiant (*prabhā*); and (8) highest (*parā*). In addition to his well-known eightfold Yoga, Patañjali also includes a threefold Yoga at the beginning of the second section of the *Yoga Sūtra*. Known as Kriyā Yoga, it specifies three core practices for the attainment of Yoga: austerity, study, and devotion (*tapas, svādhyāya, īśvara-praṇidhāna*). Haribhadra Yākinī Putra also includes a threefold system, which he describes as Icchā, Śāstra, and Sāmarthya Yoga. These terms are similar to the list of Icchā, Jñāna, Kriyā found in the Tantric traditions that were developing and gaining popularity throughout India during his lifetime. These three refer to a desire to enter into the path of Yoga, a willingness to follow the way of knowledge as articulated in the scriptures, and a resolve to take up the practices of Yoga.

Haribhadra Yākinī Putra also provides lists for two additional eightfold Yogas. He attributes one to a Vedāntin thinker, Bandhu Bhagavaddatta. This system uses terms that resonate with key ideas from Śankara and others within the Vedānta school: (1) no aversion (*adveṣa*); (2) desire for knowledge (*jijñāsā*); (3) desirous to hear truth (*śuśrūṣa*); (4) hearing truth (*śrāvana*); (5) subtle awakening (*sūkṣmabodha*); (6) reflection (*mīmāṃsā*); (7) perception of truth (*pratipatti*); and (8) enactment of absorption (*sātmī kṛta pravṛtti*). Haribhadra Yākinī Putra also identifies a Buddhist school attributed to Bhādanta Bhāskara, who employs a sequence of negating terms before arriving at the state deemed "free of attachment." His list is as follows: (1) no distress (*akheda*); (2) no anxiety (*anudvega*); (3) no distraction (*ākṣepa*); (4) no interruption (*anuttānavatī*); (5) not muddied (*abhrānti*); (6) not finding pleasure in externals (*ananyamud*); (7) no pain (*arug*); and (8) free from attachment (*saṅga vivarjitā*).

The later Jaina scholar Hemacandra also employed the frame of eightfold Yoga, which Olle Qvarnström has noted "serves the purpose of adapting Jainism to the prevailing religious environment as well as to the larger pan-Indian intellectual debate" (Qvarnström 2002: 9). Hemacandra's *Yogaśāstra*, one of the earliest handbooks to include information later popularized in the Hatha Yoga texts, starts with an exposition of correct behavior correlating to Patañjali's *yama* and *niyama* (Chapters 1–3), moves into a description of Yoga postures (end of Chapter 4), and describes various forms of breath control in great detail (Chapters 5 and 6) and inwardness and concentration (also in Chapter 6) before itemizing stages of meditation (Chapters 7–11) and the final state of release (Chapters 11 and 12).

The *Yogavāsiṣṭha* sets forth seven stages of Yoga as follows: (1) renunciation (*nivṛtti*); (2) deep thinking (*vicāraṇa*); (3) non-attachment (*asaṃsaṅga*); (4) the world as dream (*svapna loka*); (5) non-dual as if in deep sleep (*advaita suṣupta*); (6) living liberation (*jīvan mukta*); and (7) freedom from the body (*videha mukta*).[2] This sevenfold Yoga begins with disenchantment, dramatically posed in the critical question, "How can I go on living out these stale old karmas?" (YV VI:126.5). At this stage of renunciation, one decides to change and improve oneself. In the second stage, deep thinking, one cultivates concentration and meditation and fully takes on an ethical life. The third stage, non-attachment, signals a radical split from one's former identity. In this state, the ego dissolves, bringing great peace. All three of these stages of Yoga are said to happen within the realm of waking consciousness. By living in this manner, one assumes great dignity, earning the respect of others. In the fourth stage, all things appear as if they were in a dream. In the fifth stage one gains deep peace, as if one were engaged in deep sleep. The sixth stage is described as being liberated while still in the body. In the seventh stage, one's body dissolves, and one merges with or returns to the universal consciousness.

In many ways, the first three stages are similar to the first three stages of Tantra and Haribhadra Yākinī Putra's threefold Yoga. In Icchā Yoga, one desires to leave behind the sufferings and pains of the world. In Śāstra/Jñāna Yoga, one diligently dwells in the modality of correct insight and behavior. In Sāmarthya/Kriyā Yoga, non-attachment arises spontaneously, allowing one to move through the world, unaffected by its negativities, like the non-attachment Yoga of the *Yogavāsiṣṭha.*

The latter four phases demonstrate the special philosophy of the *Yogavāsiṣṭha.* Having disengaged from the fixity of things in the world, at the fourth stage one sees all things as if they are merely a dream. At the fifth stage, one is able to go beyond even the dream itself into a realm of utter peace. In a sense, these stages reflect verse 2.67 of the *Bhagavad Gītā*: "When others are awake, it is like night to the restrained one; when others are asleep, this person awakens." At the sixth stage, one resumes activity in the world, but only apparently so; in truth, one is liberated while yet living. At the seventh stage, one passes beyond, into the ultimate reality, safe from rebirth.

Jaina Yoga according to the *Guṇasthāna* system

Jaina Yoga differs from that found in the *Maitri Upaniṣad*, Patañjali's threefold and eightfold Yoga, and the sevenfold Yoga of the *Yogavāsiṣṭha* in regard to one specific point: the physical reality of karma. The *Maitri Upaniṣad* states that all involvement with *saṃsāra* arises from thought and that everything stems from the soul and will return to the soul. Patañjali merely tips his hat (or turban) to acknowledge the colors of karma but otherwise cleaves to the Sāṃkhya philosophy of *puruṣa* and *prakṛti* and does not give further details about the nature of karma, other than to associate it with impurity and affliction (*kleśa*), as mentioned above. The *Yogavāsiṣṭha* blends the Yogācāra Buddhist philosophy of mind-only (*citta-mātra*) with the Advaita Vedāntin notion of the dream quality of all existence and gives even less weight to the significance of karma. Similarly, the *Bhagavad Gītā*, though dealing with the psychological depression of Arjuna, does not explain his situation as being due to a surfeit of karma. Krishna mentions karma in the context of Karma Yoga, an attitude he encourages Arjuna to adopt so he can be free from attachments to the fruits of action and enter into battle (again, not a very Jaina undertaking). In contrast, each of the Jaina texts mentioned above, the *Yogabindu*, the *Yogadṛṣṭisamuccaya*, and the *Yogaśāstra*, relies upon the realist cosmology of the *Tattvārtha Sūtra*, which it describes in significant detail in Chapters 5–10. For the purposes of understanding the *Yogabindu*, two key aspects of the *Tattvārtha Sūtra* will be summarized: the eight karmas and the 14 *guṇasthānas*.

The eight karmas are classified as follows: (1) knowledge obscuring (*jñānāvaraṇīya*); (2) insight obscuring (*darśanāvaraṇīya*); (3) feeling producing (*vedanīya*); (4) deluding (*mohanīya*); (5) age determining (*āyus*); (6) body determining (*nāma*); (7) heredity determining (*gotra*); and (8) power hindering (*antarāya*).[3] The categories are further expanded to outline from 148 to 168 varieties of karma, referred to as *prakrti-s*.[4]

The 14 *guṇasthānas* begin with ignorance (*mithyā-dṛṣṭi*) and ascend to total freedom (*ayoga kevala*) (Figure 6.1). The entry point is *saṃyag-dṛṣṭi*, an experience of insight that can set one on the spiritual path.[5] Of particular note for our discussion of Haribhadra Virahāṅka's *Yogabindu* will be the attention given to stage eight, action uninfluenced by prior karma (*apūrva karaṇa*), achieved after assiduous practice of the five vows (*vratas*). At this state, one is said to be unbound by past action (*apunar bandhaka*) and prepared for the final ascent. However, after one rises above the gross passions and subtle passions on levels nine and ten, a critical juncture appears. If one ascends to the 11th *guṇasthāna* one will be revisited by delusion and fall back to the sixth, fifth, fourth, or second stage. This path is referred to as the "suppression ladder" (*upaśama śreṇi*), indicating that karmic influences have been suppressed but not totally quelled. If one skips the 11th stage and moves to the 12th stage, one climbs the "elimination ladder" (*kṣapaka śreṇi*), thereby gaining entry to a diminished state of delusion that will lead to living liberation (*sayoga kevala*) and ultimately to total freedom (*ayoga kevala*), whereby one's soul separates eternally from all remnants of karma (specifically life span, name, feeling, family: *āyus*, *nāma*, *vedanīya*, *gotra*). The fivefold Yoga of the *Yogabindu*, as we will see, most likely begins at the eighth *guṇasthāna*, a stage where one has achieved a mastery over the base karmic passions.

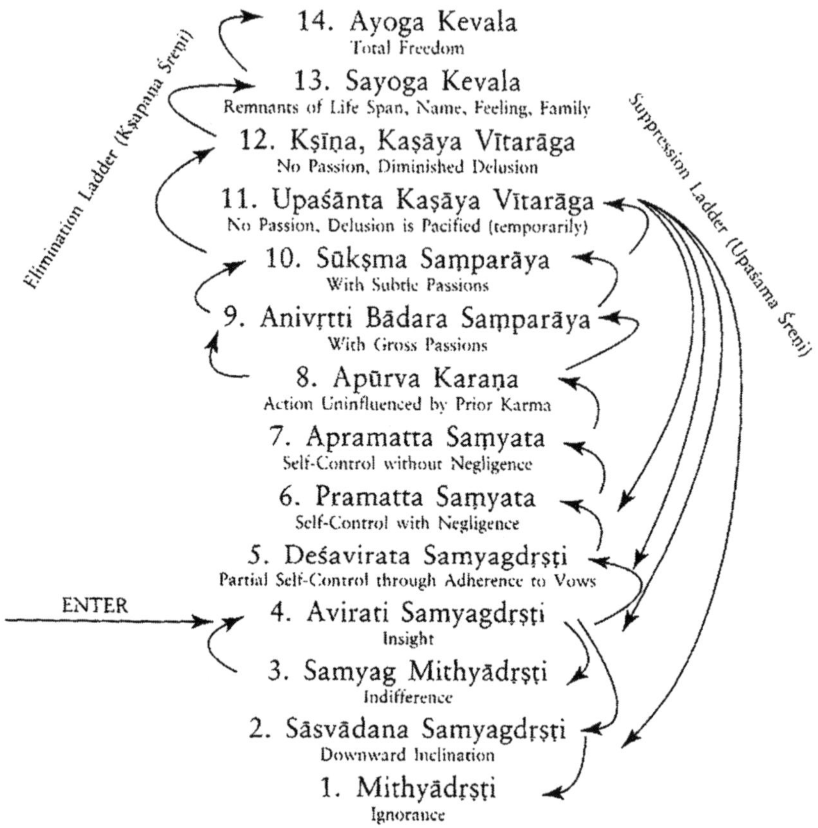

Figure 6.1 Spiritual ascent through the *guṇasthānas*. Reproduced with permission from Chapple, Christopher Key. *Reconciling Yogas: Haribhadra's Collection of Views on Yoga. With a New Translation of Haribhadra's* Yogadṛṣṭisamuccaya *by Christopher Key Chapple and John Thomas Casey.* Albany: State University of New York Press, 2003.

Haribhadra Virahāṅka's articulation of Karma as "other"

Jainism posits a pluralistic universe. Countless souls since time without beginning have taken birth due to their karma in incalculable different forms. Ultimately, the goal of the faith is to separate one from all the impulses that compel an individual to seek out yet more experience and enter another birth. However, in order to do so, one must purge oneself (*nirjarā*) of all karmic matter. This worldview differs radically from that of Vedānta, which posits emergence from and return to a singular universal consciousness or Brahman from which every soul (*jīva* or *ātman*) is born. It also differs from Buddhism, which does not accept the eternality or fixity of the soul. The Buddha taught the triple doctrine of *duḥkha*, *anitya*, and *anātman* or suffering, impermanence and no-self. At the start of the *Yogabindu*,

Haribhadra Virahāṅka argues against the unchanging notion of the soul taught by the Vedāntins and against the no-self doctrine of the Buddhists.[6] He presents his case to affirm the reality of the three key Jaina teachings: the reality of the soul, the reality of the karma that afflicts the souls, and the reality of the path of purification leading toward liberation from karma. In the *Yogabindu* he refers to this path as Yoga, declaring the purpose of Yoga to be liberation and describing it to be "the purified, true system, beneficial to one's being" (YB 4).

In the opening verses of the text, Haribhadra Virahāṅka uses the term "other" (*anya*) in two provocative ways, both of which affirm his commitment to Jaina theology. The first reference clumps all things pertaining to the eight groups of karma as "other." Anything that impedes the energy, consciousness, and bliss of the soul falls into this camp. He writes:

> Due to the linking of the self [*ātma*] with the other [karma],
> one is trapped in *saṃsāra.* When one disconnects from that [karma],
> then one becomes liberated through knowing the essence of
> these two functions [linking and disconnecting from karma] (YB 6).

He also uses this image of the "other" to criticize the notion that reliance upon an external deity can advance one on the path of Yoga (YB 7, 12), underscoring the Jaina insistence on self-reliance and the practice of austerity as the only method for reducing karma. However, in terms of the arguments made in defense of the fivefold path of Yoga later in the text, the following verses put forth key premises:

> As long as one is in the state of being connected [with karma],
> then one is not linked with the interior self [soul].
> It is said that this situation is real
> and that this linking has no beginning (10).
> Even though this process of karma connecting with the soul
> is both impure and contrary to the true nature of the soul,
> it happens repeatedly,
> according to statements made by those in a position of authority (11).
> Connection with karma defines the notion of a "doer."
> Attachment cannot exist otherwise.
> If one were not [attached], this would be
> the world of accomplishment [liberation] (13).
> . . . . . The "other" is characterized as
> ignorance, *prakṛti*, and karma (17).
> Confusion, activity, and bondage
> are known to be the results of [karmic] linking. . . . (18).
> A Yoga that addresses this issue of karmic connections
> would be consistent with both worldly experience and with scripture . . . (22).[7]

The introductory passages establish an enduring theme taken up throughout the text: connecting with karma causes bondage. Dissolution of this connection provides release.

The fivefold Yoga of the *Yogabindu*

In three distinct sections of the *Yogabindu*, the author refers to three types of persons: *apunarbandhaka*, *samyagdṛṣṭi*, and *cāritrin.*[8] All types are clearly committed to the spiritual path. The first person wants to not again return to the realm of bondage[9]; the second person has had a revelatory experience and has achieved the fourth *guṇasthāna*, the entry point for spiritual life; the third person has entered the fivefold path of Yoga. Each of these individuals seems to demonstrate the hallmark of spiritual aspiration, denoted in Jainism as *bhinna-granthi* or untying the knot of karma. The untying of the knot (*granthi bheda*) occurs first at the time of insight (*samyagdṛṣṭi*) and inspires the individual to renounce all karmas.

This brings us to the section of the text that describes the fivefold Yoga. It begins with an assessment of what qualifies one to be a pathgoer, emphasizing the need to rid oneself of karma:

> 352. The one who relinquishes karmas
> one at a time or in bunches
> attains the state of pathgoer (*cāritrin*).

This person demonstrates several qualities that indicate sincerity and effort:

> 353. The marks of a pathgoer are:
> quickly pursuing the path, keeping the faith,
> obtaining the blessings of wisdom,
> being colored with the qualities of a great being,
> and going with haste toward the truth that empowers.

Even though the way may not always be clear, a pathgoer proceeds on intuition and continues to make the correct choices by holding to the vows of purification:

> 354. A blind person, lost in an empty forest,
> though experiencing anxiety,
> is able to find the way
> through the intuitive avoidance of holes and ditches.
>
> 355. Similarly, the one who does penance
> in the wilderness of this worldly existence
> and is free regardless of what one hears and sees there
> approaches the experience of the pleasure of truth.

Karma remains an impediment to some who are unable to rise above their past karmas:

> 356. However, some people who do not have these qualities
> are referred to as "pathgoers in name only."
> This is due to their weakness caused by their various karmas.

However, those who have self-understanding and a willingness to be honest about their situation qualify as entering the first of the five paths, self-reflection (*adhyātma*):

> 357. The great souls identify these places of weakness
> and understand their various qualities.
> The Yoga referred to in ancient times is thus set in motion,
> beginning with self-reflection (*adhyātma*).
>
> 358. For the wise one who is free from delusion,
> self-reflection consists of linking oneself to suitable actions,
> thinking about truths that have been spoken,
> and flowing endlessly in the practice of
> loving kindness, [compassion, sympathetic joy, and equanimity].
>
> 359. From this, sin is destroyed and illumination (*sattva*) arises.
> Morality (*śīla*) and knowledge become second nature.
> Thus there is an experience of perfection (*siddham*),
> indeed, even of immortality.

Just as each of the four sections of Patañjali's *Yoga Sūtra* includes descriptions of the ultimate goal of Yoga, so also do we find the *Yogabindu* claiming that total liberation can be obtained by simply practicing the first phase of this five-fold Yoga. Self-reflection, by its very name, signifies that one has plumbed the depths of one's authentic being (*ātma*). To do so would require the extirpation of all karma, and hence one would arrive at perfection (*siddham*). This section also names the Brahma Vihāra, the ethical practices starting with loving kindness described in great detail in Buddhist literature that not only lay out a set of behaviors to which one should aspire, but also describe the actual behavior of the Arhats who have achieved the state of *nirvāṇa*.[10] The *Yoga Sūtra* also includes this list (I:33).

Another approach may be taken through cultivation (*bhāvanā*). This term, used by the Buddhists to denote meditation, indicates a link between ethical practice and spiritual advancement. Jainism emphasizes the application of the vows as the primary practice. Through this, one cultivates a mindfulness that releases one from the grip of karma.

> 360. Through repeated merit, one arrives at cultivation (*bhāvanā*).
> The mind is connected in *samādhi*.
> This connectivity is to be strengthened every day.
> This, indeed, is the practice to be known.
>
> 361. From this practice, there is a reduction of impurity
> and one is inclined toward the practice of purity.
> Therefore, the good mind increases.
> This is understood to be the benefit of cultivation.

The word *bhāvanā* comes from the causative form of the verb root *bhū*, cognate with the English verb "be." By carefully constructing how one presents oneself to the world and interacts with the world, purity and the good mind arise.

With images similar to those used in the sixth chapter of the *Bhagavad Gītā*, the *Yogabindu* states that holding to purity results in a stable mind, a mind accomplished in meditation, the third Yoga:

> 362. A mind state singularly residing in purity
> is called meditation (*dhyāna*) by the sages.
> It resembles an unflickering lamp.
> It endows a person with enjoyment of the subtle.
>
> 363. The wise thus say:
> "the conclusion of this is
> separation from all attachment,
> stability in the midst of existence,
> and mastery at all times."

From this steady mind state, all attachment dissolves.

With the relinquishment of attachment, one goes beyond the realm of like and dislike, beyond the pairs of opposites (*dvandva*), as stated in the *Yoga Sūtra* (II:48). One also abides in the state lauded in the *Bhagavad Gītā* (II:56–57) as "steadfast, free from attachment, fear, and anger."

> 364. Equanimity (*samatā*) is called equanimity
> because it arises when, due to understanding,
> one abandons one's likes and dislikes within the realm of things
> which are manufactured by ignorance.
>
> 365. The fruit of this [equanimity] is declared
> when one cuts the thread of expectation.
> Thus, one destroys subtle karma
> and strengthens the process of disengagement.

The meaning of the word equanimity (*samatā*) literally means seeing things equally. It also resonates with the Buddhist tradition, where the same term is used to denote the state of meditation wherein the mind reaches quiescence. The fifth and final stage marks the truly Jaina character of Haribhadra Virahāṅka's Yoga. It entails the quieting or destruction (*saṃkṣaya*) of all the fluctuations (*vṛtti*) that arise due to karma. In this verse he refers back to his earlier definition (verse 17) of karma as other (*anya*), indicating that it needs to be removed.

> 366. The one who stops the fluctuations (*vrtti*)
> that result from involvement with karma (*anya*),
> it is believed, destroys (*saṃkṣaya*) those karmas
> and no longer re-enters the form of existence.

367. This indeed is liberative knowledge.
Here one attains total freedom.
One obtains liberation from all obstacles.
One reaches [eternal] existence and bliss.

The accomplishment of this state places one in a state of liberation, free from all obstacles.

These five ways of Yoga may be seen as more complementary than hierarchical or strictly progressive. The text indicates that perfection can be attained by the process of introspective self-reflection. With cultivation and meditation, one actively engages in a process that wears away karma. According to the text, the practice of equanimity also destroys karmas (*karma-kṣaya*). All four "preliminary" phases are necessary and in fact may include the final goal of quieting fluctuations, with the distinction that all karmic connections would be broken in the fifth phase, possibly indicating an ascent to the 12th *guṇasthāna.* In verses 376 and 377, the *Yogabindu* indicates that certain individuals in fact will be able to overcome the most difficult forms of karmic bondage (*saṃparāya* or *kaṣaya karma*).

The text provides details on particular practices that are to be taken up in the name of self-reflection. The first is the practice of prayer or mantra recitation (*japa*), which should be practiced with mala beads in front of an image or in a grove of trees (YB 385). One's attention needs to be focused on the meaning of the mantra and to aspire to take on the qualities of the intended object. The practice of *japa* is discussed in eight verses, far greater than its one *Sūtra* mention in Patañjali's *Yoga Sūtra* (I:28).

Another practice recommended as part of self-reflection is what appears to be an internal moral inventory. One take a clear look (*alocana*) at one's own thoughts and qualities (*svaucitya*) and then takes appropriate remediative action (YB 389–393). If one is not able to discern the proper course of behavior, then one is urged to approach a teacher (*guru*) for advice.

Two additional practices are recommended as part of the process of self-reflection. The first is the regular practice of what in English might be rendered the confession of sins (*pratikramaṇa*, YB 397–401). The other practice, expanding its mention in verse 358 above, is to take up the Brahma Vihāra, to actively develop the feelings of loving kindness, compassion, sympathetic joy, and equanimity (YB 402–404). It further specifies that one should develop loving kindness (*maitri*) toward all living beings, sympathetic joy (*pramoda*) for those who are superior to oneself, compassion (*karuṇā*) toward those who suffer, and equanimity or even-mindedness (*madhyastha*) toward those who are incapable of being taught (*aprajñapyagocaram*).

The further description of quieting the fluctuations indicates that this is to take place on both the gross and subtle levels, indicating the ninth and tenth *guṇasthānas* (YB 406). Haribhadra Virahāṅka invokes the image of cutting off a tree at its roots (YB 408–409) to describe the stoppage of all karma. He reiterates the importance of meditation (*dhyāna*) and wisdom (*prajña*) in this process (412), as well as restating yet again the need for untying the knot of karma (*granthibheda*) (416). At the end of this section, he correlates these practices to the *Samprajñāta Samādhi* of the Yoga system (YS I:17) and the elimination ladder (*kṣapaka śreni*) of the *Guṇasthāna* system. In verses 421 and 422 he repeats his assertion that Yoga of any path will lead to deliverance, and names various appellations from different traditions for its accomplishment: *Asaṃprajñāta Samādhi* and *Dharma Megha Samādhi* from the Yoga system, eternal self (*amṛtātman*) of the Vedāntins, the arising of the state of strength in Śiva (*bhavasakrasivodaya*), the purest bliss (*sattvānanda*), and the highest (*para*). Invoking Vyāsa's commentary on the *Yoga Sūtra*, he proclaims that all seeds of karma have been burned (*vṛtti-bījam dagdhvā*) and that all great souls (*mahātma*) know that cutting off karma sets one free.

Although the *Yogabindu* takes up numerous other topics, its description of fivefold Yoga sends a clear message. An observant Jaina desiring freedom must first recognize the reality of karma's binding power. Whether a postulant, a novice, or an experienced practitioner of the Jaina religious vows, one must take an honest inventory of one's qualities and if necessary seek advice from others about penances that might be undertaken to bring about purification. The practice of prayer and devotion as well as confession are important beginning practices. From these, one then needs to develop a practice of returning to and abiding in states of *samādhi* everyday. This cultivation will lead to a state of meditation, allowing one to arrest the seeds of karma. As one matures into equanimity and develops an even-mindedness that allows one to not become easily upset, one begins to prepare for the final stage of Yoga: the quieting or destruction (*kṣaya*) of the seeds of karma. All of this would ultimately transpire at the upper rungs of the ladder to liberation, ideally culminating in the ascent to the state of "having one's owṇ mountain peak" (*śailesi*) at the 14th and final rung.

Conclusion

The practice of yoga at the time of *Yogabindu* was an engrained part of India's spiritual landscape. Numerous levels and stages of yoga were articulated by Hindu, Jaina, and Buddhist philosophers. Haribhadra Virahāṅka was clearly familiar with a variety of Yogas, as indicated by his references to various traditions throughout the text. However, rather than trying to make his own particular Jaina view acceptable to others, he works at subsuming all other forms of Yoga under the Jaina umbrella. He argues against Vedāntin eternalism and the Buddhist no-self teachings repeatedly. He upholds the notion of correct behavior as central to the path of spiritual ascent, repeatedly condemning the affliction of karma as the culprit that must be apprehended and annihilated. Although he applauds the great souls and the Bodhisattvas, and certainly supports the Yogic and Buddhist practice of the Brahma Vihāra, he does not stray from the fundamental principles and practices of the Jaina faith, giving support even to the overtly ritual practices of image worship and prayer. Unlike Patañjali, he insists on a particular religious path as essential for liberation, and unlike Patañjali, who describes the goal in at least four different ways, offering multiple practices, Haribhadra puts forth only one process that will lead to liberation: the extirpation of karma.

Notes

1 This word does not even appear in the Monier-Williams Sanskrit Dictionary with this range of meaning. See Monier-Williams, Monier, Sir, *A Sanskṛit-English Dictionary* (Oxford, Clarendon Press, 1899/1995), p.1102.

2 For more details, see Chapple, Christopher Key. "The Sevenfold Yoga of the *Yogavāsiṣṭha*" in *Yoga in Practice*, David Gordon White, ed. Princeton, New Jersey: Princeton University Press, 2011.

3 Yajneswar S. Shastri, ed. and tr., *Acarya Umāsvāti Vacaka's Praśamaratiprakaraṇa* (Ahmedabad: L.D. Institute of Indology, 1989), pp. 36–38.

4 See Helmut van Glasenapp, *The Doctrine of Karma in Jain Philosophy*, tr. G. Barry Gifford (Bombay: Bai Viibhai Jivanlal Pannalal Charity Fund, 1942) and N.L. Jain, *Jaina Karmology: English Translation with Notes on Chapter Eight of Tattvartha-Raja-Vartika of Akalanka* (Varanasi: Parshvanath Vidyapeeth, 1998).

5 See Chapple (2003), pp. 26–38.

6 See Chapple (2003), pp. 60–63.

7 These translations from the *Yogabindu* and those that follow are based on three sources: K.K. Dixit, tr., *The Yogabindu of Acarya Haribhadrasuri* (Ahmedabad: Lalbhai Dalpatbha Bharatiya Sanskriti Vidyamandira, 1968), the published edition by Luigi Suali (Bhāvānagar: Jaina Dharma Prasaraka Sabha, 1911), and the 1940 edition (Ahmedabad: Jain Grantha Prakashaka Sabha). The latter verses were translated with assistance from Jodi Shaw, Wijnanda Jacobi, Randall Krause, and Viresh Hughes.

8 The *apunarbandhaka* is described in verses 178–251, though this overlaps somewhat with the next section, devoted to the *samyagdṛṣṭi* (verses 251–351). The *cāritrin* is described in verses 352–378, followed with additional verses on fivefold Yoga (379–424).

9 I disagree somewhat with K.K. Dixit, who states that the *apunarbandhaka* is at the level of ignorance (*mithyadṛṣṭi*), based on the elevated status Haribhadra Virahāṅka accords to this individual. Haribhadra quotes Gopendra, who states that anyone interested in liberation is on the right track (YB 201).

10 Richard Gombrich, *How Buddhism Began: The Conditioned Genesis of the Early Teachings* (Delhi: Munshiram Manoharlal, 1997), p. 60.

Bibliography

Bangali Baba. *YogaSūtra of Patañjali with the Commentary of Vyasa.* Delhi: Motilal Banarsidass, 1976.

Chapple, Christopher Key. *Reconciling Yogas: Haribhadra's Collection of Views on Yoga. With a New Translation of Haribhadra's* Yogadṛṣṭisamuccaya *by Christopher Key Chapple and John Thomas Casey.* Albany: State University of New York Press, 2003.

Chapple, Christopher Key Chapple. *Yoga and the Luminous: Patañjali's Spiritual Path to Freedom.* Albany: State University of New York Press, 2008.

Chapple, Christopher Key. "The Sevenfold Yoga of the *Yogavāsiṣṭha*" in *Yoga in Practice*, David Gordon White, ed. Princeton, New Jersey: Princeton University Press, 2011.

Dixit, K.K., tr., *The Yogabindu of Acarya Haribhadrasuri*. Ahmedabad: Lalbhai Dalpatbha Bharatiya Sanskriti Vidyamandira, 1968.

Eliade, Mircea. *Yoga: Immortality and Freedom.* Princeton: Princeton University Press, 1958.

Glasenapp, Helmut van. *The Doctrine of Karma in Jain Philosophy*, tr. G. Barry Gifford. Bombay: Bai Viibhai Jivanlal Pannalal Charity Fund, 1942.

Gombrich, Richard. *How Buddhism Began: The Conditioned Genesis of the Early Teachings*. Delhi: Munshiram Manoharlal, 1997.
Haribhadra. *Yogabindu*. Ahmedabad: Jain Grantha Prakashaka Sabha, 1940.
Hume, Robert Ernest. *The Thirteen Principal Upaniṣads*. London: Oxford University Press, 1931.
Jain, N.L. *Jaina Karmology: English Translation with Notes on Chapter Eight of Tattvartha-Raja-Vartika of Akalanka*. Varanasi: Parshvanath Vidyapeeth, 1998.
Qvarnström, Olle, translator. *The Yogaśāstra of Hemacandra: A Twelfth Century Handbook on Śvetāmbara Jainism*. Cambridge. Massachusetts: Department of Sanskrit and Indian Studies, Harvard University, 2002.
Shastri, Yajneswar S., ed. and tr. *Acarya Umāsvāti Vacaka's Praśamaratiprakarana*. Ahmedabad: L.D. Institute of Indology, 1989.
Suali, Luigi, ed. *The Yogabindu of Haribhadra*. Bhāvanāgar: Jaina Dharma Prasaraka Sabha, 1911.
Timalsiha, Sthaneshwar. *Seeing and Appearance*. Aachen, Germany: Shaker Verlag, 2006.

7 Hemacandra on Yoga

Olle Qvarnström

Introduction

When the author of the *Yogaśāstra* completed his scholastic summa of Śvetāmbara Jainism and presented it to king Kumārapāla, not only was his name inscribed in the royal chronicles of the Caulukya dynasty, he also became a famous and respected scholar for those future generations, Jainas and non-Jainas, who came to regard his exposition as the arguably most systematic and clear work of its kind.[1] Born in a town located 60 miles southwest of Ahmedabad during the latter part of the eleventh century, Hemacandra[2] grew up in a region where the spread and development of religious ideas were not impeded by Islam, even though the region was still marked by the political destabilization which had resulted from Mahmūd Ghaznī's invasions at the beginning of the century.[3] Under the reign of the Śaivite king Karṇa and his wife Mayaṇallādevī, Hemacandra and his fellow Jainas lived in relatively peaceful coexistence with various Śaiva denominations, all profiting from royal patronage in compliance with ancient Indian royal ideology.

At the age of eight Hemacandra left his parental home in Dhandhukā for Stambhatīrtha (modern Cambay), unaware that this journey would mark the starting-point of a career as an outstanding monk-scholar, which would earn him the honorific title Kalikālasarvajña, "The Omniscient of the Degenerate Age," among his co-religionists, as well as a place of honor in general Sanskrit literature. At Stambhatīrtha, the young Cāṅgadeva[4] was initiated into a mendicant order by his teacher Devacandra. Under the name of Somacandra he was now a Jaina monk of the Vajraśākha of the Koṭikagaccha, the famous Śvetāmbara order known afterwards as the Tapāgaccha.[5] Judging from his future literary production, Somacandra, during the following years, received an education, the basic elements of which he shared with most of his Indian and, for that matter, European colleagues. Like the convent schools of medieval Europe and the various North Indian Buddhist and Brāhmaṇical seats of learning, the basic elements of his Jaina education consisted of grammar, dialectics, and rhetoric. In addition, and as a further supplement to the purely confessional training, various arts and sciences of Jaina as well as Buddhist and Brāhmaṇical provenance were studied.[6] Nonetheless, the sole object of the education, mediated through a learned *lingua franca*,[7] was ideally not to produce a man of extensive reading, however eloquent and deliberate, but a wise man (paṇḍita), a "Sanskritist," whose insights were morally grounded, emanating from rational argumentation, personal experience, and humble respect for the teacher and his teaching.

Once Somacandra had completed his basic education, which he obviously did with the highest aspirations since he even addressed Brāhmī, the patroness of learning, for her grace,[8] his teacher appointed him as his successor. At the age of 19 and under the clerical name of Hemacandra Sūri,[9] he was now authorized to provide his own exegesis of the Śvetāmbara canonical scriptures.[10] The greater part of his life was spent at Aṇahillapāṭaka, at that time the capital of Gujarat. Here he became the court scholar and court annalist of the Caulukya king, Siddharāja Jayasiṃha (1093–1142), under whose reign the Digaṃbaras were defeated by the Śvetāmbaras[11] and in honor of whom he prepared his first major work, the *Siddha[rāja-]hema[candra],* which still is in use among Śvetāmbara mendicants.[12] The king, who shared the same persuasion as Cāciga, Hemacandra's father, died without a son and was succeeded by his grand-nephew, Kumārapāla (1142–1173).[13] The accession was, however, not unproblematic. Jayasiṃha several times tried to kill the future king, and if we are to believe the Jaina biographers, it was due to the efforts of Hemacandra that he eventually ascended the throne, an event which in his *Triṣaṣṭiśalākāpuruṣacaritra* a Jaina teacher portrays Mahāvīra as having prophesied.[14]

The motive behind Kumārapāla's conversion and the extent to which he actually adopted the faith of the man who is claimed to have saved his life, and who was instrumental in his accession, are difficult to establish.[15] Apart from personal reasons, Kumārapāla may, like so many others of his royal colleagues, have sought alliance with a religious group that favored his own warrior-king caste (kṣatriya), the prerequisite of being a king, and thus contended the Brāhmaṇical claim of ascendancy.[16] He may also have had an economic motive behind his alliance with the Jainas, who, due to their standing in industry, commerce, and banking in Gujarat were capable of improving the finances of the state which supposedly had suffered from costly wars.[17] In any case, as a result of Kumārapāla's conversion, Hemacandra kept his royal appointment and the Jaina congregation received financial support as well as access to the court. This enabled Jaina ministers and financiers to come even closer to the political power,[18] though not without opposition from the Brāhmaṇical establishment.[19] Irrespective of whether Kumārapāla was totally committed to Jainism or, as some of his activities suggest, he remained true to the faith of his predecessors in matters related to the state while viewing Hemacandra as his personal guru, all available accounts, Jaina and Brāhmaṇa,[20] certify that he took the minor vows of a Jaina layman and consequently sought to turn Gujarat into a model Jaina state. He erected temples and urged its citizens to abstain from meat, liquor, hunting and gambling,[21] and instead to give priority to literary and scientific pursuits.[22] Following Kumārapāla's conversion, and at his request, Hemacandra wrote the *Vītarāgastotra*,[23] *Triṣaṣṭiśalākāpuruṣacaritra*,[24] *Yogaśāstra*, and *Svopajñavṛtti*.[25] Kumārapāla died heirless and was succeeded by his nephew, Ajayapāla, a Śaiva who during his short reign (1175–1178) presumably was responsible for severe persecution of the Jainas, including the execution of a Jaina minister as well as of Hemacandra's successor, Rāmacandra.[26] The situation improved later with two Jaina ministers serving under Ajayapāla's successor, but no royal patronage was ever received from the state. Instead, merchant princes, such as Vastupāla and Tejaḥpāla, came to the rescue and through their financial support temples such as Girnar and Abu were built.[27] In 1172, Hemacandra died by fasting to death and soon after, a new wave of Muslim invasions erupted. Under Muḥammad of Ghorī, supremacy was established over most of northern India, including Aṇahillapāṭaka.[28] It was not until the fourteenth century, however, that Muslim rulers entered Gujarat, some of whom the Tapā and Kharatara Gacchas tried to influence.[29] From then on Jainism was not connected to the state authority and no proselytizing took place. Furthermore, the Sanskritization and spreading of Sanskrit culture in Śvetāmbara Jaina circles gradually diminished, as this to a great extent had been the work of Hemacandra.[30]

The *Yogaśāstra*

The *Yogaśāstra* with its voluminous auto-commentary, the *Svopajñavṛtti*, is the most comprehensive treatise on Śvetāmbara Jainism known to us. Its influence extended far beyond confessional and geographical borders, especially the first four chapters.[31] The thirteenth-century Digambara author, Āśādhara, incorporated, for example, whole passages from these chapters of the *Yogaśāstra* into his *Sāgāradharmāmṛta*,[32] and the description of Jainism (Ārhatadarśana) in the standard doxographical work, the *Sarvadarśanasaṃgraha* of Mādhava, is partly based on the same chapters of Hemacandra's magnum opus.[33] They also came to serve, and still do, as a handbook for the Mūrtipūjak community in Gujarat and among Śvetāmbara Jainas in East Africa, Great Britain and North America.[34]

Such an achievement would, however, not have been possible if it were not for the Jaina community and its persistent endeavor to preserve the cultural and religious heritage of Jainism in memory and writing.[35] Nevertheless, it still required a man of eminent erudition to be able both to systematically document the Jaina doctrine and to present it in an attractive and accessible way both to the Jaina congregation and to the non-Jaina religious communities – especially those of Śaiva provenance – without endangering or misrepresenting it. In using old and well-proven methods of survival and growth, such as seeking government patronage and adapting to the prevailing religious environment by appropriating non-Jaina terminology, metaphorical language, compositional principles as well as making use of verbal ambiguity, points of common dogmas, and tenets professed by the opponents' authorities, Hemacandra was able to defend and propagate Śvetāmbara Jainism.[36] Hemacandra, like many of his predecessors, must also have been carried by the conviction that if he did not firmly establish what he reckoned as Jaina orthodoxy and orthopraxy, the unity of the dogma was endangered and thus liable to being overshadowed by Śaivism and Islam. Even if there was no immediate threat, either from within Śvetāmbara Jainism or from outside, Hemacandra's intention behind such a comprehensive project as the *Yogaśāstra* and the *Svopajñavṛtti* must have been to propagate a coherent Jaina creed among the Jainas themselves as well as among ordinary people, intellectuals, and state officials. He was thereby also able to check certain extreme tendencies within Jaina ritualism, such as worshipping and propitiating the already dead and granting the worship of yakṣas almost the same status as that of the Jinas themselves.[37] Inner disintegration was certainly not conducive to Jainism becoming a state religion or receiving support and respect from the surrounding religious communities, a prerequisite for a secure, if not flourishing, future.

Before I commit myself to a paraphrase of the *Yogaśāstra* as it unfolds itself, I shall attempt to bring out its fundamental doctrines and basic structure in order to lend meaning and function to the specific ideas in their individual ramifications as well as to tie them together into a systematic whole.

Hemacandra's account of Jainism consists of a systematic presentation of a set of ideas and practices originally belonging to the Śvetāmbara canonical scriptures (*śruta*)[38] and tradition (*sampradāya*), but molded by Hemacandra into a coherent whole with the help of the intellectual efforts of a long row of scholastic thinkers, including Umāsvāti and Haribhadrasūri.[39] In addition, the author of the *Yogaśāstra* integrates innovations of his own,[40] as well as non-Jaina elements of pan-Indian and Śaiva provenance, attesting to a strong Tantric influence on medieval Jainism.[41] Some of these elements came to be perpetually included within Śvetāmbara orthopraxy and orthodoxy due to the normative status that came to be acquired by the *Yogaśāstra*.

Like many of his predecessors, Hemacandra uses the tripartite structure of the three jewels (*ratnatraya*) – correct belief (*darśana*), knowledge (*jñāna*), and conduct (*cāritra*) – as an organizing principle in the *Yogaśāstra*. Although the terminology is borrowed from early Buddhism, this threefold structure seems to be unique to Jainism and occurs already in the canonical *Sūtrakṛtāṅgasūtra* and *Uttarādhyayanasūtra*. It was, however, first systematically utilized by the author of the post-canonical *Tattvārthasūtra* in his attempt to epitomize the canonical teachings.[42]

Underlying this tripartite structure is the doctrine of a twofold dharma or teaching (*dvidharma*)[43] which at its center has the idea of a perfect human being – a *Homo divinus* or "real God" – whose belief, knowledge, and conduct serve as the prime authority and role model. The Jaina perfected human being offers a norm or teaching (dharma) which has neither been created by himself, nor by another human being or by a god, but is eternally present within every being as his or her own Self (*jīva*) and is thus available to all. The teaching has two main aspects, moral (*karman*) and cognitive (*jñāna*). The moral aspect is concerned with activity (*pravṛtti*) in the form of proper conduct, the cognitive aspect with non-activity (*nivṛtti*) in the form of a correct understanding of reality: intellectual and experiential. The former aspect is thus devoted to improving activity, the latter to diminishing and finally suppressing activity. The former includes instructions about how mental, verbal, and physical activity should be performed, the latter how these activities should be concluded. The fundamental components of Jainism as depicted by Hemacandra under the labels of the three jewels, Ratnatraya, or the two aspects of dharma consist, accordingly, of Karmayoga and Jñānayoga accompanied by Bhaktiyoga[44] in the form of a general acceptance or confidence in the latter two and its discoverer or communicator: the Jina or the Tīrthaṅkara. These aspects were supplementary to each other and applied to both mendicants and lay persons, differing in emphasis, mode of expression, and purpose. Cultivation of mainly the moral aspect, as in the life of the lay person, leads at best to temporal happiness (*sukha*) and rebirth in heaven (*svarga*), whereas refinement of the cognitive aspect in the form of advanced intellectual and meditative practices, as in the case of the mendicant, results in eternal bliss, supernatural powers (siddhi), and liberation from cyclic existence (*mokṣa*). Except for certain qualities which are restricted to those few chosen who are to become a Tīrthaṅkara or Jina,[45] such as the ability to teach, every human is therefore capable of reaching the same level of perfection as the Jina and thus verify through his or her own reason and experience what has been taught – orally or in written form – by the Jina and his innumerable predecessors and successors.

Apart from the three jewels, Ratnatraya, and the doctrine of a double dharma (*dvidharma*), Hemacandra applies yet another organizing principle in the *Yogaśāstra*: the eight limbs of Yoga Aṣṭāṅgayoga.[46] This well-known device, classically formulated by Patañjali in his *Yogasūtra*, forms, as it were, a window dressing on top of the three jewels and its foundation, the double dharma. Viewed as a rhetorical stratagem, as in the case of the *Yogadṛṣṭisamuccaya* by the other great exalter (*prabhāvaka*) of Śvetāmbara Jainism, Haribhadrasūri,[47] it serves the purpose of adapting Jainism to the prevailing religious environment as well as to the larger pan-Indian intellectual debate. Thereby it was instrumental in converting non-Jainas, including the Śaivites of Gujarat, to Jainism.[48]

The fundamental principle of a double dharma, and from this derived doctrines of three jewels and an eightfold path, shows structural and doctrinal similarities with various Brāhmaṇical traditions and their doctrines of a twofold dharma related to the two parts (*kāṇḍa*) of the Vedic corpus, the Karmakāṇḍa and the Jñānakāṇḍa.[49] Irrespective of its historical origins, this idea was conceptually captured and defined in opposition to the Vedic tradition and its insistence on an authorless scriptural authority, and was used by Hemacandra in his critique of Vedic ritualism and Brāhmaṇical theism. Whether these similarities stem from a Śramaṇa influence on the Vedic tradition or are the result of parallel developments,[50] karman was understood by the Jaina, Buddhist, and Brāhmaṇical traditions as predominantly moral[51] and required *jñāna* for its proper implementation. Ritual activity was, however, not completely abandoned; only the violent and thereby immoral ritual practices were condemned as well as those which instead of being oriented towards mundane benefits promised liberation.

The first three chapters of the *Yogaśāstra* constitute, according to Hemacandra, a summary (*saṃkṣepa*) of the three jewels (Ratnatraya), also designated Yoga and thus elucidating the second title given to the work: *Yogopaniṣad*.[52] It begins with a set of benedictory verses (*maṅgala*) addressed to the last Jina or Tīrthaṅkara, Mahāvīra, who as an embodiment and communicator of the eternal Jaina teaching forms the object of right belief (*samyagdarśana*). Then follows a brief definition of each of the three jewels. The rest of the three initial chapters, though attempting to cover all three jewels or both main aspect of Jainism, are in substance devoted to a description of the jewel of correct conduct (*samyakcāritra*), especially the corpus of rules regulating the daily life of the lay disciple.[53] The proper conduct of the mendicant (*yatyācāra*) is summarized in the form of five great vows (*mahāvrata*) – non-harm (*ahiṃsā*), truthfulness (*satya*), honesty (*asteya*), continence (*brahmacarya*), and propertylessness (*aparigraha*) – of which the first is the paramount and all-inclusive ethical principle. These vows should be cultivated in thought, word, and action, and fostered, either through five exercises (*bhāvanā*) or through five kinds of care (*samiti*) and three kinds of control (*gupti*). The proper conduct of the lay disciple (*śrāvakācāra*) is modeled on that of the mendicant, but differs as to the degree to which the vows are to be implemented, and the extent to which other rules are to be followed. The lay vows are therefore viewed as lesser or minor and thus designated aṇuvratas. A distinction is further made between the morality of the householder (*gṛhastha*) or lay person (*śrāvaka*) and that of the exceptional layman (*mahāśrāvaka*), such as king Kumārapāla. The lay disciple, whether exceptional or not, should reinforce the five vows by means of the three virtues (*guṇa*) and the four educational vows (*śikṣāvrata*), including instructions on food, meditation, and fasting, avoiding the different infractions (aticāra), particularly those related to prohibited occupations. The exceptional disciple should furthermore follow a daily routine (*dinacaryā*) and at the end of his life ideally observe the ritual of dying through fasting (*saṃlekhanā*). A life dominated by this "jewel of correct conduct" (*samyakcāritra*) or the moral aspect of the double dharma (*dvidharma*), which by Hemacandra is equated with the first two limbs (*aṅga*) of the eightfold path,[54] leads to temporal happiness (*sukha*), rebirth in heaven (*svarga*), and for the mahāśrāvaka to liberation within eight lifetimes.[55]

The other main aspect of the Jaina teaching, the jewel of correct knowledge (*samyagjñāna*) or the cognitive aspect of the double dharma, is the prime concern of the fourth chapter of the *Yogaśāstra.* Contrary to the description of the three jewels (Ratnatraya) offered in Chapters 1–3, the fourth chapter views dharma, in the form of the three jewels, not as distinct from the human being who enjoys this teaching (*dharmin*) and who pursues its moral knowledge, but instead as identical with the human being and his Self (*jīva*): the agent (*kartṛ*) and enjoyer (*bhoktṛ*). In order for faith, knowledge, and conduct to be "correct" (*samyak*), and thus ultimately conducive to the eradication of karma and suffering, their common source, the Self, has to be known. Hemacandra, therefore, prescribes how to acquire knowledge of the Self (*ātman*). For this the passions (*kaṣāya*) have to be controlled and this is only possible if one controls the senses (*indriya*), for which mental purity (*manaḥśuddhi*) is required. The latter is obtained once attachment (*rāga*) and aversion (*dveṣa*) are eliminated through equanimity (*samatva*). Equanimity results from non-attachment (nirmamatva), which in turn results from contemplation (*bhāvanā*). Equanimity and meditation are mutually interdependent, and to even attempt to practice meditation without equanimity is, according to Hemacandra, nothing but mockery. After this description, Hemacandra urges the adept to cultivate benevolence (*maitrī*), appreciation (*pramoda*), compassion (*kāruṇya*), and tolerance (*mādhyastha*), as a direct means of assisting with respect to the practise of meditation (*dhyāna*). Meditation is twofold, virtuous (*dharmya*) and pure (*śukla*), and requires for its performance yogic postures (*āsana*) depicted at the end of the fourth chapter.

The following seven chapters may be viewed as an exegesis of the fourth chapter, particularly of meditation and its prerequisites, thus also covering the remaining limbs of the eightfold path. The fifth chapter describes various forms of breath control (*prāṇāyāma*), classic and Tantric. Breath control in itself leads to physical health (*kāyārogya*) and ability to determine the time of death (*kālajñāna*), but it may also be included as a complementary soteriological tool conforming to the recommendations of Patañjali and others. The major part of the fifth chapter is devoted to various pan-Indian and Śaiva, yogic and divinatory exercises, amalgamated with Jaina doctrine and practice. These are categorized under *prāṇāyāma* since they partly involve knowledge of the breath and its movement in the three arteries (*nāḍī*) and four operational fields (*maṇḍala*). Hemacandra also records divination based on the knowledge of medicine (*āyurveda*), astrology (*jyotiṣa*), oneiromancy (*svapnaśāstra*), oracle voices (*upaśruti*), animal portents (*śakuna*), interrogations (*praśna*), mental installment of spells on the body (*aṅganyāsa*), and mystical diagrams (*yantra*). Most of these activities are related to the settlement of a person's longevity, but they also concern warfare, harvest, and offspring, topics supposedly of concern to king Kumārapāla as a private citizen and as the head of state. The chapter concludes with a depiction of how to enter into another's body (*parakāyapraveśa*).

The sixth chapter contains a critique of the practice of breath control, which cultivated exclusively forms an impediment to the attainment of liberation, and a brief description of the practice of *pratyāhāra*, the withdrawal of the senses from their objects, and *dhāraṇā* or concentration. Analogous to *prāṇāyāma*, both of these are defined in accordance with the classical Yoga tradition and advocated as parts of the liberating path. Chapter 7 opens with a depiction of the qualifications of a meditator (*dhyātṛ*) followed by a portrayal of the first of four kinds of meditation categorized as virtuous meditation (*dharmadhyāna*). The other three varieties are outlined in Chapters 8, 9, and 10, respectively, and have as their objects holy syllables (*pada*), the external characteristics (*rūpa*) and the intrinsic nature (*rūpātīta*) of the Jina, in addition to imagined objects (*piṇḍa*) distinctive of the first variety, presented in Chapter 7. These four chapters thus express classical Jaina teachings in a hitherto unknown terminology and compositional structure, probably stemming from "Kashmirian" Śaivism, and also introduce new forms of meditation of Tantric provenance. The tenth chapter is also devoted to a description of the strictly canonical form of virtuous meditation (*dharmadhyāna*) and its four types. The succeeding 11th chapter outlines the fourfold pure meditation (*śukladhyāna*), its physical and psycho-physical preconditions, as well as the requirement of a Jina being present and knowledge of the Pūrva-scriptures acquired in order to perform this direct means to final liberation (*nirvāṇa*). In the 12th and last chapter, Hemacandra presents his own religious experience (*svasaṃvedana*) couched in a nomenclature unknown to the rest of the work. Hemacandra's highly formalized personal narrative gravitates around the practice of meditation as defined by the *Uttarādhya-yanasūtra* and the *Tattvārthasūtra* in terms of the cessation (of the activity) of the mind (cittanirodha).[56] It thus conforms with the earliest known definition of Yoga found in the *Kaṭhopaniṣad* and systematized in the classical Yoga tradition. The terminology, however, bears witness to the Nāth Siddha tradition, with which the Śvetāmbara Jainas of Gujarat also shared various cult centers.[57] Under the supervision of a teacher (guru), and through the cultivation of indifference (*audāsīnya*) and practice (*abhyāsa*), the mind reaches the state of no-mind (*unmanībhāva*/*amanaska*(tā)/*vimanaska*) and comes to rest as the Self (*jīva*) is realized and Reality (*tattva*) uncovered. In the last verses of the 12th chapter, forming the closing paragraphs of his handbook on Jainism, *Yogaśāstra*, or *Yoga Upaniṣad*, Hemacandra sums up all the wisdom that he has acquired from the scriptures, his teacher, and own personal experience, by addressing the very Self (*jīva*), urging it not to seek happiness and success from outside, but instead to please itself, realizing its inner glory and universal sovereignty.

Notes

1 This chapter is a slightly revised version of the introduction to my translation of Hemacandra's *Yogaśāstra* (Harvard Oriental Series, vol. 60. Cambridge: Harvard University Press, 2002).
2 For the available sources on the life of Hemacandra, see Bühler (1936:ix–xi, 1–5); Cort (1998:108 n. 16).
3 Cf. Kulke and Rothermund (1990:164–167). In a book by Davis (1997:92–99), it is argued that the accounts of Mahmud of Ghaznī's invasions are rhetorical and do not refer to on-the-ground conquest.
4 There are various explanations for the name Cāṅgadeva or Caṅgadeva. Bühler (1936:63 n. 12) refers to Merutuṅga, who argues that, since Hemacandra's mother, Pāhini, belonged to the Cāmuṇḍāgotra, her son's name therefore begins with Cā°. As for the complete name, Bühler thinks that it is connected with the Deśī word caṅgam, Sindhī caṅgu and Marāthī cāṃgalā, all meaning "good."
5 According to Hemacandra in his *Pariśiṣṭaparvan*, the Śvetāmbara gacchas derive their origins from one of four lineages (kula) of monastic succession. Each of these lineages was established by one of the four pupils of Vajra, the final person in the pupillary succession stemming from Jambū and the last to have gained omniscience and final liberation in this age. Vajra was initiated by Sudharman who together with Indrabhūti Gautama were the only chief disciples (gaṇadhara) out of 11 to survive Mahāvīra. The Śvetāmbara gacchas thereby derive their authority from their adherence to an unbroken tradition which originated with Mahāvīra and subsequently was transmitted by the gaṇadharas and the pupillary succession from Jambū to Vajra (Fynes 1998:xix–xxi, xxvi). Inscriptional evidence indicates that Hemacandra gave his name to a gaccha: Hemacandrāmnāyagaccha (Deo 1956:51, 65–66). On the different gacchas and their origins, see Deo (1956:231ff., 372–375, 463ff.); Granoff (1989:195 n. 1, 1991a:75 n. 1); Dundas (1993:251, 259 n. 70); and Cort (1995a:15–17).
6 Cf. the seven liberal arts (*septem artes liberales*): *trivium* and *quadrivium*. The *Prabhāvakacaritra* of Prabhācandra and *Pradyumnasūri* states that Hemacandra studied logic, dialectics, grammar, and poetics (Bühler 1936:9). On Hemacandra's

scholarly contributions to grammar, lexicography, poetics, and metrics, see Maji (1968); Sternbach (1974); Scharfe (1977); Vogel (1979); and Lienhard (1984).

7 On Jaina attitudes towards the Sanskrit language, see Granoff (1991b); Deshpande (1993: 1–16); and Dundas (1996b).

8 Bühler (1936:10).

9 See Deo (1956:232) (sūri).

10 On scriptural commentary in medieval Śvetāmbara Jainism, see Dundas (1996a).

11 The drama *Mudritakumudacandraprakaraṇa* by Yaśaścandra describes how the Digambara teacher Kumudacandra was defeated by his Śvetāmbara colleague, Devasūri, in a disputation which is said to have occurred in 1124 A.D. See Winternitz (1972:525 with n. 6).

12 For this grammar of Sanskrit and Prākrit, along with its auto-commentaries, see Scharfe (1977:169); and Jambūvijaya (1994).

13 On Kumārapāla, see Majumdar (1956:89–125); Granoff (1994) (containing a review of the numerous biographies of Kumārapāla in Sanskrit, Prākrit, and various medieval vernaculars); and Cort (1998:96–102, 106–110, 237–241).

14 See *Triṣaṣṭiśalākāpuruṣacaritra* (TC) VI.308–312. The various biographies included in Rājaśekhara's Prabandhakoṣa narrate that Kumārapāla, prior to ascending the throne, for several years lived outside of Gujarat disguised as a Kāpālika in order to avoid the death threat from the departing king, Jayasiṃha Siddharāja. See Bühler (1936:26). On the Kāpālikas, see Lorenzen (1972).

15 Many inscriptions describe Kumārapāla as a Śaiva and Hemacandra narrates in his *Dvyāśrayakāvya* how he renovated a Śaiva temple at Badrinath. Furthermore, TC VI.308–312 describes that Kumārapāla's conversion was preceded by a miracle staged by Hemacandra in the Śaiva temple of Somnātha on the southern coast of Gujarat. A similar story is narrated by the biographers of the Śvetāmbara monk, Siddhasena, who is claimed to have converted King Vikramāditya by using a similar device. See Majumdar (1956:121); Granoff (1991a:82); Dundas (1992:116); and Cort (1998:97).

16 See Jaini (1994:xxxv).

17 Cf. Majumdar (1956:122).

18 On the Jaina participation in the political discourse of pre-Islamic medieval Western India and the formulation of a Jaina theory of politics, see Cort (1998). The first Śvetāmbara to become a king was, according to Hemacandra's *Kumārapālacarita*, the mendicant Śīlaguṇasūri, who under the name of Vanarāja reigned over Gujarat from 746 to 806, after which his successors returned to Śaivism (Jaini 1994:xxxvi–xxxviii). The Jainas claim, however, several notable kings and dynasties as their own. See Jaini (1982:46).

19 Bühler (1936:38).

20 Cort (1998:96).

21 According to the drama, *Moharājaparājaya*, Kumārapāla was approached by representatives of four religious sects – Kaula, Kāpālika, Rahamāṇa, and Ghaṭachaṭaka – in connection with his prohibition against animal slaughter. See Majumdar (1956:294).

22 Two different stories explain the conversion, the *Prabhāvacaritra* of Prabhācandra/Pradyumnasūri and the *Prabandhacintāmaṇi* of Merutuṅga. See Bühler (1936:28, 123–133); and Cort (1998:97). In praise of Kumārapāla's deeds, Hemacandra wrote the *Kumārapālacarita* or *Dvyāśrayakāvya* in Sanskrit and Prākrit, thereby also illustrating the rules laid down in his grammar, the *Siddha[rāja-]hema[candra]*.

23 According to Bühler (1936:39, 94–95 n. 81), the *Vītarāgastotra* (VRS) may have been the first text on Jainism which Hemacandra introduced to Kumārapāla in

an attempt to briefly teach him about Jainism before bestowing on him the comprehensive *Yogaśāstra* (YŚ) and subsequently with the extensive *Svopajñavṛtti* (SV). Apart from VRS, Hemacandra composed two other devotional hymns, the *Anyayogavyavacchedadvātriṃśikā* and the *Anyayogavyavacchedikā*. These were also combined into a single hymn in two parts, with 32 verses each, and consequently entitled the *Dvātriṃśaddvātriṃśikā*. Malliṣeṇa wrote his famous commentary, the *Syādvādamañjarī,* on the *Anyayogavyavacchedikā.*

24 TC belongs to a class of works divided into four categories, sometimes styled the four Vedas of the Jainas, and constituting the Śvetāmbara secondary canon or Anuyoga. More specifically, TC is included in the "primary exposition" (prathamānuyoga) which contains biographies of the Jinas and of certain mythological figures. See Jaini (1979:78). TC is thus classified as a Mahāpurāṇa and as such the most important within the Śvetāmbara tradition. On Jaina purāṇas, see Jaini (1984, 1991b, 1993a, 1997a, b, 1999); Cort (1993). On the Jaina concept of history and Jaina historiography, see Cort (1995b).

25 SV draws on both TC and VRS and was thus composed subsequent to these two texts. The former is extensively quoted in SV primarily to elucidate important moral concepts; the latter is occasionally referred to mostly in connection with the definition of God and the devotion of the Jina. For references to TC, see Jambūvijaya's critical edition (J) of the YŚ and SV; for VRS, see SV II.7 (J:I.172, l. 7=VRS 6.8), III.119 (J:II.566, ll. 2–3=VRS 19.3), III.123 (J:II.603, ll. 1–3=VRS 12.4–6), IV.67 (J:II.848, ll. 3–4=VRS 7.5), XII.26 (J:III.1193, ll. 5–6=VRS 14.2).

26 Cort (1998:108 n. 13) questions this traditional view of Ajayapāla as an anti-Jaina.

27 See Majumdar (1956:320).

28 Kulke and Rothermund (1990:115, 164–167).

29 See Cort (1998:105).

30 Williams (1963:xii, xxv).

31 The fact that the circle of readers of the first four chapters exceeded that of the following seven is evident from the number of manuscripts (see Winternitz 1972:545 n. 1; Bühler 1936:93 n. 80; Cort 1995c) and the nature of their doctrinal content.

32 See Williams (1963:27, 289–296). According to Winternitz (1972:546), the subject matter of YŚ I–IV coincides with that of Amitagati's *Subhāṣitaratnasaṃdoha* (tenth century A.D.). Hertel's assumption (referred to by Winternitz 1972:546 n. 2), and Sternbach's (1974:58 n. 296), that Amitagati exerted an influence on Hemacandra is, however, improbable. First of all, Hertel only had access to Windisch's edition and translation of the verse-text, not to the auto-commentary. Secondly, the main Jaina sources of Hemacandra's treatise are the Śvetāmbara canonical scriptures and the tradition stemming from the *Tattvārthasūtra,* not Digambara secondary sources. To the best of my knowledge, there are also no verbatim quotes from YŚ in Amitagati's work.

33 See Qvarnström (1999).

34 On Jaina migration, see Banks (1994a, 1994b).

35 The commissioning and actual copying of manuscripts were regarded as meritorious acts. On Jaina libraries (bhāṇḍāra) and the illumination of manuscripts, see Guy (1994); Johnson (1999).

36 See Qvarnström (1998, 2003).

37 See Williams (1963:xxiv); Jaini (1991b); Granoff (1992). Even though Hemacandra in YŚ II.41–47 strongly criticizes the Brāhmaṇical offerings to the manes (śraddhā), the *Prabandhacintāmaṇi* speaks about the lavish funeral that Hemacandra had conducted for his mother, who had become a nun. Furthermore, the *Kumārapālapratibodha* of

Jinamaṇḍanagaṇi narrates how Kumārapāla also worshipped the dead. See Granoff (1992:187–188, 193 with n. 35). On various reform movements, see Dundas (1987–1988, 1993) and Cort (1995a).

38 Dundas (1987–1988:193 with n. 47) points out with reference to Kapadia (1941) that there seem to have been a variety of rival textual groupings as well as a tradition of lost scriptures during this time. On the distinction between canon and exegetical works, see Bruhn (1981:11–12); on scripture and canon, see Charpentier (1922:9–32); Folkert (1989, 1993:35–83, 85–94); Dundas (1992:53–73); and Cort (1994).

39 On the question of Hemacandra's originality, see Tubb (1998:53–55, 62–63).

40 Hemacandra's inventive ability is displayed in YŚ III.121–47. Based upon the Dharmabindu, he introduced a "daily routine" (dinacaryā) designed for the exceptional layman (mahāśrāvaka), but including the six obligatory duties of a mendicant (āvaśyaka). Furthermore, the list of 35 śrāvakaguṇas, which were to serve as the preconditions of taking the 12 vows of a layman, as well as the systematization of the seven fields (kṣetra) of charity (dāna), were also Hemacandra's creations. See Cort (1991:391–396).

41 YŚ displays an influence from "Kashmirian" Śaivism (YŚ VII-X.6) and medieval Siddha traditions (YŚ XII.22–26 n). See Qvarnström (1998, 2003). On Jaina medieval Tantrism, see Cort (1997); Dundas (1998, 2000); and Qvarnström (2000).

42 See *Tattvārthasūtra* (TAS) I.1–4. On this text, its date, and authorship, see Williams (1963: 1–4, 18); Ohira (1982); and Bronkhorst (1985).

43 Hemacandra refers in SV I.40 (J:I.270, ll. 1–2) to the twofold dharma resulting in happiness (abhyudaya) and liberation (niḥśreyasa). This notion is also found in Haribhadrasūri's *Śāstravārtāsamuccaya* (I.20, 23) and is possibly based on the *Vaiśeṣikasūtra* I.1.2: abhyudayaniḥśreyasasiddheḥ sa dharmaḥ. See Qvarnström (1999:170–171, 180).

44 On Jaina bhakti, see Sogani (1966); Shāntā (1985:72–75); Malvania (1986); and Cort (2002).

45 For the special karma generating the birth as a Tīrthāṅkara or Jina, see YŚ XI.48 n.; Wiley (2000: ch. 3).

46 See Qvarnström (1998).

47 See Chapple (1998).

48 The classical paths for lay persons and mendicants, the 11 pratimās and the 14 guṇasthānas, do not have any bearing on the composition of YŚ.

49 Cf. e.g. Śaṅkara's introduction to the *Bhagavad Gītā* (BhG): *sa bhagavān sṛṣṭvedaṃ jagat tasya ca sthitiṃ cikīṛsuḥ marīcyādīn agre ṣṛṣtvā prajāpatīn pravṛttilakṣaṇaṃ dharmaṃ grāhayām āsa vedoktam | tato 'nyāṃś ca sanakasanandanādīn utpādya nivṛttilakṣaṇaṃ dharmaṃ jñānavairāgyalakṣaṇaṃ grāhayām āsa | dvividho hi vedokto dharmaḥ pravṛttilakṣaṇo nivṛttilakṣaṇaś ca jagataḥ sthitikāraṇam* | "That Lord, having created this world and desiring its continued existence, first created the progenitors, headed by Marīci, and made them accept the dharma characterized by activity, as taught in the Veda. He then brought forth others, headed by Sanaka and Sanandana, and made them accept the dharma characterized by cessation, [that is], characterized by wisdom and dispassion. For twofold is the dharma taught in the Veda: characterized by activity and characterized by cessation, [and it is] the cause of the continued existence of the world."

50 See e.g. Jaini (1970); Bronkhorst (1993).

51 The fundamental principles of Jaina ethics are pan-Indian (cf. e.g. Manusmṛti (MS) X.63; Kauṭīlya's *Arthaśāstra* I.3.13, XIX; Baudhāyana's *Dharmasūtra* II.10.18.2–3; *Yogasūtra* (YSū) II.30; *Dīghanikāya* I.63). The five Jaina mendicant rules (mahāvrata)

are attested already in the canonical *Ācārāṅgasūtra* and had developed out of the far older sect of the Nigaṇṭhas described in the earliest strata of the Pāli canon. They were later systematized in TAS (VII.5–6). The earliest description of ideal lay practice (śrāvakācāra) is in the seventh Aṅga of the Śvetāmbara canon, the *Upāsakadaśā,* and the earliest Śvetāmbara text devoted exclusively to the description of lay practice is the fifth-century A.D. *Śrāvakaprajñapti* of Umāsvāti. See Williams (1963:1–4); and Cort (1991a:391).

52 In equating the term ratnatraya with Yoga, Hemacandra adopts a linguistic usage which was introduced into the Śvetāmbara Jaina tradition by Haribhadrasūri in his *Yogaviṃśikā.* Hemacandra thus employs the term Yoga both as a generic term for all kinds of activity – mental, verbal, and physical – and more specifically as synonymous with the three main constituents of the path of liberation. On the concept of Yoga and ayoga(tā) in Śvetāmbara Jainism, see Qvarnström (2003: with references).

53 As noticed by Jaini (1979:160 with n. 5; 1994:xxxviii with n. 9), we only possess one Theravāda text on lay conduct, the *Upāsakajanālaṅkāra* (Twelfth century A.D.), and one Mahāyāna text, i.e. a small portion of Śāntideva's *Śikṣāsamuccaya* (ninth century A.D.). Medieval Śvetāmbara Jainism produced a large number, of which more than 40 are listed and discussed by Williams (1963). In this connection the first four chapters of YŚ formed the standard for future Śvetāmbara Jaina texts on lay conduct (śrāvakācāra). This also explains why YŚ was categorized under the third part of the Anuyoga designated as caraṇānuyoga or "exposition on discipline" and oriented towards inner and outer tapas. See Jaini (1979:80). Apart from the Śvetāmbara Jaina canon and tradition some aspects of lay activity were influenced by local customs (deśācāra) and formed common law. See YŚ I.48. Cf. Somadeva's distinction in his *Upāsakādhyayana* 477 (quoted by Jaini 1991a:188; Lath 1992:27–29) between laukika- and pāralaukikadharma.

54 See YŚ/SV IV.34.

55 On the specific ideals of laywomen and nuns, see Shāntā (1985).

56 See YŚ IV.115 n., XII.

57 See Qvarnström (2003).

Bibliography

Banks, M. *Bhagavadgītā.* Ed. with Śaṅkara's commentary in *Śrīmadbhagavadgītā*[bhāṣya]. Poona: Ānandāśrama Sanskrit Series 34, 1896.

Banks, M. *Organizing Jainism in India and England.* Oxford Studies in Social and Cultural Anthropology. Oxford: Oxford University Press, 1994a.

Banks, M. "Why Move? Regional and Long Distance Migrations of Gujarati Jains." In *Migration: the Asian Experience.* Ed. by J. M. Brown and R. Foot. Oxford: St. Martin's Press, pp. 131–148, 1994b.

Bronkhorst, J. "On the Chronology of the Tattvārtha Sūtra and Some Early Commentaries." *Wiener Zeitschrift für die Kunde Südasiens*XXIX:155–184, 1985.

Bronkhorst, J. *The Two Sources of Indian Asceticism*, 1993. Bern: Peter Lang.

Bruhn, K. "Āvaśyaka Studies I." In *Studium zum Jaiṅismus and Buddhismus: Gedenkschrift für Ludwig Alsdorf.* Ed. by K. Bruhn and A. Wezler. Wiesbaden: F. Steiner, pp.11–49, 1981.

Bühler, G. *The Life of Hemacandrācārya.* Tr. by M. Patel from the German original (*Über das Leben des Jaina-Mönches Hemacandra. Des Schülers des Devachandra aus der Vajraśākhā.* Vienna, 1889). Santiniketan: Singhī Jaina Jñānapīṭha, 1936.

Chapple, C. K. "Haribhadra's Analysis of Pātañjala and Kula Yoga in the Yogadṛṣṭisamuccaya." In *Open Boundaries. Jain Communities and Cultures in Indian History*. Ed. by J. E. Cort. Albany: State University of New York Press, pp. 15–30, 1998.

Charpentier, J. Uttarādhyayanasūtra. Ed. by J. Charpentier. *Archives d'Études Orientales* 21–22. Uppsala, 1922.

Coburn, T. B. "Devī. The Great Goddess." In *Devī. Goddesses of India*. Ed. by J. S. Hawley and D. M. Wulff. Berkeley: University of California Press, pp. 31–48, 1996.

Commissariat, M. S. *Studies in the History of Gujarat*. Ahmedabad: Saraswati Pustak Bhandar,

Cort, J. E. "Medieval Jaina Goddess Traditions." *Numen* XXXIV:235–255, 1987.

Cort, J. E. *Liberation and Wellbeing: A Study of the Śvetāmbar Mūrtipūjak Jains of North Gujarat*. Unpublished dissertation. Harvard University, 1989.

Cort, J. E. "Two Ideals of the Śvetāmbara Mūrtipūjak Jain Layman." *Journal of Indian Philosophy* 19:391–420, 1991a.

Cort, J. E. "Mūrtipūja in Śvetāmbar Jain Temples." In *Religion in India*. Ed. by T. N. Madan. Delhi: Oxford University Press, pp. 212–223, 1991b.

Cort, J. E. "An overview of the Jaina Purāṇas." In *Purāṇa Perennis. Reciprocity and Transformation in Hindu and Jaina Texts*. Ed. by W. Doniger. Albany: State University of New York Press, pp. 185–206, 279–284, 308–315, 1993.

Cort, J. E. "Śvetāmbar Mūrtipūjak Jain Scripture in a Performative Context." In *According to Tradition. Hagiographical Writing in India*. Ed. by R. Snell and W. M Callewaert. Wiesbaden: Harrasowitz Verlag, pp. 171–194, 1994.

Cort, J. E. *Defining Jainism: Reform in the Jain Tradition*. The 1995 Roop Lal Jain Lecture. Toronto: University of Toronto. Centre for South Asian Studies, 1995a.

Cort, J. E. "Genres of Jain History." *Journal of Indian Philosophy* 23:469–506, 1995b.

Cort, J. E. "Jain Knowledge Warehouses: Traditional Libraries in India." *Journal of the American Oriental Society* 115:77–87, 1995c.

Cort, J. E. "Tantra in Jainism: The Cult of Ghaṇṭākarṇ Mahāvīr, the Great Hero Bell-Ears." *Bulletin d'Études Indiennes* 15:115–133, 1997.

Cort, J. E. "Who is a King? Jain Narratives of Kingship in Medieval Western India." In *Open Boundaries. Jain Communities and Cultures in Indian History*. Ed. by J. E. Cort. Albany: State University of New York Press, pp. 85–110, 1998.

Cort, J. E. "Bhakti in the Early Jain Tradition: Understanding Devotional Religion in South Asia." *History of Religions* 42, 59–86, 2002.

Davis, R. *Lives of Indian Images*. Princeton: Princeton University Press, 1997.

Deo, S. B. *History of Jaina Monachism*. Poona: Deccan College Post-graduate and Research Institute, 1956.

Deshpande, M. M. *Sanskrit and Prakrit. Socio Linguistic Issues*. Delhi: Motilal Banarsidass, 1993.

Dundas, P. "The Tenth Wonder: Domestication and Reform in Medieval Śvetāmbara Jainism." *Indologica Taurinensia* XIV:181–194, 1987–1988.

Dundas, P. *The Jains*. London: Routledge, 1992.

Dundas, P. "The Marginal Monk and the True Tīrtha." In *Jain Studies in Honour of Jozef Deleu*. Ed. by R. Smet and K. Watanabe. Tokyo: Hon-No-Tomosha, pp. 237–259, 1993.

Dundas, P. "Somnolent Sūtras: Scriptural Commentary in Śvetāmbara Jainism." *Journal of Indian Philosophy* 24:73–101, 1996a.

Dundas, P. "Jain Attitudes towards the Sanskrit Language." Ideology and Status of Sanskrit. Contributions to the History of the Sanskrit Language. Ed. by J. E. M. Houben. Leiden: Brill, pp. 137–156, 1996b.

Dundas, P. "Jain Attitudes Towards the Sanskrit Language." In *Ideology and Status of Sanskrit. Contributions to the History of the Sanskrit Language*. Ed. by J. E. M. Houben. Leiden: Brill, 137–156, 1998.
Dundas, P. "Becoming Gautama. Mantra and History in Śvetāmbara Jainism." In *Open Boundaries. Jain Communities and Cultures in Indian History*. Ed. by J. E. Cort. Albany: State University of New York Press, pp. 31–52, 2000a.
Dundas, P. "The Jain Monk Jinapati Sūri Gets the Better of a Nāth Yogī." In *Tantra in Practice*. Ed. by D. G. White. Princeton: Princeton University Press, 231–238, 2000b.
Folkert, K. W. "The 'Canons' of 'Scriptures'." In *Rethinking Scripture*. Ed. by M. Levering. Albany: State University of New York Press, pp. 170–179, 1989.
Folkert, K. W. *Scripture and Community. Collected Essays on the Jains*. Ed. by J. E. Cort. Harvard University. Center for the Study of World Religions. Studies in World Religions, No. 6. Atlanta: Scholars Press, 1993.
Fynes, R. C. C. See *Pariśiṣṭaparvan* of Hemacandra, 1998.
Granoff, Ph. "Religious Biography and Clan History among the Śvetāmbara Jains in North India." *Philosophy East and West* 39:195–215, 1989.
Granoff, Ph. "The Politics of Religious Biography: The Biography of Balibhadra the Usurper." *Bulletin d'Études Indiennes* 9:75–91, 1991a.
Granoff, Ph. "Buddhaghoṣa's Penance and Siddhasena's Crime: Remarks on Some Buddhist and Jain Attitudes Towards the Language of Religious Texts." In *From Benares to Beijing: Essays on Buddhism and Chinese Religion*. Ed. by K. Shinohara and G. Schopen. Oakville: Mosaic Press, pp. 17–33, 1991b.
Granoff, Ph. "Worship as Commemoration: Pilgrimage, Death and Dying in Medieval Jainism." *Bulletin d'Études Indiennes* 10:181–202, 1992.
Granoff, Ph. "Biography Writing among the Śvetāmbara Jains." In *According to Tradition: Hagiographical Writing in India*. Ed. by R. Snell and W. M Callewaert. Wiesbaden: Otto Harrassowitz, pp. 131–159, 1994.
Guy, J. "Jain Monumental Painting." In: *The Peaceful Liberators. Jain Art from India*. Ed. by P. Pal. New York: Thames and Hudson; Los Angeles: Los Angeles County Museum of Art, pp. 77–99, 1994.
Jaini, P. S. "Śramaṇas: Their Conflict with Brahmanical Society." In *Chapters in Indian Civilization I*. Ed. by J. W. Elder. Dubuque, Iowa: Kendall Hunt, pp. 40–81, 1970.
Jaini, P. S. *The Jaina Path of Purification*. Berkeley: University of California Press, 1979.
Jaini, P. S. "The Buddhist and Jaina Concepts of Man and Society as Revealed in their Religious Literature." *Sambodhi* 9:40–51, 1982.
Jaini, P. S. "Mahābhārata Motifs in the Jaina Pāṇḍava-Purāṇa." *Bulletin of the School of African and Oriental Studies* XLVII:108–115, 1984.
Jaini, P. S. *Gender and Salvation. Jaina Debates on the Spiritual Liberation of Women*. Berkeley: University of California Press, 1991a.
Jaini, P. S. "Bhaṭṭāraka Śrībhūṣaṇa's Pāṇḍava Purāṇa: A Case of Jaina Sectarian Plagiarism?" *Middle Indo-Aryan and Jaina Studies*. Ed. by C. Caillat. Leiden: E. J. Brill, pp. 59–68, 1991b.
Jaini, P. S. "Jaina Purāṇas: A Purāṇic Counter Tradition." In *Purāṇa Perennis. Reciprocity and Transformation in Hindu and Jaina Texts*. Ed. by W. Doniger. Albany: State University of New York Press, pp. 207–249, 279–293, 1993.
Jaini, P. S. "The Jaina Faith and its History." *Tattvārtha Sūtra. That Which Is*. London: Harper Collins Publishers, xxv–xxxxiv, 1994.
Jaini, P. S. "Pāṇḍava-Purāṇa of Vādicandra: Text and Translation." (Cantos I and II). *Journal of Indian Philosophy* 25:91–127, 1997a.

Jaini, P. S. "Pāṇḍava-Purāṇa of Vādicandra: Text and Translation." (Cantos III and IV). *Journal of Indian Philosophy* 25:517–560, 1997b.

Jaini, P. S. "Pāṇḍava-Purāṇa of Vādicandra: Text and Translation." (Cantos V and VI). *Journal of Indian Philosophy* 27:215–278, 1999.

Jambūvijaya, Muni. *Śrī Siddhahemacandra Śabdānuśāsana*. Pātan: Śri Hemacandrācārya Jaina Jñanamandira, 1994.

Johnson, D. C. "Jaina Collections and Libraries: Past and Present." In *Approaches to Jaina Studies: Philosophy, Logic, Rituals and Symbols*. Ed. by N. K. Wagle and O. Qvarnström. Toronto: University of Toronto, Centre for South Asian Studies, pp. 372–378, 1999.

Kapadia, H. R. *A History of the Canonical Literature of the Jainas*. Surat: H. R. Kapadia, 1941.

Kulke, H. and Rothermund, D. *A History of India*. London: Routledge, 1990.

Lienhard, S. *A History of Classical Poetry. Sanskrit Pali Prakrit*. A History of Indian Literature III:1. Ed. by J. Gonda. Wiesbaden: Otto Harrassowitz, 1984.

Lorenzen, D. N. *The Kāpālikas and Kālāmukhas: Two Lost Śaivite Sects*. Delhi: Motilal Banarsidass, 1972.

Maji, M. "A Comprehensive List of the Published Works of Hemacandra (from the Catalogue of the India Office Library)." *Jain Journal* 2:262–274, 1968.

Majumdar, A. K. *The Chaulukyas of Gujarat*. Bombay: Bharatiya Vidya Bhavan, 1956.

Malvania, D. See *Viśeṣāvaśyakabhāṣya* of Jinabhadra. Prakrit text with Sanskrit autocommentary, ed. by D. Malvania. Parts I–III. Ahmedabad, 1966–1968.

Malvania, D. "Bhaktimarga and Jainism." In *Jainism (Some Essays)*. Tr. into English by A. S. Gopani. Jaipur: Prakrit Bharati Academy, pp. 76–88, 1986.

Ohira, S. *A Study of Tattvārthasūtra with Bhāṣya*. L. D. Series 86. Ahmedabad: L. D. Institute of Indology, 1982.

Pariśiṣṭaparvan of Hemacandra. Tr. by R. C. C. Fynes as *Hemacandra. The Lives of the Jain Elders*. Oxford World's Classics. Oxford: Oxford University Press, 1998.

Qvarnström, O. "Stability and Adaptability: A Jain Strategy for Survival and Growth." *Indo-Iranian Journal* 41:33–55, 1998.

Qvarnström, O. "Haribhadra and the Beginnings of Doxography in India." In *Approaches to Jaina Studies: Philosophy, Logic, Rituals and Symbols*. Ed. by N. K. Wagle and O. Qvarnström. Toronto: University of Toronto, Centre for South Asian Studies, pp. 169–210, 1999.

Qvarnström, O. "Jain Tantra: Divinatory and Meditative Practices in the Twelfth Century *Yogaśāstra* of Hemacandra." In *Tantra in Practice*. Ed. by David G. White. Princeton: Princeton University Press, pp. 595–604, 2000.

Qvarnström, O. "Losing One's Mind and Becoming Enlightened. Some Remarks on the Concept of Yoga in Śvetāmbara Jainism and its Relation to the Nāth Siddha Tradition." In *Yoga: The Indian Tradition*. Ed. by D. Charpenter and I. Whicher. London: RoutledgeCurzon, 2003.

Scharfe, H. *Grammatical Literature*. A History of Indian Literature V:2. Ed. by J. Gonda. Wiesbaden: Otto Harrassowitz, 1977.

Shāntā, N. "The Concept of Devotion in Jainism." *Vishveshvaranand Indological Journal* 4:65–71, 1966.

Shāntā, N. *La voie jaina: Histoire, spiritualité, vie des ascètes pèlerines de l'Inde*. Paris: Paris: F.-X. de Guibert Oeil, 1985.

Sogani, K. C. "The Concept of Devotion in Jainism." *Vishveshvaranand Indological Journal* 4:65–71, 1966.

Sternbach, L. *Subhāṣita, Gnomic and Didactic Literature*. A History of Indian Literature IV:1. Ed. by J. Gonda. Wiesbaden: Otto Harrassowitz, 1974.

Tattvārthasūtra of Umāsvāti Tattvārthasūtra together with the combined commentaries of Umāsvāti/Umāsvāmī, Pūjyapāda and Siddhasenagaṇi. Ed. and tr. by N. Tatia as *That Which Is*. New York: Harper Collins Publishers, 1994.

Triṣaṣṭiśalākāpuruṣacaritra of Hemacandra. Tr. by H. Johnson as *The Lives of Sixty-three Illustrious Persons*. 6 Vols. Baroda: Baroda Oriental Institute, 1931–1962.

Tubb, G. A. "Hemacandra and Sanskrit Poetics." In *Open Boundaries. Jain Communities and Cultures in Indian History*. Ed. by J. E. Cort. Albany: State University of New York Press, pp. 53–66, 1998.

Vogel, C. *Indian Lexicography. A History of Indian Literature V:4*. Ed. by J. Gonda. Wiesbaden: Otto Harrassowitz, 1979.

Wiley, K. L. *Jain Karma Theory*. Unpublished dissertation. Berkeley, CA: University of California at Berkeley, 2000.

Williams, R. *Jaina Yoga. A Survey of the Mediaeval Śrāvakācāras,* vol. 14. Oxford: London Oriental Series, 1963.

Winternitz, M. *History of Indian Literature. Vol. II: Buddhist and Jaina Literature*. Delhi: Motilal Banarsidass, 1972.

Yogaśāstra of Hemacandra *The Yogaśāstra of Hemacandra. A Twelfth Century Handbook on Jainism*. Tr. By Olle Qvarnström. Harvard Oriental Series, Vol. 60. Cambridge: Harvard University Press, 2002. Revised and enlarged eition: Pandit Nathuram Premi Research Series Volume 29. Mumbai: Hindi Granth Karyalay, 2012

Yogaśāstra and *Svopajñavṛtti*, ed. by Muni Jambūvijaya. Vols. I–III. Bombay: Jaina Sāhitya Vikāsa Maṇḍala, 1977, 1981, 1986.

Yogasūtra of Patañjali Yogasūtra of Patañjali with the *Yogasūtrabhāṣya* of Vyāsa and the *Tattvavaiśāradī* of Vācaspatimiśra. Poona: Ānandāśrama Sanskrit Series, 1932. Tr. by J. H. Woods as *The Yoga System of Patañjali*. Harvard Oriental Series 17. Cambridge: Harvard University Press, 1911.

8 Ethics and mysticism in Jaina Yoga spirituality

Kamal Chand Sogani

This chapter will examine the 12 incentives that inspire an individual to take up the path toward sainthood, the five vows well known within the Yoga and Jaina traditions, and the stages of meditation (*dhyāna*) taught within the *Jñānārṇava* of Śubhacandra. The chapter will end with a study of mysticism as explained through the Jaina levels of spiritual ascent (*guṇasthānas*). The primary textual sources drawn upon include the *Sarvārthasiddhi* of Pūjyapāda, his commentary on the *Tattvārthasutra*, the *Mūlācāra* of *Vaṭṭakera*, the *Kārttikeyānuprekṣā* of Svāmī Kumāra, the *Pravacanasāra* of Kundakunda, and especially the *Jñānārṇava* of Śubhacandra.[1]

The incentives to spiritual life (*anuprekṣās*)

Before we set out to deal with the nature of the spiritual and ethical duties of the Jaina saint or yogī, we shall deal with the nature and importance of 12 incentives of spiritual life (*anuprekṣās*), which prepare the layperson and the monk alike for dissipating the metaphysical, the ethical, and the spiritual states of ignorance and for overcoming all those obstacles which impede moral and spiritual advancement. These incentives may possess the potency to push the layperson into the realm of complete renunciation. They also serve as guides for the monk who leads the life of complete renunciation. The first nine incentives (*anuprekṣās*) offer the following insights: (1) of perpetual flux or transitoriness of things (*anitya*); (2) of inescapability from death (*aśaraṇa*); (3) of transmigration (*saṃsāra)*; (4) of loneliness (*ekatva*); (5) of the metaphysical distinction between the self and the non-self (*anyatva*); (6) of bodily impurity (*aśuci*); (7) of the constitution of the universe (*loka*); (8) of the difficulty of attaining the right path (*bodhidurlabha*); and (9) of the inflow of the karman (*āsrava*). The next three incentives are the means of escape from the stress and storm of worldly career, namely: (10) the incentive of the stoppage of the inflow of karman (*saṃvara*); (11) the incentive of the shedding of karmas (*nirjarā*); and (12) the incentive of the dharma preached correctly (*dharmasvākhyātatva*). These three provide the proper way of channeling the energies toward the higher path. In other words, if the first nine *anuprekṣās* are negative incentives, the last three are positive ones, i.e., the former presents a true picture of man in the world and of his surroundings, while the latter prescribe the practical path for enabling the aspirant to advance morally and spiritually.

Incentives to spiritual practice require repeated reflection (*anucintana*). According to Pūjyapāda's commentary on the *Tattvārthasūtra*, incentives arise beginning when one ponders on the nature of the body. The *Kārttikeyānuprekṣā* presents it as reflections on the noble principles leading upward. The difference in characterization is due to the difference in emphasis. The former lays stress on the negative incentives, while the latter, on the means of escape from the turmoil of the world, i.e., on positive incentives. The incentives have been contemplated upon to subserve the noble cause of spiritual progress, to engender detachment, and to lead the aspirant from the domain of passion to that of dispassion. They have also been recommended for the attainment of the purity of thoughts, for the growth of the desire for salvation, for the development of detachment and self-control, and lastly, for the experience of tranquility as a result of the extinction of passions. According to the *Mūlācāra* these cultivations or contemplations (*bhāvanās*) bring about detachment. The one who identifies with them attains liberation as a result of the consequent disruption of karmic bondage. In general, these contemplations lift the mind of the aspirant above profane relations and considerations, and thereby prepare the self for meditation and emancipation.

Account of each incentive

Let us now turn to explain the nature of each incentive.

1 The incentive of perpetual flux or transitoriness of things (*anityānuprekṣā*) states that everything is subject to change and mutation. Birth accompanies death; youth is tied up with senility; wealth and prosperity may disappear at any time; and the body may fall victim to various kinds of ills and diseases. Thus impermanence of the state of things stares us in the face. Whatever form is born must necessarily perish. Attachment to ever-transforming modifications leads a person astray and clouds the spiritual and veritable aspect of life. Friends, beauty, spouse, children, and wealth – all these things which in general captivate one's mind and energy are fraught with transitoriness, thus are not the eternal associates of the self. Besides, body, fame, pleasures of the senses and other things of enjoyment (*bhoga*) and enthrallment (*upabhoga*) are unstable in character like a bubble of water, or lump of ice, or rainbow or lightning. Keeping in mind the transient character of the mundane pleasures and objects, the aspirant should part with fraudulent company and utilize this inherent challenge of the process of the world for spiritual beneficence so that happiness par excellence may sprout. Kundakunda tells us that body, possessions, pleasure and pain, friends and enemies are not the enduring accompaniments of the self, unlike the eternality of the conscious soul itself; and whether a householder or a monk, whoever derives inspiration from this meditates upon the supreme ātman and destroys the knot of delusion. This expression is indicative of the way of the utilization of the incentive of transitoriness of things for superb attainments.

2 The incentive of inescapability from death (*aśaraṇānuprekṣā*) serves as a potent incentive to spiritual life. One experiences helplessness with the onset of imminent death. Death knows no partiality. It behaves equally and indiscriminately with the young and old, the rich and the poor, the brave and the cowardly, and the like. Nothing mundane, whatsoever is capable of resisting the challenge of death. Neither earthly powers nor heavenly gods can save us from the clutches of death. Besides, there is no place where death cannot stretch its wings. Every stratagem and contrivance is impotent in rescuing a living being who is breathing his last. Thus, those who want to evolve an incentive to spiritual life through the consideration of inescapability from death are necessarily prompted to seek a life which will be forever beyond its ordinarily irresistible grip.

3 The incentive of transmigration (*saṃsārānuprekṣā*) teaches that every creature under the sway of perverted belief and passions falls victim to births and deaths. The transmigrating soul leaves one body and resorts to another incessantly and uninterruptedly. Under the constraint of karmic bondage the mundane falls an easy prey to repeated birth and death. Briefly speaking, four categories of post-existence have been recognized (human, celestial, hellish, and sub-human) where a transmigrating soul is born and is involved in distressing anguish and affliction. The formidable sufferings associated with the hellish and sub-human beings need no further explanation. The celestial beings may be deemed comparatively happy, but their pleasures of the senses end in ever-increasing hunger for more, which entails mental agony and perturbation, hence they may be considered only ostensibly happy. The sufferings of the human form of existence are very evident. The pains of womb, parentless childhood, diseased body, destitution, quarrelsome spouse, undutiful son and daughter, and the like are so manifest that every human being has to undergo and bear incalculable suffering. Thus the suffering consequent upon these four forms of existence afford an incentive to the seeker to transcend these miseries of life enduringly.

4 The incentive of loneliness (*ekatvānuprekṣā*) hinges on the insight that his soul is all alone without any companion to suffer the consequences of good and evil deeds. Neither friends nor relations, howsoever nearest and dearest they might be, are capable of sharing one's sufferings and sorrows, the result of past karmas, though they may run to enjoy one's wealth. One may feed one's dependants by earning dishonestly, but, at the time of fruition, one alone will suffer. The one who constantly reflects thus becomes absolved from the trammels of attachment and aversion.

5 The incentive of the metaphysical distinction between the self and the not-self (*anyatvānuprekṣā*) stems from the perception that the self is permanently distinct from the body. Though empirically one with the body, the self transcendentally is different from it. The body is sensuous, unconscious, impermanent, and with beginning and end, while the soul is supra-sensuous, conscious, permanent, and without beginning and end. When one is alien even to this body so nearest to the self, the question of its distinction with

other objects of the world around does not arise. The realization of such basic instinct would naturally tend to withdraw one's mind from the externalities and to fix in the depths of one's own self.

6 The incentive of bodily impurity (*aśuci-anuprekṣā*) arises from the view that the physical body is the center of all filth and impurities. The impure nature of the body may be understood by gleaning from several considerations. In the first place, the antecedent conditions of its origination, for example, semen and blood, are themselves abominable. So also are the consequent conditions, for instance, flesh, fat, and blood, which are stored from the transformation of food particles. Secondly, it is the storehouse of all sorts of nasty things like bile, phlegm, perspiration, and filth of ear, nose, and throat. Thirdly, it constantly discharges excreta through its several openings. Fourthly, its impurity cannot be removed by bathing, perfumes, incense, and other means. Thinking like this in all earnestness will encourage one to sever ties of attachment to the body, which will turn the mind toward crossing this ocean of existence.

7 The incentive of the constitution of the universe (*lokānuprekṣā*) requires reflection on the portion of space, which includes the living and non-living substances (*loka*), and the rest of the empty space (*aloka*). This universe is beginningless, self-evident, and indestructible, and needs no creator, as is assumed by some other systems of philosophy. The nature of the constitutive substances of the universe has already been discussed elsewhere in this book. Besides, the characteristic nature of the self from different standpoints has also been dwelt upon. Such philosophical reflection would enable the aspirant to know his or her real status which would necessarily yield spiritual inspiration.

8 The eighth incentive points to the difficulty of attaining the right path (*bodhidurlabhānuprekṣā*). The three jewels, which are capable of unfolding the divine potentialities, are very difficult to attain on account of the rarity of adequate qualifications. A human being has the potential to attain salvation but to be born as a human being is not guaranteed, nor can one count on being born with the necessary accompaniments for practicing austerities and meditation. Somadeva remarks that:

> unceasingly wandering on the ocean of transmigration, a sentient creature is born as a human being by chance. Even then, birth in a family respected by the world and association with the good are as rare as the coming of a quail within a blind man's grasp . . . Released from birth in the plant world, after much sufferings a sentient being is again born in the hells on account of his sins, then in genus of animals, mutually hostile, and then again among uncouth men resembling animals . . . The person who wastes human birth, obtained after cherished desire, with thoughts of disease, sorrows, fear, pleasures, spouse and children, might as well consign a heap of jewels to the flames for the sake of ashes; verily such a soul is blackened by mighty ignorance. Even if by a stroke of fortune one is again born as a human being with all the material facilities,

that person may lack right instruction. Even if that be obtained, sensual pleasures may while away the time.

(Sogani: 125)

Again, even if one gets rid of the sensual enjoyments, the performance of austerities and meditation is met with difficulties. Keeping in view, therefore, these formidable obstacles in the practicing of holy asceticism, one should resolve to traverse the path of spiritual realization and set aside indolence and inaction in this very life, here and now.

9 The incentive of the inflow of karman (*āsravānuprekṣā*) regards the influx of the auspicious and inauspicious *āsravas* to be the root cause of mundane existence. To dwell upon the consequences of karma would encourage an aspirant to rise above the realm of good and evil.

10–12 We have expounded the different negative incentives that lead us to the pursuit of spiritual life. We shall now close this topic by dwelling upon the positive incentives which enable one to transcend the miseries of mundane existence. The tenth anuprekṣā entails the stoppage of karma (*saṃvarānuprekṣā*). The 11th comes from the shedding of karma (*nirjarānuprekṣā*). The 12th arises when dharma is preached and heard correctly (*dharmasvākhyātatvānuprekṣā*). The stoppage of karma results from *gupti*, *samiti*, *dharma*, *anuprekṣā*, *parīṣahajayā*, and *caritra* (meditation on the self). The shedding of karma is effected by *tapas*. The Dharma preached correctly (*dharmasvākhyātatva*) recognizes *ahiṃsā* as its veritable characteristic, associated with modesty, forgiveness, continence, self-control, and non-acquisition.

Formal attainment of saintly life

Now, being prompted by the incentives mentioned above, the aspirant cherishes a negative attitude toward worldly actions and acquisitions, and a positive enlightened, tenacious, and resolute attitude towards the life of the spirit. The aspirant bids *adieu* to all sorts of profane relations, including spouse, children, and elders. Permeating the mind with the five types of ascetic discipline, namely good comportment in the areas of knowledge (*jñānācāra*), insight (*darśanācāra*), conduct (*cāritrācāra*), austerity (*tapācāra*), and resoluteness (*vīryācāra*), he or she prostrates before a great saint who is adorned with mystic characteristics, who abounds in virtues, who is associated with a family of distinction, who possesses an attractive physical form, who is endowed with mature age, who is bereft of mental insobriety, and who is honored and extolled by other saints. This individual seeks initiation into a religious order. In consequence, consecrated favor is gained and the monk or nun takes up the five great vows.

The five great vows of Jaina Yoga

The life of asceticism aptly illustrates the existence and operation of Śubha Yoga (purified practice), Śubha Dhyāna (purified meditation), and Śubha Leśyā (purified karma), which, in the life of the householder, are never found unmixed with their contraries. These are cultivated through the five vows, listed below.

Ahiṃsā-Mahāvrata

The first *mahāvrata* consists of the due observance, even in dreams, of the principle of non-injury to all living beings (mobile and immobile, gross and subtle) by avoiding threefold ways of acting, commanding, and consenting through the triple agency of mind, body, and speech. Broadly speaking, the four fundamental passions, when they are combined with three stages of action, namely, *saṃrambha*, *samārambha*, and *ārambha*, committed by dint of mind, body, and speech in the threefold ways of *kṛta*, *kārita*, and *anumodanā*, cause 108 kinds of hiṃsā or violence. The monk who renounces these, and extends active friendship to all living beings as such for the purpose of purifying one's *bhāvas*, and curbing one's passions, is said to observe *ahiṃsā-mahāvrata*. In order that this vow may be properly observed, the monk or nun is required to be cautious regarding movement, speech, mental thoughts, handling of things, food and drink.

Satya-Mahāvrata

This *mahāvrata* consists in always abandoning all forms of falsehood, since the allowance of any kind of falsehood points to the presence of intense passion, which is repugnant to the life of the saint. The false and oppressing words likely to be uttered under the constraint of attachment, aversion, jest, fear, anger, and greed should be renounced along with the improper pronouncement of scriptural meaning. The five kinds of longing that strengthen the vow of truthfulness are recognized as thoughtfulness in speech and as restraining from anger, greed, fear, and joking.

Asteya-Mahāvrata

This *mahāvrata* consists in renouncing all forms of stealing. To express it differently, the renouncement of the possession of all "*para dravyas*" lying in a village or in a town or in a wood without their being offered comes within the purview of *asteya-mahāvrata*. The perfection of this vow consists in getting books etc., after one has asked one's superiors, in seeking the permission for necessary things from the possessor, in purging all attachment to things taken, in allowing oneself to accept faultless articles, and in handling things of co-religionists according to the prescribed rules. According to the *Ācārāṅga*, it is brought out by restricting oneself to limited alms, seeking the permission of superiors before consuming food and drink, taking possession of limited part of the ground for a fixed time, renewing permission, and begging for a limited ground for one's co-religionist. According to the *Tattvārthasūtra*, it consists in staying in the deserted places of adobe, and secluded places like caves, in not denying the other person's intention to stay, in maintaining purity of food, and in not developing the habit of quarrelsomeness.

Brahmacarya-Mahāvrata

This fourth great vow for men prescribes avoidance of sexual intercourse with four kinds of females – human, animal, celestial, and artificial – along with the denial of seeking sexual gratification in "unnatural" ways. The adherent of the *brahmacarya-mahāvrata* ought to renounce the following also for the purpose of facilitating the observance of the vow: bodily makeup, sense indulgence, use of passion-exciting food articles, taking excessive food, attending to song and dance, association with women, exciting residence, passionate thinking about a woman, seeing the sexual organs, holding to their after-effects, reviving the memory of past sexual enjoyments, planning for future sexual enjoyment, and seminal discharge. The accomplishment of this vow consists in refraining from discussing matters concerning females, contemplating the lovely forms of women, remembering former sexual enjoyment, eating seasoned meals, or eating too much, decorating the body, and having a habitation associated with women.

Aparigraha-Mahāvrata

This fifth great vow consists in detaching oneself root and branch from internal and external attachments or from intrinsic impurities and extrinsic sentient and non-sentient *parigraha* (paraphernalia). It has been pointed out that the person who performs activities invigilantly cannot escape internal *hiṃsā*, no matter whether a living being is injured or not, while careful performance of actions never binds one by mere external hiṃsā. Consequently, that person remains forever uncontaminated like the lotus in water. Thus, bondage may or may not accrue when the *prāṇas* of a being depart on account of physical activities, but the thralldom to karman is inevitable in the presence of *parigraha*: that is why ascetics give up all *parigrahas*. In other words, it is inconceivable that in spite of the association with any kind of *parigraha* one does not become the victim of infatuation, of mundane engagements and of unrestraint; and one who is preoccupied with the profane things is incapable of realizing the true self. Considered from the highest perspective, *parigraha* includes the slightest attachment even to the body; and those who are desirous of liberation have been preached non-attention and non-attachment to the body. It follows, then, that the other kinds of *parigraha* cannot be appreciated even in the least. This is the ideal state and the real pharma; but until the saint is short of this achievement, he or she may accept that parigraha which does not cause bondage, is not longed for by others, and does not engender psychical impurity like infatuation. In other words, when the shining summit of spiritual experience is enduringly climbed, any kind of *parigraha* has no meaning, but below that a saint may keep that *parigraha* which is compatible with *śubhopayoga*, or which does add to the sustenance and enhancement of *śubha bhāvas*.

This kind of *parigraha* is indispensable for the maintenance of sainthood. Such *parigraha* includes the body with which one is born, the spiritual words of the guru, the sacred texts capable of unfolding the true nature of self, and devotion and modesty towards spiritually developed souls. The celebrated book *Mūlācāra* describes the nature of *aprigraha-mahāvrata* by saying that it consists in renouncing the sentient and non-sentient *parigraha*, and in adopting an attitude of non-attachment to other unforbidden and sinless *parigraha*. Thus a muni may possess a book (*jñānopadhi*), a peacock-feather broom (*saṃyamopadhi*), and a pot for water, (*śaucopadhi*). Just as the *śubha bhāvas* in the absence of *śuddha bhāvas* adorn the life of the saint, so do these paraphernalia without any contradiction. The pot for water is used for answering calls of nature. The peacock-feather broom serves the purpose of avoiding hiṃsā of living beings. This sort of broom possesses five characteristics. It does not get soiled with either dust or with sweat; it has the qualities of softness, non-injuriousness, tenderness, and lightness. In contrast to the Nirgrantha Digambara monk, the Śvetāmbara monk had been allowed to keep with him clothes, alms bowl, *kambala*, and broom. Besides, he may keep *mukhapati* (mouth cloth) and *gocchaga* (cloth for cleaning the alms bowl). These are not regarded as *parigraha*. We are not concerned here with the details of these. This vow is properly followed when the monk adopts an attitude of indifference towards the pleasures of hearing, seeing, smelling, tasting, and feeling.

General nature and types of meditation (*dhyāna*)

Having discussed the nature of the five kinds of internal *tapas*, we now proceed to dwell upon the nature of meditation or *dhyāna*. It will not be amiss to point out that all the disciplinary practices form an essential background for the performance of *dhyāna*. Just as the storage of water which is meant for irrigating the corn field may also be utilized for drinking and other purposes, so the disciplinary practices like *gupti* and *samiti*, which are meant for the cessation of the inflow of the fresh karman, may also be esteemed as forming the background of *dhyāna*. In other words, all the disciplinary observances find their culmination in *dhyāna*. Thus *dhyāna* is the indispensable integral constituent of right conduct, and consequently, it is directly related to the actualization of the divine potentialities. It is the clear and single road by which the aspirant can move straight to the supreme good.

Dhyāna represents the concentration of one's mind on a particular object. This concentration is possible only for an *antarmuhūrta* (time below 48 minutes) at most and that, too, in the case of such souls as are possessing bodies of the best order. The stability of thoughts on one object is recognized as *dhyāna* and the passing of mind from one object to another is deemed to be *bhāvanā* or *anuprekṣā*, or *cintā*. Now, the object of concentration may be profane or holy in character. The mind may concentrate either on the debasing and degrading object, or on the object which is uplifting and elevating. The former, which causes the inflow of inauspicious karman, is designated as inauspicious concentration (*apraśasta*), while the latter, which is associated with the potency of karmic annulment, is called auspicious concentration (*praśasta*). To be brief, *dhyāna* is capable of endowing the individual with resplendent jewels or with the pieces of glass. When both can be had, which of these will a person of discrimination choose?

Śubhacandra distinguishes three categories of *dhyāna*: good, evil, and pure, in conformity with the three types of purposes – the auspicious, the inauspicious, and the transcendental. Any one of these may be owned by a self. At another place he classifies *dhyāna* into *praśasta* and *apraśasta*. These two modes of classification are not incompatible, but evince difference of perspectives; the former represents the psychical or psychological view, the latter, the practical or ethical view. In a different way, the *praśasta* type of *dhyāna* may be considered as including good and pure types of *dhyāna* within it; and this will again give us the two types of *dhyāna*, namely, *praśasta* and *apraśasta*. The former category is divided into two types, namely, *dharma-dhyāna* and *śukla-dhyāna*, and the latter also into two types, namely, *ārta-dhyāna* and *raudra-dhyāna*. The *praśasta* category of *dhyāna* has been deemed to be potent enough to make the aspirant realize the emancipated status. On the contrary, the *apraśasta* one forces the mundane being to experience worldly sufferings. Thus those who yearn for liberation should abjure *ārta* and *raudra-dhyānas* and embrace *dharma* and *śukla* ones. In dealing with *dhyāna* as tapa, we are completely concerned with praśasta types of *dhyāna*, since they are singularly relevant to auspicious and the transcendental living. But in the previous we have frequently referred to the avoidance of *apraśasta* types of *dhyāna* without revealing their nature. At this stage, we propose, in the first instance, to discuss the nature of *apraśasta* types of *dhyāna*, the exposition of which would help us to understand clearly the sharp distinction between the two categories of *dhyāna*. To speak in a different way, if *praśasta dhyāna* is the positive aspect of *tapas*, the *apraśasta* one represents the negative one.

Apraśasta dhyāna

Ārta-Dhyāna

The word *ārta* implies anguish and affliction, and the dwelling of the mind on the thoughts resulting from such a distressed state of mind is to be regarded as *ārta-dhyāna*. In this world of storm and stress, though there are illimitable things which may occasion pain and suffering to the empirical soul, yet all of them cannot be expressed by limited human understanding. Four kinds of *ārta-dhyāna* have been recognized. The first concerns itself with the fact of one's being constantly occupied with the anxiety of overthrowing the associated undesirable objects of varied nature. In a different way, when the discomposure of mind results in the account of the baneful association of disagreeable objects which are either heard or perceived or which occur in mind owning to previous impressions, we have the first type of *ārta-dhyāna*, namely, *aniṣṭa-saṃyogaja*. The parting with agreeable objects may also occasion discomposure of mind. To be overwhelmed by anxiety for restoring the loss is called the second type of *ārta-dhyāna*, namely, *iṣṭa-viyogaja*. The constant occupation of mind to remove the distressing state of mind resulting from the diseased condition of the body is called the third type of *ārta-dhyāna*, namely, *vedanā-janita*. To yearn for agreeable pleasures and to contrive to defeat and slander the enemy constitutes the fourth type of *ārta-dhyāna*, namely, *nidāna-janita*. Again, to make up one's mind for and to dwell upon the way of getting objects of sensual pleasures are termed the fourth type of *ārta-dhyāna*, namely, *nidāna-janita*. It may be noted here that the *ārta-dhyāna* in general is natural to the empirical souls on account of the evil dispositions existing from an infinite past. It discovers itself owning to the presence of inauspicious *leśyas* like *kṛṣṇa*, *nīla*, and *kāpota* in the texture of the worldly self, and brings about sub-human birth where innumerable pain-provoking things inevitably arise. The *ārta-dhyāna* with its fourfold classification occurs in the perverted, the spiritually converted, and the partially disciplined personalities. Even the saint associated with *pramāda* sometimes is influenced by the above types, except the fourth. It will not be amiss to point out that, just as the householder cannot escape the *hiṃsā* of one-sensed *Jīvas*, so he cannot avoid *ārta-dhyāna*. No doubt, he can reduce it to an irreducible extent, but cannot remove it altogether, unlike the saint of a high order.

Raudra-Dhyāna

We now proceed to explain the *raudra-dhyāna*, which also admits of four kinds. To take delight in killing living beings, to be felicitous in hearing, seeing, and reviving the oppression caused to sentient beings, to seek ill of others, to be envious of other men's prosperity and merits, to collect the implements of *hiṃsā*, to show kindness to cruel persons, to be revengeful, to wish defeat and victory in war – all these come within the purview of the first kind of *raudra-dhyāna*, namely, *hiṃsānandi raudra-dhyāna*. The individual whose mind is permeated by falsehood, who desires to entangle the world in troubles by dint of propagating vicious doctrines, and writing unhealthy literature for the sake of his own pleasure, who amasses wealth by recourse to deceit and trickery, who contrives to show faults fraudulently in faultless persons in order that the king may punish them, who takes pride and pleasure in cheating the simple and the ignorant through fraudulent language, may be considered to be indulging in the second type of *raudra-dhyāna*, namely, *mṛṣānandi raudra-dhyāna*. Dexterity in theft, zeal in the act of thieving, and the education for theft should be regarded as the third type of *raudra-dhyāna*, namely, *cauryānandi raudra-dhyāna*. The endeavor a man does to guard paraphernalia and pleasures of the senses is called the fourth type of *raudra-dhyāna*, namely, viṣayānandi raudra-dhyāna. It deserves our notice that the undisciplined and partially disciplined persons are the subjects of *raudra-dhyāna*. Though the partially disciplined persons are the victims of this *dhyāna* on account of their observing partial conduct, i.e., partial *ahiṃsā*, partial truth, partial non-stealing, partial non-acquisition, and partial chastity, yet *raudra-dhyāna* in their case is incapable of leading them to experience miseries of hellish beings. The life of a saint is exclusive of this *dhyāna*, since in its presence conduct degenerates. This *dhyāna* also occurs in the self without any education and is the result of the intensest passions, or of the *kṛṣṇa*, *nīla*, and *kāpota leśyās*.

Prerequisites of *praśasta dhyāna*

Next in order comes the praśasta type of *dhyāna*, which may be called *dhyāna* proper. This type of *dhyāna* is conducive to *mokṣa* or final release. Before we directly embark upon study of the types of *praśasta dhyāna*, it is of primary and radical importance to delineate their prerequisites, which will enforce banishment of all the inimical elements robbing the soul of the legitimate disposition and proper conduct for spiritual advancement. In consequence the self will gain strength to dive deep into the ordinary unfathomable depths of the mysterious self. Indubitably, in the initial stages the purity of empirical and psychical background is the indispensable condition of *dhyāna*. The necessary prerequisites of *dhyāna*, in general, may be enumerated by saying that the subject must have the ardent desire for final liberation, be non-attached to worldly objects, possess unruffled and tranquil mind, and be self-controlled, stable, sense-controlled, patient, and enduring. Besides, one should steer clear of: (1) the worldly; (2) the philosophic-ethical; and (3) the mental distractions, and look to the suitability of: (4) time; (5) place; (6) posture; and (7) to the attainment of mental equilibrium, before one aspires to *dhyāna* conducive liberation. We now deal with them in succession.

The worldly

The life of the householder is fraught with numberless disturbances, which impede the development of his meditational disposition. Śubhacandra holds an antagonistic attitude towards the successful performance of *dhyāna* in the life of the householder. He says that we may hope for the presence of the flower of the sky, and horn of the donkey at some time and place, but the adornment of the householder's life with *dhyāna* is never possible. All this must not imply that the householder is outright incapable of performing *dhyāna*, but it should mean that he cannot perform *dhyāna* of the best order, which is possible only in the life of the saint.

The philosophical-ethical

If the aspirant, despite his saintly garb, suffers from philosophical and ethical delusions, he will likewise lose the opportunity to perform *dhyāna*. In other words, right belief and right conduct cannot be dispensed with, if *dhyāna* is to be performed.

Control of mental distractions

The control of mind which in turn leads to the control of passions and senses is also the essential condition of *dhyāna*. Mental distraction, like mental perversion, hinders meditational progress, and to achieve liberation without mental purity is to drink water from there where it is not, i.e., from the river of mirage. That is *dhyāna*, that is supreme knowledge, that is the object of *dhyāna* by virtue of which the mind after transcending ignorance submerges in the self's own nature. A man who talks of *dhyāna* without the conquest of mind is ignorant of the nature of *dhyāna*. On the reflective plane, the recognition of the potential divinity of the empirical self, and the consciousness of the difference between the empirical self and the transcendental self will unequivocally function as the mental prerequisite condition of *dhyāna*. The practice of the fourfold virtues of *maitrī* (friendship with all creatures), *pramoda* (appreciation of the merits of others), *karuṇā* (compassion and sympathy) and *mādhyastha* (indifference to the unruly) has also been represented as the mental prerequisite conditions of *dhyāna*. These quadruple virtues, when practiced in an earnest spirit, cause to disappear the slumber of perversion, and to set in eternal tranquility.

Time, place, and posture

The selection of proper time, place, and posture is of no less importance for the performance of *dhyāna*. The aspirant should avoid those places which are inhabited by the vicious, hypocrites, and acutely perverted persons, and by gamblers, drunkards, and harlots, and should also avoid those places which may be otherwise disturbing. He should choose those places which are associated with the names of holy *tīrthaṅkaras* and saints. A bank of a river, a summit of a mountain, an island, and a cave, and other places of seclusion and inspiration, should be chosen for practicing spiritual concentration. As regards the posture for *dhyāna*, for the people of this age who are generally deficient in energy, *paryaṅka* or padma and *kāyotsarga* postures are especially recommended. For him, whose mind is immaculate, stable, enduring, controlled, and detached, every place and every time is fit for meditation. A place may be secluded or crowded, the saint may be properly or improperly seated; the stability of the saint's mind is the proper time for meditation. Śubhacandra very beautifully portrays the mental and the physical picture of a saint preparing for meditation. The mind of the saint should be purified by the waves of the ocean of discriminatory enlightenment, be destitute of passions, be like an unfathomable ocean, be undeviating like a mountain, and should be without all sorts of doubts and delusions. Besides, the posture of the saint should be such as to arouse suspicion in the mind of a wise man regarding his being a stone statue or a painted figure. The yogī who attains sturdiness and steadfastness in posture does not get perturbed by being confronted with the extremes of cold and heat and by being harassed by furious animals.

Mental equilibrium

The saint who has controlled the mind and purged it of perversion and passions is said to have attained initial mental equipoise by virtue of which he is not seduced by the sentient and non-sentient, pleasant and unpleasant objects. The consequence of this is that his desires vanish. Ignorance disappears, and his mind is calmed. And above all he can sweep away the filth of karman within a twinkle of an eye. The great Ācārya Śubhacandra is so overwhelmed by the importance of this sort of mental poise that he esteems this as the *dhyāna* of the best order. Thus mental equanimity precedes *dhyāna*.

Process of *Dhyāna*

After dealing with the prerequisites of *dhyāna* we now propose to discuss the process of *dhyāna*. For the control of the mind, and for the successful performance of *dhyāna* the process of breath control (*prāṇāyāma*) may be necessary, but it being painful engenders *ārta-dhyāna*, which consequently deflects the saint from his desired path. Besides, the process of breath control develops diverse supernormal powers, which hinder to the healthiest development of the spirit. Hence the better method is to withdraw the senses from the sensual objects and the mind from the senses, and to concentrate the mind on the forehead (*lalāṭa*). This process is called *pratyāhāra*. Ten places in the body have been enumerated for mental concentration, namely, the two eyes, the two ears, the foremost point of the nose, the forehead, the mouth, the navel, the head, the heart, the palate, and the place between the eyebrows. The yogī should think over his or her original underived potency of the self, and compare the present state with the non-manifested nature of the self. The yogī should regard ignorance and sensual indulgence as the causes of the fall. Then, he or she should be determined to end the obstructions to the manifestation of the transcendental self by dint of the sword of meditation. The yogī should express resolution by affirming that he or she is not a hellish being, an animal, a human being, or a celestial being, but a transcendental being devoid of these mundane transformations, which result from the karmic association. And again, being possessed of infinite power, knowledge, intuition, and bliss, that yogī must not go away from his or her original nature. Having determined in this manner, the patient, enduring, steadfast, and crystal pure yogī should meditate upon the material and non-material objects as possessing the triple nature of origination, destruction, and continuance, as also upon the omniscient souls, embodied and disembodied. Having meditated upon the six kinds of *dravyas* in their true nature, the yogī should either acquire the spirit of non-attachment or enrapture the mind in the ocean of compassion. Afterwards the yogī should begin to meditate upon the nature of paramātman, who is associated with a number of original and unique characteristics. The yogī gets engrossed with these characteristics, and endeavors to enlighten his own self with spiritual illumination. He or she becomes immersed in the nature of paramātman to such an extent that the consequence of the distinctions of subject, object, and the process vanishes. This is the state of equality (*samarasībhāva*) and identification (*ekīkaraṇa*) where the self submerges in the transcendental self and becomes non-different from it. This sort of meditation is called *savīrya-dhyāna*.

There is another way of speaking about the process of *dhyāna*. Of the three states of self, namely, the external, the internal, and the transcendental, the yogī should renounce the external self and meditate upon the transcendental self by means of the internal self. In other words, after abandoning the spirit of false selfhood and attaining spiritual conversion, the yogī should ascend higher through the ladder of the latter with steps of meditation. The ignorant are occupied with the renunciation and possession of external objects, while the wise are occupied with the renunciation and possession of internal ones; but the superwise transcend the thoughts of the external and the internal. Hence, in order to attain this last state, the yogī after isolating the self from speech and body should fix the mind on his or her own self, and perform other actions by means of speech and body without mental inclination. The constant meditation upon the fact, "I am that, I am that" results in the steadfastness of ātmanic experience.

The author of the *Jñānārṇava*, in addition, elaborately expounds the process of *dhyāna* by classifying *dhyāna* into: (1) *piṇḍastha*; (2) *padastha*; (3) *rūpastha*; and (4) *rūpātīta*. Though the credit of their lucid exposition devolves upon Śubhacandra, yet the credit of suggestion and enumeration in the history of Jaina literature goes to Yogīndu, who is believed to have lived in the sixth century A.D., much earlier than Śubhacandra. We shall now dwell upon this fourfold classification.

Piṇḍastha-Dhyāna

The Piṇḍastha-Dhyāna comprises the five forms of contemplation (*dhāraṇās*) which have been explained in the following way.

Earth concentration

The yogī should imagine a motionless, noiseless, and ice-white ocean in Madhyaloka. In the center of the ocean one should imagine a finely constructed, resplendent, and enchanting lotus of a thousand petals, as extensive as Jambūdvīpa. The center of the lotus should then be imagined as having a pericarp which emanates yellowish radiance in all ten directions. In the pericarp the yogī should imagine a raised throne resembling the resplendence of the moon. And therein one should imagine oneself seated in a serene frame of mind. One should then firmly believe that the self is potent enough to sweep away all the filth of passions and to demolish all the karmas. This type of contemplation is called Pārthivī-Dhāraṇā.

Fire concentration

Afterwards the yogī is required to imagine a beautiful, well-shaped lotus of 16 petals in the region of the navel. The yogī should then imagine that each petal is inscribed with one of the 16 vowels, a, ā, i, ī, u, ū, ṛ, ṝ, ḷ, ḹ, e, ai, o, au, aṃ, aḥ, and that the pericarp of this lotus is inscribed with a holy syllable, arhaṃ. Afterwards one should imagine that the smoke is slowly coming out of the upper stroke of the holy syllable arhaṃ, and that after some time the smoke turns into a flame of fire which burns the lotus of eight petals situated in the region of the heart. After this lotus, which represents the eight kinds of karmas, has been reduced to ashes, the yogī should imagine a fire surrounding the body. After the body is reduced to ashes, the fire, in the absence of anything to burn, is automatically extinguished. This type of contemplation is called Āgneyī-Dhāraṇā.

Wind concentration

The yogī should then imagine the powerful winds, which are capable of blowing away the ashes of the body. After the ashes are imagined to be blown away, the yogī should imagine the steadiness and calmness of the wind. This type of contemplation is called Śvasanā-Dhāraṇā.

Water concentration

The yogī should then imagine a heavily clouded sky along with lightning, thundering, and rainbows. Such imagination should culminate in a constant downpour of big and bright raindrops like pearls. These raindrops are required to be imagined as serving the holy function of washing away the remnants of ashes of the body. This type of contemplation is called Vāruṇī-Dhāraṇā.

Transcendent concentration

Afterwards the yogī should think over his own soul as great as an omniscient, as bereft of seven constituent elements of the body, as possessed of radiance, which is as immaculate as the full-orbed moon. He should, then, consider his soul as associated with supernormal features, as seated on the throne, as adored and worshipped by devas, devils, and men. After this he should regard his soul as free from all kinds of karmas, as possessed of all the divine attributes and qualities. This is called *tattvarūpavatī-dhāraṇā*. With this finishes the practicing of the *piṇḍastha-dhyāna*, which leads to the blissful life, enduring and everlasting.

Padastha-Dhyāna

The *padastha-dhyāna* means contemplation by means of certain mantric syllables, such as "om" and "arahanta." Śubhacandra draws attention to the number of such syllables, which need not be dealt with here.

Rūpastha-Dhyāna

The *rūpastha-dhyāna* consists in meditating on the divine qualities and extraordinary powers of the arahantas. The yogī by virtue of meditating on the divine qualities imagines his own self as the transcendental self and believes that "I am that omniscient soul and not anything else."

Rūpātīta-Dhyāna

The *rūpātīta-dhyāna* implies the meditation on the attributes of *siddhātman*. In other words, the *rūpātīta-dhyāna* is when the yogī meditates upon the self as blissful consciousness, pure and formless. We have thus dwelt upon the various processes of *dhyāna*. These different processes, which may be brought under *praśasta-dhyāna*, are capable of leading one to the supreme state of transcendental existence.

Meditation on Dharma (*Dharma-Dhyāna*)

The word "dharma" implies the veritable nature of things, the ten kinds of dharma, the triple jewels, and the protection of living beings. Four types of meditation on dharma have been recognized. The first is when the aspirant relies upon self-insight (*ajñā-vicaya*). The purpose of this meditation (*dhyāna*) is to maintain intellectual clarity regarding the metaphysical nature of the objects propounded by the arahanta. The second meditation (*apāya-vicaya*) gives rise to serious contemplation on the questions of "Who am I?" Why are there inflow and bondage of karmas? How can karmas be overthrown? What is liberation? And what is the manifested nature of the soul on being liberated? In contrast, first meditation establishes oneself in truth, and the second meditation lays stress on the means of realizing the essential nature of truth. Pondering over the adequate ways and means of emancipating souls from the worldly suffering caused by the perverted belief, knowledge, and conduct, and meditating on the means of ascending the ladder of the spiritual welfare, constitutes the second meditation. In the third meditation, the aspirant is obstructed by the rise of karmas (*vipāka-vicaya*). This causes reflection on the effects which karmas produce on the diverse empirical souls. Finally, in the fourth meditation one is struck by the subtleness of objects and experiences the deficiency of evidence and illustration in upholding and vindicating any doctrine. In this meditation, one adheres to the exposition of the arahanta after believing that the arahanta does not misrepresent things (*saṃsthāna-vicaya*). This entails reflection on the nature and form of this universe. This kind of concentration impresses upon the mind the vastness of the universe and the diversity of its constituents. By this meditation the aspirant realizes his or her own position in the universe.

These four types of meditation serve twofold purposes, of auspicious reflection and self-meditation. They supply the material for the intellect and offer inspiration to the self for meditation. Though they do not seem to suggest any process of meditation, their subject-matter is such as to evoke active interest for nothing but self-realization through self-meditation. Thus in this process of meditation as well as reflection, the latter may pass into the former and the former may lapse into the latter. In other words, the four kinds of *dhyāna* are reflective when intellectual thinking is witnessed, and meditative when the mind attains stability in respect of them. The best practice is to meditate upon the self by fixing one's mind in it after renouncing all other thoughts.

Pure meditation (*Śukla-Dhyāna*)

The meditations on dharma which have so far been expounded prepare a suitable ground and atmosphere for ascending the loftiest spiritual heights. These meditations claim to have swept away every iota of inauspicious dispositions from the mind of the aspirant. The yogī has achieved self-mastery to the full, and has developed a unique taste for the accomplishment of that something which is unique. The yogī, having brushed aside the unsteadiness of his mind, now resorts to pure meditation, *śukla-dhyāna*, which is so called because of its origination after the destruction or subsidence of the filth of passions. There are four types of pure meditation: variegated thought, one-pointed thought, subtle action, and sublime action (*pṛthaktva-vitarka-vicāra*, *ekatva-vitarka-avicāra*, *sūkṣmakriyāpratipātin*, and *vyuparatakriyānivartin*). The first two occur up to the 12th level of spiritual attainment (*guṇasthāna*) with the help of conceptual thinking based on scriptural knowledge, and the last two crown the omniscient where conceptual activity of the mind abates to the last.

The first type (*pṛthaktva-vitarka-vicāra*) is associated with manyness, scriptural knowledge, transition from one aspect of entity to another, for example, substance to modifications and vice versa. In this state, one goes from one verbal symbol to another, and from one kind of *yoga* (activity) to another. In the second type (*ekatva-vitarka-avicāra*), oneness displaces manyness. The mind shortens its field of concentration to the effect that the yogī meditates upon one substance, an atom, or a modification of substance with the assistance of only one kind of *yoga*. With the performance of this second type of meditation, the yogī reduces to ashes the four types of obscuring (*ghātin*) karmas. In consequence the yogī experiences infinite intuition, knowledge, bliss, and energy. Thus the state of liberation (*jīvanmukti*) is attained through the third and fourth meditations, which lead to the 13th and 14th levels of spiritual attainment (*guṇasthāna*). The omniscient is occupied with the third type of pure meditation (*sūkṣmakriyāpratipātin*) when an *antarmuhūrta* remains in final emancipation. After being established in gross bodily activity in the prior 12 levels, the ascetic makes the activities of mind and speech subtle. Then after renouncing the bodily activity, the ascetic becomes fixed in the activities of mind and speech, and makes the gross bodily activity subtle. Afterwards mental and vocal activities are stopped and only subtle activity of body is left. In the last type of pure meditation (*vyuparatakriyānivartin*), even the subtle activity of the body is stopped. The soul now becomes devoid of mental, vocal, and physical vibrations, and immediately after that time attains disembodied liberation.

Spiritual evolution (*guṇasthānas*) and the nature of mysticism

Before we commence to reckon with the nature of the *guṇasthānas*, we propose to discuss the nature of mysticism, which will enable us to evaluate the Jaina conception of morality. The word "mysticism" does not possess any uniform and consistent meaning in spite of a noble history to its credit. It has been variously used and diversely interpreted. To dwell upon these various expressions and interpretations of the word "mysticism" is not our objective. We simply note that, notwithstanding its manifold meanings, the note of concordance found in them is greater than that of discordance. Professor Ranade rightly says: "the mystics of all ages and countries form an eternal divine society."[2] "There are no racial, no communal, no national prejudices among them. Time and space have nothing to do with the eternal and infinite character of their mystical experience."[3] "They may weave out their mysticism with the threads of any metaphysical structure, but they always try to go behind the words and realize a unity of significance."[4] The equivalent expression in Jainism for the word "mysticism" is "*śuddhopayoga*."

According to Kundakunda, mysticism consists in realizing the transcendental self through the internal self after renouncing the external self; i.e., after relinquishing the *bahirātman* and by turning to the *antarātman*, one should realize the supra-ethical state of the *paramātman*. In other words, non-conceptual and perpetual meditation on the supreme self ought to be effected after abandoning the *bahirātman* through the inter-meditation of the *antarātman*; i.e, *bahirātman* is to be of necessity renounced to attain *antarātman*, which will in turn lead us to an unimaginable transformation into *paramātman* through the medium of meditation and other practices of moral nature. Kundakunda, Yogīndu, Pūjyapāda, Śubhacandra, and Kārttikeya have endorsed this very statement. It will not be idle to point out here that in realizing the transcendental self, the whole of the existence is intuited on account of the spontaneous efflux of omniscience. The realization of self and intuition of other substances are synchronal. According to Ranade, "Mysticism denotes that attitude of mind which involves a direct, immediate, first-hand, intuitive apprehension of God."[5] This definition as a given by Ranade is in keeping with the Jaina exposition of mysticism, provided that the word "God" is understood in the sense of the transcendental self as recognized by Jainism. Thus mysticism is not mere speculation, but action. It is transition from the life of sense to the life of spirit, which is tantamount to achieving the immortal heritage of man. This amounts to realization of the transcendental self. The limited character of the individual self is disrupted and invaded by the absolute self which the individual feels as his own. We may sum up by saying that mysticism culminates in the heightened and completed form of life, which is accomplished by that transcendental belief, knowledge, and conduct which in our life remains ordinarily below the threshold of consciousness.

Characteristics of the three kinds of self

Outward-oriented self (bahirātman)

The characteristic of the *bahirātman* may, in the first place, be accounted for by affirming that the outward-oriented person identifies with the physical body, spouse, and children, silver and gold, and so forth. Such a person is constantly obsessed with fear of self-annihilation on the annihilation of the body and the like. Secondly, this person remains engaged in the transient pleasures of the senses, feels elated in getting the coveted things of the unsubstantial world, and becomes dejected when they depart. Thirdly, this soul is desirous of getting a beautiful body and physical enjoyment in the life hereafter as a result of penances, and is tormented even by the thought of death. The attitude of the Cārvāka materialist sums up the meaning of the *bahirātman*.

The spiritually oriented self (antarātman)

The spiritually oriented self has undergone a conversion through which one relinquishes pride and regards outward physical dwelling places as unnatural and artificial. This person renounces all identification with spouse and children as well as wealth and property. The spiritually oriented person is the only self that has acquired the right of *mokṣa* and consequently adopts an attitude to safeguard spiritual status and interest. Endowed with spiritual resolution, one sounds the bugle of triumph after defeating the treacherous foes of attachment and aversion in the outward-oriented state.

There are three types of spiritually oriented persons. The first one has attained a spiritual conversion, is devoted to the Jinendra, possesses the attitude of self-censuring, is disposed to the adoption of virtues, is affectionate toward the meritorious, but lacks pursuance of the moral path. The second one, in the householder state, follows partial vows and is loyal to the words of the Jina. Saints comprise the third type, steadfast in dharma and *śukla-dhyāna*.

The supreme self (paramātman)

The *paramātman* is the supreme self, the consummation of an aspirant's life, the terminus of spiritual endeavors. The embodied *paramātman* is *arhat*, while the disembodied one is *siddha*. The *Mokṣa Pāhuḍa* proclaims the *paramātman* to be without defects, body, and senses, and to be associated with omniscience and purity, free from birth, old age, and death, supreme, pure, devoid of eight karmas, possessing infinite knowledge, intuition, bliss, and potency (5, 6). Such a one is indivisible, indestructible, and inexhaustible: super-sensuous and unparalleled, free from obstructions, merit, demerit, and rebirth, eternal, steady, and independent.

The mystic way

The outward-oriented self, which is the perverted self, is to be renounced; the *antarātman* is the converted self, the awakening of the consciousness of the transcendental self within. It is separated from the body, the external world and psychical states, both auspicious and inauspicious. The *paramātman* is the true goal of the mystic quest. The journey from external self to the supreme self is traversed through the medium of moral and intellectual preparations, which purge everything obstructing the emergence of potential divinity. Thus the whole mystic way may be put as follows: (1) awakening of the transcendental self; (2) purgation; (3) illumination; (4) dark night of the soul; and (5) transcendental life. According to Underhill, "Taken together, they constitute phases in a single process of growth, involving the movement of consciousness from lower to higher levels of reality, the steady remaking of character in accordance with the independent spiritual world."[6] In Jaina terminology, right knowledge, right conduct, which includes will and feeling, and right belief are indispensable for mystical endeavor.

In Jainism, the mystic follows a 14-fold path to freedom, from the dark period of the self prior to its awakening (*mithyātva guṇasthāna*) to the state of total freedom, discussed elsewhere in this volume. For the purpose of this chapter, we will investigate the upper rungs of this spiritual staircase, beginning with the seventh level (*apramattavirata*). The second part of the seventh *guṇasthāna* and the rest of the higher *guṇasthānas* up to the 12th are the meditational stages or the stages of illumination and ecstasy. The ladder steps are ascended by the aid of deep meditation. It is through the medium of contemplation that the mystic pursues the higher path. By this time, the aspirant has developed a power of spiritual attention, of self-merging, and of gazing into the ground of the soul. He or she has developed a deep habit of introversion. The mystic abundantly experiences the pure states of the self, and, after the expiry of one *antarmuhūrta*, comes to the eighth stage, namely, *apūrvakaraṇa*, where it is realized such states as this were unprecedented in the history of the soul. The maximum sojourn of the self in this stage is one *antarmuhūrta*. Here the self engages itself either in subsiding or annihilating the residual of conduct-deluding karma according to the ladder it chooses to climb up.

After the end of the aforementioned duration, it performs the process of *anivṛttikaraṇa* where exists the state of profound purity, the ninth stage. In the tenth *guṇasthāna*, known as *sūkṣmasāmparāya*, there is only subtle greed that can disturb the soul. The self which has chosen the ladder of subsidence for its spiritual ascent suppresses even this subtle greed in the 11th *guṇasthāna* and absolves itself from the rise of all types of passions. This stage is known as *upaśāntakaṣāya gūṇasthāna*. This height has been arrived at by the first type of *śukla-dhyāna*. It is the culmination of the first type of white contemplation, *śukla-dhyāna*. Pūjyapāda observes that contemplation produces supreme ecstasy in a mystic who is firmly established in the self and who has withdrawn from worldly intercourse. Such ecstatic consciousness is potent enough to burn the karmic fuel; and then the person remains unaffected by external troubles and never experiences discomposure. All the stages described above are undoubtedly the stages of illumination.

The last stage is the termination of the "first mystical life." If the ladder of annihilation has been ascended, the self, instead of entering the 11th *guṇasthānas* from the tenth, rises directly to the 12th one, known as *kṣīṇakaṣāya guṇasthāna*. Here the residual of conduct deluding karma is destroyed instead of being suppressed. All other characteristics are identical with the 11th stage. The soul remains for one antarmuhūrta in this stage. With the help of the second type of *śukla-dhyāna*, the self in the last instant of this stage annuls all the remaining destructive karmas; and the mystic enjoys the transcendental life, which shall be presently dealt with.

Dark night of the soul post-illumination

The mystic who possesses the fresh fruits of contemplation may encounter a state of outright putrefaction, and experience a swing-back into darkness. This divides the "first mystic life" or illuminative way from the "second mystic life" or transcendental life. It is generally a period of utter blankness and stagnation, so far as mystical activity is concerned. "The self is tossed back from its hard-won point of vantage." Technically speaking, the Dvitīyopaśama Samyagdṛṣṭi, i.e., one who attains the designation of illuminated consciousness in the 11th *guṇasthāna*, falls to the lowest stage of *mithyatva* step by step after completing the period of stay in each stage. This may be accounted for by saying that the suppressed passions gain strength after the lapse of one *antarmuhūrta*; and the mystic has to suffer unhappy consequences. The ecstatic awareness of the transcendental self, which was the governing characteristic of illumination, is negated. The illuminated consciousness is perfectly content and tranquil, but after the lapse of the aforementioned period, the state of illumination begins to break up; and an overwhelming sense of darkness and deprivation envelops the mystic. "This sense is so deep and strong that it inhibits all consciousness of transcendent and plunges the self into the state of negation and misery which is called the Dark-Night."[7] The dark night experienced by the Kṣāyika Samyagdṛṣṭi is not as intense as it is experienced by the Dvitīyopaśama Samyagdṛṣṭi, inasmuch as the latter may fall to the first *guṇasthāna*, in contradistinction to the former who cannot go beyond the fourth one. Those who are great contemplatives emerge from this period of destitution, but those who are less heroic succumb to its dangers and pains. It may be noted here that not all the mystics experience this dark night. Those of them who ascend the ladder of annihilation escape this tragic period, and forthwith succeed in materializing the final accomplishments, in relishing the fruits and transcendental life, in comparison with those who ascend the ladder of subsidence. Mystics of the latter type no doubt will also reach the same heights, but they do so only when they climb up the ladder of annihilation either in this life or in some other to come. As a matter of fact, the soul, which has once attained spiritual conversion, is entitled to be the inhabitant of the holy world. The question is only of time and not of certitude. To sum up, some souls are confronted with darkness of three types in their life: first, before conversion; secondly, after conversion; and thirdly, after the ascension of the ladder of subsidence. In the first, though the self is overwhelmed by utter darkness, he or she is not aware of it; in the second, the fall from spiritual conversion is not consciously recognized; in the third, the self, having touched the sublime heights, falls to the ground; hence the invasion of darkness is naturally most perturbing and painful.

Transcendental life, or (A) *Sayoga Kevalī*, (B) *Ayoga Kevalī*

The slumbering and the unawakened soul, after passing through the stages of spiritual conversion, moral and intellectual preparation, now arrives at the sublime destination by dint of ascending the rungs of meditational ladder. The dormant self, prone to the renouncement and choice of external things, and who, when awakened, is occupied with the rejection of inner evil desires and the acceptance of auspicious psychical states, now by virtue of his metamorphosis into the transcendental self neither abandons nor adopts anything, but rests in eternal peace and tranquility. The self which was swayed by perversion, non-abstinence, spiritual inertia, and the *samjvalana* types of passion and quasi-passions refuses now to be deflected by them; and possesses the dispassionate vocal and physical activities (*yogas*) which cannot deprive the soul of mystical experience. Activity is not incompatible with transcendent experience. It is a state of *jīvanmukta*, an example of divine life upon earth. In the transitional stages, the auspicious *bhāvas*, which were used as temporary structures for taking refuge, have now, succumbed, and the Śuddha Bhāvas, which will now serve as a permanent dwelling, have emerged. The *antarātman* has been displaced by the *paramātman*. Potentiality has been turned into an actuality. The disharmony between belief and living has vanished. This is transcendental life, a super-mental state of existence. It is the final triumph of the spirit, the flower of mysticism, the consummation towards which the soul of the mystic strenuously engaged itself from the commencement of the spiritual pilgrimage. Technically it is termed "*sayoga kevalī*" *guṇasthāna*," since it is accompanied by *yoga* (activity) and *kevalajñāna* (omniscience). The *Gommaṭasāra* proclaims that in this *guṇasthāna* the *ātman* is called "paramātman."

The next stage is called "*ayoga kevalī guṇasthāna*," as there the soul annuls even the vibratory activities, but preserves omniscience and other characteristics; and afterwards attains disembodied liberation in contradistinction to the two types of embodied liberation enjoyed by the self in the previous *guṇasthānas*. However, the difference in the state of liberation (embodied and disembodied) does not create the difference in spiritual experience, inasmuch as the four types of obscuring karmas (*ghāti karmas*), namely, the knowledge-covering, the intuition-covering, the deluding and obstructive, have ceased to exist in the embodied state of emancipation. Even the influx of karmas, which is due to the presence of Yoga, cannot operate in a polluted manner owing to the absence of passions. When the self lands in the "*sayoga kevalī guṇasthāna*," he may be credited with the designation of "*arhat*" and it holds good before the attainment of *siddha* state.[8] To be clearer, the self in the *sayoga kevalī* and the *ayoga kevalī guṇasthānas* bears the title of "*arahanta*."

The *arahanta* is the ideal saint, the supreme guru, and the divinity-realized soul; hence he may be designated as paramātman or God. *Siddha* has also been called God. But:

> neither *arhat* nor *siddha* has on him the responsibility of creating, supporting and destroying the world. The aspirant receives no boons, no favours, and no curses from him by way of gifts from the divinity. The aspiring souls pray to him, worship him and meditate on him as an example, as a model, as an ideal that they too might reach the same condition.[9]

But it should not be forgotten that unified, single-minded devotion to arahantas or siddhas accumulates in the self the *puṇya* of the highest kind, which, as a natural consequence, brings about material and spiritual benefits. Samantabhadra observes that the adoration of *arahanta* deposits great heap of *puṇya*.[10] He who is devoted to him relishes prosperity, and he who casts aspersions sinks to perdition; in both these *arahanta* is astonishingly indifferent. The aspirant, therefore, should not breathe in despondency for the aloofness of God (*arahanta* and *siddha*). Those who are devoted to him are automatically elevated. The ultimate responsibility of emancipating oneself from the turmoil of the world falls upon one's own undivided efforts, upon the integral consecration of energies to the attainment of divine life. Thus every soul has the right to become *paramātman*, who has been conceived to be the consummate realization of the divine potentialities.

Characteristics of the *arahanta*

We shall now dwell upon the characteristics of *arahantas*, the effects of transcendental life, the effects which the realization of *paramatman* produces upon the perfected mystic. The *Ācārāṅga* tells us that the *arahanta* is established in truth in all directions. The liberated being is free from anger, pride, deceit, greed, attachment, hatred, delusion, birth, death, hell, animal existence, and pain. *Arahantas* lead a life of supermoralism but not of amoralism. It is inconceivable that the saint who has attained supremacy on account of the realization of perfect *ahiṃsā* may in the least pursue an ignoble life of *hiṃsā*, a life of vice. This person is no doubt beyond the category of virtue and vice, good and evil, *puṇya* and *pāpa*, auspicious and inauspicious psychical states, yet may be pronounced to be the most virtuous soul, though the pursuit of virtuous life is incapable of causing bondage to the cycle of life and death. Technically speaking, *sātāvedanīya* karma in the absence of deluding karma cannot sow the seeds of mundane career. Samantabhadra ascribes inconceivability to the mental, vocal, and physical actions of arhat, since they are neither impelled by desire nor born of ignorance. Whatever issues from the arahant is potent enough to abrogate the miseries of tormented humanity. Hundreds of souls are spiritually converted by the mere sight of a liberated being, forsaking their skeptical and perverted attitude towards life.

The presence of an *arahant* is supremely enlightening. The embodiment of mystical virtues, the *arahant* is the spiritual leader of society, beyond attachment, aversion, and infatuation. By virtue of intuitively apprehending the nature of reality, as also the implications of the sacred texts, all doubts have been resolved. The perfected mystic has become through self-effort with self-control. The abandonment of all violence (*hiṃsā*) allows one to resist the temptations of senses and mind, including anger, lust, and greed by performing internal and external austerities. In mystical language we may say that, with the emergence of the *ātmanic* experience and steadfastness in it, the conquest over mind, the senses, and the passions becomes natural, i.e., a thing flowing from the intrinsic nature of the freed soul. By virtue of self-realization, and of having achieved sublime concentration and owing to the simultaneous establishment in the triune path of right belief, right knowledge, and right conduct, the *arahant* has transcended the dualities of friends and enemies, pleasure and pain, praise and censure, life and death, sand and gold. And yet in spite of this transcendence, the freed soul embraces reconcilable contradictions. Self-established yet all-pervading, knowing all things yet detached, the *arahant* is associated with great longevity, yet devoid of senility. The transcendent mystic has manifested pure consciousness, destroyed the destructive karmas, and attained supersensuous knowledge, infinite potency, and unique resplendence. As a consequence of this, all desires for bodily pleasures and pains vanish immediately.

The infinite life of the mystic has rendered possible the emergence of omniscience which possesses the potency of completely, simultaneously and intuitively or unassistedly apprehending all the substances along with their present and absent modifications in contradistinction to the limited life of sensuous knowledge which cognizes substances incompletely, successively, and intellectually or assistedly.

The omniscient being neither accepts nor abandons, nor transforms the external objectivity, but only witnesses and apprehends the world of objects without entering them, just as the eyes see the objects of sight. Yogīndu, in a similar vein, proclaims that the universe resides in the *paramātman* and the freed soul resides in the universe, but the soul is not the universe. The pure soul, according to him, is all-pervading, in the sense that when delivered from the karmas the soul comprehends, by omniscience, physical and super physical worlds.[11] The knowledge which is independent, perfect, immaculate, intuitive, and extended to infinite things of the universe may be identified with bliss on account of the absence of discomposure arising from the knowledge which is dependent, imperfect, maculate, mediate, and extended to limited things. In other words, the consciousness of the perfected mystic is not only omnipotent and intuitive but also blissful. Bliss is naturally consequent upon the destruction of the undesirable and accomplishment of the desirable. The consummate mystic experiences unprecedented bliss, which originates from the innermost being of self, and which is supersensuous, unique, infinite, and interminable.

A legitimate question is apt to be asked: what does the culminant mystic who has swept away the dense destructive karmas, who intuits all the entities, who does not allow even an infinitesimal fragment of the objects to escape his all-comprehensive knowledge, and who is free from doubts, meditate upon? This may be replied to by saying that the consummate ātman who is super-sensuous, bereft of senses, free from all hindrances, permeated by knowledge and happiness meditates upon the happiness supreme. According to Kundakunda the real contemplator of the ātman, after removing the filth of delusion, overthrowing attachment and aversion, and detaching from the objects of pleasure, restrains the mind, and attaining indifference to pleasure and pain, is established in the intrinsic nature of the ātman, thus attaining inexhaustible bliss. The perfected mystic is the exemplary illustration of this sort of living. Thus the mystical or spiritual consciousness is intuitive, blissful, and all-powerful. We may conclude by saying that the cognitive, conative, and affective tendencies of the perfected mystic reveal their original manifestation in the supreme mystical experience, which is ineffable and transcends all the similies of the world.

The religious consciousness of the transcendent mystic that there is "intimate interpenetration of the non-rational with the rational elements like the interweaving of warp and woof,"[12] ineffability being the non-rational element and the evaporation of bodily urges, the emergence of omniscience, obtainment of infinite power, abolition of all fear, enjoyment of illuminate joy, resolution of all doubts, and the consummation of virtues.

Samudghāta* in *Sayoga Kevalī Guṇasthāna

The acme of the ladder, the 14th stage of absolute motionlessness, the *ayoga kevalī guṇasthāna* is arrived at when the perfected mystic gets over the vibratory activities of the body and speech by resorting to the two types of *śukla-dhyāna* when the small duration of longevity-determining karma remains. Though the self has annulled the four *ghāti* karmas, yet the four *aghāti* karmas, namely, feeling producing (*vedanīya*), longevity determining (*āyus*), body making (*nāma*), and status determining (*gotra*) exist and function in the structure of the self. When the duration of three karmas lacks equality with the duration of *āyu* karman and an *antarmuhūrta* remains for the soul to attain disembodied liberation, a certain process of equalization, technically known as *samudghāta*, takes place in the omniscient being. The term *samudghāta* implies the emanation of the *pradeśas* of the soul along with karmic and electric bodies from the gross body without leaving it. Now, the self before taking recourse to the stoppage of vibrational activities undergoes the process of samudghāta in the 13th *guṇasthāna* for accommodating the other three karmas to *āyuḥkarman*.

When the equalization process has come to an end, the omniscient soul in the 13th *guṇasthāna* turns to the cessation of vibrational activities, and just after doing this enters the 14th stage of spiritual evolution, called *ayoga kevali guṇasthāna*, where the soul stays for the time required to pronounce five syllables – a, i, u, ṛ, lṛ. After this, disembodied liberation results. In this *guṇasthāna* the ātman has become self-crowned with a great number of mystical virtues, has attained steadiness like the Meru mountain, has stopped the influx of all sorts of karmic particles, and has become devoid of *yogas* (activities of body, mind, and speech).

***Siddha* state or transcendental life par excellence**

This stage is immediately followed by final emancipation, which is the same as disembodied liberation, the last consummation of the spirit, the attainment of siddhahood, transcendental life par excellence, and the state of videha mukti. This state of self is beyond *guṇasthānas*. Just after the termination of the last stage of spiritual evolution, the soul in one instant goes to the end of the *loka*, since beyond that there is no medium of motion in the *aloka*. The upward motion of the self is on account of the fourfold reasons. First, it is due to the persistence of the effects of previous strenuous endeavors for disenthralment, just as the wheel of the potter continues to move even when the force of hand is removed. Secondly, it is on account of the fact of freedom from the karmic weight, just as there is the upward motion of the *tumaḍī* in water after the dissolution of the burden of clay. Thirdly, it results owing to the destruction of all karmas, just as there is the upward movement of castor seed after the bondage of cover is removed. Lastly, it is due to its intrinsic nature, which manifests owing to the absence of the aberrant power of karmas, like the upward direction of the lamp flame in the absence of the deflecting wind. In other words, the original dwelling place of the ātman is the top of the loka; and it is only due to the karmic encumbrance that the ātman has been forced to bear the mundane form; and when one has attained supreme consciousness of his inherent nature, one resorts to freedom.

Characteristics of the *siddha* state

The *siddha* state transcends the realm of cause and effect, inasmuch as the *dravya* and *bhāva* karmas and the consequential four types of transmigratory existence have ceased to exist. The category of causality is applicable only to mundane souls and not to the siddha, who is an unconditional being. Kundakunda announces that the *siddha* is neither the product of anything nor produces anything, hence neither effect or cause. According to the *Ṣatkhaṇḍāgama,* he who has destroyed all the karmas, who is independent of external objects, who has attained infinite, unique, intrinsic, and unalloyed bliss, who is not attached to anything, who has achieved steady nature, who is devoid of all sorts of mal-characteristics, who is the receptacle of all virtues, and who has made the top of the universe his permanent abode, is siddha.[13] The acquisition of siddhahood is indistinguishable from the accomplishment of nirvana, where, negatively speaking, there is no pain, nor pleasure, nor any karmas nor auspicious and inauspicious *dhyānas*, nor anything such as annoyance, obstruction, death, birth, senses, calamity, delusion, wonder, sleep, desire, and hunger and, where, positively speaking, there is perfect intuition, knowledge, bliss, potency, immateriality, and existence. The *Ācārāṅga* pronounces:

> All sounds recoil thence where speculation has no room, nor does the mind penetrate there . . . The liberated is without body, without resurrection, without contact of matter; he is not feminine, nor masculine, nor neuter; he perceives, he knows, but there is no analogy; its essence is without form; there is no condition of the unconditioned.
>
> (I: 5:6, 3–4)

The state of self is the termination of the mystic's journey. It is the final destination for which the self was all along struggling. In other words, the history of the siddha state of self is the history of the mystic's trials and tribulations in the march from bondage to freedom. Also, it is the history of the triumphant conclusion of moral and spiritual exertions.

Conclusion

In our discussion of the mystical significance of Jaina ethics, we have pointed out how the human self-emerging from the cave of passions rests in the abode of transcendental consciousness. The outward-oriented self (*bahirātman)* accepts everything as one's own, the spiritually oriented self (*antarātman*) negates all, but the supreme self (*paramātman*) neither accepts nor negates but transcends these dualities of acceptance and negation.

First, this chapter has explained the Jaina conception of mysticism and its relation to metaphysics. Second, the plight of the self steeped in ignorance and the nature and the process of emergence into spiritual conversion as distinguished from the ethical and the intellectual conversion have been expounded. Third, we have shown the necessity of purgation and moral preparation. Fourth, the conception of illumination, and the possibility of the two types of fall, first, from spiritual conversion and, secondly, from illumination, have been dealt with. And, fifth, the characteristics of transcendental life in the form of embodied and disembodied liberation have been portrayed. To sum up, we have delineated all the above states of the self under the 14 stages of spiritual evolution, including the siddha state, which transcends these stages.

Notes

1 For specific text references, consult Kamal Chand Sogani, *Ethical Doctrines in Jainism* (Solapur: Jaina Samskriti Samraksaka Sangha, 2001).
2 R. D. Ranade, *Mysticism in Mahārāṣṭra* (Bombay: University of Bombay), p. 2.
3 R. D. Randade, *Pathway to God-Realization in Hindu Literature* (Sāṅglī: Adhyātma Vidyā Mandira), p. 2.
4 *Paramātmaprakāśa of Yogīndu* (Bombay: Rāyacandra Jaina Śāstramālā), p. 26.
5 Ranade, *Mysticism in Mahārāṣṭra*, p. 1.
6 Evelyn Underhill, *Mysticism* (London: Methuen), p. 169.
7 Underhill, *Mysticism*, p. 382.
8 See Chainasukhadas, *Bhāvanā Viveka* (Jaipur: Sadbodha Grantamālā).
9 Upadhyaye, Introduction, *Paramātmaprakāśa*, op. cit., p. 36.
10 Samantrabhadra, *Svayambhūstotra* (Delhi: Vīrasevā Mandira), 58.
11 Yogīndu, *Paramātmaprakāśa*, op. cit., 52.
12 Rudolf Otta, *The Idea of the Holy* (London: Oxford University Press), p. 23.
13 Puṣpadanta and Bhūtabalī, *Ṣatkhaṇḍāgama, with Commentary Dhavalā of Vīrasena, Vol.* I (Amaroti: Jaina Sahitya Uddharaka Fund), p. 200.

Bibliography

Jñānārṇava of Śubhacandra. Bombay: Rāyacandra Jaina Śāstramālā.
Kārttikeyānuprekṣā. Bombay: Rāyacandra Jaina Śāstramālā.
Mūlācāra of Vaṭṭakera. Bombay: Anantakīrti Digambara Jaina Granthamālā.
Pravacanasāra of Kundakunda. With the commentaries of Amṛtacandra and Jayasena. Bombay: Rāyacandra Jaina Śāstramālā.
Pūjyapāda's commentary on the *Tattvārthasutra*.
Pūjyapāda. *Sarvārthasiddhi*. Kāśī: Bhāratīya Jñāna Pīṭha.

9 Yaśovijaya's view of Yoga

Jeffery D. Long

Introduction

This paper will explore the distinctive perspective on Yoga developed by the seventeenth-century Śvetāmbara sage, Yaśovijaya, focusing specifically on points of both contrast and overlap between Yaśovijaya's perspective and those of other Jaina and non-Jaina thinkers and movements. In terms of Jaina intellectual history, Yaśovijaya's view is of particular interest due to his location at the cusp of what are widely known as the "classical" and "modern" periods. This paper will emphasize ways in which Yaśovijaya can be seen as a transitional figure between these two periods, with aspects of his thought demonstrating strong continuity with classical Jaina (especially Śvetāmbara) philosophy, and other aspects anticipating modern trends, such as an emphasis on yogic experience (*anubhāva*) as a valid source of authentic knowledge.

Inasmuch as Yaśovijaya emphasizes direct experience of the soul (*jīva*), he can be seen as similar to the classical Digambara master, Kundakunda. Yaśovijaya, however, is more in line with classical Śvetāmbara metaphysical realism in rejecting Kundakunda's claim that the soul is already, in some sense, liberated, being inherently and intrinsically pure. Kundakunda's understanding of the soul, with the distinctively Jaina version of the "two truths" doctrine that is connected with it, is both structurally and substantively like the view of Śaṅkara, a view typically rejected by Śvetāmbara thinkers for its *ekānta* focus on continuity over change. At the same time, though, Yaśovijaya shows continuity with Śaṅkara in identifying the *jñāna yoga* as the supreme path to liberation, with *karma yoga* playing a more preliminary, purificatory role in this path. Finally, Yaśovijaya shows very strong continuity with Haribhadra, as well as anticipating a modern Jain approach to the concept of *anekāntavāda*, in his emphasis on a spirit of impartiality towards the various systems of thought of his time, utilizing the *Bhagavad Gītā* and Brahmanical terminology in his account of Yoga.

Yoga in Yaśovijaya's *Jñānasāra*

The view of Yoga found in Yaśovijaya's *Jñānasāra*, or *Essence of Wisdom,* shows a strong continuity with Haribhadra's view of Yoga. First, in terms of his definition of Yoga, Yaśovijaya begins by saying that, "Yoga refers to all practices that are desirable because of their association with liberation."[1] Haribhadra has similarly defined Yoga in both his *Yogabindu* and *Yogaviṃśikā*, as any practice that is "instrumental in bringing about final liberation."[2]

Next, Yaśovijaya specifies Yoga as consisting of five types of practice: *sthāna*, *ūrṇa* (or *varṇa*), *artha*, *ālambana*, and *anālambana*.[3] This, again, follows Haribhadra's specification of five types of Yoga practice in his *Yogaviṃśikā*.[4] *Sthāna* refers to physical posture. *Ūrṇa* (or *varṇa*) refers to vocal utterances, such as the chanting of prayers or *mantras*. *Artha* means properly grasping the meaning of that which one chants or recites. *Ālambana* is concentration on the external characteristics of one's deity – the chosen focus of one's meditation. This would seem to refer to a process of visualization of the deity as described in authoritative texts or as represented iconographically. *Anālambana* refers to concentration on the spiritual qualities of one's deity – inner qualities, such as compassion and wisdom, in contrast with visible characteristics.[5] Yaśovijaya also follows Haribhadra in categorizing *sthāna* and *ūrṇa* as types of Yoga characterized by physical activity, or *karma yoga*, and *artha*, *ālambana*, and *anālambana* as types of Yoga that take the form of knowledge, or *jñāna yoga*. He goes on to say that all these types of Yoga are manifested among those who are detached. Among others, these types of Yoga are in a "seed state," or a state of potential.[6] Yaśovijaya seems to be asserting here that everyone is either a practitioner or a potential practitioner of Yoga.

This last point is significant, because it suggests at least some measure of doubt on Yaśovijaya's part regarding the notion that some beings are *abhavya*, or incapable of liberation. If all beings have the potential to practice Yoga – the practices associated with and instrumental in bringing about liberation – then it logically follows that all beings can conceivably attain liberation. This is not, of course, the same as saying that all beings definitely will, or must, attain liberation. But it is in keeping with the overall irenic thrust toward inclusivism that Yaśovijaya and Haribhadra share to presume a universal potential for liberation, in contrast with the more exclusivist strand of Jain thinking which asserts that there are some beings who will definitely not attain liberation because they *cannot* do so. In the view of Yoga suggested here, all beings *might* attain liberation, though not all will necessarily do so. To be sure, in another text – his *Adhyātmamataparīkṣā* – Yaśovijaya states, with regard to the question of whether they are *bhavya* or *abhavya*, that beings should be given the benefit of the doubt – at least those beings who question whether they are *bhavya* or *abhavya* (since an *abhavya* would presumably not ask this question in the first place) [7] In his *Upadeśarahasya-svopajña-ṭika*, Yaśovijaya explains that *bhavyatva*, the capacity for liberation, is different for all beings. This accounts for the fact that different beings attain liberation at different times, as well as the fact that only some become Tīrthaṅkaras.[8] If one may generalize from all of this, the suggestion seems to be that Yaśovijaya, while not explicitly rejecting the notion of *abhavya*, prefers to err on the side of a non-judgmental approach to this issue. While some beings may never achieve liberation, it is better to say nothing definitive in this regard about any particular case.

Next, Yaśovijaya tells us that, "[The practice of Yoga] gives rise to compassion, detachment, the desire for liberation, and serenity."[9] These qualities are, indeed, attested effects of many years of regular meditation and Yoga practice, as described, for example, in Lola Williamson's recent (2010) study of long-time meditation practitioners in America.

Yaśovijaya then divides each type of Yoga practice into four successive stages: "aspiration (*icchā*), manifestation (*pravṛtti*), stability (*sthira*), and perfection (*siddhi*)."[10] Elaborating upon these, he explains that:

> In the stage of aspiration, one enjoys hearing stories of those who have achieved the goal. In the stage of manifestation, one engages in the Yoga practices most assiduously. In the stage of stability, one has abandoned all fear of doing harm. And in the stage of perfection, one works for the good of others.[11]

The stage of aspiration, it seems, is one in which one possesses and cultivates enthusiasm for the practice by listening to and reflecting upon accounts of other practitioners who have, through their practice, attained liberation. The stage of manifestation is one of intensive and diligent practice.

The stage of stability seems to be one in which the practice has become second nature. One has "abandoned all fear of doing harm" because one has, through the serious and intensive practice of the second stage, cultivated the characteristics of compassion, detachment, desire for liberation, and serenity to which the practice of Yoga gives rise. In reflecting upon this stage, one recalls the statement attributed to Confucius that, by the age of 70, he could follow his heart's desire without committing any transgressions.

"In the stage of perfection, one works for the good of others." While Jainism has no precise equivalent of the Mahāyāna Buddhist concept of the bodhisattva path, in the sense of a path that individual Jains consciously strive to cultivate as distinct from the path to liberation broadly conceived,[12] this line of Yaśovijaya's is certainly evocative of the idea that one pursues liberation not for one's benefit alone, but for the good of all beings. One recalls here Mahātma Gāndhī's belief "that if one man gains spiritually, the whole world gains with him and if one man falls the whole world falls to that extent . . . I do not believe . . . that an individual may gain spiritually while those around him suffer."[13]

Returning to the specifics of the various Yoga practices, Yaśovijaya explains that reflection upon the meanings of one's prayers and *mantras* (or *artha*) and on the external characteristics of one's deity (*ālambana*) should be done in the context of worship in the temple.[14] Posture (*sthāna*) and vocal utterances of prayers and *mantras* (*ūrṇa* or *varṇa*), on the other hand, are for one's individual practice.[15]

Yaśovijaya holds the fifth Yoga practice, *anālambana*, or reflection on the internal characteristics of one's deity, to be the highest. Of the two practices involving reflection upon the characteristics of one's deity – *ālambana* and *anālambana* – the first focuses upon the physical form of the deity, and so is called, by Yaśovijaya, *rūpi*, or "with form." But *anālambana*, reflection on the internal characteristics of one's deity, is *arūpi*, or "without form." Yaśovijaya holds this latter form of reflection on the deity to be the highest, due to the fact that it leads to communion with one's deity through the absorption of its inner qualities.[16]

The manner in which one performs the yogic practices, according to Yaśovijaya, is of four types: that in which one enjoys the practice, that in which one has developed a sense of *bhakti*, or devotion, that in which one has understood the authoritative textual basis of the practice, and that in which the practice has become a part of one's nature. A practice pursued progressively in each of these ways, culminating in the last, gradually leads to *ayoga*, the final stage of the spiritual path, or *guṇasthāna*, and the ultimate goal: liberation from the cycle of rebirth.[17] As in his account of the five types of yogic practice and their division into the categories of *karma yoga* and *jñāna yoga*, Yaśovijaya, in this fourfold division of the ways in which Yoga is to be practiced, closely follows the model set out by Haribhadra in his *Yogaviṃśika*.[18]

In the final verse of the Yoga section of the *Jñanasāra*, Yaśovijaya also follows Haribhadra in asserting that improper engagement in yogic practices leads to great harm for the practitioner and for the community. Even to protect the religious community from dying out, one must not teach yogic practices to those who are not properly prepared.[19] If a person lacks faith and does not have the proper foundation in the moral observances of the Jain path, then yogic practice will either be fruitless, or even lead to positive harm. A concern of many Indic traditions is the cultivation of various abilities, or *siddhis*, on the part of those who engage in yogic practice but lack the moral and spiritual foundation to handle these abilities. An image from contemporary popular culture for such a person is the Jedi knight, from the *Star Wars* films, who succumbs to the "dark side of the Force." That paranormal powers can arise from yogic practices, even if pursued by persons who lack spiritual maturity, is not denied. But the harm of which such persons are capable, if they develop such powers, is potentially great, and a source of highly destructive karmas. For the protection of both the community and the practitioner, yogic practices should not be taught to those who are not ready for them. This is even the case, both Haribhadra and Yaśovijaya maintain, if one fears that the religious tradition is in danger of dying out due to a lack of disciples – a fear likely harbored by many Jain teachers throughout history, given the status of the Jain community as a tiny minority during most of its existence.

How consistent is this concern with Haribhadra's and Yaśovijaya's impartial and irenic stance toward non-Jain traditions? For one could easily interpret the statements of these masters in this regard as an insistence that all yogic practice outside the boundaries of Jainism is destructive, and that only yogic practice in a Jain context can be conducive to liberation. This would be a mistaken interpretation, however; for, as Paul Dundas has pointed out, in his *Dharmaparīkṣā*, Yaśovijaya argues that other spiritual traditions can be, with regard to some of their particulars, "effectively no different from Jainism."[20]

Yaśovijaya's view of Yoga is therefore, with regard to the question of the efficacy of practice pursued in non-Jain contexts, structurally no different than inclusivist views found in Hindu and Buddhist traditions, as well as in the teaching of the Roman Catholic Church with regard to other traditions, as found in the documents of the Second Vatican Council. The fact that one's own tradition is seen as wholly and exhaustively true and its practices the most reliably efficacious for the attainment of salvation does not logically preclude that specific truths and specific efficacious practices present within one's own tradition might also be present in other traditions. On this view, the other traditions are not seen, in their totality, as being on the same level as one's own in regard to the truths they affirm or the efficacious practices they commend. But the fact that they do affirm at least some truths and commend at least some practices that can issue in the same positive results as one's own is not thereby denied. Yaśovijaya is not a relativist. But neither is he insistent that religion be an all-or-nothing proposition.

Yoga in Yaśovijaya's *Adhyātmasāra*

One indication of Yaśovijaya's openness to the presence of useful truths in non-Jain traditions is his frequent use of ostensibly non-Jain terminologies and categories, and even non-Jain texts, in presenting his view. His early immersion in the study of Navya Nyāya and his representation of Jain logic in Navya Nyāya terminology and utilizing the Navya Nyāya form of argumentation is famous. Indeed, it is his best-known contribution to the Jain intellectual tradition. It is also the case that the just-examined *Jñānasāra* is replete with Hindu terminology. Its categorization of the five types of Yoga into the two categories of *karma yoga* and *jñāna yoga* has been mentioned. And, in addition to using the term *paramātman*, or "Supreme Self," to refer to the nature of the liberated soul – a use not uncommon among Jain authors – there are several points throughout the text in which Yaśovijaya also refers to the liberated soul as *Brahman*. He does not thereby subscribe to the monistic metaphysics of Advaita Vedānta. But he certainly presents his Jain view in way that a Vedāntin could appreciate.

Another example of Yaśovijaya's willingness to tap into non-Jain sources in the service of Jainism is his extensive use of the *Bhagavad Gītā* as a proof text in his other major work on Yoga, the *Adhyātmasāra*, or *Essence of the Inner Self*.

On the analysis of N.M. Kansara, Yaśovijaya's reading of the *Gītā* is influenced heavily by Advaita Vedānta, a current of thought quite strong in the city of Bānāras in the seventeenth century, when Yaśovijaya studied Navya Nyāya there. Again, it is not that Yaśovijaya endorses the monistic metaphysics of Śaṅkara. But his reading of the *Gītā* is in tune with Śaṅkara's inasmuch as he sees the text as commending the *jñāna yoga* as the Yoga that brings about liberation, with *karma yoga* in the subservient or auxiliary role of bringing about the mental purification needed to create the conditions in which true *jñāna* can occur. This is certainly not a universally held interpretation of the *Gītā* among Hindu commentators, many of whom see this text as being primarily about *bhakti yoga*, seeing the culmination of the yogic path as the ecstatic and loving union of the devotee with the Lord. And in the modern or "neo" Vedānta of Sri Ramakrishna and Swāmī Vivekānanda, *karma yoga*, *jñāna yoga*, *bhakti yoga*, and Patañjali's *dhyāna* or *rāja yoga* are seen as just so many equally valid and efficacious paths for different types of practitioner, or as parts of the holistic practice of just one. It seems that, for Yaśovijaya, the *Bhagavad Gītā* is the *Bhagavad Gītā* of Śaṅkara, in which *jñāna yoga* reigns supreme. Yaśovijaya's task, then, is to press this text into the service of Jain Yoga.

In viewing *jñāna* as the supreme and final Yoga – the one Yoga that issues directly in liberation – Yaśovijaya can be seen to echo not Haribhadra so much as another of his Jain predecessors, the Digambara mystical philosopher Kundakunda. Kundakunda, like Śaṅkara and like the Buddhist master, Nāgārjuna, develops a "two truths" model of Yoga, in which the *vyavahāranaya*, or perspective of ordinary existence, is wholly subordinated to the *niścayanaya*, the absolute, ultimate perspective of the liberated soul. A potential source of controversy is the extent to which some of Kundakunda's pronouncements can be seen to downplay the *karma yoga* aspect of the Jain path, elevating gnosis over praxis.

The danger here, one could well argue, is that Kundakunda's "two truths" model is susceptible to the same misuses as its Buddhist and Vedāntic counterparts, from a Jain perspective. If liberation is purely a matter of saving knowledge, of perceiving reality in a particular way – in other words, if the bondage of the soul is merely apparent – then the very strong emphasis that the Jain tradition places upon right conduct and the freeing of the soul from karmic bondage through ascetic practice might be undermined. For saving knowledge might then arise through other means, such as the antinomian practices of the left-handed Tantric traditions, which are condemned even by the famously tolerant and irenic Haribhadra as leading to nothing but the accumulation of destructive karmas.[21]

On a metaphysical level, Kundakunda's elevation of one *naya*, or perspective, to the level of absolute truth, while relegating the other to the status of an inferior mode of perceiving reality, did not sit well with the ideal of impartiality expressed in *anekānta-vāda*. The Buddhist and Vedāntic versions of the "two truths" model are also critiqued by Jain authors as examples of *ekāntatā*, or one-sidedness, with their respective claims that the true nature of reality is either a web of impermanent moments or a single, eternal, unchanging being, with the contrary dimension relegated to the realm of illusion or *māyā*. *Māyāvāda*, the doctrine of illusion, runs directly contrary to the metaphysical realism of Jainism, in part due to its perceived ability to undermine spiritual practice. Put bluntly, if all is illusion, then what is the point of striving so hard for liberation?

Although Kundakunda himself did not see his "two truths" doctrine as leading to this conclusion, a movement taking him as its inspiration – the *Adhyātma* movement – did, questioning the need for traditional Jain practice, such as the worship practices associated with temples and the strict asceticism of monks and nuns. If one had experienced the true nature of the soul and the dawn of spiritual consciousness, was this not sufficient to attain liberation?

The followers of the Adhyātma movement were contemporaries of Yaśovijaya, and his criticism of them was relentless. Though he concurs with Kundakunda in seeing *jñāna* as the proximate cause of liberation, and so the supreme and final Yoga, part of the point of his citations of the *Bhagavad Gītā* is to show the necessity of *karma yoga* for the purification that is a necessary (though not sufficient) condition for the arising of *jñāna*. In keeping with the mainstream of Jain thought, Yaśovijaya is deeply suspicious of any conception of the self as lacking any need for purification that might undermine religious practice. Kansara accurately – and bluntly – summarizes Yaśovijaya's position as follows: "As to the view of those that hold the Supreme Self as eternally pure, Yaśovijaya thinks it is useless and hence not acceptable."[22]

Conclusion: Yaśovijaya – The Rationalist Mystic

Both Paul Dundas and Krishna Kumar Dixit have described Yaśovijaya as the last great intellectual of pre-modern Jainism. He is also a transitional figure, towering over modern Jain discourse, which tends to view his conclusions on a host of issues as having settled those issues decisively, and as the definitive Jain view. This is particularly so for the Śvetāmbara tradition and the various traditions that have sprung from it in the last few centuries.

Aspects of Yaśovijaya's thought demonstrate strong continuity with classical Jain philosophy – particularly, as we have seen, the thought of Haribhadra. Indeed, the work of Yaśovijaya can be seen, in many respects, as a restatement and extension of Haribhadra's work. As Dundas affirms, Yaśovijaya "saw himself as Haribhadra's successor."[23]

At the same time, there are aspects of Yaśovijaya's thought that also anticipate modern trends, such as a rationalistic impartiality (or *madhyastha*) toward the views of different traditions, and an emphasis on yogic experience (*anubhāva*) as a valid source of authentic knowledge.

In terms of rationalistic impartiality, this dimension of Yaśovijaya's thought is both an anticipation of modern thought and a strong point of continuity with Haribhadra, who himself famously stated that he harbored no special partiality toward Mahāvīra, nor any animus against Kāpila (the founder of the Sāṃkhya system of Hindu philosophy), but that he accepted any view that was in harmony with reason (*yukti*). If we define *modern* in purely conceptual rather than chronological terms, it could be said that a strong modern streak has existed in Jainism for many centuries. If *modernity* refers to a worldview that takes as its authoritative basis reason reflecting on experience, as opposed to an arbitrary partiality toward a particular text, teacher, or tradition, then Haribhadra and Yaśovijaya are both thoroughly modern figures. Both display a spirit of openness toward the various systems of thought of their time, with Yaśovijaya, as we have seen, using the *Bhagavad Gītā* and Hindu terminology in his account of Yoga. The particular strand of Jain thought that Yaśovijaya picks up and builds upon from Haribhadra has been widely adopted by many contemporary Jains, who characterize Jainism as a tradition of intellectual openness and tolerance.

Inasmuch as Yaśovijaya emphasizes the direct experience of the soul, he can be seen as similar to the classical Digambara master, Kundakunda, who is as important for contemporary Digambara Jainism as Yaśovijaya is for Śvetāmbaras.

Both view a direct, mystical realization as constitutive of liberation. This emphasis on direct experience is, like an impartial rationalism, a mark of Jain modernity.

Yaśovijaya, however, is more in line with classical Jain metaphysical realism in rejecting Kundakunda's claim that the soul is already, in some sense, liberated, being inherently and intrinsically pure, and the claim of Kundakunda's followers that action is not a necessary step on the path to the highest realization. For Yaśovijaya, *karma yoga* is a necessary, albeit subordinate, preliminary to the higher *jñāna yoga*, consisting of *artha*, *ālambana*, and finally, *anālambana* meditation.

It has been said that in the later half of his life, after composing his great works on logic, Yaśovijaya came under the influence of the Gujarati mystic, Ānandghan.[24] It was during this period that Yaśovijaya composed his major works on Yoga – the *Jñānasāra* and the *Adhyātmasāra*, which we have very briefly examined here, and the *Adhyātmopaniṣat-prakaraṇa*, or *Elucidation of the Secret Doctrine of the Inner Self*, which we have not. Unlike Thomas Aquinas, another great religious intellectual who is said, later in life, to have pursued a more mystical path, viewing his philosophical work at that point as "mere straw," Yaśovijaya remained a rationalist to the end. The view of Yoga that he develops in his later works reflects this simultaneously rationalistic and mystical orientation.

Notes

1 *mokṣeṇa yojanādyogaḥ sarvo'pyācāra iṣyate* (*Jñānasāra* 27:1a).
2 *Yogabindu* 1:3a, Kansara trans. Also *Yogaviṃśikā* 1a.
3 *viśiṣya sthānavarṇārthālambanaikādyagocaraḥ* (*Jñānasāra* 27:1b).
4 *Yogaviṃśikā* 2a.
5 Dixit (1970, p. 11).
6 *karmayogaṃ dvayaṃ tatra jñānayogaṃ trayaṃ/viduḥ virateṣveṣa niyamād bījamātraṃ pareṣvapi* (*Jñānasāra* 27:2).
7 *Adhyātmamataparīkṣā* 172, as explained in Jaini (2000, p. 109).
8 *Upadeśarahasya-svopajña-ṭīkā* 188, as explained in Jaini (2000, p. 109).
9 *kṛpānirvedasaṃvegapraśamotpattikāriṇaḥ* (*Jñānasāra* 27:3a).
10 *bhedāḥ pratyekam atrecchāpravṛttisthirasiddhayaḥ* (*Jñānasāra* 27:3b).
11 *icchā tadvatkathāprītiḥ pravṛttiḥ pālanaṃ param/sthairya bādhakabhīhāniḥ siddhiranyārthasādhanam* (*Jñānasāra* 27:4).
12 Jaini (2000, pp. 111–119).
13 Gandhi (1982, p. 23).
14 *arthālambanayoścaityavandanādau vibhāvanam* (*Jñānasāra* 27:5a).
15 *śreyase yoginaḥ sthānavarṇayoryala eva ca* (*Jñānasāra* 27:5b).
16 *ālambanamiha jñeyaṃ dvividhaṃ rūpyarūpi ca/arūpiguṇasāyujyayogo'nālambanaḥ paraḥ* (*Jñānasāra* 27:6).
17 *prītibhaktivaco'saṅgaiḥ sthānādyapi caturvidham/tasmādayogayogāptermokṣayogaḥ kramād bhavet* (*Jñānasāra* 27:7).
18 *Yogaviṃśika* 18.
19 *sthānādyayoganastīrthocchedādyālambanādapi/sūtradāne mahādoṣa ityācāryāḥ pracakṣate* (*Jñānasāra* 27:8). See also *Yogaviṃśika* 15–16.
20 Dundas (2004, p. 131).

21 Chapple (2003, pp. 75–85).
22 Kansara (1974, p. 41).
23 Dundas (2004, p. 131).
24 Wiley (2004, p. 239).

Bibliography

Chapple, Christopher Key. *Reconciling Yogas: Haribhadra's Collection of Views on Yoga* (Albany, NY: State University of New York Press, 2003).

Dixit, Krishna Kumar (trans.) *Yogadṛṣṭisamuccaya and Yogaviṃśikā of Ācārya Haribhadrasūri* (Ahmedabad: L.D. Institute of Indology, 1970).

Dixit, Krishna Kumar. *Jaina Ontology* (Ahmedabad: L.D. Institute of Indology, 1971).

Dundas, Paul. *The Jains* (second edition) (London: Routledge, 2002).

Dundas, Paul. "Beyond Anekāntavāda: A Jain Approach to Religious Tolerance," in Tara Sethia, Ed. *Ahiṃsā, Anekānta and Jainism* (Delhi: Motilal Banarsidass, 2004).

Gandhi, Mohandas K. (Richard Attenborough, ed.) *The Words of Gandhi* (New York: Newmarket Press, 1982).

Jaini, Padmanabh S. *Collected Papers on Jaina Studies* (Delhi: Motilal Banarsidass, 2000).

Kansara, N.M. "The Yoga in the *Bhagavadgītā* and in Yaśovijaya's *Adhyātmasāra*," in *The Adyar Library Bulletin*, Vol. 38, 1974 (*Mahāvīra Jayanti Volume*).

Wiley, Kristi L. *Historical Dictionary of Jainism* (Lanham, MD: The Scarecrow Press, 2004).

Williamson, Lola. *Transcendent in America: Hindu-Inspired Meditation Movements as New Religion* (New York: New York University Press, 2010).

Yaśovijaya. *Jñānasāra* (Jaipur: Prakrit Bharati Academy, 1995).

10 When will I meet such a guru? Images of the *yogī* in Digambar hymns

John E. Cort

What a difference a single vowel can make. In a book dedicated to the study of Jain Yoga, this essay addresses Jain *yogīs*. While the two cannot be completely separated, neither should the connections between the two be overemphasized. Yoga refers to a large number of technical embodied spiritual disciplines in South Asia (and for many centuries elsewhere in Asia, and increasingly nowadays everywhere in the world). In this sense, anyone who practices Yoga can be described as a *yogī*.

The term *yogī* also refers more generally in South Asian religious culture to anyone who has in some way renounced the world, and thereby engages in conduct that runs counter to the norms of the householder. Someone who is a *yogī* is not necessarily a practitioner of a formal Yoga. South Asian literature is replete with descriptions of *yogīs* in this second sense. In other words, we can analyze "*yogī*" as a literary trope. These include Jain *yogīs*.

David White (2009) has recently shown, with his characteristic insightful brilliance, that there can be significant differences between Yoga and a *yogī*. Whereas we usually consider a practitioner of Yoga to be a peaceful, irenic person, in popular South Asian understanding most *yogīs* are powerful and dangerous wonder-working characters who are as likely to demand money as anything else.[1] *Yogīs* are practitioners of difficult spiritual disciplines aimed at conquering the senses and ultimately conquering death itself. They are also *jogīs* and *fakīrs*, who could be alchemists, healers, poisoners, purveyors of aphrodisiacs, soldiers, spies, long-distance traders, power-brokers, and princes. While the standard literary accounts of Yoga present it as "a disengagement of the senses, mind and intellect from the outside world in favor of concentration on the transcendent person within," accounts of *yogīs*, "the presumptive agents of Yoga, *never* portray their practice as introversive or introspective – but rather always as extrovert, if not predatory" (White, 2009: 38).

White's observations are an important call to distinguish more clearly between Yoga as a practice and *yogī* as a person in South Asian history. We will see, however, that the *yogī* as portrayed in Digambar Jain literature does not fit White's characterization. A Jain *yogī* is not the same as a Hindu *yogī*. A Digambar *yogī* is not a wonder-working street performer who inspires awe, fear, and suspicion on the part of the general public. Instead, the Digambar literary *yogī* is an ideal spiritual practitioner, who represents and enacts in his practice the highest renunciatory ideals of the tradition.

The trope of the *yogī* is an ancient one in Digambar literature. At the center of this essay are Hindi *pad*s or *bhajans* composed by a number of Digambar poets in north India in the seventeenth through nineteenth centuries. In these *pad*s the poets articulate a vision of the ideal Digambar yogī. The poets also use the terms guru, *muni*, and *sādhu* in ways that are largely synonymous. The poets articulate a longing to see such a yogī, for the institution of the naked Digambar *muni* had been absent in north India for many centuries. This literary trope, I argue, played an important role in the twentieth-century revival of the naked *muni* tradition, as it provided an oft-sung memory of how a real Digambar *muni* should act. At the same time, we will see that there are some significant differences between the literary description of the yogī and the contemporary institutionalized mendicant practice of the Digambar *muni*.

The Prākṛt and Sanskrit *Yogī Bhaktis*

The trope of the yogī extends back at least a millennium-and-a-half, to the early levels of the development of a distinct Digambar renunciatory ritual culture. At the heart of Digambar mendicant practice is a set of recitations known as the Bhaktis. These exist in both Śaurasenī Prākṛt and Sanskrit forms. They are distinctly different texts, and in no sense can they be seen as linguistic translations of each other. While there are traditionally said to be ten Bhaktis, only seven of these are fully extant in Prākṛt, and there are ten in Sanskrit.[2] The *Sanskrit Bhaktis* exist in both longer and abbreviated forms, the latter known as *Laghu Bhaktis*. One Bhakti that is extant in all three forms – Prākṛt, long Sanskrit and short Sanskrit – is the *Yogī Bhakti*.

According to the sixteenth-century *Kriyākalāpa* commentary on the Bhaktis, written by Prabhācandra, the *Prākṛt Bhaktis* were composed by Kundakunda, and the *Sanskrit Bhakti*s by Pūjyapāda.[3] Neither of these attributions, however, can be accepted uncritically. The texts themselves, as seen by their unstable lengths in the manuscripts, appear to be more compilations of earlier materials for the purpose of ritual performance than original compositions. The best we can say in terms of dating the texts is that both their Prākṛt and Sanskrit versions date to some time in the middle of the first millennium C.E.

A. N. Upadhye (1935:xxviii) noted that the Prākṛt prose passages, which he argued are older and not from the same author as the Prākṛt metrical passages, "when carefully read, remind us of closely similar passages in Śvetāmbara canonical texts, in their *Pratikramaṇa* and *Āvaśyaka Sūtras* and texts like *Paṃcasutta*." The Prākṛt prose Bhaktis date back to the early years of the Jain mendicant tradition. Upadhye was of the opinion that the metrical *Prākṛt Bhakti*s were "composed, or rather compiled . . . to explain and amplify the prose Bhaktis." Later, "to supplement the *Prākṛt Bhaktis* and to keep pace with the growing popularity of classical Sanskrit among the Jaina monks, Pūjyapāda appears to have composed the *Sanskrit Bhaktis*" (Upadhye, 1935: xxviii–xxix).

The text of the *Prākṛt Bhakti* in 23 verses lists the virtues (*guṇa*) of the mendicant.[4] After beginning with a praise of the *yogī* as homeless (*anagāra*) and virtuous (*guṇadhara*), the text lists sets of virtues with increasing numbers from two through 14. Some examples of these are that the *yogī* is freed of the two faults (*doṣa*, i.e., rāga and *dveṣa*); is without the three modes of violence (*daṇḍa*, i.e., by mind, speech or body); grinds the four passions (*kaṣāya*, i.e., anger, pride, delusion, and greed); preserves his celibacy (*brahmacarya*) in nine ways; upholds the tenfold dharma; can cross the ocean made up of the 11 scriptures (*aṅga*); and practices the 13 forms of conduct (*kriyā*, i.e., the five great vows (*mahāvrata*), the five self-regulations (*samiti*), and the three restraints (*gupti*)). The text then describes the conduct of the true Jain yogī. He fasts for 6 months, and stands in the sun to perform penance at dawn and noon. He remains in various postures, and neither spits nor scratches. He stands at the base of a tree in all weather, and pulls out his hair. His hair is covered with dirt, but his soul is pure of karmic dirt. His nails and hair grow long. He bathes in the water of knowledge (*jñāna*), he is adorned with morality (*śīla*) and virtue (*guṇa*), and he is fragrant with asceticism (*tapas*). He practices various austerities in which asceticism (*tapas*), equanimity (*saṃyama*), and accomplishments (*ṛddhi*) are conjoined. Due to his asceticism his body has become like a plant. The text lists all the spiritual powers and forms of knowledge exhibited by the yogī. Like a deity, he travels four fingers above the surface of the ground. He has conquered all fear, all obstacles, all sensory distractions, all harassments, all impurities, the duality of passion and aversion, and the duality of pleasure and suffering. The text concludes with a verse of veneration of the homeless yogīs who are purified of passion and aversion.

The *Prākṛt Bhakti* contains a description of the ideal Jain yogī, but embeds it within a recitation of praise. The *Sanskrit Bhakti*, on the other hand, is more within the genre of poetry. The author employs his skills as a Sanskrit littérateur to paint a picture of the ideal Jain yogī. The Prākṛt text is a straightforward unembellished description, while the Sanskrit text is full of striking images.[5]

The poet describes the yogī as painfully aware that he burns from the sufferings of birth, old age, death, and disease.[6] The yogī is also aware that the universe is teeming with life. As a result he goes to the forest (*vana*) for shelter. He observes the great vows, the self-regulations, and the restraints. The poet paints a picture of the naked yogī standing in the full sun atop mountains during the hot season, with his body smeared with dirt, as he wears away his faults. This king of mendicants (*munīndra*) drinks the nectar (*amṛta*) of true knowledge (*jñāna*) and the milk of forbearance (*kṣānti*), and stands beneath a sheltering umbrella of contentment (*santoṣa*).

In the rainy season the yogī looks like a peacock, and in the dark he looks like a rainbow. In the rainy season lightning flashes and thunder roars all around him. He stands in meditation all night despite the heavy rains, and sits in meditation at the base of a tree. The *muni* is described as a lion among men (*nṛsiṃha*), who doesn't move even when buffeted by wind and rain. He remains standing in meditation through the night even in winter, when the ground is covered by snow.

In this manner, says the poet, the yogī practices the threefold discipline (*yoga*) of mind, body, and speech. His asceticism renders his body meritorious. He enters into *samādhi*, and experiences the pleasure of supreme bliss (*paramānanda*).

The Yogī in the Hindi *pads*

Let me now jump forward a millennium or more from the time of the *Prākṛt* and *Sanskrit Bhaktis,* to the evocations of the true Digambar yogī and the true Digambar guru in the hymns (*pad*) composed by the many Hindi poets of the late medieval and early pre-modern period in the urban centers of north India. I am not arguing that the Hindi poets were directly influenced by the Prākṛt or Sanskrit *Yogī Bhakti*s. Given the relative scarcity of manuscripts of the Bhaktis in Digambar libraries, and their performance largely, if not exclusively, within mendicant practice, it is likely that there was not a direct influence. Instead, the trope of the yogī was passed down through a large number of texts, and a full history of the trope would involve a careful analysis of the many texts that interceded between the Bhaktis and the Hindi pads.[7]

In this essay I analyze *pads* by the following poets. Five of them are the most popular of the Digambar Hindi poets: Dyānatrāy (1676–1726), Bhūdhardās (fl. 1724–1749), Budhjan (fl. 1778–1838), Bhāgcand (fl. 1850–1856), and Daulatrām (1798/99–1866). These poets were active in the Digambar urban centers of Agra, Mathura, Delhi, Jaipur, and Gwalior. To these I have added *pads* by Jagrām Godikā, a largely unknown poet who lived in Kama some time before 1789. His poems show how widespread the trope of the Digambar yogī was.

The poets describe the yogī as living in the forest, not in the city. Jagrām says that he is devoted to the forest-dwelling *sādhu*.[8] Budhjan sings that the renouncer (*tyāgī*) has renounced his home and lives in the forest,[9] and that the *muni* has come to the forest.[10] Since the yogī now understands that the body is a prison, physical enjoyment is a snake, and dependants and society are his foes, he has renounced them all to dwell in the forest. He has become a forest-dwelling *muni* in order to destroy karma.[11] Daulat says that the *muni* lives for 6 months in the forest performing a fast,[12] and that he lives in the forest, where he is firm in his meditation.[13] The poets here play upon a long-standing moral dichotomy in Jain practice, between the *caityavāsī*, the domesticated monk who lives in the city in a temple compound, and the *vanavāsī* (or, in Braj, *banavāsī*), the true mendicant who lives in the forest.

Some of the poets pair the forest and the mountain. Bhāgcand says that the king of *munis* is *giri-vana-vāsī*, one who lives in the hills and in the forest.[14] The same compound is employed by Dyānat.[15]

Other poets omit the reference to the forest and focus on the mountain – but where there are mountains there are also caves, so the combination of mountain peaks and mountain caves is common. Bhūdhar says, "He lives outside on mountains and in the forest, he considers the mountain cave to be his palace."[16] Daulat says that the *muni* stays in empty buildings, on mountains, and in deep caves, where he remains seated in the lotus position.[17]

A key feature of the yogī is his ability to remain outdoors regardless of whatever harsh weather the seasons bring. He stands aloof even though it rains and thunders all around him during the rainy season. Budhjan says,

> The monsoon clouds hang low & heavy.
> The *muni*s stand firm under the trees.
> Clouds gather round with fearsome rain.
> They feel no more fear than of a wooden puppet.[18]

Dyānat echoes this when he says, "The monsoon rains pound him, the lightning flashes and thunders."[19] In a similar vein, Jagrām says,

> Dense clouds gather overhead
> the rain falls in sheets
> the lightning flashes.
> Squalls lash the land
> and the trees bend low.[20]

Then there is the cold and snow in the winter. Bhūdhar sings,

> When it snows in winter
> & the whole forest is covered in ice,
> the water is frozen
> & everyone's body shivers –
> then he dwells naked in a field
> or the bank of a river.[21]

Finally, the yogī can withstand the fierce midday sun of the hot season. Bhāgcand says,

> When the sun is above him at midday
> the fierce heat falls on him like burning coals.
> This is when his knowledge shines with purifying power
> and sparks fly out from the flames of his meditation.[22]

The three seasonal hardships are often combined into one extended trope of the naked yogī who is able to withstand all extremes of weather. Daulatrām says, "He stands on the hills in the heat, on the river banks in the snow, beneath a tree in the rains."[23] Dyānat employs the same three seasonal settings: "[He stands] on the mountain peaks in the heat of summer, and on river banks in the winter. He bears the rains in the monsoon."[24] Budhjan provides a longer description, in which he explicitly ties the settings to the names of the months, and thereby makes a passing reference to the genre of the *Bārahmāsā* or "Twelve Month" poem:

> He sits on the river bank in the cold winter of Poṣ.
> He meditates on the naked form of the Jina.[25]

> He stands on a mountain peak in the hot days of Jeṭh,
> with his face turned toward the sun.
> [He stands] beneath a tree when the rains come in Sāvan,
> constantly harassed by horse-flies and mosquitoes.[26]

The yogī also can withstand all sorts of other discomforts, since the ability to withstand afflictions (*parīṣaha*) is a mark of his equanimity. Jagrām says that the yogī "conquers desire, greed and the other afflictions,"[27] and Daulat that he "burns up the afflictions like foes."[28] An example of such an affliction is the insect bites that the yogī must withstand. We have already encountered this image in the passage from Budhjan. Dyānat invokes the same two oppressive insects, the horse-fly (*ḍaṃs, ḍāṃs*) and the mosquito (*masak*, *machar*):

> Horse-flies & mosquitoes are a cause of much suffering.
> But, says Dyānat, the *muni* just keeps working on his self.[29]

This pair, emblematic of the insects that emerge with the rains, also appear in a poem by Jagrām: "His body burns from the sharp bites of horse-flies and mosquitoes." Jagrām adds that these are explicitly among the afflictions that a yogī is expected to withstand.[30]

Wealthy, wealthy is that yogī

A phrase one finds in many of these songs is that the possession-less yogī, standing in his ascetic pose in the wilderness, is the truly wealthy person (*dhani*). Dyānat says, "The *sādhu* is wealthy who lives in the forest,"[31] "wealthy, wealthy is the *muni* who lives in the hills and in the forests,"[32] and "Brother, the *muni* is wealthy who stands firm in meditation."[33] Budhjan says, "Wealthy are the faithful ones in this world who live like a lotus in the water."[34] Bhāgcand says, "Wealthy, wealthy is the Jain *sādhu*."[35] Daulat says, "Wealthy is the *muni* who is attached to liberation,"[36] "Wealthy is the *sādhu* who recognizes the spirit,"[37] and "Wealthy is the *muni* who works on the welfare of his soul."[38]

In each case this is the first line of the poem, which therefore serves as the *ṭek*, the refrain that is recited after every verse and thereby establishes the content foundation of the poem. The poets here play on a well-established contrast in South Asian religious culture between worldly wealth and religious poverty, and between the enjoyer (*bhogī*) and the renouncer (*yogī*). From a worldly perspective, renouncing worldly wealth is a foolish thing to do. From a religious perspective, however, it is only by renouncing worldly physical wealth that one can find the real wealth, which is spiritual realization. The man in the world is constantly involved in consumption, and so is a consumer and enjoyer (*bhogī*). To find spiritual liberation, he must renounce consumption and become a yogī. This contrast is especially marked in the case of the Jains, most of whom come from merchant castes and have been among the more prosperous communities in South Asia for centuries. The Jain yogī, by contrast, gives up everything, including his clothes.

Jagrām Godikā

Two short poems by Jagrām Godikā bring these various motifs together into a more comprehensive portrait of the ideal Jain yogī. Jagrām, a Khaṇḍelvāl layman who lived in Kama sometime in the mid eighteenth century, is one of the lesser-known Digambar Hindi poets.[39] Nothing is known of him except that he lived in Kama, and once organized a festival in which a Jina icon was processed on a chariot. The relative rarity of his poems, however, allows us to see how thoroughly the trope of the Digambar yogī had penetrated the Digambar religious *imaginaire*. In his collection of 159 poems is a section of six poems on yogī bhakti.[40]

The first of the two poems by Jagrām that I translate here refers to the yogī as a forest-dwelling *sādhu*. It then describes him in meditation, and explains that for a Digambar mendicant the proper topic of meditation is to realize that in ultimate truth he is nothing but soul, by uttering the Digambar mystical phrase "I am that" (*so'ham*). The poet describes the yogī as standing in meditation like a tree. He also describes him grazing here and there like a deer, in reference to the requirement that a Jain mendicant strive not to let intention enter into his food-gathering round. Finally, Jagrām asserts that the Jain yogī is superior to gods and men, who bow at the yogī's feet while Jagrām sings his praises.

> Forest-dwelling *sādhu*, you are my devotion.
>
> You cut the net of delusion,
> you show the path to liberation.
>
> At the proper times you adopt the postures and fast,
> Month after month you are firm in your austerities.
>
> In your heart you remember, "I am that, I am that,"
> you weave the colors of the difference between Self and Other.
>
> You stand like a tree immersed in meditation.
> You graze here & there like a deer.
>
> Gods & man bow to the dust from your feet.
> Jagaṭ sings your glories.[41]

The first poem by Jagrām is largely a poetic description of the yogī, and given that the Digambar mystical invocation "I am that, I am that" (*so'ham so'ham*) could apply equally well to a yogī of almost any religious tradition in South Asia, there is nothing distinctly Jain about it. The second poem, however, is more closely tied to Jain doctrine. Jagrām describes someone who is obviously a Digambar mendicant, standing naked with his two arms hanging down in the distinctively Jain meditative pose of *kāyotsarga*. The yogī understands everything external, including the physical mental facilities, to be karmic dirt. He therefore turns his meditative gaze inward by fixing it on the tip of his nose. Through this meditation he overcomes attachment to sense objects and the passionate responses that the senses engender. By severing these external connections he also severs the bonds of karma. While this is standard Jain language, it again could apply to a yogī in a number of spiritual traditions. In the penultimate verse, Jagrām returns to a more distinctly Jain description, when he describes the yogī overcoming hunger, greed, and other afflictions. The word he uses here is *parīsaḥ* (Sanskrit *parīṣaha*), a technical Jain term found rarely in non-Jain contexts.

> The *jogī* is firm in his practice.
>
> His body is naked, his two arms hang down;
> the *jogī* stands staring at the tip of his nose.
>
> The master sees that his outer mind is only dirt
> and so remains within.
>
> The master stands firm to defeat sense objects and passions
> and to break the bonds of karma.
>
> The master conquers hunger, greed, & the other afflictions;
> he is filled by the color of his soul.
>
> Jagrām describes how the gods and men
> loudly say "Hail hail" to the master.[42]

Bhūdhardās

The two most widely recited and sung poems to the Digaṃbar yogī are by Bhūdhardās. He lived in Agra, and was active as a poet in the second quarter of the eighteenth century.[43] We know that he regularly gave sermons at the Digaṃbar temple in the Syāhgañj neighborhood of the city, and that he was considered to be a leader of the circle of Digaṃbars interested in *adhyātma*, the spiritual style of the time. In addition to composing many independent poems that were gathered together into the *Bhūdhar Vilās* ("Sport of Bhūdhar"), he composed the *Jain Śatak*, a set of 100 poems on religious themes, and a *Pārśvapurāṇ*. It is evident that he was well trained in both Braj-bhāṣā and Sanskrit, as he translated the Sanskrit *Caturviṃśati* of Bhūpāla and the Sanskrit *Ekībhāva Stotra* of Vādirāja into Braj-bhāṣā. He was well trained in Jain doctrine, as a result of which his poems are frequently rather heavily ladened with Jain technical vocabulary.[44]

Two poems by Bhūdhar are found in many Digambar anthologies and hymnals. The first of these is titled "Guru Stuti" ("Praise of the Guru") and "Guru Vinati" ("An Invitation to the Guru"). It is more popularly known by its first two words, "Bandoṃ Digambar," "I Venerate the Naked Mendicant."[45] The second is more simply entitled "Guru Vinati." In both poems Bhūdhar provides a lengthy and praising (*stuti*) description of the ideal Digambar yogī. The yogī is his true guru, whom he requests or invites to "reside in my heart and take away my sins,"[46] and to "come live in my mind."[47] While neither of these poems explicitly calls the Digaṃbar mendicant a yogī, the descriptions are parallel with those found in other poems I have discussed, and the range of terms Bhūdhar uses could clearly include yogī as a synonym. In just the opening verses of these two poems – and the verses, therefore, that serve as the refrains – he calls the mendicant Digaṃbar, guru, *vaidya* (Hindu physician), *sādhu* (Jain mendicant), *pīr (*Sufi master), and *ṛṣi* (sage), indicating that a wide range of spiritual terms apply to the person who is the object of Bhūdhar's veneration.

In the eight verses of "Bandoṃ Digaṃbar," Bhūdhar gives a generic description of the ideal Digambar yogī, but in language, like that in the first of Jagrām's poems, that could apply to a Hindu naked renouncer as well. The yogī dwells in the forest, where he has renounced all attachments – including, obviously, clothing. He has attained a state of equanimity toward all dualities, so that he looks without any emotional or intellectual judgment upon glass and gold, foes and friends, censure and praise, the forest and the city, pleasure and suffering, life and death. He views them all as equivalent (*sarūp*, *anūp*), and feels neither enjoyment (*khuśī*) nor attraction (*dilgīr*) in any of them. He lives outside, in the mountains and in the forest, and thinks of his mountain cave as a palace. He views the slab of rock on which he practices meditation as his fellow practitioner (*sahacarī*), and uses the moon as a lamp. The deer are his friends. He eats asceticism (*tap*) for food, and drinks knowledge (*vijñān*) for water.

In three verses, which I have already mentioned above, Bhūdhar describes the conduct of the yogī in the three seasons. In the hot, dry season, when the water in the lakes and rivers evaporates, he remains on the mountain top, practicing asceticism. Here Bhūdhar uses *tap* as both verb and object, so he says literally that the yogī "heats heat." In the monsoon there is thunder, lightning, rain, and cold winds, but during them all he stands unmoving beneath a tree. In the winter, when everyone and everything suffers from the cold, he remains naked, in the snow in a field or on a riverbank. Bhūdhar ends his poem by asking, "When will I meet such a king of renouncers" (*kaba milaiṃ voha munirāja*)?

Guru Stuti / Guru Vinati / Bandoṃ Digambar

I venerate the feet of the naked guru,
known for saving the world.
He is the royal physician
for those who wander the world in sickness.
Without his mercy
there is no way to cut off karma.
Sādhu, reside in my heart;
Master, take away my sins.

This body is defiled & impure,
it is totally absorbed in saṃsār.
I eat poison that is well-cooked –
I need to think about this.
The blessed *muni* who lives in the forest
has considered this.
The renouncer
has abandoned everything.
Sādhu . . .

He counts glass & gold as of equal value,
sees no difference between foe & friend.
He looks upon criticism & praise,
the forest & the city, as the same.
He finds neither joy
nor satisfaction
in pleasure or pain,
life or death.
Sādhu . . .

He lives outdoors on hills and in the forest,
he considers the mountain cave as a palace.
The slab of rock practices equanimity like him,
he uses the moon as a lamp.
Deer are his friends, his food is made of asceticism,
knowledge is his pure water.
Sādhu . . .

The lake dries up
the river runs dry
the path is impassable
his abode is hot –
this is the time the excellent *muni* heats himself
standing firm on the mountain peak.
Sādhu . . .

The thunder roars and booms
the rain pours down
lightning flashes in all directions
the cold wind blows.
Then the *jātī* stands under a tree
his body focused and unmoving.
Sādhu . . .

When it snows in winter
& the whole forest is covered in ice,
the water is frozen
& everyone shivers –
then he dwells naked in a field
or the bank of a river.
Sādhu . . .

Bhūdhar folds his hands and sings,
"When will I meet such a king of *munis*?
When will my mind's hope come to fruition,
my efforts be successful?
For no good reason, Vīr,
I live in the painful foreign land of *saṃsār*."
Sādhu . . .

The second "Guru Vinati" is longer, at 14 verses, and employs technical Jain language to describe a yogī who could only be Jain. Bhūdhar begins with a more generic description of a naked renouncer, who has abandoned all the cares of a householder to live naked in the forest, where he is concerned only with his real being, his pure soul (*ātma śuddh*).[48] He rejects the body as though it were a snake, and so renounces *saṃsār*.

Bhūdhar then moves the poem into a more specifically Jain setting. The yogī holds the three gems (*ratnatraya*), or right faith, right perception, and right conduct, in his heart. He has adopted the five great vows (*mahāvrata*) of a Jain renouncer, along with the eight matrices of practice: the five vigilances (*samiti*s) of care in walking, speech, accepting food, picking up and putting down objects, and excretory functions; and the three restraints (*gupti*) in mind, speech, and body. He follows the tenfold dharma and practices the 12 reflections (*bhāvnā*), and withstands the 22 afflictions (*parīsah*).[49]

In this poem Bhūdhar again employs a seasonal theme, devoting a verse each to the difficulties the *yogī* faces in hot season, the monsoon, and winter. The yogī focuses on the present, as he neither dwells fondly on pleasures from earlier times nor worries about what is to come. Instead, he fears the suffering that is inherent in all four of the possible realms of rebirth (here again using a specifically Jain phrasing of the world of rebirth). In two verses Bhūdhar contrasts the yogī's present renunciatory condition with his former life as a prince or king. Since all 24 Jinas renounced royalty, Bhūdhar elides the difference between the career of a past Jina and the practice of a contemporary mendicant. Whereas he used to sleep on a soft bed in a palace, he now sleeps on the ground; and whereas he formerly rode an elephant at the head of an army, he now walks barefoot and carefully observes every footfall. Bhūdhar concludes by saying that wherever such a guru travels is a pilgrimage shrine (*tīrath*), employing a common Jain understanding that there are two kinds of pilgrimage shrines: immobile (*sthavar*) temples with Jina icons, and mobile (*jaṅgam*) living mendicants.

Guru Vinati

Guru, come dwell in my mind
a river for the ocean of rebirth.
You cross & bring others across
you are the blessed king of sages.

You defeated the great foe delusion,
abandoned all the concerns of home.
You live naked in the forest
focused on your pure soul.

You count this body as a snake of disease,
enjoyment like a serpent.
Saṃsār is like a banana tree
so a wise man abandons it all.

You hold the three gems in your heart,
you are unbound in the three times.

You have overcome all bad lust:
Lord, you are the supreme compassion.

You treasure the five great vows
Along with the five observances (*samiti*).
You always follow the three guards (*gupti*).
These are the cause of the undecaying, undying state.

You uphold the tenfold dharma
and consider the twelve reflections.
You withstand the twenty-two afflictions,
you are a treasury of conduct.

You stand in the burning sun of Jeṭh
when lakes & rivers are dry.
The *muni* heats himself on mountain peaks
you heat your naked body.

In fearsome monsoon nights
when the rains overflow,
& the storms howl
the *yati* dwells at the root of a tree.

When the snow falls & the monkeys become restless
when all the great trees are frozen
you stand on the bank of a pond or river
and maintain your meditation.

You heat your difficult asceticism in the proper way
in all three seasons
in your body you attain the supreme state
devoid of body or ego.

You don't dwell on past pleasures
nor worry about what's to come.
You fear the suffering of the four states of birth
& strive to shine in liberation.

He slept in a royal palace,
he lay in a soft bed.
Now he spends his nights on the ground
keeping his body in equanimity.

He proudly rode on an elephant
at the head of an army of four divisions.
Now he carefully measures every step,
his limbs a means of compassion.

Wherever that guru walks
is a shrine in the world.

I raise that dust onto my head –
This is Bhūdhar's desire.

When will I meet such a guru?

Bhūdhar concludes his "Bandoṃ Digambar" by asking, "When will I meet such a guru?" This is a frequent question in the Digambar poems of the ideal yogī. In the refrain of another poem, Bhūdhar asks, "When will I meet that excellent *muni* who is beneficent?"[50] Budhjan concludes one poem by asking, "When will I have *darśan* of such a guru? Budhjan says it would bring joy to his heart."[51] In another he asks in the refrain, "When will I see that king of *munis*?"[52] Bhāgcand begins a poem with the refrain, "When will I meet such a *sādhu* who is a true guru?"[53] Daulat begins a poem with the refrain, "When will I meet my blessed guru, the excellent *muni*, who will ferry me across the ocean of rebirth?"[54]

Asking when one will meet a true guru is a widespread trope in South Asian devotional literature. The spiritual seeker has gone from teacher to teacher, but has yet to find one who truly knows and can teach the path to spiritual freedom. In the case of the Digambar Jains of north India in the seventeenth through early twentieth centuries, this was more than a literary trope: it was a very real situation. The institution of the naked *muni* was largely extinct in late medieval and early pre-modern north India, and it is likely that none of our poets ever met one.

There are scattered reports of naked *munis*, who appear to have been freelance Digambar renouncers outside the control of the *bhaṭṭārakas*, but they were very few at best. Kāmtā Prasād Jain (1962:265–266) wrote that a Muni Narsiṃh was reported in Dacca in 1813, that there was a report of a Muni Vinaysāgar near Itava sometime in the first half of the nineteenth century, and that his own ancestors had seen a naked *muni* from South India in Phagi in Jaipur state around 1823.[55]

Anūpcand Nyāytīrth (2002) wrote that when he was a boy of ten years of age, Ācārya Śāntisāgar (1872–1955), one of the three *munis* who in the twentieth century revived the tradition of naked *munis* in north India, came to Jaipur to spend the 4-month rains retreat (*cāturmās*) in 1932 with seven other *munis*. He wrote, "I heard from people that no Digambar *muni* had come before this." Nyāytīrth, however, indicated that this was a faulty history. He summarized an incomplete manuscript from 1833, containing the record of the 1832 visit to Jaipur and Amer of two *munis*, named Vṛṣabhsen and Bāhubali. The initial section of the manuscript is lost, so it is not known whence the two *munis* came to Jaipur. They were on their way to Sammet Shikhar. They were accompanied by several laymen who had been appointed by a congregation in Karnataka to look after their needs, so presumably they were Kannada Jains by birth. Vṛṣabhsen had taken initiation as a *muni* at age 40, and Bāhubali at age 28. After Jaipur, they went to the village of Sunara in Kota state, and then to Mathura. Their example inspired a 35-year-old man from Uvara village near Mathura to remove his clothes and thereby initiate himself as Muni Balbhadra. After a pilgrimage to Mount Girnar to confirm his initiation, he joined the other two on their trip to Sammet Shikhar. En route to Girnar he was imprisoned for 3 days in Alwar by local authorities who thought that this naked man was mentally disturbed.

Renunciation among Digaṃbars had become a highly domesticated institution. Instead of naked mendicants, there were robed *bhaṭṭāraka*s, and their equally robed followers, known as *pāṇḍes* and *brahmacārīs*. The *bhaṭṭāraka*s lived in monasteries, and controlled much of the ritual and intellectual culture of Digambar Jainism.

In such a setting, the vernacular *pads* that described the form and practice of the ideal *muni* played a powerful role in the Digambar religious *imaginaire*. On the one hand, these poems were a form of what we might call *viraha bhakti*: devotion to an absent lord, in which the very absence of the divine figure whom the singer longs to see intensifies the religious emotions.[56] But these poems also kept alive an understanding of what a "real" *muni* should look like, in contrast to the *bhaṭṭāraka*s, *pāṇḍe*s and *brahmacārī*s that the poets encountered in their local temples and monasteries.

Conclusion

The trope of the Digambar yogī as a radical renouncer, who abandons everything, including his clothes, to seek liberation by practicing rigorous asceticism in all sorts of inhospitable weather atop mountains, in forests, and on the banks of rivers, is an ancient one. Similar images of the Digambar yogī are found in Prākṛt and Sanskrit texts from the middle of the first millennium C.E. and in Hindi texts from the past several centuries. These poetic images kept alive the ideal of the Digambar *muni*, and the central role of nudity (*digaṃbaratva*) itself in the conduct of the "true" mendicant, during the many centuries when the realities of Digambar mendicancy were dominated by the domesticated *bhaṭṭāraka*s who wore robes, lived in urban monasteries that approximated more to royal palaces than sites of asceticism, and in manifold other ways stood in stark contrast to the ideals enunciated in the poems.[57] When the institution of the naked *muni* was revived in the early twentieth century, the poems provided a template against which Jains could judge the conduct of the longed-for true guru, true *muni*, true *yogī*.

There is much in the portrait of the *yogī* that is not unique to the Digambar tradition. Much, however, is specifically Jain. The classical Bhaktis in particular are framed in the technical language of Digambar Jain mendicancy, but there is also much in the Hindi *pads* that clearly signals that the poet is singing about a Digambar Jain yogī.

It is noteworthy, however, that the *yogī-muni*s as described in the poems exhibit some important differences from contemporary Digambar *munis*. The poems all describe the yogīs as naked, as this is a sine qua non for "real" Digambar mendicancy, and it is nudity that most demonstrably distinguishes a *muni* from a *bhaṭṭāraka*. Many poems describe the yogī standing in the distinctive Jain meditative pose known as *kāyotsarga*, his two arms hanging parallel to the body and the eyes focused on the tip of the nose. One poem by Budhjan describes some of the technical specifics of the *muni*'s begging round. When the *muni* comes to the house, his lotus-feet are washed in water. He walks and takes his food according to the rules (*vidhi*) for such conduct. When on his food-begging round, the *muni* does not ignore any house.[58] All of these, however, are also practiced by a *bhaṭṭāraka* on the ritualized occasions when he goes on a food-begging round, so the degree of technical specificity is not surprising.

The poems dwell upon the physical hardships the yogī willingly undergoes. While contemporary naked *munis* are well known for their asceticism, rarely, if ever, do they dwell alone on mountain tops or in caves, braving the elements in the effort to burn away karmic defilement. Instead, the lives of the contemporary *munis* are much more routinized and integrated into the lives of their lay supporters and followers.

Another defining conduct of a Digambar *muni* is the act of regularly pulling out the hair on the head, an act known as *keś locan*. This rite is mentioned in the *Prākṛt Yogī Bhakti*, but is absent from any of the poems. Also absent are any references to two of the defining visual signs of a Digambar *muni*, the *kamaṇḍalu* or gourd used to hold water, and the *picchi* or peacock-feather whisk. These two items are so closely identified with the Digambar *muni* that many Jains, when referring in the abstract to a group of mendicants, will indicate how many are in the group by saying how many *picchi*s are present. Finally, a modern sign of a Digambar *muni* is the scriptures (*śāstra*) each mendicant is expected to study on a regular basis. These are all essential signs of the routinized conduct of a contemporary *muni*, and all notably absent from the idealized description of a yogī as found in the *pads*.

In trying to understand the many ways that the Jain tradition for over 2,000 years has intersected with the broader South Asian traditions of Yoga, it is necessary to investigate a wide array of texts oriented both to the articulation of doctrines and the demonstration of techniques. These texts, however, do not exhaust the resources available to us for understanding either Yoga in general or Jain Yoga in particular. By shifting our scholarly focus from *yoga* as a system of doctrines and techniques to the yogī (and, in this case, the Digambar yogī) as a literary trope, we can expand our understanding of how both concepts and images of Yoga and the yogī have been expressed in Jain settings, and thereby come to a richer understanding of Yoga as a central South Asian religious concept.

Notes

This paper is based in significant part on research conducted in India in 2007 and 2008 under the auspices of a senior short-term grant from the American Institute of Indian Studies.

1 This is perhaps more obvious if we consider the north Indian vernacular *jogī*, who seems to have clearer connections with the popular and powerful wonder-worker than with the formal spiritual techniques of Patañjali and the other classical theorists of *yoga*.

2 An indication of the primacy of the Sanskrit over the Prakrit forms is seen in that one of the mendicant manuals I have used (Jain 1982) includes only the Sanskrit verses and the Prakrit prose passages.

3 Dates for Kundakunda range from the first through the eighth centuries C.E. Pūjyapāda probably lived in the seventh century C.E. Since it is unlikely that either was the

"author" of a set of Bhaktis, the scholarly and sectarian disagreements concerning their dates need not detain us.

4 The text of the Prakrit *Yogī Bhakti* is found at Kundakunda (1960:162–168; 2006: 290–293), and Jñānmati and Ganini (1991:538–545). I give all terms from the Prakrit *Bhakti*s in their Sanskrit equivalents.

5 The text of the Sanskrit *Yogī Bhakti* is found at Jain (1982:124–126) and Jñānmati and Ganini (1991:171–175 and 480–483).

6 The text describes the yogīs in the plural; for the sake of continuity, throughout this essay I generally refer to the yogī in the singular.

7 See, for example, Colette Caillat's (2003) discussion of the portrait of the yogī by the medieval Apabhramsha poet Yogīndu. Rameścand Jain (1997:46) cites the use of the term yogī in several classical Digambar texts.

8 Jagrām Godikā, p. 6: *banavāsī sādhu mohi bhāvai.*

9 Budhjan, p. 197: *sadana tyāgi vanavāsa kiyau hai.*

10 Budhjan, p. 208: *muni bana āye.*

11 Budhjan, p. 211:

tana kārāgṛha bhoga bhujaṅgasā parikara śatru samājā /
aisī jāni tyāga bana basikai . . .
karmavināsī muni vanavāsa.

12 Daulatrām (all citations to V. Jain ed.), p. 91: *māsa cha māsa upāsa vāsa vana.*

13 Daulatrām, p. 95: *rahatā hai vanakhaṇḍa meṃ dhari dhyāna kuṭhārā.*

14 Bhāgcand, p. 88: *girivanavāsī munirāja.*

15 Dyānatrāy, p. 322: *dhani dhani te muni girivanavāsī.*

16 Bhūdhardās (all citations to T. Jain ed.), p. 68: *je bāhya paravata vana vasaiṃ girī guhā mahala manoga.*

17 Daulatrām, p. 92: *śūnya sadana giri gahana guphā meṃ padmāsana āsīnā.*

18 Budhjan, p. 210:

lūma jhūma barasai badaravā munijana ṭhāṛe taruvara taravā /
kārī ghaṭā taisī bīja ḍarāvai ve nidharaka mānoṃ kāṭha putaravā //

19 Dyānatrāy, p. 323: *masūla bhārasī dhāra parai hai bijulī kaṣakata sora karai hai.*

20 Jagrām Godikā, p. 7:

umaḍa umaḍa ghana barasata ati jahāṃ capalā camaka ḍarāī /
jhañjhāvata calata jiha siyarī tarū ṭapakata adhikāī //

21 Bhūdhardās, p. 69:

jaba śita māsa tuṣārasoṃ dāhai sakala vanarāya /
jaba jamai pānī pokharāṃ tharaharai sabakī kāya //
taba nagana nivasaiṃ cauhaṭaiṃ athavā nadīke tīra /

22 Bhāgcand, p. 80:

tahaṃ madhyānhamāhiṃ nija ūpara āyo ugra pratāpa pataṅga /
kaidhauṃ jñāna pavanabala prajvalita dhyānānalasauṃ uchali phuliṅga //

23 Daulatrām, p. 91: *grīṣama giri hima saritā tīreṃ pāvasa tarutara ṭhārā ho.*

24 Dyānatrāy, p. 321: *grīṣama śaila śikhā hima taṭinī pāvasa varaṣā adhika sahāhīṃ.*

25 This line could also be read: "Naked, he meditates on the Jina." In either case, Budhjan makes a direct correlation between the nakedness of the Jina and that of the yogī.

26 Budhjan, p. 197:

> *poṣa niśā saritā taṭa baiṭhe nagana rūpa jina dhyāna liyā //*
> *jeṭha divasa giri ūpara ṭhāṛe sūraja sanamukha vadana kiyā //*
> *virakha talaiṃ sāvana jaba varaṣata ḍāṃsa macharkī vipati sayā //*

27 Jagrām Godikā, p. 7: *kṣudhā tṛṣādi parīsaha vijaī.*
28 Daulatrām, p. 92: *pariṣaha sahata arī nā.*
29 Dyānatrāy, p. 323: *ḍaṃsa masaka bahu dukha uparājaiṃ dyānata lāga rahe nija kājaiṃ.*
30 Jagrām Godikā, p. 7: *ḍaṃsa masaka kāṭata tana cāṭata sahata parisā āī.*
31 Dyānatrāy, p. 321: *dhani te sādhu rahata vanmāhīṃ.*
32 Dyānatrāy, p. 322: *dhani dhani te muni girivanavāsī.*
33 Dyānatrāy, p. 323: *bhāī dhani muni dhyāna lagāyake.*
34 Budhjan, p. 156: *dhani saradhānī jagmaiṃ jyoṃ jala nivāsa.*
35 Bhāgcand, p. 78: *dhana dhana jainī sādhu.*
36 Daulatrām, p. 94: *dhani dhani muni jinkī lagī lau śiva ora nai.*
37 Daulatrām, p. 93: *dhani muni jina yaha bhāva pichānā.*
38 Daulatrām, p. 92: *dhani muni jina ātamahita kīnā.* T. Jain (p. 65) gives a slightly different reading of this line: *dhani muni nija ātamahita kīnā.* V. Jain recognizes this as an alternate reading. It would read in translation, "Wealthy is the *muni* who works on the welfare of his own soul."
39 Gaṅgārām Garg edited 159 *bhajan*s, a *Nām Mahimā*, and a *Pūjāṣṭak Gīt* on the basis of a manuscript dated VS 1846 (1789 C.E.).
40 It is not clear if the titling of this section of six poems as *yogī bhakti* was done by the poet or the editor.
41 Jagrām Godikā, p. 6:

> *banavāsī sādhu mohi bhāvai /*
> *moha jāla niravāri chāri graha mukati pantha ko darasāvai /*
> *yathākāla āsana upavāsana māsa māsa tapa thira thāvai /*
> *sohaṃ sohaṃ sumari ura nija para nati raṅg jhara lāvai /*
> *dhyānālīna tarū ṭhūṭa jāṃni kari mraga chāvā khasi khasi jāvai /*
> *sura nara pada raja vandata jākī tākaiṃ sujasa jagata gāvai /*

42 Jagrām Godikā, p. 7:

> *jogī kai sādhyāna dharā hai rī /*
> nagana rūpa dauu hātha jhulāye nāsādiṣṭa kharā hai jogī /
> bāhira mana malīna sā dīsata antaraṅga ujarā hai jī /
> viṣaya kasāya jīti dhari dhīraja karamana saṅga arā hai jī /
> kṣudhā tṛṣādi parīsaha vijaī ātama raṅga bharā hai jī /
> jagatarāma sura nara laṣi jākūṃ namo namo ucarā hai jī /

43 Information on Bhūdhardās comes from Jain (1997).
44 For another example of a more doctrinally oriented poem by Bhūdhardās, see Cort (2009). His extensive use of technical vocabulary makes his poetry very challenging to translate into contemporary English verse.
45 This is the spelling given by Jain (1997:166) and SPS (159–160). The version given by T. Jain (Bhūdhardās 1999:68–69) reads *bandau digambar*. As is the case with almost all Digambar Hindi literature, there is no critical edition of any of Bhūdhar's compositions.

46 Bhūdhardās, p. 68: *mere ura baso merī haro pātaka*. T. Jain recognizes *mana* (mind) as an alternative reading for *ura* (heart), and SPS gives only *mana*. In South Asian spiritual physiology, the heart is the location of spiritual intelligence as well.

47 Bhūdhardās, p. 71: *mere mana baso*.

48 Paul Dundas (forthcoming) has argued against translating either *ātman* or *jīva* as "soul," on the grounds that "for many modern readers this has become either an excessively overcoded or near meaningless term." While I agree with the main thrust of his argument, in my estimation the alternative of "self" lacks the spiritual and emotional power of "soul," and so have retained the latter term in my English translations.

49 See Jaini (1979:247–250) on these classical practices of a Jain mendicant.

50 Bhūdhardās, p. 58: *ve munivara kaba mili hai upagārī*.

51 Budhjan, p. 197: *kaba darśana hvai aise guru kau budhjana ke ura haraṣa bhayā*.

52 Budhjan, p. 213: *hūṃa kaba dekhūṃ ve munirāīa ho*.

53 Bhāgcand, p. 87: *aise sādhu suguru kaba mila haiṃ*.

54 Daulatrām, p. 91: *kabadhoṃ mileṃ mohi śrīguru munivara karihaiṃ bhavodadhi pārā ho*.

55 See also Flügel (2006:347–348).

56 The same point was made by Divākar (1997:2–3), although he did not use the language of *viraha bhakti*. He wrote that Bhūdhar expressed a great thirst (*pyās*) and longing (*lālsā*) to see the true *muni*, who exhibited the proper signs of the Jina (*jinamudrā*), i.e., who was a naked ascetic.

57 Both Kāmtā Prasād Jain (1962) and Rameścand Jain (1997) make the nudity of the mendicant the centerpiece of their studies of Digambar Jainism, and, by extension, true religiosity.

58 Budhjan, p. 207.

Bibliography

Bhāgcand. *Bhāgcand Bhajan Saurabh*. With Hindi paraphrase by Tārācand Jain. Mahavirji: Jain Vidyā Saṅsthān, 2003.

Bhūdhardās. *Bhūdhar Vilās*. Calcutta: Jain Pustak Bhavan, n.d.

Bhūdhardās. *Bhūdhar Bhajan Saurabh*. With Hindi paraphrase by Tārācand Jain. Mahavirji: Jain Vidyā Saṅsthān, 1999.

Budhjan. *Budhjan Bhajan Saurabh*. With Hindi paraphrase by Tārācand Jain. Mahavirji: Jain Vidyā Saṅsthān, 2006.

Caillat, Colette. A Portrait of the Yogi (*joi*) as Sketched by Joindu. In Piotr Balcerowicz (ed.), *Essays in Jaina Philosophy and Religion*, pp. 239–252. Delhi: Motilal Banarsidas, 2003.

Cort, John E. The Cosmic Man and the Human Condition. In Phyllis Granoff (ed.), *Victorious Ones: Jain Images of Perfection*, pp. 34–47. New York: Rubin Museum of Art; and Ahmedabad: Mapin Publishing, 2009.

Daulatrām. *Daulat Vilās*. Ed. Vīrsāgar Jain. New Delhi: Bhāratīya Jñānpīṭh, 2000.

Daulatrām. *Daulat Bhajan Saurabh*. With Hindi paraphrase by Tārācand Jain. Mahavirji: Jain Vidyā Saṅsthān, 2001. .

Divākar, Pt. Sumerucand. *Cāritra Cakravartī: Śramaṇ-śiromaṇi Ācārya Śāntisāgar Mahārāj kā Puṇya Caritra*. Beawar: Ācārya Jñānsāgar Vāgarth Vimarś Kendra; and Sanganer: Śrī Digambar Jain Atiśay Kṣetra Mandir Saṅghījī. Seventh printing, 1997.

Dundas, Paul. Forthcoming. A Digambara Jain Description of the Yogic Path to Deliverance. In David Gordon White (ed.), *Yoga in Practice*. Princeton: Princeton University Press, 2000.

Dyānatrāy. *Dyānat Bhajan Saurabh*. With Hindi paraphrase by Tārācand Jain. Mahavirji: Jain Vidyā Saṅsthān, 2003.

Flügel, Peter. Demographic Trends in Jaina Monasticism. In Peter Flügel (ed.), *Studies in Jaina History and Culture: Disputes and Dialogues*, pp. 312–398. London: Routledge, 2006.

Jagrām Godikā. *Jagrām Godikā Padāvalī*. Ed. Gaṅgārām Garg. Bharatpur: Pāras Pāṇḍulipi Prakāśan Samiti, 2000.

Jain, Kāmtā Prasād. *Digambaratva aur Digambar Muni*. Ambala: Jain Śāstrārth Saṅgh. Orig. Ambala: Campāvatī Jain Pustakmālā Prakāśan Vibhāg, 1962.

Jain, Lallūlāl (chief ed.). *Humbuj Śramaṇ Siddhānt Pāṭhāvali*. Jaipur: Śrī Digambar Jain Kunthu Vijay Granthmālā Samiti, 1982.

Jain Śāstrī, Narendrakumār. *Mahākavi Bhūdhardās: Ek Samālocanātmak Adhyayan*. Ajmer: Paṅ. Sadāsukh Granthmālā antargat Śrī Vītrāg Vijñān Svādhyāy Mandir Ṭrasṭ, 1997.

Jain, Rameścand. *Digambaratva kī Khoj*. New Delhi: Ahiṃsā Mandir Prakāśan, 1997.

Jaini, Padmanabh S. *The Jaina Path of Purification*. Berkeley: University of California Press, 1979.

Jñānmati, Mātā, and Gaṇinī, Āryikā (eds.). *Municaryā (Munikriyākalāpa)*. Hastinapur: Digambar Jain Trilok Śodh Saṅsthān, 1991.

Kundakunda. *Kundakunda Prābhṛta Saṅgraha*. Ed. Kailāś Candra Jain (Śāstrī). Sholapur: Jain Saṃskṛti Saṃrakṣak Saṅgh, 1960.

Kundakunda. *Kundakundaganthāvalī*. Ed. Bhagchandra Jain Bhaskar. Shravanabelegola: National Institute of Prakrit Studies and Research, 2006.

Nyāytīrth, Anūpcand. 170 Varṣ Pūrv Uttarī Bhārat meṃ Digambar Jain Muniyoṃ kā Vihār. *Anekānt* 55/4, 2002, 25–34.

SPS. *Stotra Pāṭh Saṅgrah*. Jaipur: Vīr Pustak Bhaṇḍār, n.d.

Upadhye, A. N. *Kundakundācāya's Pravacanasāra*. Bombay: Parama Śruta Prabhāvaka Maṇḍala, 1935.

White, David Gordon. *Sinister Yogis*. Chicago: University of Chicago Press, 2009.

11 Prekṣā Dhyāna in Jaina Yoga

An archetypal ritual for the proper ordering of the soul

Smita Kothari

Introduction

In this chapter I will examine the practice of *dhyāna* (meditation) as a ritual within Jaina Yoga through a case study of Prekṣā Dhyāna, a late-twentieth-century innovation of the Terāpanthīs. According to the Terāpanthīs, *dhyāna* in general, and Prekṣā Dhyāna in particular, aims towards the purification of the soul and is considered a *lokottara* (transcendental) activity. I will argue that, for the Terāpantha, meditation, in particular Prekṣā meditation, is not only a bodily technique that leads to communication with the divine, as Mauss (1973) has suggested, but it is also a ritual gesture, a "discipline of the body that is aimed at the proper ordering of the soul" (Asad 1993: 139). I will also argue that the founding of Prekṣā in 1975 was not a mere coincidence. It was, rather, a movement influenced by and capitalizing upon the popularity of other Yoga movements of the time, such as the Buddhist Vipassanā meditation movement. Like other Yoga reform movements before them, the Terāpantha claim to have revived their meditation, Prekṣā, from an *Ur* or pristine past by finding canonical sources to support their claim. However, unlike other contemporary Yoga groups, the Terāpanthīs do not accentuate the bodily; they remain committed to the body, mind, and spirit connection in which the body is an instrument for a higher goal. A full exploration of these differences would provide a rich study, but it is beyond the scope of this paper. Furthermore, I argue, that, by going back to Mahāvīra and forward to contemporary science articulating the neurological dynamism and medical benefits, the Terāpanthīs have a structure that is regulated and shaped by authoritative discourses in order not only to secure meaning for the ritual (Asad 1993: 155), but also to promote it to a worldwide audience.

Why is it significant to study Jaina Yoga and Prekṣā Dhyāna? I will argue that for the Terāpanthī Śvetāmbara Jaina community Yoga and, in particular, Prekṣā Dhyāna are the driving forces behind the movement. They are the strongest dynamics that have allowed the Terāpanthī movement to not only become a pan-Indian phenomenon, but to also become a transnational movement with presence in the United Kingdom, continental Europe, and the United States. Prekṣā Dhyāna along with *aṇuvrata* (small vows) and *jīvan vijñāna* (science of living) allow the Terāpanthīs to enter into the global discussion on universal concerns of ecology, economy, and social justice. In order to be able to answer the above question it is important to determine what constitutes Jaina Yoga. While past scholarship relating to Jaina Yoga, both traditional and Western, has focused on the textual tradition, my objective in this study will be to augment the textual study with a critical examination of the lived tradition, for it is only through examining both that a meaningful picture will emerge.[1] Such a study will contribute to the ongoing debate as to whether there has been a continuous Jaina Yoga tradition, as the Jainas themselves claim, or if there have been periodic ruptures and revivals.

I will begin by contextualizing the ritual practice of meditation through what Talal Asad has identified as the two ways of looking at ritual, as both a virtue-making activity that stipulates regimes of behavior, and as symbolic. I will do this by looking at the ritual as a performative through fieldwork data, and by examining the prescriptive manuals. I will then discuss the Terāpantha as a reform movement and the authoritative discourses they use to secure meaning for Prekṣā Dhyāna as a ritual.

Prekṣā Dhyāna: a performative ritual

It is late afternoon on October 10, 2009 and I am in the offices of the Tulsī Adhyātma Needam residence and the center for meditation in Ladnun, Rajasthan, where I have been for the past two weeks. I notice a flurry of activity and discover that it is registration for a Prekṣā meditation camp starting the next day, a meditation camp in Hindi that I was not aware of. I had arrived to spend the next four months doing research amongst the Terāpantha Rāja Sangha (the group of ascetics traveling with the *ācārya*), and was aware of and planned to attend the international camp in November 2009. So this camp in Hindi is a bonus in terms of research. For the next week I am totally immersed in the meditation camp as a participant/observer. There are about 50 participants who are roughly divided between the sexes. A majority of the participants are Terāpanthīs, and those who are not Terāpanthīs are, at least, Jains. There are a handful of participants who are Hindus from a variety of sects. Some have attended previous camps, while others are first timers. With the exception of the family of four Indo-Americans and myself, the rest of the participants are from all over India and come from a fairly well-to-do background. There are a few young couples who have decided to participate in the camp together. There is a team of a mother-in-law and daughter-in-law who make an interesting pair as subjects for my research. The mother-in-law lives abroad and is a Terāpanthī both by birth and marriage. The daughter-in-law, on the other hand, is a Bengali Hindu who seems to have come to the camp to please her husband and her in-laws and as the camp progresses seems to be under significant stress due to particular pressures from the mother-in-law.

The camp begins with an orientation package, which includes a welcome letter, a Prekṣā meditation experience survey form, and a detailed daily itinerary. Our camp begins this very evening with Gamana Yoga (a walking meditation) to the *paṇḍāla* (a semi-enclosed outside space with a roof and a huge stage that is used as a dais from which the *ācārya* gives his daily sermon) for *Gurū Vandanā* (obeisance to the guru). The *ācārya* gives us a short speech and recites a *Maṅgala*

Bhāvanā (auspicious blessing), following which we make our way back to the meditation center for an evening meditation session. The next day, October 11, 2009, the camp officially begins, and ends on the 18th. The camp has a full daily schedule of structured regimes of behavior designed to inculcate the discipline necessary for the "proper ordering of the soul."

Every aspect of the participant's life is scheduled for the next 8 days from 4:30 in the morning to 9 o'clock at night. By coming to the meditation camp, each participant has taken a particular stance that separates the everyday actions from the ritual actions. Caroline Humphrey and James Laidlaw underscore this point in their work on ritual. According to them, actions may be said to be ritualized when the actor has made a "ritual commitment," "a particular stance with respect to his or her own action" (Humphrey and Laidlaw 1994: 88). Thus, when one sits in meditation it is the intentionality, the commitment to meditate, that makes the cross-legged position of sitting in meditation different from everyday sitting. In the case of the Prekṣā meditation camp, the actor has taken a particular position from the time she decides to attend the camp. She reaffirms this on a daily basis throughout the camp as she wakes up each morning to get ready for the meditation. When she enters the meditation hall she reiterates this commitment.

Everything about the meditation hall – the physical space – makes it conducive for her to take this stance.[2] As she enters the dimly lit hall her mind is already transposed and conditioned to be in a meditative state. The front of the room, where the *muni* will shortly arrive to lead us into Prekṣā meditation, has several large square blue wooden boxes with the front facing the audience, painted with circles in several different colors that represent the colors used in *Leśyā Dhyāna* (a type of meditation focusing on visualizing specific colours on specific *caitanya kendras* or meridian points). The hall is large, with framed posters related to Prekṣā meditation all around on the walls. There are at least 15 posters on the wall, of which a few are worth a closer mention. There is a poster titled "Prekṣā Meditation," which depicts an iconographic image of a figure in meditation, representing the *tīrthaṅkara* in the *dhyāna mudrā* (a figure in the sitting lotus position with the hands resting on the feet with the right hand on top). There are concentric circles from dark to light, representing auras on this figure. There is another poster titled "Kāyotsarga" that shows two very vivid pictures of a man with tension (*tanāv yukta*) with a snake wrapped around his waist about to bite him,[3] and a man without tension in a meditative posture (*tanāv mukta*) with the caption underneath stating, "my body from the toes to the top of the head is completely free from tension." Another poster depicts a pyramid with the 12 limbs of Prekṣā meditation beginning with *kāyotsarga* (complete relaxation or separation of attachment to the body) and ending with *ekāgrata* (single-minded concentration). Within the same poster to the side of the pyramid are two figures, one on top of the other. The one on top is the prominent Jaina *pratīka*, a symbol of the Jaina faith officially adopted ecumenically by all Jaina sects during the 2,500th anniversary of Mahāvīra's *nirvāṇa* (1975). The palm of the hand bears the word *ahiṃsā*; the swastika topped by the three dots and the crescent represent the four destinies (*gati*) – gods (*devas*), humans (*manuṣya*), hell beings (*nāraki*), and animals and plants (*iryañca*) – the threefold path, and the abode of the liberated souls, respectively; the slogan below the figure of *loka-ākāśa* (the inhabited universe) calls for the mutual assistance of all living beings (*parasparopagraho jīvānām*). Underneath this symbol is a wheel with several circles within it. The middle circle represents the seven necessary steps in Prekṣā meditation – yogic physical exercise, *prāṇāyāma* (breathing exercises), *kāyotsarga, prekṣādhyāna, japa* Yoga (chanting of mantras), discourses, and yogic *āsanas* (postures). The two innermost circles depict social health and individual health. These two images of the Jaina faith and the wheel of Prekṣā meditation are in many of the posters, which indicate that for the Terapantha these are important.

The symbol of Jaina faith in the figure of *loka-ākāśa* corresponds to the Jaina universe and is significant in helping us understand how meditation can play a role in the liberation of the soul. According to Jaina theories of karma, human life is the only life one can attain liberation from, and birth in a Jaina household is not to be frittered away. Jaina cosmography sees the universe in the shape of a cosmic man. At the apex is a crescent-shaped space called *Siddhaloka,* where all liberated souls reside as individual jīvas. The soul never loses its identity as an individual jīva, unlike certain Hindu traditions like Advaita Vedānta. Below *Siddhaloka* are the seven heavens (*ūrdhvaloka*) where the gods reside, in the middle or terrestrial world (*Madhyaloka*) is where humans (*manuṣya*), animals and plants (*tiryañca*) reside, and below this is the lower world (*Adholoka*) of the seven hells the abode of infernal beings (*nāraki*).[4] Beings move up or down in this universe, depending on their action (karma) – good karma leading to a life as a human being or a god perhaps in one of the seven heavens, and bad karma leading to the animal kingdom or one of the seven hells. The path to liberation involves mental practices of meditation, physical practices of self-denial and austerities, and avoidance of harm to all living beings. Jainism believes that these practices are necessary for the individual to be rid of the effects of karma – accumulated over many lifetimes – and to minimize the accumulation of new karma. According to Padmanabh Jaini, these actions proceed from the soul's passions for nourishment (*āhāra*), reproduction (*maithuna*), and the accumulation of worldly goods (*parigraha*) for the attainment of power over others (Jaini 2002: 142). In order to get rid of the karmas two things need to happen – stop the influx of new karmas (*saṃvara*), and shed existing karmas (*nirjarā*). Ultimately, the goal is to not create any actions, good or bad, so one can get out of the cycle of *saṃsāra* or transmigration. A good way to get out of this cycle is by following the five vows, the *mahāvratas*, which are absolute for the Jaina ascetics, and are less absolute for the laity, because living in this world inherently involves violence. However, meditation, according to the Terāpanthīs, is an activity par excellence for the shedding of karmas or *nirjarā*. The Prekṣā wheel underscores this point by showing that not only does Prekṣā lead to the physical health of an individual, but also to his/her mental and spiritual health, and healthy individuals lead to a healthy society, which is important when we look at the applied ethics of *dāna* and *dhyāna*, a point I develop in my larger work.

While the importance of the visuals on the wall in the meditation hall is clear, both from the broader Jaina perspective and from the Terāpantha perspective, nevertheless, when I ask the camp attendees about the importance of these visuals I get mixed responses. For the four Indo-Americans in the Hindi camp these visuals are so important that they have had the official Terāpantha photographer make a DVD of all the posters, which are then distributed to the camp attendees for a fee of Rs.50, and most of the camp attendees buy the DVD. However, for some participants these visuals seem to have very little long-term impact. In follow-up interviews in 2011, some could barely remember these posters. Also in 2011, in a follow-up interview with Jitmalji, the lay *upāsaka* who runs the meditation classes during the year, I ask about the posters, which seem to have disappeared from the walls. Jitmalji's response is that he follows instructions from the Terāpantha leadership. Other senior ascetics, too, seem to have a short memory about the posters. However, when I ask Samaṇi Chāritraprajñaji, the current vice-chancellor of the Jain Vishva Bharati University who taught a Prekṣā meditation course for 4 years at the Florida International University in Miami, she has a very positive spin on the visuals. I believe, and the Samaṇi confirms this, that the crucial point here is not whether the participants remember the posters at a later date or not; the point is that the posters are part of the aids that help put the participants into the meditative zone in a particularly Jaina way with thoughts of shedding one's karma by just being there in that moment. It is part of the ambience that makes it conducive for the participant to make a "ritual commitment."

Just as the physical space is conducive for the camp participant to make a "ritual commitment," so, too, is the physical body an instrument in this commitment. The camp participants are divided into two groups, men sitting on the far left and women on the right closer to the entrance. They are seated in rows about five across, one behind the other on cotton mats with pillows to sit on. There is a wide gap in the center between the men and women. There are two rows of plastic chairs at the back of the room for people who cannot sit in a cross-legged position. This is important, for the body needs to be in a relaxed mode for the next hour during the meditation. The body here is the instrument for the development of the soul. Talal Asad, following Mauss' famous essay, "Techniques of the Body," states that in the case of medieval Christian monastics, "discourse and gesture are viewed as part of the social process of learning to develop aptitudes, not as orderly symbols that stand in an objective world in contrast to contingent feelings and experiences that inhabit a separate subjective one" (Asad 1993: 77). I will employ Mauss' concept of the "*habitus*" and Asad's analysis of Mauss' concept to show that within the Terāpantha, the discourse and gesture related to Prekṣa meditation are part of the social process of learning to develop aptitudes.

In his essay, Mauss asserts, "The body is man's first and most natural instrument. Or more accurately, not to speak of instruments, man's first and most natural technical object at the same time technical means, is his body" (Mauss 1973: 75). Mauss sought to focus his attention on human behavior as learned capabilities and how these are connected to authoritative standards and regular practice:

> Hence I have had this notion of the social nature of the '*habitus*' for many years. Please note that I use that word . . . *habitus*. The word translates

> infinitely better than '*habitude*' (habits or custom), the '*exis*', the 'acquired ability' and 'faculty' of Aristotle (who was a psychologist). [. . .] These habits do not just vary with individuals and their imitations, they vary, especially between societies, educations, proprieties and fashions, prestiges. In them we should feed the techniques and work of collective and individual practical reason rather than, in the ordinary way, merely the soul and its repetitive faculties.
>
> (Mauss 1973: 73)

The concept of *habitus*, according to Asad, "invites us to analyze the body as an assemblage of embodied aptitudes, not as a medium of symbolic meanings" (Asad 1993: 75). James Laidlaw (1995: 151–159) develops this point in the context of Jainism and the ascetic imperative – practices of fasting, strict dietary regimes, and the like. Although meditation is part of this ascetic imperative, still not much is discussed in contemporary ethnographies on this issue. It is this notion that I wish to explore in the context of Prekṣa meditation. Mauss himself is aware of this with regard to yogic practices within India. Following Marcel Granet's study of techniques of the body and breathing in particular, within Taoism, Mauss asserts:

> I have studied the Sanscrit texts of yoga enough to know that the same things occur in India. I believe precisely that at the bottom of all mystical states, there are techniques of the body which we have not studied, but which were perfectly studied by China and India even in very remote periods. This socio-psycho-biological study should be made. I think that there are necessarily biological means of entering into 'communication with God'. Although in the end breath technique, etc., is only the basic aspect in India and China, I believe this technique is much more widespread.
>
> (Mauss 1973: 86–87)

Thus, as Asad rightly states, the inability to communicate with God becomes "a function of untaught bodies" (1993: 77).

But what does this mean in a religion where communication is not with a monotheist god? While the Jainas are not theists (they do not believe in a creator god) in the same sense as the medieval Christian monastics that Asad talks about, nevertheless communion with the Jinas (beings who have achieved complete victory over attachments and aversions)[5] is an important aspect within Jainism. Paul Dundas writes:

> While Jainism is, as we have seen, atheist in the limited sense of rejection of both the existence of a creator god, and the possibility of the intervention of such a being in human affairs, it nonetheless must be regarded as a theist religion in the more profound sense that it accepts the existence of a divine principle, the *paramātma*, often in fact referred to as 'God' (e.g. ParPr 114–116), existing in potential state within all beings.
>
> (Dundas 2002: 110–111)

This is also echoed by Kendall Folkert (1993: 24), who speaks of a temple cult developing around the figure of the Jina. However, worship of the Jinas is not a two-way communication, as Dundas points out, even amongst the temple-worshipping Jainas. For them worship is more about the creation of *bhāva* and about the emulation of the Jinas who are exemplars. So what does this mean for the "taught bodies" in Prekṣā meditation? Amongst the Terāpanthīs, where idol worshiping is not permitted, *bhāv pūjā* (mental obeisance) and Guru *pūjā* are an important aspect of worship. In her detailed study of the Terāpanthīs, Ann Vallely suggests that devotion to and connection with divinity are an important part of Jaina ascetic life that are "sometimes masqueraded as something else, more along the lines of self-realization. [. . . Such practices] are not treated (in the public ideology) as efforts to connect with something greater than the self, but rather as utilitarian tools of spiritual self-help" (2002: 180). While I would concede that, amongst the Terāpantha, devotion to the *ācārya* and senior ascetics might fit into Vallely's characterization of devotion "masqueraded" as "utilitarian tools of spiritual self-help," yet I would argue that Prekṣa meditation is less about masquerading and more about actually being a utilitarian tool of spiritual self-help and more.

Prekṣā meditation, as a virtue-making ritual, is comprised of 12 limbs, as depicted in the poster hanging on the wall in the meditation hall. The *muni* guides us at every step of the 1-hour meditation. There are three full sessions of meditation per day that include all the 12 limbs, and throughout the day there are longer sessions of individual limbs, such as a long session of *kāyotsarga* before lunch and a long session of *anuprekṣā* later in the afternoon. Some days the young and rather shy Jay Muni leads the morning meditation and other days it is Kishan Muni, the more gregarious and senior ascetic. The instructions are precise. We, my camp cohorts and I, begin by gently closing our eyes (not shut tight). We repeat three times: "I am practicing Prekṣā meditation for the purity of my consciousness (*citta*)," followed by three Mahāprāṇa dhvani, a breath technique that entails inhaling through the nose and creating a sound like a buzzing bumble bee while exhaling. This is followed by *kāyotsarga* (a guided relaxation from the toes to the head). The next limb is called *antaryātrā* (internal trip), which involves taking a deep breath in, and drawing the *prāṇa* (energy) to the base of the spine to the *śakti kendra* (energy center) and exhaling, drawing the prāṇa to the top of the head to the *jñāna kendra* (knowledge center). In this way one continues to be led into contemplating on the breath (*śvāsa prekṣā*), on the body (*śarīra prekṣā*), on meridian points with color (*leśyā dhyāna*), on the impermanence of all things (*anitya anuprekṣā*), and so on. At each stage one is gently asked to auto-suggest. For example, when practicing the ritual of *leśyā dhyāna* on the *jyoti kendra* (the center for illumination at the top of the forehead in the middle) while contemplating on the whiteness of a full radiant moon, one feels one's passions, such as anger, greed, delusion, attachment, and aversion, subsiding. The meditation ends with three long breaths and the *śaraṇa sūtra*, paying obeisance to the five superior beings – the arhats, the *siddhas* (liberated souls), the *sādhus* (ascetics), the *ācāryas*, and the *upādhyayas* (teachers) – and the *śraddhā sūtra*, *vande saccam*, or bowing to the truth.

According to the Terāpanthīs, daily practice of the Prekṣā meditation ritual along with the cultivation of five observances of (1) *bhāvakriyā* (single-mindedly living in the present moment); (2) *pratikriyā virati* (cessation of reactionary behavior); (3) *maitrī* (universal friendship); (4) *mitāhāra* (moderation in food); and (5) *mitabhāṣaṇa* (speaking measuredly) creates vibrations (*kampana*) that allow for the shedding of karma (*nirjarā*).

So far I have been narrating my observances and experiences in the Prekṣā Hindi camp, which has the atmosphere of a local camp although the participants have come from all over India. Granted, the food in the Needam residence kitchen during the camp has improved over the food served during normal times in terms of quality and variety; however, camp attendees still eat their meals in the traditional Indian style, cross-legged on the floor, though there are two small, ramshackle wooden tables with a couple of plastic chairs, for those who cannot or will not sit on the floor. Camp participants share their meals with other visitors who are living in the residence and who eat their meals in the residence and eat out of stainless-steel traditional *thālis*, which they wash themselves after each meal. Moreover, there are no other noticeable differences in the appearance of either the residence or the rest of the Jain Vishwa Bharati campus. In fact, except for the participants who reside in the upscale Sāgar, a much smaller and, by Ladnun standards, fairly luxurious residence, the camp participants complain about the lack of cleanliness and basic hygiene in the Needam residence.

While I only accidentally find out about the Hindi camp the day before the camp starts during guest registration, in contrast, the approaching date of the international camp which begins on November 4th, 2009, is announced with a great deal of flourish. All over the campus, I see banners and posters announcing the forthcoming camp and welcoming its attendees. At the Needam residence there is a great deal of activity with contractors running in and out. The rooms get individual water heaters for the bathroom, a point that registers with me, as the hot summer days are waning and the coolness of the Rajasthan winter approaches. I know that the rooms were upgraded from my two Russian friends who had arrived 2 weeks prior to the international camp and are residing in the Needam residence. When they arrived they had no hot water until just prior to the beginning of the camp. These two Russian (they are actually Ukrainian, but no distinction is made by the Terāpantha between the Russians and the Ukrainians) women and a young Japanese woman and I become close friends as they learn to practice and teach *yoga āsanas* (postures) from the young Samaṇi, Āgamaprajñaji, every morning. I tag along for the morning Yoga sessions and sometimes if the Samaṇi is too busy she entrusts me to lead the sessions, since I am a practicing Yoga teacher.

A few days before the camp begins, the young, mostly male volunteers start arriving for the camp. These young men are trained *upāsakas*[6] who are kept very busy over the next week – from performing administrative tasks, to teaching morning Yoga classes, to being tour guides for the international camp attendees. Besides the volunteers, there are the two translators for the Russian and Japanese groups, respectively. As the international crowd starts arriving they are greeted with garlands placed around their necks. This reception is quite different from the reception given to the Hindi camp attendees. The guests are divided into three groups by language – Russian, Japanese, and English. The Russian group, the largest of the three groups at 50 members coming from four different countries, mainly from the Ukraine, Russia, Uzbekistan, and Kazakhstan, is housed in the Needam residence; the Japanese group, the smallest group at 15 members, is housed in the slightly more upscale Shubham residence, and the English group, which is comprised primarily of about 25 ex-pat Indians with a few rich locals, is housed in the upscale Sāgar residence. With the exception of meals and the morning Yoga *āsana* classes, which are segregated by sex, these groups are trained separately in their respective languages through translators. After the first day, the English group decides that they want their instructions in Hindi, since all of them are Indian by birth. However, the three groups collectively form a lineup, each morning and evening, in front of the Needam residence to go for *gaman* meditation (walking meditation), and *Guru Darśana.*

It is the first morning of the camp and the international crowd, in their white Prekṣā uniforms, gathers in front of the Needam residence for a photo opportunity with the local press and then they walk to the *ācārya's* residence, with the press in tow, to receive his blessings. The photograph taken at this event of the crowd, with their hands joined together in obeisance to the *ācārya*, and a story announcing the eighth international camp make front-page news in the local paper.[7]

Aside from this, there are other differences between the Hindi camp and the international camp. The daily food is served in the upscale Shubham restaurant where the food is richer and more suited to the Western palate. The international participants are given the option of going on a day-long guided tour of some of the local sites, such as local Jaina temples, a charity institution run by the Terāpantha, and other notable Terāpantha sites. Another day there are bullock cart rides around the campus, giving the campus a circus-like atmosphere. For all of these extras, the price of the international camp, at Rs.14,000 (about $330), is double that of the Hindi camp. One can conclude from all of the above that the marketing for the international camp is on a whole different scale than that of the Hindi camp.

The fact that the Russian-language group, as I stated above, is the largest group is not an accident. The Ukraine and Russia are particular target markets for the Prekṣā camps. My two Ukrainian friends, in 2009, hosted a team of two trained Prekṣā meditation specialists – a Samaṇa (male middle-order ascetic, of which there are only four in total during my time in Ladnun in 2009) and a young lay follower, with whom they toured all over the Ukraine, conducting Prekṣā meditation camps in existing Yoga studios. My friends told me this was grueling work for them, not only housing the two young men, but also preparing suitable Jaina meals for them. Thus, Prekṣā has opened up doors for the Terāpantha not only to teach meditation techniques, but also to proselytize Jainism for the first time in its history.

While the guided meditation is more about how to than why for, the meaning making occurs during the lectures and the question-and-answer sessions, held each day during the camp. For example, in a lecture session called "Body Science," one is taught about the living cells in the body that are susceptible to suggestion. The self-styled lay "expert" teaching this component states that in kāyotsarga one needs to do three things: internal travel (*antarayātra*), suggest (*sujāva*), and experience (*anubhava*). Observe the breath, for if the breath is controlled then the mind will quiet down, and this will lead to the purity of one's consciousness and also increase the lungs' working capacity, making it disease-free. What is the relationship with meditation? According to him, breath is a tool used in meditation to calm the mind; it shortens the wandering.[8]

On another day Muni Kumārśramaṇa explains the scientific nature of Prekṣā. He states, "today's life is very stressful; we are always in the fear and flight syndrome causing an overactive adrenalin. [. . .] Prekṣā balances the sympathetic and parasympathetic systems" (October 13, 2009). He goes on to explain how when we meditate on the *jyotikendra* through *leśyādhyāna*, we can control our anger. The scientific reason, according to the *muni*, is that it controls the pineal, pituitary, and adrenal glands. The notion that Prekṣā helps in anger management is reiterated by several of the young interviewees, mostly male, during my research both in Delhi (at the Adhyātma Sādhana Kendra, a Terāpantha Satellite Centre) and in Ladnun.

Raj and Kiran,[9] the two young men I interview on the third day of my stay in Delhi, are charming and very amiable. Neither is Terāpanthī, nor Jaina for that matter. They are both in training to become Prekṣā teachers. In my interview with him, Raj reveals that he was a very angry young man who used to break dishes when he got angry. His family members were at the end of their rope, but when he started Prekṣā meditation there was a transformation in him, which was gradual, but a huge improvement over his former self. His family members could not believe the new person he had become. Today, he tells me, there is nothing that fazes him and he seems the picture of perfect calmness. He attributes the calmness, this change in demeanor, all to Prekṣā and is such a believer in the power of the meditation that he has decided to become a teacher and help others. Kiran also tells me a similar story, but his transformation does not seem to be dramatic. For a young man, he seems quite bitter about his experiences at the Jain Vishwa Bharati Institute, where he did an M.A. in "Prekṣā Meditation and the Science of Living." His bitterness seems to stem from the fact that he has not been able to secure a job as a Prekṣā meditation teacher, which he feels entitled to, and tells me that he was led to believe that Prekṣā would open up doors for him.

However, by and large, the people I interview are positive about their experiences with Prekṣā meditation. Most offer stories of transformation, and often when I interview couples or families their spouses or family members will vouch for their transformation. This leads me to conclude that, while Prekṣā may or may not get one closer to salvation, it does serve as a virtue-making tool, in the same manner as the disciplinary practices employed by the medieval Christian monastics were tools for the "proper ordering of the soul" in Talal Asad's writing.

Prescriptive manuals: Prekṣā Dhyāna theory and practice

While the daily regimes of behavior within the group setting of the camp serve to inculcate patterns for bodily techniques to transform the soul, still the Terāpanthīs recognize that this may be a difficult pattern to observe left to one's own devices at home in the daily grind of contemporary living. Thus, they leave nothing to chance. Each camp attendee receives a Prekṣādhyāna theory and practice text. These texts are prescriptive manuals that play a supportive role to the foundations laid in the meditation camp. Although the theory in these texts is carefully culled from ancient sources, nevertheless the texts themselves are contemporary, since Prekṣā meditation is a contemporary form of Jaina meditation. The text provided in the Hindi camp is considerably different from the text provided in the international camp. The English manual, *Prekṣādhyāna: Theory and Practice*,[10] at 128 pages is almost twice as long as the Hindi manual, *Prekṣādhyāna Prayoga Paddhati* (*Treatise for the Practice of Prekṣādhyāna Rite*), and devotes less space to actual meditation techniques than the philosophical and scientific basis of Prekṣā Dhyāna and its benefits. In contrast, the Hindi text devotes 20 pages to an appendix consisting primarily of inspirational Prekṣā songs (*gīta*), rules of conduct (*ācāra saṃhitā*), and of further reading lists. This scripted text stays close to the techniques taught in the meditation camps without going into philosophical or scientific explications. A closer examination of the two texts may shed some light on the variance between the texts. In what follows I will begin by analyzing the Hindi manual, and in particular the songs, followed by the English manual.

The Hindi work *Prekṣādhyāna Prayoga Paddhati* opens with the following *prastuti* (eulogium):

> *Dhyāna* is not done; it happens. It is believed that there is no technique (*paddhati*) for *dhyāna*. *Dhyāna* is not innate. Not everyone is able to enter into dhyāna without knowing the technique. [. . .] The technique is useful at the commencement of the practice of dhyāna. Through development the technique may not be required, but whenever it is needed, it should not be considered unessential. Keeping this viewpoint in mind, the technique of Prekṣādhyāna is produced as a collection in this short book. This will be useful for teachers of 'the Science of living' and 'Prekṣādhyāna.
>
> (Ācārya Mahāprajña 2007)

This *prastuti* debunks the myth that meditation is an innate state that just happens. According to the Terāpantha, it is learned behavior and this handbook is just the tool to help with such a practice. Besides the *prastuti*, three sections in the Hindi manual distinctly stand out. The first section consists of a list of Prekṣā aphorisms in Prākṛt with Hindi translations, beginning with the aim Sutra (*dhyeya sūtra*), which translates as "Through the Self see the Self."[11] There are three additional sutras – the wisdom sutra (*vivekasūtra*), the refuge sutra (*śaraṇasūtra*), and the faith sutra (*śraddhā sūtra*). Each of these *sūtra*s is in Prakṛt, culled from Āgamic sources, with Hindi translations. The second section consists of the initiatory vows (*upasaṃpadā*) for Prekṣā and the resolve (*saṃkalpa*) *sūtra*s for the initiation. The term *upasaṃpadā* literally means the act of entering into the order of monks, so it is interesting that the camp attendees take this temporary vow. This does raise the question of why *upasaṃpadā*? Does one have to be an ascetic to practice Prekṣā Dhyāna? The vows are: (1) "I dedicate myself to the practice (*sādhanā*) of Prekṣādhyāna"; (2) "I initiate myself into the path of spiritual practice" (*adhyātma sādhnā kā mārg*); (3) "I initiate myself into the practice of internal perception" (*antardarśana*); and (4) "I initiate myself into the practice of spiritual experience"(*ādhyātmika anubhava*) (Ācārya Mahāprajña 2007: 2, Also see English Manual 2008: 3).

These four vows, followed by the resolve (*saṃkalpa*) *Śāstras*, which I have already mentioned above as the five observances, are the basis for the practice of meditation, and they supposedly help create vibrations (*kampana*) that allow for the shedding of karma. The five resolves are worth looking at in some detail. The first resolve is *bhāva kriyā*, by which the Terāpanthīs mean to keep the mind engaged in all actions. Specifically they give three meanings for this type of action: to live in the present moment, perform actions with awareness, and to always remain vigilant. The next resolve, *pratikriyā virati*, literally means refraining from reactionary behavior. The manual goes on to explain that all our daily actions are a result of our reactions. In spiritual practice one should remain free from reactionary behavior. The *sādhaka* (practitioner) should act, not react. The third resolve, *maitrībhāva*, is about awakening and cultivating the *bhāva* of friendliness towards all at all times. The fourth resolve of *mitāhāra* or moderate eating is important because its power is felt not only on the body, but also its effect is felt on *dhyāna* and even on one's consciousness. It saves one from carelessness (*pramāda*) and laziness (*ālasya*). The final resolve of *mitabhāṣaṇa* is about moderation in speech. The manual goes on to elaborate that one should save oneself from unnecessary speech; practice the observance of silence most of the time; speak only when it is necessary to speak; and converse in a soft voice. The observance of these five resolve *sūtra*s must be diligently maintained during the duration of the camp (Ācārya Mahāprajña 2007: 2–3). Essentially, the manual elaborates on the discourse given by the muni during the question-and-answer sections of the Hindi camp. The manual, which is read by the attendees during the camp, serves as a reinforcement of what they are told to observe throughout the camp. In this way, it solidifies the learning.

I now come to the final section of this manual, which is an appendix primarily consisting of songs (*gīta*) and a few suggested Prekṣā practice sessions. These songs are supposed to create *bhāva* in the same manner as bhakti or devotional songs do in other traditions, although the emotions expressed are not towards a deity, but rather towards the Self. In what follows I translate in full the Prekṣādhyāna Song (Ācārya Mahāprajña 2007: 56).

Through Prekṣā meditation, occurs the Self-realization
Through this approach may occur dream realization. (Chorus)
Perceiving Self through Self, intuition is this itself
Truth, being established in one's inner self.
Through waning may *saṃskāra*s undergo destruction. (Repeat chorus)

Mental equanimity, awakening and psychic bliss
Comes near, and goes away physical, mental and emotional illness.
Through Self-discovery spreads tenderness. (Repeat chorus)

Changes occur in biochemical and glandular hormone
Changes too occur in behavior, as well as emotion.
Through breath regulation one's own world undergoes transformation. (Chorus)

In this world of difficulties, the problem is one of anger
And enslavement to one's habits is pervasive in one's every fiber.
Through this glorious achievement [meditation] occurs polite behavior. (Chorus)

Through contemplation, color meditation, and repose
Through perception of breathing, Heaven is on the globe.
Through omniscience may the heart be free from *ahiṃsā*.
Through Tulsī *dhyāna* may the heart be free from *ahiṃsā*. (Chorus)

The instruction at the end of the song indicates that the song must be sung in the melody of a popular Hindi film song, which the Indian audience would be quite familiar with. It is clear from the above that the song expresses everything a practitioner may expect to undergo in terms of transformation through the practice of Prekṣā meditation. The transformation is supposed to be at every level of the Self – the spiritual, mental, and physical right down to chemical and hormonal changes. Here we see that both scripture and science are used as authoritative discourse, a point I will elaborate upon in the next section. One last thing about this manual is the direct English translation of this work. The English translation is significantly missing the first two sections, as well as the appendix. Buried in the text of the English translation is the "Aim *Sūtra*," and at the end of a particular meditation technique section are the aphorisms for "wisdom," "taking refuge," and "faith." The initiation vow and the five resolves are not translated and neither are the songs. What is curious about the English translation is that at the end of the translation is a section on "Practice of Prekṣā Dhyāna for Freedom from Drug Addiction," which does not exist in the original Hindi. It would seem from this that drug addiction is perceived to be a problem in the West, or at least a problem within English-speaking audiences.

I now come to the English manual, which, as I said earlier, lacks the appendix of songs that are in the Hindi manual. When I ask Muni Mahendra, the senior scholar and translator of much of these works, why the songs are missing, he dismisses the question by undermining the appendix saying, "It is only an appendix." However, I suspect that the *muni*, who admittedly is not a poet, might have found the songs difficult to translate, and hence their omission. Nevertheless, the English manual has substantial space devoted to the philosophical basis, the scientific basis, and the benefits of Prekṣā Dhyāna, which are totally missing in the Hindi manual. When I ask the *muni* about this difference in the two manuals he points out that there is a Hindi translation of the English manual and all camp attendees are expected to know the philosophical and scientific basis of Prekṣā Dhyāna. When I press on the point as to why the Hindi translation is not the manual handed out in the Hindi camp, he just shrugs and dismisses my suggestion that perhaps there is an economic reason, the less substantial Hindi manual being cheaper.

I want to discuss the scientific rhetoric in this manual, as part of the Terāpantha authoritative discourses. But before I do that I want to give a brief history of the Terāpantha as a reform movement and how they use both scriptural and scientific discourses to achieve this reform.

The Terāpantha reform and authoritative discourses

The Terāpantha is considered to be a reform movement. This notion of reform is perpetuated both by the tradition itself and is further aided by some Western scholars who use the term rather uncritically in separating the fifteenth- and seventeenth-century aniconic movements of Sthānakvāsi (hall dwellers) and Terāpanthī, for example, as reformed, whereas the Mūrtipūjaka (temple-worshipping) Śvetāmbara and Digambara movements as unreformed.[12] The term "reform," according to John Cort (2000: 170), is not value-neutral as some scholars use it, but rather prescriptive, and highly contentious. When traditions introduce change, they rarely call it new. Rather they hail the changes as a return to a pristine and original state. This idea of reform is particularly true of the Terāpanthīs, who, according to Flügel, do not have a *paṭṭāvali* (a genre of text) tracing their lineage to the Sthānakvāsis, since Bhikṣu (the founder of the Terāpantha) split from the Sthānakavāsī Ācārya Raghunāthji.[13] By deliberately not tracing such a lineage, the Terāpantha, in effect, are claiming a direct lineage to Mahāvīra (the historical founder of the tradition). Moreover, the Terāpanthīs claim that Prekṣā Dhyāna originated with Mahāvīra, and draw their inspiration from Mahāvīra's meditation, as described in the *Ācārāṅga Sūtra*.[14]

Given the paucity of references to meditation in the early history of Jaina Yoga, it is noteworthy that the Terāpanthīs by-passed medieval Jaina Yoga influences, such as that of Haribhadra and Hemacandra, two leading figures in medieval Jaina Yoga. Johannes Bronkhorst (1993a, b), Paul Dundas (2002: 166–167), and Padmanabh Jaini (1979: 252) all agree on the lack of material in early Jaina sources, although their explanations for this lack are different. I conjecture that this lack of material reference encourages a re-reading of the past and gives the Terāpanthīs the freedom to re-read the *Āgamic* (canonical) sources to return to the "fundamentals" of a pristine past. But what is this pristine past? Scholars have varying opinions on what constitutes meditation during this period. There are two schools of thought – that coming from within the tradition, and that coming from Western scholarship. Indian scholarship argues that in early Jainism meditational practices were well developed; and right faith, right knowledge, and right conduct ultimately led to liberation, whereas Western scholarship sees the focus less on meditation and more on cessation of activity. In Prekṣā Dhyāna, *aṇuvrata*, and *jīvan vijñāna*, the Terāpanthīs are seemingly saying that the "revival" of ancient meditation practices along with right conduct and the "art of right living" bring the practitioner closer to the goal of liberation.

Bronkhorst and Dundas are of the opinion that there was less emphasis on meditation in the early sources, and that the teachings were more concerned with the cessation of mental and physical activity rather than their transformation (Bronkhorst 1993b: 36; Dundas 2002: 166). According to Dundas, it is only in the early medieval period that it became necessary for the Jains to have a more theoretical development (2002: 166–167). Like the medieval *ācārayas* Haribhadra[15] and Hemacandra, who, with the popularity of Tantric Yoga during their times, felt the need to produce elaborate treatises on Jaina Yoga, the Terāpanthīs felt a similar need in the contemporary social milieu. I intend to show that, given the contemporary popularity of Yoga in general and of Buddhist *vipassanā* meditation in particular, the Terāpanthīs felt it necessary to have a more theoretical development of Jaina meditation, which they claim has always been in Jainism, but lost over time. Although Jaini concurs with Bronkhorst and Dundas, he states that the traditional emphasis on austerities was more within reach of the majority of aspirants, whereas the trance-like states were achievable by only the few. Moreover, the very nature of meditation did not lend itself to written exposition, esoteric teaching being best conveyed in person from teacher to disciple (Jaini 1979: 252). Both these views are important with respect to the Terāpantha reinterpretation of "original" doctrines because their reinterpretation is more about transformation. Moreover, if the ancients thought that esoteric teaching was best conveyed from teacher to disciple, as Jaini argues, then the mass-audience Prekṣā Dhyāna camps are an antithesis to secret, esoteric knowledge.

Despite the paucity of material, it is important to see that Nathmal Tatia, who comes from within the tradition, is able to cull from the early Āgamic sources, such as the *Āyaro*, *Bhagavati*, and *Uttaradhyayaṇa Sūtras*, a picture of meditation from various angles; broadly speaking he divides the physical and the mental development for such a practice (1986: xvii).[16] Tatia's description of physical postures from these sources, such as *kāyotsarga* (literally meaning abandonment of the body, but it is a form of detachment from the body), which leads to equanimity of the mind for a meditator, is important. It shows that the Terāpanthīs have carefully chosen to cull a pristine past. *Kāyotsarga*, as I have shown above, is an important process within the practice of Prekṣā Dhyāna, in which complete abandonment of the body is a precursor to meditation.

Finally, I come to the scientific discourse that the Terāpanthīs use both in the meditation camps and in the prescriptive manuals. Moreover, science is not limited to discourse. The Terāpantha have actively sought to encourage scientific experiments on the physiological and neurological effects of Prekṣā Dhyāna.[17]

Here the Terāpanthīs are not alone. In his work *Buddhism and Science*, Donald Lopez asserts that, "over the past 25 years, the effects of Buddhist meditation have begun to be measured by neurologists, adding a new dimension to the Buddhism and Science discourse" (Lopez 2008: 207). According to Lopez, these studies have sought to measure the physiological and neurological effects of Buddhist meditation. The claim made here is that "Buddhist meditation works," but as Lopez rightly asserts, in order to understand the laboratory results of such claims,

> one must first identify what is *Buddhist* about this meditation, describe what the term *meditation* encompasses in this case, and explain what *works* means, especially in the context of the exalted goals that have traditionally been ascribed to Buddhist practice. Although these goals are numerous and variously articulated across the tradition, it can be said that their ultimate aim is not self-help but traditional reorientation toward the world – and in many articulations, a liberation from it – either for oneself or for all beings.
>
> (Lopez 2008: 207)

What Lopez is saying about Buddhist meditation can be easily applied to the Terāpantha claim of Prekṣā Dhyāna as a particularly Jaina meditation. What makes Prekṣā Dhyāna different from Buddhist *vipassanā* meditation, or for that matter other forms of meditation in Hinduism, Buddhism, or even Christian traditions of meditation? Since *vipassanā* and Prekṣā both mean "to see," the Terāpantha, as I have shown above, have carefully culled Prekṣā meditation from authoritative canonical sources and have gone as far as putting together a whole text that refer to the sources of Prekṣā within the Jaina canon.[18] While the canonical sources lend authority and give meaning to the ritual for the people within the tradition, nevertheless since, as Lopez has argued, science is the new authoritative discourse, the scientific discourse and experiments that the Terāpantha employ lend a more secular authority, which allows them to promote Prekṣā to a worldwide audience, as evident from the international camps.

In conclusion, I have shown in this chapter how Prekṣā Dhyāna as a performative ritual is conducive for the "proper ordering of the soul." I have argued that it is a ritualized action because the "actor" takes a particular stance to her action, making it a "ritual commitment," and how not only the physical space contributes towards this commitment, but also the body is an instrument that assists in this commitment. I have also demonstrated how the Terāpantha, by going back to Mahāvīra and the canon and forward to contemporary science, have developed a structure that is regulated and shaped by authoritative discourses in order not only to secure meaning for the ritual, but also to promote it to a worldwide audience. However, despite the Terāpanthī attempt to keep Prekṣā Dhyāna anchored to Jaina theology, still the opening up to science and other contemporary influences raises the question of how this leaves the possibility of an erosion of Jaina theology within the Terāpantha.

Notes

1 There have been no ethnographic studies focused on Jaina meditation rituals that I have been able to uncover. For a historical, textual perspective on Jaina yoga and meditation, see Bronkhorst (1986, reprinted 1993a, b), as well as Tatia (1986).

2 My sources for what follows, unless stated otherwise, are my own observations as a participant/observer in the camp and also field notes for sessions that were lectures, discussion groups, or question-and-answer sessions.

3 This image of the man with a snake wrapped around him bears a very close resemblance to, if not a spitting image of, the representation of Laocoon and his sons in Greek mythology. The sculptural grouping of Laocoon and his sons depicts an event in Vergil's *Aeneid* (Book 2). I am indebted to Christoph Emmrich for bringing this to my attention. I am not sure if the Terāpantha were aware of this imagery or came up with the imagery on their own.

4 For a more detailed explication of the cosmography and the mechanism of bondage, see Jaini (1979: 107–130).

5 For a detailed discussion on the Jina, see Laidlaw (1995) and Babb (1996).

6 The term *upāsaka* means a lay follower or worshiper, but within the Terāpantha these lay followers are highly trained individuals who sometimes act as preachers during the *Paryuśana* festival in small places where there may be no Terāpantha ascetics to give daily sermons. These *upāsakas* dedicate their time and energy to whatever is required of them by the Terāpantha leadership.

7 *Cūrū Patrikā* a publication of *Rajasthan Patrikā*, Friday November 6, 2009. The story in Hindi, headlines "International Prekṣādhyāna commences: 'Adopt the Prekṣā sūtra (aphorism) for a life time' – Mahāśramaõa." citing *Yuvācārya* (ācārya designate in waiting) Mahāśramaõa. The article goes on to say that at the commencement ceremony in the presence of His Holiness, Ācārya Mahāprajña, the *Yuvācārya* impressed upon the camp attendees the necessity to observe at all times the five important vows of *bhāva kriyā, pratikriya virati, maitri, mitāhara*, and *mitabhāùaõa*. For a detailed explanation of these vows, see above.

8 Field notes: Prekṣā meditation camp, October 11, 2009.

9 These are not their real names. I have used pseudonyms to protect the identity of my subjects, but in this particular case, they also represent the type of young men who shared similar stories.

10 There is a direct translation of this work in Hindi called *Prekṣādhyāna Siddhānta aur Paddhati*. I found it interesting that the original English work is actually a selected compilation of Ācārya Mahāprajña's writings on Prekṣā scattered in various works. There was obviously a perceived need for a concise English manual and that the Hindi version was an afterthought. However, the detailed manual in Hindi is not the manual given in the Hindi camp. I am not sure of the reasons for this variance. Is it because it might be easier for the Indians to learn the devotional songs, and experience the *bhāva* (feelings) generated through such devotion or is there a mundane economic reason?

11 *saṃpikkhae appagamappaeṇaṃ*: *DasveāliyaṃCūliyā* 2.12. The Hindi translation is "*ātmā ke dvāra ātmā ko dekhe*," cited in *Prekṣādhyāna Āgama aur Āgametara Stotra* (Muni Dharmesh. Ladnun, Rajasthan: Jain Vishva Bharati, 1996, 2006, p.56).

12 Cort (2000, 170) rightly points out that this uncritical use by scholars like Banks (1992:30–32), and others cited by Cort (170 n. 8) is a critique based on pre-understandings of Protestant critique of image-worshipping cults. Thus the image-worshipping Śvetāmbara and Digambara sects are considered unreformed. I am with Cort that a more critically appropriate approach is one taken by Humphrey and Laidlaw (1994:47).

As Humphrey and Laidlaw state, there is no unreformed sect today in Jainism. All of them claim to have returned to an earlier form of Jainism. In his article Cort traces the reform in the Śvetāmbara Mūrtipūjak Jain community in the early twentieth century.

13 Flügel (2003). Dundas (2002) also states that, although the Terāpanthīs share certain aspects of the Sthānakavāsī teachings, such as the permanent wearing of a *muhpattī* (mouth covering) for ascetics and the rejection of image worshipping, they do not trace their lineage to the Sthānakavāsī." Raghunāthji is viewed as Bhikṣu's teacher only in the most provisional sense . . . the only true authority was vested in the scriptures, the expression of eternal truth, and Mahāvīra and his disciples" (256).

14 This is the first work in the Śvetāmbara canon and the ninth chapter of this work, which many scholars believe to be a later interpolation, describes Mahāvīra's meditation. See *Sacred Books of the East – Jaina Sūtras Part 1* (Hermann Jacobi (trans.) Oxford: Oxford University Press, 1884). Also see Mahāprajña's translation and commentary *Acharanga Bhasyam* (Ladnun, Rajasthan: Jain Vishva Bharati, 2001).

15 Christopher K. Chapple. *Reconciling Yogas: Haribhadra's Collection of Views on Yoga* (Albany: SUNY Press, 2003). Chapple makes this point with regard to Haribhadra and Olle Qvarnström makes a similar claim in his translation of *The Yogaśastra of Hemacandra*. (Harvard Oriental Series, 60, Cambridge: Harvard University Press, 2002).

16 It is possible that Nathmal Tatia who, for a while, was a director of the Jain Vishwa Bharati Institute (the deemed university founded by the Terāpantha) may have had his own biases, as a scholar who was also a practicing Jain, which may have informed his reading of these passages. I am not saying that this diminishes his scholarship in any way, but as scholars we sometimes bring our biases, and one needs to just be aware of this.

17 During my research stay in Delhi at the Adhyātma Sādhanā Kendra (a Terāpantha center) I met a cardiologist who was conducting a study on the effects of Prekṣā on cardiac patients. There were also at least two Ph.D. dissertations out of the Jain Vishva Bharati Institute on the physiological effects of Prekṣā. All of these were actively sought by the Terāpantha leadership to claim that, "Prekṣā works," not only on the spiritual level, but also on the physical and neurological levels.

18 *Prekṣādhyāna Āgama aur Āgametara Stotra*. (Muni Dharmesh. Ladnun, Rajasthan: Jain Vishva Bharati, 1996, 2006).

Bibliography

*texts in Hindi

Asad, Talal. *Genealogoes of Religion*. Baltimore, MD: The Johns Hopkins University Press, 1993.

Babb, Lawrence A. *Absent Lord Ascetics and Kings in a Jain Ritual Culture*. Berkeley, CA: University of California Press, 1996.

Banks, Marcus. *Organizing Jainism in India and England*. Oxford: Clarendon Press, Oxford University Press, 1992.

Bronkhorst, Johannes. "Remarks on the History of Jaina Meditation." In Smet, R & Watanabe, K. (eds.), *Jain Studies in Honour of Josef Deleu*. Tokyo: Hon-No-Tomosha, 1993a.

Bronkhorst, Johannes. *The Two Traditions of Meditation in Ancient India*. Delhi: Motilal Banarsidass Publishers Private Limited, 1986, reprinted 1993b.

Chapple, Christopher C. *Reconciling Yogas: Haribhadra's Collection of Views on Yoga*. Albany: State University of New York Press, 2003.

Cort, John D. "Defining Jainism: Reform in the Jain Tradition." In O'Connell, J. T. & Wagle, N. K. (eds.) *Jain Doctrine and Practice: Academic Perspectives.* . Toronto: University of Toronto Centre for South Asian Studies, 2000, pp. 165–191.

*Dharmesh, Muni. *Prekṣādhyāna Āgama aur Āgametara Strota.* Ladnun, Rajasthan: Jain Vishva Bharati, 2006, first published 1996.

Dundas, Paul. *The Jains*, 2nd ed. London: Routledge, 2002, first published 1992.

Flügel, Peter. "The Ritual Circle of the Terāpanth Śvetāmbara Jains." In: *Bulletin d'Etudes Indiennes*, 13, 1996, 117–176.

Flügel, Peter. "Spiritual Accounting: The Role of the Kalyānaka Patra in the Religious Economy of the Terāpanth Śvetāmbara Jain Ascetics." In Qvarnström, O. (ed.) *Jainism and Early Buddhism in Indian Cultural Context: Festschrift in Honour of P.S. Jaini.* Freemont, CA: Asian Humanities Press, 2003, pp. 167–204.

Folkert, Kendall. *Scripture and Community. Collected Essays on the Jains.* ed. John Cort. Atlanta: Scholars Press, 1993.

Humphrey, Caroline & James Laidlaw. *The Archetypal Actions of Ritual: A Theory of Ritual Illustrated by the Jain Rite of Worship.* Oxford: Clarendon Press, 1994.

Jacobi, Hermann (trans.). *Sacred Books of the East – Jaina Sūtras Part 1.* Oxford: Oxford University Press, 1884.

Jaini, Padmanabh S. *The Jaina Path of Purification.* Delhi: Motilal Banarsidass, 1979.

Jaini, Padmanabh S. "Ecology, Economics, and Development in Jainism." In: Chapple, Christopher Key (ed.) *Jainism and Ecology: Nonviolence in the Web of Life.* Cambridge, Mass: Harvard Divinity School, 2002, pp. 141–158.

Laidlaw, James. *Riches and Renunciation: Religion, Economy and Society Among the Jains.* Oxford: Clarendon Press, 1995.

Lopez, Donald. *Buddhism and Science: A Guide for the Perplexed.* Chicago: The University of Chicago Press, 2008.

Mahāprajña, Ācārya. *Acharanga Bhasyam.* English Translation of the Original Text of Āyaro together with its Roman Transliteration and Bhasyam (Sanskrit Commentary). Commentator: Acharya Mahaprajna. English Rendering: Dr. Nathmal Tatia, Muni Dulharaj, Muni Mahendra Kumar. Ladnun, Rajasthan: Jain Vishva Bharati, 2001.

Mahāprajña, Ācārya. *A Handbook of Preksha Meditation for the Trainers.* trans. Muni Mahendra Kumar. Ladnun, Rajasthan: Jain Vishva Bharati, 2004.

*Mahāprajña, Ācārya. *Prekṣādhyāna Prayoga-Paddhati.* Ladnun, Rajasthan: Jain Vishva Bharati, 2007.

Mahāprajña, Ācārya. *Prekṣādhyāna: Theory and Practice.* trans. Muni Mahendra Kumar. Ladnun, Rajasthan: Jain Vishva Bharati, 2008.

*Mahāprajña, Ācārya. *Prekṣādhyāna Siddhānta aur Paddhati.* Ladnun, Rajasthan: Jain Vishva Bharati, 2008.

Mauss, Marcel. "Techniques of the Body." *Economy and Society,* 2 (1), 1973, 70–88.

Qvarnström, Olle (trans.) *The Yogaśāstra of Hemacandra.* Harvard Oriental Series, 60 Cambridge, Mass: Harvard University Press, 2002.

Tatia, Nathmal. *Jaina Meditation: Citta-Samādhi, Jaina-Yoga.* Ladnun, Rajasthan: Jain Vishva Bharati, 1986.

Vallely, Ann. *Guardians of the Transcendent: An Ethnography of a Jain Ascetic Community.* Toronto: University of Toronto Press, 2002.

12 Jain modern Yoga

The case of Prekṣā Dhyāna

Andrea R. Jain

> If we look from a comparative point of view, then there is no difference between asserting any particular qualities of yoga and [those of] physiology.[1]
>
> (Mahāprajña, *Prekṣā Dhyāna: Siddhānta aur Prayoga*, 32)

Introduction

Beginning in the nineteenth century, Yoga was reconstructed anew in light of modern ideas and values. Religious reformers prescribed their idiosyncratic versions of modern Yoga usually not as all-encompassing religious worldviews or systems of practice, but as one part of self-development that could be combined with other worldviews and practices. Indians, Europeans, and Americans attributed benefits to Yoga that reflected the dominant anatomical and physiological paradigms of modern biomedicine. In short, they used biomedical discourse to discuss Yoga ideas and practices that were traditionally read through metaphysical lenses.[2] By the early twentieth century, proponents of Yoga appropriated fitness techniques and their valorization as a part of self-development from Western European and North American proponents of physical culture.[3] Furthermore, the very method through which people learned Yoga changed when, instead of relying on transmission through the traditional guru–disciple relationship in the isolated context of an *ashram*, proponents began to disseminate Yoga to mass audiences and attempted to convince people to choose their particular system as opposed to others in the increasingly plural and global Yoga market.[4]

By the mid-twentieth century, there emerged many modern Yoga systems that aimed at psychological and physiological control and transformation according to modern conceptions of anatomy, physiology, and psychology through modern relaxation and fitness techniques that were accessible to the masses. These systems, according to Elizabeth de Michelis, can be categorized into two main types: modern meditational Yoga and modern postural Yoga.[5] Modern meditational Yoga, such as Satya Narayan Goenka's (b. 1924) Vipassanā or Insight Meditation, which was prescribed as a universal Buddhist system, stresses concentration and meditation techniques. The most prominent form of Yoga, however, focused on physical techniques. Modern postural Yoga, such as Iyengar Yoga, focuses on *āsana* or "posture" synchronized with prāṇāyāma or "breath control." By the 1970s, postural Yoga was popularized in urban centers across the world.

In the fast-growing transnational Yoga market, Jain modern Yoga became one choice among many when Muni Nathmal, a Jain monk of the Śvetāmbara Terāpanth (henceforth, Terāpanth) took leave from his regular monastic duties in order to formulate a system of Jain Yoga. After studying Jain scriptures and engaging in personal experimentation in solitude at the Jain Viśva Bhāratī center in Lāḍnūn, a town in the Nāgaur district of Rājasthān, he systematized Prekṣā Dhyāna, literally, "concentration of perception," but most often translated by insiders to the Terāpanth as "insight meditation."[6] Prekṣā Dhyāna is a systematic, hybrid program of modern meditational Yoga and modern postural Yoga.[7] It shares important similarities with other forms of modern Yoga, especially Vipassanā.[8] Nathmal asserted that Prekṣā Dhyāna was universal and scientific, and, though Nathmal constructed Prekṣā Dhyāna in light of modern ideas and values, he claimed that it was not new, but had been central to Jain orthodoxy before it was gradually lost over time. He thus viewed his systematization of Prekṣā Dhyāna as a process of rediscovery.

The introduction of Prekṣā Dhyāna was only one step in the Terāpanth's reformation process during the ācāryaship of Tulsī (1914–1997), the ninth *ācārya* of the Terāpanth, who increased the sect's engagement in worldly affairs by expounding solutions to global concerns regarding social and individual ethics, education, and health. All of these reforms were dramatically innovative given Terāpanth orthodoxy as established by Bhikṣu (1726–1803), the founder and first *ācārya* of the Terāpanth. Bhikṣu was a Śvetāmbara reformer who left his order in 1759 because he thought that Jain monastic practice had become too lax. He interpreted Jain orthodoxy through an exclusively ascetic lens, arguing that the preeminent Jain virtue of ahiṃsā or "non-violence" is about the purification of the self from karmic matter. Because all participation in worldly affairs perpetuates violence, true spiritual practice requires total ascetic withdrawal from physical and social action. Bhikṣu thus distinguished between two realms of value. The worldly realm consists of any physical or social action directed toward worldly benefits. The spiritual realm includes ascetic behavior that aims at the purification of the self. Bhikṣu established the new Terāpanth order in 1760, asserting that this order returned to the logical end of Jain orthodoxy's dualist ontology by calling for the reduction and eventual elimination of all action for the sake of purifying the self from karmic matter.[9]

Although the Terāpanth upholds Bhikṣu's teaching that purification requires withdrawal from physical and social action, the reformation process that Tulsī initiated was premised on the idea that the Terāpanth should increase its engagement in worldly affairs. For Nathmal's contribution toward this end through the rediscovery of Prekṣā Dhyāna, Tulsī honored him with a new name, Mahāprajña or "Great Wisdom." He would eventually be initiated as the tenth *ācārya* in 1994 and would continue in that role until his death in 2010.[10]

Confident that Prekṣā Dhyāna was the solution to the perceived problems of the modern world, especially rampant ill health, Tulsī decided that Prekṣā Dhyāna's global dissemination to Jains and non-Jains was necessary. This led to an additional reform on the part of the Terāpanth since the sect needed representatives to disseminate this unique form of Yoga. Thus, beginning in 1980, Tulsī introduced the *samaṇ* monastic order, made up of novice monastics charged with this mission. In 1986, four *samaṇas* or male *samaṇ* and six *samaṇīs* or female *samaṇ* underwent initiation. Today, almost all *samaṇ* are *samaṇīs.*[11]

The rules governing the *samaṇ* are more lax than those for fully initiated monastics. The *saman* are allowed to travel by means of mechanical transportation; they live in buildings constructed or purchased especially for them; they generally do not wear the *muhpattī* or mouth-shield; and they can establish long-lasting relationships with lay people.[12] All of this enables the *samaṇīs* to travel throughout India and abroad in order to work toward the global dissemination of Prekṣā Dhyāna. The existence of this order makes it possible for the Terāpanth to maintain the Jain ascetic ideal as Bhikṣu prescribed it while sustaining participation (through the intermediary role of the *samaṇīs*) in worldly affairs by means of the dissemination of Prekṣā Dhyāna.

The construction and implementation of Prekṣā Dhyāna itself also make it possible for the Terāpanth to remain soteriologically committed to the Jain ascetic ideal while also affirming worldly values. In theory, Prekṣā Dhyāna is a highly systematized meditational and postural program based on aspects of Jain doctrine and practice as well as Hatha Yoga and what are perceived as the universalizing systems of modern anatomy and physiology. In practice, however, the form of Prekṣā Dhyāna varies depending on context. For advanced practitioners, on the one hand, the aim of Prekṣā Dhyāna is soteriological. It advances the practitioner along the path of purification of the self from karma and the perception of the self as ontologically distinct from the body. Prekṣā Dhyāna is an ascetic, meditational program that includes posture and breathing exercises, but these serve to enhance meditation. Even the achievements of physical and psychological health are means to the soteriological aim. On the other hand, for non-advanced practitioners, Prekṣā Dhyāna is prescribed as fitness and encapsulates the worldly aims of modern postural Yoga, such as improved health and stress reduction, as valuable ends in themselves. The emphasis is on postural practice, and in this way it intersects with the most popularized varieties of modern Yoga.[13]

By constructing Prekṣā Dhyāna in a way that interprets aspects of Jain meditation and Haṭha Yoga through modern biomedical and fitness lenses as well as prescribing it in both modern meditational and modern postural forms, reformers made it possible for the Terāpanth to increase its worldly engagement by attracting individuals in pursuit of the aims of modern postural Yoga, consequently growing in numbers and influence around the globe, while simultaneously remaining compatible with Jain soteriological orthodoxy as expounded by the founder of the Terāpanth, Bhikṣu.

Prekṣā Dhyāna as modern meditational Yoga

In his construction of Prekṣā Dhyāna, Mahāprajña appropriates many ideas and practices from Haṭha Yoga and Jain meditation and interprets them through the lens of modern biomedicine. Whereas Haṭha Yoga is believed to result in supernatural powers, Prekṣā Dhyāna is believed to result in the preliminary aims of physiological and psychological health as well as enhanced virtue, and the final soteriological aim of an improved perception of the self.

Mahāprajña relies on a conception of a subtle body composed of *prāṇa* or subtle energy that resembles that of Haṭha Yoga. He appropriates the term *chakra* (common in Haṭha Yoga literature) to refer to each center of concentrated energy, but more often uses *chaitanya kendra* (literally, "center of consciousness"), which his disciples translate as "psychic center."[14]

Prāṇa is believed to become concentrated in different *chaitanya kendras*, and the area where it is most concentrated reflects one's psychological state. Mahāprajña provides a way of categorizing different people based on the area where *prāṇa* is concentrated.[15] A person whose *prāṇa* is active around or below the navel is an *ichhā puruṣa*, meaning "one possessed by preponderant desire." A person whose *prāṇa* moves between the navel and the nostrils is a *prāṇa puruṣa*, "one possessed by preponderant subtle energy." Finally, a person whose *prāṇa* moves between and above the eyebrows is a *prajñā puruṣa*, meaning "one possessed by preponderant wisdom." Because the location of *prāṇa* determines one's psychological disposition, the manipulation of *prāṇa* functions to transform that disposition.

Unlike the well-known Indian guru, Ramana Maharshi, who prescribed asking oneself "Who am I?" as the best way to spiritual progress, Mahāprajña says that the more important question is "In what part of the body do I usually reside?"[16] In Prekṣā Dhyāna, one must first perceive in which parts of the body one's *prāṇa* is fixated before one can resolve to improve the state of the self by adjusting the flow of *prāṇa* in order to suppress harmful psychological qualities.

The preliminary goal of Prekṣā Dhyāna is to redirect *prāṇa* away from the lower *chaitanya kendras* and toward the higher ones in the heart, throat, nose, tip of the tongue, forehead, and top of the head. Consequent transformations result in an improved state of the self. This is possible because, when one is no longer subject to negative emotions or desires, one purifies the self from the effects of previously accumulated karma as well as prevents the accumulation of new karma. With less karmic obstruction, one can increasingly perceive the self.

In order to understand Prekṣā Dhyāna as a meditational program that enhances the perception of the self, one must evaluate its primary stages.[17] Regular participation in the gradual progression through such stages is necessary for the monastic and serious lay practitioners who seek to purify the self from karma, consequently enhancing the perception of the self.

Before the practitioner begins the formal stages, she must go through certain preliminary ones. The first stage is to adopt an appropriate *āsana*. In contrast to the beginner who may adopt a sitting *āsana*, ideally, the practitioner adopts a standing one. She must also adopt a particular *mudrā*, a position of the hands, with palms open and facing the body, and fingers straight and facing down. Mantra is another preparatory stage and is considered potent because it stimulates the flow of subtle energy and enhances concentration.[18]

The first formal stage in the meditational program is *kāyotsarga* or "abandonment of the body."[19] Appropriated from Jain meditation, *kāyotsarga* traditionally functions to end the practitioner's identification with the body by simulating death. In the context of Prekṣā Dhyāna, however, *kāyotsarga* is relaxation. The practitioner stands or lies down in the *āsana* described above and, in a way that resembles a form of mindfulness meditation or relaxation therapy prevalent in biomedical contexts, alternately concentrates on different parts of the body, consciously willing the relaxation of each part.

The next stage is *antaryātrā* or "internal trip."[20] *Antaryātrā* requires the practitioner to direct the flow of subtle energy in an upward direction. Because negative emotions, such as fear and hate, as well as sexual and other bodily drives are believed to result from concentrated energy in the lower *chaitanya kendras*, *antaryātrā* is believed to eliminate such emotions and drives by moving *prāṇa* to the highest *chaitanya kendra*. Using visualization techniques, the practitioner wills her concentrated energy at the bottom of the spine to move upward along the spinal column to the top of the head.

The next four stages of Prekṣā Dhyāna aim at the extraordinarily precise perception of four things: breath, body, psychic centers, and psychic colors. *Śvas prekṣā* or "perception of breath" includes three steps appropriated from the prāṇāyāma techniques of Haṭha Yoga: deep breathing, breathing through alternate nostrils, and breathing through alternate nostrils coupled with retention of breath. *Śarīra prekṣā* or "perception of body" requires the practitioner to, with indifference to pleasure or pain, concentrate on the gross body in increasing degrees of depth and subtlety: from the superficial sensations of the skin, to muscular sensations, to sensations of the internal organs, and finally to subtle vibrations of the electrical impulses in the nervous system. *Chaitanya kendra prekṣā* or "perception of psychic centers" requires the practitioner to meditate upon the *chaitanya kendras* in order to become directly aware of the vibrations of subtle energy at each one.

Once the practitioner directly perceives the subtle body, she practices *leśya dhyāna* or "meditation on color." Jain karma theory maintains that action leads to the accumulation of karma, and karma in turn produces *leśya*. There are many different *leśyas* and the specific type depends on the mental state behind the action that produced that karma, such as whether or not the individual was motivated by anger or equanimity when performing the action. Mahāprajña appropriates this traditional Jain idea and reinterprets it, arguing that a particular *leśya* is believed to characterize each *chaitanya kendra*. The practitioner thus meditates on one of the five highest *chaitanya kendras* and its constituent *leśya* in order to become decreasingly subject to negative emotions (and thus the deleterious effects of karma) and to attain full conscious control over her emotional state. What makes this possible is the association between auspicious *leśyas* and virtuous emotions. By focusing on auspicious *leśyas* as opposed to inauspicious ones (unsurprisingly associated with the lower *chaitanya kendras*), the practitioner blocks certain deleterious emotional effects of karma, such as anger and fear, as well as sexual and other bodily drives.

Prekṣā Dhyāna culminates in *anuprekṣā* or contemplation.[21] The practitioner increasingly focuses on the distinction between the self and its transient associations, including one's surroundings, one's clothing, one's body, one's bodily and psychological processes, one's emotions, one's behaviors, and one's karma. This stage ends with meditation on three particular *chaitanya kendras* and their concomitant *leśyas* and virtues. The practitioner concentrates on the *ānanda kendra* (pink), and contemplates fearlessness, the *jyoti kendra* (blue) and contemplates equanimity, and finally, the *śānti kendra* (white) and contemplates modesty.

Prekṣā Dhyāna is a meditational program based on an empirical inquiry into the self. The perception of the self requires that the practitioner engage in ascetic control over and eventual transcendence of the body, including its subtle and physiological components. In short, the stages outlined above are believed to improve the practitioner's psychological disposition and virtues, which enhances her ability to disassociate from the body and to perceive the self, the soteriological aim according to Jain doctrine.

Practitioners of Prekṣā Dhyāna are not just concerned with soteriological aims but also with what are believed to be its physiological and psychological health benefits. With regard to such concerns, Mahāprajña appropriates modern biomedical discourse on anatomy and physiology to explain the effects of Prekṣā Dhyāna on health. Mahāprajña's construction of Prekṣā Dhyāna demonstrates the phenomenon whereby modern Yoga, by appropriating the physiological and anatomical discourse of biomedicine, somaticizes the subtle body, which was metaphysical in premodern varieties of Haṭha Yoga. Basically, the movement of *prāṇa* by means of the techniques described above is believed to change the psychological disposition through the mechanism of the endocrine system. According to Mahāprajña, as *prāṇa* moves to different parts of the body, it stimulates the release of hormones by different endocrine glands, and those hormones enter the blood stream and stimulate responses in the sympathetic and parasympathetic nervous systems.

The idea that the movement of *prāṇa* could have physiological effects is consistent with Jain doctrine's ontological distinction between the self and the material world. Since everything that is not the self is a component of the material world, *prāṇa* is a component of the material world and, more specifically, a component of the body. When *prāṇa* releases *leśya*, the process is believed to affect physiological functioning by means of the physical vibrations of color waves, made up of colors linked to particular emotions and desires.[22] In other words, *leśya* is believed to function as the intermediary force between the subtle body and gross physiology in the same way that the visual perception of a particular color, via color waves, might stimulate a particular mood in a person. Just as color waves affect visual perception (and potentially, stimulation), they are also believed to affect the endocrine glands. Upon stimulation of the endocrine glands by particular *leśyas*, the glands release hormones, and those hormones enter the blood stream and interact with the nervous system.

The neuroendocrine system is responsible for the production of a particular emotive state, which has physiological effects. Relaxation, for example, may lead to a decreased heart rate. Such physiological effects may prevent diseases that, according to mainstream biomedicine, stress is believed to exacerbate, such as heart disease. In fact, most diseases, according to Mahāprajña and his disciples, are psychosomatic.[23] Mahāprajña even adopts biomedical discourse on stress to talk about *kāyotsarga*. Though *kāyotsarga* is an ancient, ascetic Jain practice believed to enhance meditative capacities, Mahāprajña adds that the meditative effects intersect with its relaxation effects, which also result in health benefits.

Mahāprajña and his disciples prescribe Prekṣā Dhyāna as a healing technique especially suitable for what he deems illnesses of modernity and especially urban lifestyles linked to a diet of unhealthy non-vegetarian foods, lack of exercise, over-consumption, and most of all, stress. In this way, he participates in the modern biomedical discourse on stress and reflects the trends of modern Yoga, which in various forms is prescribed as a program for relaxation.

The biomedical discourse on stress, which maintains that stress is both a psychological and physiological syndrome, is itself a modern one.[24] It has only been since the 1930s that stress entered the vocabularies of numerous languages. Hans Selye produced the earliest scholarly work on stress and argued that stress is associated with urban life.[25] Since then, biomedical physicians and researchers have continued to associate stress with urban lifestyles, emphasizing the need to change lifestyle as a top-down strategy for treating stress.[26] They further connect chronic stress caused by lifestyle choices to numerous diseases, especially heart disease.

Stress is believed to result when the body stimulates hormones in response to the cognitive signal of danger, and those hormones affect the parasympathetic and sympathetic nervous systems. Those responses, over time, cause chronic wear and tear on the cardiovascular system.[27] In mainstream biomedicine, since the introduction of the discourse on stress, behavioral patterns or "lifestyle" have been key to constructing preventive and treatment therapies.

Mahāprajña appropriates the biomedical discourse on stress in an attempt to explain Prekṣā Dhyāna and thus validate it as a therapeutic practice that is scientific and universally accessible as well as original to the Jain tradition. This serves as a key component of mythologizing Prekṣā Dhyāna. In modern Yoga, mythologizing simultaneously involves validating Yoga based on its ties to both ancient origins and modern science.[28] Proponents of Prekṣā Dhyāna mythologize the system by locating its origins in the practices of Mahāvīra, the historical founder of the Jain tradition, but also by arguing for its compatibility with modern medicine. Many proponents of modern Yoga often participate in the biomedical discourse on stress by arguing that Yoga is a scientifically legitimized lifestyle choice that reduces stress. As is characteristic of proponents of modern Yoga generally, proponents of Prekṣā Dhyāna reify the association between modern urban lifestyles and stress and the argument that stress is responsible for both physiological and psychological diseases. They thus prescribe Prekṣā Dhyāna as prevention and treatment for such diseases given what is perceived as the effective program through which it transforms psychological dispositions and physiological functioning.

For most living beings, the force of karma and its effects on *prāṇa* are believed to produce a negative and deluding psychological state by producing an imbalanced and unregulated endocrine system, which has consequences for illness and health. For this reason, most individuals have no control over illness or health. But for the practitioner of Prekṣā Dhyāna, *prāṇa* is believed to be a mechanism that can come under one's control and consequently one gains power over illness and health. Mahāprajña associates each Prekṣā Dhyāna technique with certain physiological benefits. Some benefit the body with regard to basic aches and pains, whereas others serve to cure chronic illnesses such as heart disease and diabetes. For those practitioners of Prekṣā Dhyāna concerned with soteriological progress, such benefits are preliminary to the ultimate aim, which is the perception of the self. For most Yoga practitioners, however, physiological and psychological benefits are aims in themselves, and practitioners take a different route from that of the meditational program described above to attain them.

Prekṣā Dhyāna as modern postural Yoga

The alternative route to the perceived health benefits of Prekṣā Dhyāna is postural Yoga, and practitioners learn it under the guidance of the *samaṇīs*.[29] In ways similar to popularized forms of postural Yoga, practitioners engage in postural sequences and coordinate the body's movements with their breathing.

The *samaṇīs* disseminate Prekṣā Dhyāna by establishing Jain Viśva Bhāratī centers, which function as community centers, and offering Yoga classes there. The *samaṇīs* do not charge any fee for Yoga classes, but request donations to support the many programs held at the centers. These centers often function as important non-sectarian community spaces for members of the Jain and broader South Asian diaspora, and a number of cultural events take place there throughout the year. The *samaṇīs* have established four major centers outside of India in the following locations: London, the United Kingdom; Iselin, New Jersey; Orlando, Florida; and Houston, Texas. They chose these locations because they feature large diaspora communities whose members are willing to provide the financial support necessary for building and sustaining the centers and for meeting the basic needs of the *samaṇīs* who live and teach there.[30]

The *samaṇīs* who teach at these centers maintain that Prekṣā Dhyāna is primarily a meditational program that functions to enhance the perception of the self and that its psychological and physiological benefits are means to that end.[31] In the majority of their classes at the Jain Viśva Bhāratī centers, however, the *samaṇīs* focus on the psychological and physiological benefits of Yoga as aims in themselves. They thus respond to the desires and demands that are dominant in the wider Yoga market, which is not surprising since the introduction of the *samaṇ* order was for the sake of adapting to the reality of globalization and the need for traveling monastics to strategically disseminate Prekṣā Dhyāna. In other words, attracting students to their centers by offering Yoga classes that focus on the popular aspects of modern Yoga, specifically postural Yoga, is a strategic way to disseminate Prekṣā Dhyāna.

As demonstrated above, the Prekṣā Dhyāna meditational program does not involve posture except for the preliminary adoption of an appropriate meditative posture, though the variety of Yoga stretching and muscle-building postures associated with postural Yoga, such as the series of *āsanas* in Sūryanamaskār (sun salutation), as well as individual postures, such as Bhujangāsana (cobra posture), Sarvangāsana (shoulder-stand posture), and Chakrāsana (wheel posture), are accepted as preliminary steps because increased bodily flexibility and strength contribute to the practitioner's ability to meditate comfortably, without bodily distractions, for long periods of time.[32] Such postural practices, however, are marginal. Yet, in the Yoga classes at the Jain Viśva Bhāratī centers, there is a reversal of what is central and what is marginal. The *samaṇīs* focus primarily on postural Yoga, and the stages listed as part of the formal meditational program are marginalized. Although they often incorporate certain stages, including mantra, *kāyotsarga*, and *anuprekṣā*, they only incorporate them for a few moments at the beginning or end of class.

Sometimes the *samaṇīs* offer separate classes that focus, not on postural practice, but on the meditational program of Prekṣā Dhyāna. They also offer camps in which practitioners remove themselves from the stresses of everyday life and learn the formal meditational program of Prekṣā Dhyāna. The *samaṇīs*, however, describe how very few students come when a meditation class is offered, but several more come for Yoga classes that emphasize postural Yoga.[33] For this reason, the *samaṇīs* offer more classes that focus almost exclusively on postural Yoga.

In such classes, the *samaṇīs* address their students' body aches or chronic health issues. This reflects their students' concerns with enhancing their life through Yoga. Primarily, students mention health and fitness as the reasons they practice Yoga.[34] In addition, students often express a desire to reduce stress, improve their physical appearance, and possibly, along the way, "achieve something spiritual."[35] Few students voice an interest in Yoga as a means to advanced soteriological progress.[36] In response to their students' interests and concerns, the *samaṇīs'* teachings differ from those found in the monastic context, meditation classes, and Prekṣā Dhyāna camps for soteriologically oriented lay practitioners insofar as the focus is not on ascetic body and meditative work for the sake of the purification and perception of the self, but on body maintenance and the enhancement of life according to modern ideas about fitness, beauty, and health.

Conclusion

Modern Yoga began to emerge in the nineteenth century as a product of encounters between Indians, North Americans, Western Europeans, and dominant modern physiological and psychological paradigms. Modern Yoga underwent popularization in the late twentieth century, and the Terāpanth joined the emergent modern Yoga movement by introducing Prekṣā Dhyāna in the 1970s and taking steps toward its global dissemination. Mahāprajña integrates Haṭha Yoga, Jain meditation, and modern biomedicine in his construction of Prekṣā Dhyāna and prescribes it as a meditational program with soteriological aims, namely, the purification and perception of the self.

For advanced practitioners immediately concerned with advancement along the Jain soteriological path, Prekṣā Dhyāna is believed to have physiological and psychological benefits, but they are means to the soteriological aims of meditation. In the global dissemination of Prekṣā Dhyāna, however, the *samaṇīs* prescribe it as a fitness routine and emphasize postural Yoga for the sake of psychological and physiological benefits that have inherent value. In this context, practitioners of Yoga aim, not to reduce action as prescribed by Bhikṣu, but to engage in action, particularly postural Yoga, for the sake of worldly benefits.

By constructing a system of Jain modern Yoga that interprets Yoga, techniques through the lens of biomedicine and can be implemented in modern meditational Yoga or modern postural Yoga forms, members of the Terāpanth affirm worldly values and participate in the fast-growing modern Yoga market while also remaining committed to their traditional doctrines and soteriological path.

Notes

1 This is my translation of the Hindi text. For this point in the English-language translation of the text, see Mahāprajña, *Prekṣā Dhyāna: Theory and Practice*, trans. Muni Mahendra Kumar and Jethalal S. Zaveri, ed. Muni Mahendra Kumar (Jain Vishva Bharati: Ladnun, Rajasthan, 2004), 30.

2 For a study on the "modern mimesis" of physiology and metaphysics in modern *yoga*, see Joseph Alter, *Yoga in Modern India: The Body Between Science and Philosophy* (Princeton: Princeton University Press, 2004).

3 For a study on the construction of modern postural *yoga* as a result of appropriations of modern ideas and practices from Western European and North American physical culture, see Mark Singleton, *Yoga Body: The Origins of Modern Posture Practice* (Oxford: Oxford University Press, 2010).

4 On the global popularization of *yoga* and the emergence of a transnational *yoga* market, see Andrea R. Jain, *Selling Yoga: From Counterculture to Pop Culture* (New York: Oxford University Press, 2014).

5 Elizabeth de Michelis, *A History of Modern Yoga: Patañjali and Western Esotericism* (New York: Continuum, 2004), 187.

6 Jain Viśva Bhāratī is a global organization for disseminating Terāpanth ideology and practice while adapting the sect to changes in the modern world. The first center was built in Lāḍnūn in 1970. It eventually became the Jain Viśva Bhāratī Institute that offered degrees in 1991. Today, members of the institute are working toward establishing it as a university. Jain Viśva Bhāratī Institute, http://www.jvbi.ac.in.

7 Jain, *Selling Yoga*, 56–65.

8 For a summary of the similarities between Vipassanā and Prekṣā Dhyāna, see Olle Qvarnström and Jason Birch, "Universalist and Missionary Jainism: Jain Yoga of the Terāpanthī Tradition," *Yoga in Practice*, ed. by David Gordon White (Princeton: Princeton University Press, 2011), 378–379.

9 There are three meanings attributed to the name of this sect (*panth*) based on the dual meaning of "*tera*" in Rājasthāni. According to legend, "Terāpanth" was first applied to Bhikṣu's order because he had 13 (*tera*) monastic and 13 lay followers. It may also refer to the 13 Jain rules for ascetic discipline. Another explanation is that *tera* refers to "your" (Mahāvīra's) path (*panth*).

10 In 2010, Mahāśramaṇ (b. 1962) succeeded Mahāprajña as the 11th and current *ācārya*.

11 The first initiation of semi-monastics in 1980 included six *samaṇīs*. Today there are over 100 *samaṇīs*. Of the four *samaṇas* initiated in 1986, only two remain *samaṇas*. The other two have been initiated as *munis*, and there have been no additional initiations of *samaṇas* since 1986.

12 Fully initiated monastics wear the mouth-shield in order to prevent the undesired breathing in and consequent destruction of microscopic organisms in the air. Usually, the *samaṇīs* only wear the mouth-shield while performing morning and evening prayers. For a study on the rules regulating the contemporary *samaṇ* order, see Peter Flugel, "The Codes of Conduct of the Terāpanth Samaṇ Order," *South Asia Research* 23, no. 1 (2003): 7–53.

13 Jain, *Selling Yoga*, 56–65.

14 "*Chaitanya*" is usually translated as "consciousness," but I use "psychic" here because this is the translation that proponents of *Prekṣā Dhyāna* themselves prefer in this context. Mahāprajña assigns different titles to each *chaitanya kendra* than those most commonly assigned to the *chakras* in Haṭha Yoga. Although such terms can sometimes differ between Haṭha Yoga and *prekṣā dhyāna*, it is clear when their referents align based on their locations in the subtle body. Furthermore, in contrast to the primary seven *chakras* of most Haṭha Yoga systems, *Prekṣā Dhyāna* has 13 primary *kendras*: *śākti kendra*, located at the bottom of the spinal column; *svāsthya kendra*, located at the genitals; *taijasa kendra*, located at the navel; *ānanda kendra*, located at the heart; *viśuddhi kendra*, located at the throat; *brahma kendra*, located at the tip of the tongue; *prāna kendra*, located at the tip of the nose; *chākṣuṣa kendra*, located at the eyes; *apramāda kendra*, located at the ears; *darśana kendra*, located between the two eyes; *jyoti kendra*, located at the center of the forehead; *śāṇti kendra*, located at the front of the top of the head; and *jñāna kendra*, located at the top of the head. Mahāprajña, *Prekṣādhyāna: Caitanya Kendra Prekṣā, Jīvan-Vijñān Granthmālā* [Science of Living Series] 8 (Lāḍṇūn, Rājasthān: Jain Viśva Bhāratī, 2003), 23.

15 Mahāprajña, *Towards Inner Harmony*, trans. R.K. Seth (New Delhi: B. Jain Publishers, 2006), 3.

16 Mahāprajña, *Towards Inner Harmony*, 13.

17 For information on the specific stages of Prekṣā Dhyāna's meditational program, I rely primarily on interviews with Samaṇī Vishubh Prajña from June 22, 2009 to June 29, 2009 in Lāḍnūn, Rājasthān. Samaṇī Vishubh Prajña's peers consider her an expert on the underlying spiritual, subtle, and physiological processes involved in Prekṣā Dhyāna. My meetings with her were arranged by the *niyojikā* (chief *samaṇī*), Samaṇī Madhur Prajña, who recommended I speak to Samaṇī Vishubh Prajña on all topics regarding Prekṣā Dhyāna. Mahāprajña also provides descriptions of each stage of Prekṣā Dhyāna. For a general introduction to the stages of Prekṣā Dhyāna by Mahāprajña, see Mahāprajña, Prekṣādhyāna*: Siddhānta aur Prayoga* or the English translation, *Prekṣā Dhyāna: Theory and Practice.*

18 Although *ārhaṃ* is the most important mantra in the practice of Prekṣā Dhyāna, Mahāprajña believes in the auspiciousness of mantra generally and argues that, if one recites a mantra properly with right articulation, it is both meaningful and powerful. One cannot know the meaning or the correct articulation, however, without the guidance of a guru. Otherwise, such knowledge is "secret." See Mahāprajña, *Towards Inner Harmony*, 72.

19 The literal meaning of *kāyotsarga* is the "mental abandonment" (*utsarga*) of the "body" (*kāya*). *Kāyotsarga* is one of the six *āvaśyaka* or obligatory duties of the Jain monastic. The standing posture required for *kāyotsarga* is also one of the two postures in which the *jinas* are iconographically represented, the other being the sitting meditative posture.

20 There are a variety of ways that *antaryātrā* could be translated, such as "internal journey," but insiders to the Terāpanth translate it as "internal trip."

21 The literal translation of *anuprekṣā* is "[the stage] following perception," but insiders to the Terāpanth translate it as "contemplation" since its aim is to contemplate the distinctions between the true self and its transient associations.

22 Mahāprajña, *Prekṣādhyāna: Siddhānta aur Prayoga,* 17. For this point in the English-language translation, see Mahāprajña, *Preksa Dhyana: Theory and Practice*, trans. by Muni Mahendra Kumar and Jethalal S. Zaveri, ed. by Muni Mahendra Kumar (Jain Vishva Bharati: Ladnun, Rajasthan, 2004), 17.

23 Personal communication, Mahāprajña, Lāḍnūn, Rājasthān, July 2006. Mahāprajña also states this interpretation of illness throughout his writings on Prekṣā Dhyāna and health.

24 "Stress" is notorious for lacking a single definition. For a discussion on the ways in which people have attempted to define "stress," see Michael King, Gordon Stanley and Graham Burrows, *Stress: Theory and Practice* (Sydney: Grune and Stratton, 1987). For a critical essay on the discourse on stress, see Allan Young, "The Discourse on Stress and the Reproduction of Conventional Knowledge," *Social Science and Medicine* 14B (1980): 133–146.

25 Hans Selye, *The Stress of Life*, 2nd ed. (New York: McGraw-Hill, 1978. First published 1956).

26 Bruce S. McEwen, "Central Effects of Stress Hormones in Health and Disease: Understanding the Protective and Damaging Effects of Stress and Stress Mediators." *European Journal of Pharmacology* 583 (2008): 181–182.

27 McEwen, "Central Effects of Stress Hormones," 175.

28 On mythologizing modern postural yoga, see Jain, *Selling Yoga*, 114–115.

29 For earlier discussions of Prekṣā Dhyāna's dissemination through postural yoga, see Andrea R. Jain, "The Dual-Ideal of the Ascetic and Healthy Body: The Jain Terapanth and Modern Yoga in the Context of Late Capitalism." *Nova Religio* 15(3) (2012): 29–50; and Jain, *Selling Yoga*, 61–65.

30 Repeated personal communications with the following *samaṇīs*: Samaṇī Madhur Prajña, Lāḍnūn, Rājasthān, June 2009; Samaṇī Rohit Prajña, London, Britain, July 2009; and Samaṇī Vinay Prajña, Houston, Texas, 2006–2009.

31 Samaṇī Madhur Prajña and Samaṇī Vishubh Prajña, repeated personal communications, Lāḍnūn, Rājasthān, June 2009.

32 I encountered this notion of postural Yoga as a preliminary step to the meditational program in my conversations with numerous *samaṇīs* and also in much of the literature published by Jain Viśva Bhāratī. Two *samaṇīs* especially emphasized this notion, Samaṇī Madhur Prajña and Samaṇī Vishubh Prajña, repeated personal communications, Lāḍnūn, Rājasthān, June 2009.

33 Samaṇī Madhur Prajña, repeated personal communications, Lāḍnūn, Rājasthān, June 2009; Samaṇī Vinay Prajña, repeated personal communications, Houston, Texas, 2006–2009; and Samaṇī Rohit Prajña, London, the United Kingdom, personal communication, July 25, 2009.

34 Samaṇī Sanmati Prajña, repeated personal communications, Houston, Texas, 2006–2009; and Samaṇī Rohit Prajña, personal communication, London, the United Kingdom, July 25, 2009.

35 Samaṇī Sanmati Prajña, personal communication, Houston, Texas, October 20, 2006.

36 In London, in fact, no members of the Terāpanth and very few Jains come to yoga classes. Almost all of those in attendance are self-identifying Hindus. Samaṇī Prasanna Prajña and Samaṇī Rohit Prajña, personal communications, London, the United Kingdom, 25 July 2009.

Bibliography

Alter, Joseph S. "Celibacy, Sexuality, and the Transformation of Gender into Nationalism in North India." *The Journal of Asian Studies,* 53, no. 1 (1994): 45–66.

Alter, Joseph S. "Seminal Truth: A Modern Science of Male Celibacy in North India." *Medical Anthropology Quarterly* 11, no. 2 (1997): 275–298.

Alter, Joseph S. *Yoga in Modern India: The Body between Science and Philosophy.* Princeton: Princeton University Press, 2004.

Alter, Joseph S. "Introduction: The Politics of Culture and Medicine." In *Asian Medicine and Globalization,* edited by Joseph Alter. Philadelphia: University of Pennsylvania Press, 2005.

Chapple, Christopher Key. "Modern Yoga," *Religious Studies Review* 34, no. 2 (2008): 71–72.

de Michelis, Elizabeth. *A History of Modern Yoga: Patañjali and Western Esotericism.* New York: Continuum, 2004.

Flugel, Peter. "The Codes of Conduct of the Terāpanth Samaṇ Order." *South Asia Research* 23, no. 1 (2003): 7–53.

Iyengar, B.K.S. *Light on Yoga.* New York: Schocken, 1966.

Jain, Andrea R. *Health, Well-Being, and the Ascetic Ideal: Modern Yoga in the Jain Terāpanth.* Doctoral Dissertation. Houston, TX: Rice University, April 2010.

Jain, Andrea R. "The Dual-Ideal of the Ascetic and Healthy Body: The Jain Terapanth and Modern Yoga in the Context of Late Capitalism." *Nova Religio* 15(3): 29–50.

Jain, Andrea R. *Selling Yoga: From Counterculture to Pop Culture.* New York: Oxford University Press, 2014.

King, Michael, Gordon Stanley and Graham Burrows. *Stress: Theory and Practice.* Sydney: Grune and Stratton, 1987.

Mahāprajña. *Prekṣādhyāna: Śarīr prekṣā. Jīvan-Vijñān Granthmālā.* Science of Living Series 7. āḍnūn, Rājasthān: Jain Viśva Bhāratī, 2000.

Mahāprajña. *Lord Mahavira's Scripture of Health.* 2nd ed. Edited by Muni Dulah Raj and Muni Dhananjaya Kumar. Translated by Sarla Jag Mohan. Lāḍnūn, Rājasthān: Jain Viśva Bhāratī, 2001.

Mahāprajña. *Apnā Darshanah: Apnā Vimb.* Lāḍnūn, Rājasthān: Jain Viśva Bhāratī, 2002.

Mahāprajña. *Prekṣādhyāna: Anuprekṣā. Jīvan-Vijñān Granthmālā.* Science of Living Series 10. Lāḍnūn, Rājasthān: Jain Viśva Bhāratī, 2003.

Mahāprajña. *Prekṣādhyāna: Caitanya Kendra Prekṣā. Jīvan-Vijñān Granthmālā.* Science of Living Series 8. Lāḍnūn, Rājasthān: Jain Viśva Bhāratī, 2003.

Mahāprajña. *Prekṣādhyāna: Leśya-dhyāna. Jīvan-Vijñān Granthmālā.* Science of Living Series 6. Lāḍnūn, Rājasthān: Jain Viśva Bhāratī, 2003.

Mahāprajña. *Preksa Dhyana: Theory and Practice.* Translated by Muni Mahendra Kumar and Jethalal S. Zaveri. Edited by Muni Mahendra Kumar. Ladnun, Rajasthan: Jain Vishva Bharati, 2004.

Mahāprajña. *Towards Inner Harmony.* Translated by R.K. Seth. New Delhi: B. Jain Publishers, 2006.

Mahāprajña. *Prekṣādhyāna: Siddhānta aur Prayoga.* Lāḍnūn, Rājasthān: Jain Viśva Bhāratī, 2009.

McEwen, Bruce S. "Central Effects of Stress Hormones in Health and Disease: Understanding the Protective and Damaging Effects of Stress and Stress Mediators." *European Journal of Pharmacology* 583 (2008): 181–182.

Mukhya-Niyojika, Sadhvi Vishrutavibha. *An Introduction to Terāpanth.* Lāḍnūn, Rājasthān: Jain Viśva Bhāratī, 2007.

Pragya, Chaitanya. *Scientific Vision of Lord Mahavira.* Lāḍnūn, Rājasthān: Jain Vishva Bharati, 2005.

Pragya, Malli. *Influence of Prekṣā Meditation on Personality and Emotional States of Under Graduate Girls*. Doctoral Thesis. Department of Science of Living, Prekṣā Meditation and Yoga. Lāḍnūn, Rājasthān: Jain Viśva Bhāratī University, 2007.

Pragya, Unnata. "Body–Soul Relation: Āsana." Unpublished paper.

Qvarnström, Olle and Jason Birch. "Universalist and Missionary Jainism: Jain Yoga of the Terāpanthī Tradition." *Yoga in Practice*. Edited by David Gordon White. Princeton: Princeton University Press, 2011.

Selye, Hans. *The Stress of Life*. 2nd ed. New York: McGraw-Hill, 1978. First published 1956.

Singleton, Mark. *Yoga Body: The Origins of Modern Posture Practice*. Oxford: Oxford University Press, 2010.

Wiley, Kristi L. "Colors of the Soul: By-Products of Activity or Passions?" *Philosophy East and West* 50, no. 3 (July 2000): 348–366.

Young, Allan. "The Discourse on Stress and the Reproduction of Conventional Knowledge." *Social Science and Medicine* 14B (1980): 133–146.

13 Contemporary expressions of Yoga in Jainism

Christopher Key Chapple

The relationship between Yoga and Jainism not only can be found in the texts dating from antiquity and the medieval period, but persists in the daily life of practicing Jainas. In the two prior chapters we learned about the dissemination of Prekṣā Dhyāna as a contemporary Jaina response to the emergence of globalized meditation systems. This chapter will consider additional contemporary expressions of Jaina Yoga and meditation drawing largely from reflection on field experiences, including visits to Jaina religious sites and trainings with Jaina religious leaders.

It is important to reiterate that Yoga is not a monolithic tradition. Yoga has taken multiple expressions in various religious traditions. The term Yoga carries a range of meanings, as we have seen in earlier chapters. In the early Jaina scriptures and philosophical texts *yoga* describes the process of generating action that results in karma clinging to and hence obfuscating the pure consciousness of the soul. In the medieval period Yoga becomes a blanket term in Jainism for acts of purification and spirituality, synonymous with the word practice (*abhyāsa* or *sādhana*).

In one of the early popular modern interpretations of Yoga, Swami Prabhavananda and Christopher Isherwood (1953:15) proclaim that Yoga means the union of the lower soul (*ātman*) with the universal soul or Brahman, that "yoga is a method – any one of many – by which an individual may become united with the Godhead, the reality which underlies this apparent, ephemeral universe." This assertion differs radically from the definition given by Patañjali, who states that Yoga entails the quieting of action (*prakṛti*) to reveal an individual consciousness (*puruṣa*) not related to an "oversoul." The word Brahman does not appear in the *Yoga Sūtra*.

Buddhists deem all things empty of inherent existence, agreeing neither to existence nor its negation. Buddhist Yoga as described in the Yogācāra School emphasizes the importance of the mind in the construal of one's relationship with the world. Buddhism points to a middle path that avoids positive or negative assertions, a position that disallows the separation of consciousness from worldly activity as taught in Jainism.

Sri Aurobindo, a modern interpreter of Yoga influenced by the nineteenth-century Bengali encounter with the West, sought to reverse the presumed trajectory of Yoga that seeks to disassociate consciousness from material reality. Aurobindo described instead the descent of consciousness into the world. Similarly, Mahatma Gandhi sought to use the Yogas of the *Bhagavad Gītā* as a way to reform the world, applying the fivefold ethics of the Jaina *Ācārāṅga Sūtra* and the *Yoga Sūtra* as a gateway to personal transformation. This personal transformation in turn helped the individual to develop the power to effect social change. In the twentieth-century tradition of Aurobindo's and Gandhi's advocacy of Yoga as a tool for worldly improvement, Ian Whicher in *The Integrity of the Yoga Darśana* gives an interpretation of Yoga as world-friendly rather than world-denying. Yohanan Grinshpon rejects this position in his book *Silence Unheard*, asserting that the *Yoga Sūtra* provides a handbook for the good death rather than a call for action in the world.

David Gordon White in the book *Sinister Yogis* and Knut Jacobsen's edited volume *Yoga Powers: Extraordinary Capacities Attained through Meditation and Concentration* revisit the power-engendering aspects of Yoga. According to these studies, Yoga for centuries has been employed to bolster personal power, particularly among India's many kings throughout history. Andrea Jain (2015:65, 87, 117–120) points to abuses of power that have been inflicted by gurus of modern Yoga, though does not cite instances of Jaina teachers engaging in such activities.

For the Jain tradition, Yoga takes many forms and meanings. Its core teachings, however, do make it possible to typologize a distinctly Jaina Yoga. Jaina Yoga would not assent to the monistic worldview espoused by Swami Prabhavananda. Jainism clearly retains a commitment to philosophical pluralism due to its teachings on multiple *jīvas*, as well as its well-known teachings on perspectivalism (*anekānta, naya*). Jainism would generally not ascribe to the notion that Jaina Yoga has the power to transform society; Jaina asceticism entails removal from the world, not redemption of the world. One exception may be the Aṇuvrata Movement established by Acharya Tulsi, which seeks to bring Jaina vows into the business and political spheres. In terms of the cultivation of power through the practice of Jaina Yoga, it must be acknowledged that Hemacandra's *Yogaśāstra* does list several powers, including the ability to possess the body of another person (V:264–271). However, these powers must be tempered by the observance of Jaina precepts. Śubhacandra's *Jñānārṇava* specifies the difference between auspicious (*śukla*) meditations and inauspicious (*raudra*) meditations that must be avoided because of their concomitant violation of the Jaina vows (Chapter 26).

Swami Vivekananda found it useful to conceptualize the forms of Yoga along the lines found in the *Bhagavad Gītā.* This same schematic may be employed to assess the ways in which Jainism implicitly and explicitly conforms to these tropes of Yoga. Hence, a fourfold analysis of Jaina Yoga will be attempted below: Karma, Bhakti, Rāja, and Jñāna, drawing from some of my own personal fieldwork.

Karma Yoga takes actions in the world very seriously, suggesting that the yogi must seek to transform his or her place in the world away from attached action toward non-attached action. Karma Yoga requires effort and mindful purification through acts of personal sacrifice (*tapas, yajña*). Bhakti Yoga entails devotion to a transcendent ideal expressed in acts of ritual (*pūjā*) and chanting (*japa, mantra, kirtan, stavan*). Through Rāja Yoga one commits oneself to a regimen of spiritual practice (*sādhana*) that may follow the sixfold practice of the *Maitri Upaniṣad*, the eightfold paths of the *Yoga Sūtra* or the *Yogadṛṣṭisamuccaya* or the steps for meditation practice found in the sixth chapter of the *Bhagavad Gītā*. Through Jñāna Yoga the yogi knows that any identification with particular forms must be eschewed, that the soul, even while embodied, cannot be attached to any residue of karma. The application of one or more of these four Yogas can result in the reshaping of oneself into the state of a purified soul, in imitation of and in solidarity with the ideals presented by a Jina, a Siddha, or a Buddha. In this concluding chapter, anecdotal examples will be given of how these forms of Yoga have been expressed in the world of contemporary Jainism, both in the realm of applied faith and in light of scholarship about Jainism.

Karma Yoga

Conversations with Padmanabh S. Jaini and Nathmal Tatia began my field experiences with Jainism, followed by visits to Jaina centers throughout the United States as they began to emerge in the 1980s, participation in Jaina conventions and conferences in North America, England, and India, and travels to many Jaina sites and temples and research centers in India. In each circumstance, selfless action or Karma Yoga could be found. Instances include the generosity of Acarya Tulsi providing counsel for seemingly endless hours to his lay followers, monks, and nuns; the efforts by lay Jaina leaders such as Pravin K. Shah to establish a curriculum and training regimen for teaching Jainism in North America; the dedication of Shugan Jain in the establishment of the International Summer School for Jaina Studies; and the energetic efforts of Professor Tara Sethia in creating and maintaining the Ahimsa center at California Polytechnic University in Pomona. Countless other instances could be given of the hard work done daily by members of the Jaina community in the spirit of what might be characterized as Jaina Karma Yoga.

Bhakti Yoga

Bhakti Yoga may be regarded as closely related to the pan-Indian cultural practice of "taking *darśan*." This process has been defined by Diana Eck (1998:4) as "to stand in the presence of the deity and to behold the image with one's own eyes, to see and be seen by the deity." This practice pertains not only to standing in front of an image but to being in the company of a great teacher or guru. The central devotional prayer of the Jainas, the Namokar Mantra, celebrates veneration of the Tīrthaṅkaras and Siddhas who have left the body but can be represented in sculpture, as well as the living teachers (*ācāryas*), preceptors (*upādhyāyas*), monks (*sādhus/munis*), and nuns (*sādhvīs*). Lawrence Alan Babb has written eloquently about the non-expectational worship that characterizes Jaina religiosity in his book *Absent Lord: Ascetics and Kings in a Jain Ritual Culture*. Because of the thorough-going voluntarist philosophy of Jainism, all spiritual advancement must generate from the will of one's own soul (Chapple 2014:84). Inspiration may be found in the example of others, but no material help can be expected from liberated beings or even living monks or nuns. Whitney Kelting (2001:107) states that Jaina devotion may be seen as an act of mimesis, that Jaina women, by creating and singing hymns (*stavan*) to the saints of the tradition, hope to take on their qualities.

As a scholar and participant observer of Jaina Bhakti Yoga, I have taken *darśan* from several Acaryas, including Acarya Tulsi in Ladnun, Acarya Mahāprajña in Baroda, Carukirti Svami Bhattarak in Sravana Belgola, Acarya Vidyananda in New Delhi, and Pujya Ganini Shri Gyanmati Mataji in Hastinapur. I have also taken *darśan* in many Jaina temples in North America and India, standing, sitting, and bowing before images of the Tīrthaṅkaras and deities such as the goddess Padmāvatī.

Bhakti devotion often entails pilgrimage to a sacred place or to an ordinary place made sacred by the presence of a living teacher. The pilgrimage experience often includes all aspects of *darśan*: visitation with a living saint, contemplation of images of the Tīrthaṅkaras, and large-scale ablution (*abhiṣeka*) ceremonies. On more than one occasion, I have traveled with students and other professors to the rural village of Hastināpur, northeast of Delhi, the site of many tales from the *Mahābhārata* epic. Three founding teachers or Tīrthaṅkaras of the Jaina tradition were born in Hastināpur: the 16th, Shantinath, the 17th, Kunthanath, and the 18th, Arahnath. Mammoth images of these saints can be found in a huge temple under construction in a corner of the vast temple complex. Numerous Jaina temples and museums have been constructed there under the able leadership of Sri Pujya Ganini Shri Gyanmati Mataji, a Digambara nun.

Hastināpur has been transformed into an altered landscape of monumental architecture, vertical, circular, and horizontal. On the horizontal plane one is reminded of the complex composition of this place called earth, Jambudvīpa. Marble houses and flowing streams separated by wrought iron fences evoke the various realms and areas of this middle place in which lives take birth: the elements of earth, water, fire, and air, all considered to possess soul; the microbes; the plants; the animals; and of course human beings. Round and round, the soul takes birth due to past karma, fulfills the needs of those karmas during life, and moves instantly at death into another life form, experiencing the joys and pains of saṃsāra. In this present age, the best one can hope for is to attain human birth, the birth that allows for self-improvement and purification. This monument also moves its pilgrim physically and symbolically to another time, another Yuga, where it is possible to ascend to the state of perfect freedom, represented by the pillar of pride, Mt. Meru, the lofty point at the very top of the universe from which the liberated soul can survey the continued rounds of existence while not being tempted to fall from one's abode of eternal consciousness, energy, and bliss.

Across the moat and a few yards away, one encounters a vertical depiction of the Jaina cosmos. Towering some ten stories above the earthbound detailed likeness of Jambudvīpa, this glass-clad image of the human body dramatically presents dozens of dioramas. At the base one finds microbes and dirt. Climbing up seven floors of cramped staircases, one can rise up through the various hells where people suffer due to heinous sins and crimes. At the level of Jambudvīpa, one catches a glimpse of the much larger version outdoors, and again can gaze upon the rivers, oceans, and continents that comprise Middle Earth. From there, one ascends through the multiple stages of the heavens, seeing the joy and pleasure experienced by myriad gods and goddesses. Finally, one reaches the very top, an observation deck from which, having arrived at the top of this symbolic Mt. Meru, one can survey the vast life-filled plains of India in a moment of exhilaration.

Temples honoring Tīrthaṅkaras line the streets of Hastināpur, each ornately designed in its own style. On the horizon can be found a hulking stūpa-like form, more circular than vertical, yet rising several stories above the bustle of the village. One enters through a simple portal. The architecture guides the pilgrim to the left, up a circular ramp, into a tunnel of darkness. Every 100 feet or so a small portal allows light to filter into the passageway and if one peers through the small aperture, one can barely discern the central pillar-like altar. Step after step, round after round, not unlike the Guggenheim Museum in New York City, one ascends, the light increasing as one reaches the top after what feels like at least seven circumambulations. Finally, one breaks through into the light and enters the final abode, symbolic of the release upward, on to Mt. Meru. In this rooftop temple one finds gleaming images of the Tīrthaṅkaras and Siddhas. The light from this lofty perch filters down over the enclosed central pillar. After rejoicing in silence at the exquisite renderings symbolic of beings that have reached the perfection of total freedom, one can then walk around the plaza that surrounds the temple, gazing outward rather than inward, feeling the delight of being a watcher rather than a doer.

According to Jainism, the cosmos takes the shape of the human body; the human body takes the shape of the cosmos in an interplay of microphase and macrophase. The lower realms of the body, burdened with karmas, hold the soul tightly within saṃsāra. The middle realms of the body, a place of will and heat, allow for purification and taking up the vows that dispel karma: non-violence, truthfulness, not stealing, sexual restraint, and non-possession. The upper realms of the body provide the clarity of heaven-like experiences. Purified senses and a calm mind can erase lifetimes of stress and karma. Jaina monumental architecture brings body, mind, and senses into a space of contemplation on these Jaina teachings, evoking by their sheer size and beauty the feelings and emotions of devotion or Bhakti Yoga. Sri Pujya Ganini Shri Gyanmati Mataji, by overseeing the construction of these temples and inviting the global community to learn about the Jaina worldview through making pilgrimage to Hastināpur has demonstrated great devotion to her religious tradition. In turn, she has gathered a sizable community of disciples who sing and dance in her honor, exhibiting great bhakti for her as their "Mataji."

Rāja Yoga: Prekṣā meditation

I first received instruction in Prekṣā Dhyāna meditation during a visit to Jaina Vishva Bharati in Ladnun in December 1989. Around 5:30 a.m. I met with Muni Mahendra Kumar and we went through a sequence of breathing exercises and visualizations lasting approximately 45 minutes. The breathing included diaphragmatic breathing and alternate-nostril breathing, as outlined in the small book *Prekṣā Dhyāna: Perception of Breathing*, techniques familiar from my own training in and practice of Yoga that commenced in the early 1970s. Acharya Mahāprajña (1985: 22) sets forth these two primary techniques as "perception of slow and deep breathing or *dīrgha-śvāsa-prekṣā*" and "perception of breathing through alternate nostrils or *samavṛtti-śvāsa-prekṣā*." This book also includes biological descriptions of breath from modern science, complementing the discussion of *prāṇa* with explanations of hemoglobin, oxygen, the release of carbon dioxide, and so forth.

The color visualization technique as taught by Muni Mahendra Kumar and outlined by Acharya Mahāprajña in *Preksha Dhyana: Perception of Psychic Colours* was less familiar. Though using the Jaina term *leśyā*, this practice did not involve the progressive ascent through the *leśyā*s from dark to bright to transparent. A famous parable describes several hungry persons confronting a grove of mangoes, wherein the person of foulest temperament and densest karma *leśyā* uproots and destroys the life of the mango tree. Less violent persons cut portions of the tree or scamper up its limbs to pluck mangoes. The person free from karmic taints simply waits for the fruits to fall. This meditation sequence, rather than carrying a moral lesson, required the self-generation of five colors within one's visual field that served as a cleansing agent. Acarya Mahāprajña has linked each color to be visualized to a particular energy center (*kendra*) and accomplishment:

1 Centre of bliss (*ānanda kendra*); emerald green; freedom from psychological faults . . .

2 Centre of purity (*viśuddhi kendra*); peacock-neck blue; self-control of urges . . .

3 Centre of intuition (*darśana kendra*); rising red sun; awakening intuition – bliss . . .

4 Centre of wisdom (*jñāna kendra*); golden yellow; acuity of perception, clarity of thought . . .

5 Centre of enlightenment (*jyoti kendra*); full moon white; tranquility, subsidence of anger and other states of agitation and excitation.

(Mahāprajña, 1986: 44)

The theory given behind this practice draws heavily from the work of Faber Birren and a study conducted by Paul E. Boccunini at the San Bernardino County Probation Department in California as well as the work of Alexander Schauss of the American Institute of Bio-social Research and Harold Wohlfarth of the German Academy of Colour Science. Mahāprajña (1986: 14, 59) also discusses the physics of color spectrum and proclaims four major benefits of this practice: freedom from anguish, freedom from infatuation, attainment of wisdom, and "ability to abandon, renounce, and relinquish." Dr. Shekawat, assistant professor of meditation studies at Jaina Vishva Bharati in Ladun, lectured on Prekṣā meditation during the summer of 2014 in New Delhi, explaining how the Prekṣā meditation system blends contemporary physiology with color theory, aura assessment, *cakras*, *kuṇḍalinī*, *āsanas*, and *prāṇāyāma*. These practices fall under the general instructions given for meditation in the *Yoga Sūtra* and the sixth chapter of the *Bhagavad Gītā*, referred to collectively as Rāja Yoga.

Jñāna Yoga: So'ham, Ko'ham

During a day-long retreat in the Shanti Nagar neighborhood of north Delhi in July 2014, faculty and students from Loyola Marymount University learned and practiced a type of Jñāna Yoga with Acharya Shiv Muni and his assistant, Shri Shirish Muniji Maharaj. They taught meditation on the mantra *So'ham* (That I am), the same as the Upaniṣadic great sentence (*mahāvākya*), and on the mantra *Ko'ham* (Who am I?), the vehicle through which the twentieth-century Hindu saint Ramana Maharshi reached his enlightenment. These practices were taught through a Jaina prism. Acharya Shiv Muni, echoing the closing chapters of the *Yogaśāstra*, encouraged us to visualize our consciousness and body as identical with that of the Tīrthaṅkaras as we reflected on *So'ham*, "I am that." This process was buttressed with alternate-nostril breathing and *kapālabhāti*, a form of rapid breathing. As we entered into *Ko'ham*, or "Who am I?" we were invited to strip away all identifications such as family or profession or possessions and move into the state of mind known as no-mind (*amanaska*), lauded by Hemacandra.

As we gratefully accepted a collection of the instructional booklets created by these teachers, we discovered that their curriculum overlapped rather remarkably with our own course of study. Acharya Shiv Muni holds multiple advanced degrees in the study of Indian thought and his book *The Doctrine of the Self in Jainism* includes analysis of ideas of Self in the Upaniṣads, Sāṃkhya, Buddhism, and the *Bhagavad Gītā*. *The Jaina Pathway to Liberation* describes the eightfold path set forth by Haribhadra using the terms Mitrā Yoga, Tārā Yoga, Balā Yoga, and so forth, in correlation with Patañjali's system. Shirish Muni Ji's *Self-Meditation: Nature and Practice* includes instruction in *prāṇāyāma* and illustrations of how to perform the following āsanas: Tāḍāsana, Triyaktāḍāsana, Kaṭicakrāsana, Vajrāsana, Ardhaśalabhāsana, Purṇaśalabhāsana, Naukāsana, Bhujaṅgāsana, Dhanurāsana, Matsyendrāsana, Parvatāsana, and Yogamudrā.

The first segment of meditation focused on *So'ham* with citations from what seemed to be the concluding segment of the *Yogaśāstra*. "*So*" here refers to the perfected beings in the Siddha Loka, reflected upon in the inhaled breath. "*Ham*," the abbreviation of *Aham*, means that "I (the soul) am that perfected being," to be recalled on the exhale breath. We began with alternate-nostril breathing and did some breath of fire (*kapālabhāti*) as the meditation leader escalated the recitation of *So'ham*.

The second segment, following a delicious (and chatty) lunch replete with My Jeera Drink, a local cumin soda, brought us into the Ramana Maharshi-like practice of *Ko'ham*: Who am I? What am I? We were given a series of reminders that we are not our bodies, not our moods, not our family, and so forth. Our preceptor, Acarya Shiv Muni, emphasized that we must arrive at the place of *śūnya*, or emptiness. After the tea break, with his energy somewhat flagging (he has eaten only one meal a day every other day for 22 years), he read a prepared meditation on various topics, including the importance of reducing anger, and the results of deceit. Our closing session emphasized that the soul is not the body and nothing relating to the body. The beautiful colors many of us experienced (such as visions of peacock feathers; see *leśya* practice above) do not have anything to do with the soul, no association with God. Three men conducted the proceedings: Acarya Shiv Muni, perhaps a septagenarian; his major assistant, Shri Shirish Muniji Maharaj, probably in his 50s and also a regular faster (who guided us in stretching exercises); and a young radiant monk, tall but not yet in puberty. All sang at one point or another in the 6-hour session. The young monk was quite a talented singer.

We had originally thought we would be instructed in Prekṣā Meditation, but it was made quite clear that this was the "original" meditation as taught by Mahāvīra and not a modern hybrid. Our host in India, Dr. Shugan Jain, clarified that this meditation complex belongs to the original Sthānakavāsī branch of Śvetāmbara Jainism, established in the sixteenth century by Acarya Lonkha in the Punjab. This branch of Jainism includes no temples, no images, no fixed scripture. Its followers proclaim solely and purely to meditate on God. This movement was later reformed by Acarya Bhikshu in 1726, who reintroduced emphasis on the practice of the Jaina vows. His 11th successor, Acarya Tulsi, introduced the application of the vows to social issues, while the 12th, Acarya Mahāprajña, developed the inward science of prekṣā meditation. Acharya Shiv Muni and Shri Shirish Muniji Maharaj represent an independent Jaina movement within the Tapa Gaccha that traces itself back to Acarya Lonkha. Their emphasis on the inviolability of the soul bears strong resemblance to the Jñāna Yoga reminder that the soul cannot be killed, cannot be touched or named in any way.

Jainas and modern Yoga

Two figures from the Jaina community have made important contributions to the teaching of modern Yoga in India and beyond. Chandra Mohan Jain (1931–1990), hailing from a Jaina family, was a successful college professor who began to write and lecture independently. He took the pen name Bhagavan Rajneesh and later changed his name to Osho. One of his early works, *Yoga: The Science of Soul*, provides a close examination of Patañjali's discussion of mind states in the *Yoga Sūtra.* Osho (2002:13) declares Patañjali to be a "scientist of the soul." Though Osho generated a great deal of controversy and was deported from the United States, his writings have experienced something of a resurgence among members of the Jaina community worldwide.

The Yoga Institute, in the Santa Cruz neighborhood near the Mumbai airport, was founded by Yogendra in 1918. He had originally established it in Harriman, New York, but relocated to India with the advance of anti-Asian exclusionary policies in 1920. For generations, this center, which I first visited in 2012, has taught an integrated form of Hatha Yoga that emphasizes the Yamas of Yoga, which are identical to the Vratas of Jainism. The current managing director, Hansaji Jayadeva Yogendra, wife of the founder's son, continues to supervise the instruction of thousands each day who walk through the gates of its pristine campus. Hansaji, born into a Jaina family, began the practice of Yoga at the Yoga Institute as a young woman. She has dedicated her life to the uplift of others through the practice of Yoga and has actively trained many leaders of Modern Yoga in the United States and Europe. For her, the connections between classical Yoga and her natal Jainism can be found in the basics of a non-violent lifestyle and the insistence on the integrity and individuality of each and every soul. Through her dedication to the teachings of classical Yoga, she abides by Jaina values.

Yoga and Jainism in an age of interconnectivity

Manish Modi, a publisher and translator in Mumbai, maintains a list serve called Jain Class, with extensive distribution on the internet. Every day or two, Modi sends Jaina-themed messages as well as news notes and inspirational quotations. Modi also translates Jaina texts and, in collaboration with Muni Mangalayashavijaya, has widely distributed selected works by Yaśovijaya whose work on Yoga was the topic of Jeffery Long's chapter in this book (Chapter 9). Yaśovijaya wrote a short text called the *Yoga Ashtaka* that summarizes key teachings about Yoga in Jainism. In this particularly short work, Yaśovijaya, in the tradition of the Haribhadras and Hemacandra, uses the term Yoga to describe the path to liberation. He lists five forms of Yoga that differ significantly from the fivefold Yoga of Haribhadra Virahāṅka in the *Yogabindu* (see Chapter 6). Yaśovijaya begins the text by stating that "all conduct which connects the soul to *mokṣa* is known as *yoga*." According to Yaśovijaya's first verse of the *Yoga Ashtaka*, the first two forms of Yoga are "connected to *karma yoga*: *āsanas* (yogic poses) [and] *varṇa* (letters of the scriptures which are recited [*mantras*?])." The use of the word karma refers to actions of the body, not the non-attached action of the *Bhagavad Gītā*. The remaining three forms of Yoga as given in the third verse are connected to what Yaśovijaya refers to as Jñāna Yoga: "*artha* (understanding the inner meaning of the scriptures), *ālambana* (sustaining support, e.g. meditating upon the image of a Tīrthaṅkara), and *ekāgratā* (being engrossed in deep concentration and immersion in the soul)." This short text explains further subdivisions in the fourth verse of these four practices into increasing levels of competence (inclination, activity, firmness, and attainment: *icchā, pravṛtti, sthiratā, siddhi*) and resulting attainments described in the seventh verse (joy, devotion, speaking, and independence: *prīti*, *bhakti*, *vacana*, *asaṅga*). This last attainment, as described in the eighth and final verse, results in "cessation of all activities of mind, speech, and body . . . complete stillness (*ayoga*) is achieved." As explained in the *Tattvārtha Sūtra* and the *Yogadṛṣṭisamuccaya*, entry into *ayoga* leads to total freedom, alluding to the disjunction of the individual soul (*jīva*) from all the fettering bonds of afflicted karma.

The presentation of this text in this format proves to be doubly effective. First, Yaśovijaya telescoped and in a sense telegraphed key Yoga tropes in a succinct, easily transmitted format that utilizes vocabulary well known to those even marginally familiar with Jaina doctrine and practice. Second, by choosing this text to distribute on the internet, Manish Modi has reached a far greater audience than would be possible via the normal transmission channels of hearing a talk by a visiting monk or conducting library research. The combination of succinctness and wide distribution makes the dissemination of Jaina teachings highly effective in the globalized internet age.

Conclusion

As I have noted in my book *Reconciling Yogas*, and has been pointed out by several scholars in John Cort's edited volume *Open Boundaries: Jain Communities and Cultures in Indian History*, Jainism has participated interactively with cultural developments for millennia. This book has examined how Jaina thinkers have used the frame of Yoga as a way to describe Jaina spirituality and cosmology. By the sixth century, Jaina scholars began appropriating the word Yoga to describe their own spiritual practice, rather than adhering to their earlier use of *yoga* to explain the bondage of fettering action. By the eleventh century, Jaina scholars and monks, including the Digambara Śubhacandra and the Śvetāmbara Hemacandra, enfolded the *mantra* and *yantra* techniques popularized in Tantra into Jaina practice. In the contemporary period, Acharya Mahāprajña used the quantitative tools of modern science to affirm and augment Jaina Prekṣā Dhyāna meditation practices.

What philosophy has allowed Jainism to adapt itself to such innovations? Three terms beginning with the letter "a" have been employed to encapsulate the basic teachings of the Jaina tradition that lend themselves to a sense of openness: *ahiṃsā*, *aparigraha*, and *anekāntavāda*: non-violence, non-possession, and many-sidedness. Through the first, *ahiṃsā*, one takes the general attitude to avoid harm. Some have argued that this predisposes Jaina thinkers to learn about the views of others and consider their usefulness before summarily dismissing them. Through the second, *aparigraha*, one actively seeks to distance oneself from appropriation of ephemera. The rigor of Jaina vows has for millennia set apart this tradition from its Hindu and Buddhist cousins to the extent that a certainty arises about Jaina identity that helps mitigate any fear within the tradition of the slippery slope of syncretism that might compromise one's beliefs. In the third, *anekāntavāda*, one recognizes that no single idea or practice can be all things to each and every person.

The Yoga tradition itself may be said to hold a similar openness and dynamism. Many practices of Yoga can be found throughout Indian history, from the sixfold method of the *Maitri Upaniṣad*, the eightfold paths of Patañjali, Haribhadra Yākinī Putra, and Hemacandra, the sevenfold Yoga of the *Yogavāsiṣṭha*, and the fivefold paths of Haribhadra Virahāṅka and Yaśovijaya. Andrea Jain (2015:157), in her study of modern schools of Yoga, comments on this pluralistic approach:

> Yoga has a long history whereby adherents of numerous religions, including Hindu, Jain, Buddhist, Christian, and New Age traditions, have constructed, deconstructed, and reconstructed it anew. Symbols, practices, and ideas vary across yoga studios and ashrams within South Asia alone, thus illustrating that the quest for the essence of yoga is an impossible task.

Yoga has long identified itself as a technique, not a belief system. It fascinated the Mughals as much as the British. It found adherents among Sufis as well as Theosophists. Its movement and breathing and meditation practices now can be found on a global scale.

Hence, we have two abiding traditions that hold certain characteristics in common, and also carry divergences. Jainism, though adopting Yoga practices, remains true to its core teachings regarding karma and the soul. Jainas remain confident in the efficacy of their commitment to vegetarianism and complex fasting rituals. Although many variations appear depending upon the sect or subsect, the truths taught by Jaina religious leaders in matters of cosmology and personal ethics hold great sway in the Jaina community. Though engaging techniques that fit within the schematic of Karma, Bhakti, Rāja, and Jñāna Yoga, Jainism, though appreciative of non-Jaina views, retains its integrity and its difference from other belief systems.

Bibliography

Babb, Lawrence Alan. *Absent Lord: Ascetics and Kings in a Jain Ritual Culture*. Berkeley: University of California Press, 1996.

Chapple, Christopher Key. *Reconciling Yogas: Haribhadra's Array of Views on Yoga with a New Translation of the Yogadṛṣṭisamuccaya*. With John Thomas Casey. New York: State University of New York Press, 2003.

Chapple, Christopher Key. "Free Will and Voluntarism in Jainism." In *Free Will, Agency, and Selfhood in Indian Philosophy*. Edited by Matthew R. Dasti and Edwin F. Bryant. New York: Oxford University Press, 2014, pp. 68–84.

Cort, John. Editor. *Open Boundaries: Jain Communities and Cultures in Indian History*. Albany: State University of New York Press, 1998.

Cort, John. *Framing the Jina: Narratives of Icons and Idols in Jain History*. New York: Oxford University Press, 2010.

Eck, Diana. *Darśan: Seeing the Divine Image in India*. 3rd ed. New York: Columbia University Press, 1998.

Grinshpon, Yohanan. *Silence Unheard: Deathly Otherness in Pātañjala-Yoga*. Albany: State University of New York, 2002.

Jacobsen, Knut, ed. *Yoga Powers: Extraordinary Capacities Attained through Meditation and Concentration*. Leiden: Brill, 2012.

Jain, Andrea R. *Selling Yoga: From Counterculture to Pop Culture*. New York: Oxford University Press, 2015.

Jain, Dashrath, tr. *Shri Shubhachandracharya's Jnanarnavah*. Gems of Jaina Wisdom, vol. 8. Delhi: Granthagar, 2011.

Kelting, Whitney M. *Singing to the Jinas: Jain Laywomen, Mandal Singing, and the Negotiations of Jain Devotion*. New York: Oxford University Press, 2001.

Mahaprajña, Yuvacharya. *Preksha Dhyana: Perception of Breathing,* 2nd ed. Translated by Muni Mahendra Kumar and Jethalal S. Zaveri. Ladnun: Tulsi Adhyatma Nidam, 1985.

Mahaprajña, Yuvacharya. *Preksha Dhyana: Perception of Psychic Colours*. Translated by Muni Mahendra Kumar and Jethalal S. Zaveri. Ladnun: Tulsi Adhyatma Nidam, 1986.

Modi, Manish, translator. *Yoga Ashtaka: Eight Introductory Verses on Yoga by Upadhyaya Yashovijaya.* June 10, 2013. Received electronically Monday, August 18, 2014.

Osho. *Yoga: The Science of Soul.* New York: St. Martin's Press, 2002.

Prabhavananda, Swami, and Christopher Isherwood. *How to Know God: The Yoga Aphorisms of Patanjali.* Hollywood: Vedanta Press, 1953.

Qvarnström, Olle, tr. *The Yogaśāstra of Hemacandra: A Twelfth Century Handbook of Śvetāmbara Jainism.* Cambridge, Massachusetts: Harvard University Press, 2002.

Rodrigues, Santan. *The Householder Yogi: Life of Shri Yogendra.* Santa Cruz: The Yoga Institute, 1995.

Shirish, Muni Ji. *Self-Meditation: Nature and Practice.* 1st ed. Punjab: Bhagwan Mahavir Meditation Research Centre Trust, 2009.

Shiv, Acharya Muni. *The Doctine of Karma and Transmigration in Jainism,* 2nd ed. Chennai: Sanskar Jain Patrika, 2007.

Shiv, Acharya Muni. *The Doctrine of the Self in Jainism,* 2nd ed. Punjab: Bhagwan Mahavir Meditation Research Centre Trust, 2007.

Shiv, Acharya Muni. *The Fundamental Principles of Jainism,* 2nd ed. Punjab: Bhagwan Mahavir Meditation Research Centre Trust, 2007.

Shiv, Acharya Muni. *The Jaina Pathway to Liberation,* 2nd ed. Punjab: Bhagwan Mahavir Meditation Research Centre Trust, 2007.

Shiv, Acharya Muni. *The Jaina Tradition*, 2nd ed. Punjab: Bhagwan Mahavir Meditation Research Centre Trust, 2007.

Whicher, Ian. *The Integrity of the Yoga Darśana: A Reconsideration of Classical Yoga.* Albany: State University of New York Press, 1998.

White, David Gordon. *Sinister Yogis.* Chicago: University of Chicago Press, 2009.

Yogendra, Jayadeva and Hansaji. *The Yoga Sutras of Patanjali: Stray Thoughts.* Mumbai: The Yoga Institute, 2009.

Index